ANCIENT INDIGENOUS CUISINES

ARCHAEOLOGY OF FOOD

SERIES EDITORS

Karen Bescherer Metheny
Christine Hastorf
Tanya M. Peres

EDITORIAL BOARD

Umberto Albarella
Tamara Bray
Katie Chiou
Yannis Hamilakis
Amanda Logan
Shanti Morell-Hart
Katheryn Twiss
Amber VanDerwarker
Joanita Vroom
Richard Wilk
Anne Yentsch

Ancient Indigenous
CUISINES

Archaeological Explorations of the Midcontinent

Edited by

SUSAN M. KOOIMAN, JODIE A. O'GORMAN,
AND AUTUMN M. PAINTER

THE UNIVERSITY OF ALABAMA PRESS
Tuscaloosa

The University of Alabama Press
Tuscaloosa, Alabama 35487-0380
uapress.ua.edu

Copyright © 2025 by the University of Alabama Press
All rights reserved.

A Dan Josselyn Memorial Publication

Inquiries about reproducing material from this work should
be addressed to the University of Alabama Press.

Typeface: Arno Pro

Cover images: (*above*) wild rice (courtesy of ange1011/stock.adobe.com); (*below, left to right*) reconstructed Oneota plate, bison scapula, and stumpware (courtesy of Jodie A. O'Gorman, Mary E. Malainey, and Illinois State Archaeological Survey)

Cover design: Lori Lynch

Cataloging-in-Publication data is available from the Library of Congress.
ISBN: 978-0-8173-2220-5 (cloth)
ISBN: 978-0-8173-6182-2 (paper)
E-ISBN: 978-0-8173-9540-7

Contents

List of Illustrations vii

Acknowledgments xi

Introduction: Cuisine in the Ancient Midcontinent
SUSAN M. KOOIMAN, JODIE A. O'GORMAN,
AND AUTUMN M. PAINTER. 1

Chapter 1   Earth Oven Cuisine via Fire-Cracked Rock Cooking in
the Midcontinent
FERNANDA NEUBAUER 19

Chapter 2   Indigenous Cuisine in the Northern Great Lakes
SUSAN M. KOOIMAN AND REBECCA K. ALBERT 39

Chapter 3   Woodland Tradition Cuisines in Southeastern Wisconsin
JENNIFER R. HAAS. 63

Chapter 4   Plates, Cuisine, and Community at the Morton Site
JEFFREY M. PAINTER AND JODIE A. O'GORMAN 90

Chapter 5   Ceremonial Feasting and Culinary Practices in the Central
Illinois River Valley: A Zooarchaeological Perspective
TERRANCE J. MARTIN. 110

Chapter 6   Exploring Identity through Cuisine and Ritual at the
Morton Village Site, West-Central Illinois
KELSEY NORDINE 132

Chapter 7   Bison Hoes and Bird Tails: Reconsidering the Introduction
of Maize Farming into Manitoba
MARY E. MALAINEY. 155

CONTENTS

Chapter 8 Nixtamalization and Cahokian Cuisine
ALLEEN BETZENHAUSER 179

Chapter 9 The Archaeobotany of the East St. Louis Precinct
of Greater Cahokia
KIMBERLY SCHAEFER, MARY SIMON, AND MARY M. KING. . . . 196

Conclusion: Why Cuisine?
JODIE A. O'GORMAN AND SUSAN M. KOOIMAN 226

References 241

List of Contributors 299

Index 301

Illustrations

FIGURES

I.1. Map of archaeological sites discussed in the book 12

1.1. Idealized earth oven illustration displaying six layers 20

1.2. Location of Site 914 on Grand Island in Michigan's Upper Peninsula . . . 21

1.3. Fire-cracked rock density at Site 914 by count and weight 23

1.4. Quartzite fire-cracked rock at Site 914 28

2.1. Map of the Cloudman site and surrounding northern Great Lakes region 43

2.2. Microbotanical remains from Cloudman site pottery residues 46

2.3. Frequencies of boiling and stewing interior carbonization patterns on cooking vessels from sites and site components in the northern Great Lakes 48

2.4. Frequencies of resources found alone or together in adhered carbonized residues from discrete pottery vessels at the Cloudman site. 50

2.5. Number of discrete pottery residues containing resources and resource combinations by component 51

2.6. Frequencies of resources and resource combinations by associated cooking style. 51

3.1. Nutshell composition by component. 71

3.2. Relative frequency of mammal sizes by component. 77

viii ILLUSTRATIONS

4.1. Map showing Morton Village site along with major Oneota and Mississippian sites. 93

4.2. Examples of broad-rimmed plates from Morton Village 95

4.3. Bar chart comparing the percentage of plates at Morton Village with those of other Mississippian assemblages in the Central Illinois River Valley. 97

4.4. Stylized plate designs from Morton Village 99

5.1. Plan of Structure 25 and Feature 224 profile 112

5.2. Deer antler tool with embedded beaver incisor found in Feature 224, Zone 3 114

5.3. Morton Village site and Lamb site vertebrate faunal collections 121

5.4. Morton Village site and Lamb site avian faunal collections 122

5.5. Morton Village site and Lamb site identified fishes, percentage number of identified specimens 123

5.6. Morton Village site and Lamb site identified fishes, percentage biomass. 123

5.7. Morton Village site and Lamb site deer skeletal portions, percentage number of identified specimens. 125

5.8. Comparison of deer food utility indices for Morton Village Feature 224 and the Lamb site, percentage number of identified specimens 125

6.1. *Nicotiana* sp. recovered from external pit feature. 145

7.1. Map showing locations of sites discussed in this chapter. 157

7.2. Digital elevation map of the Olson site/DgMg-40c locale 161

7.3. Bison scapula hoe from the Olson site and Lockport 162

7.4. Examples of Thunderbird and "tail of the raptor or Thunderbird" motifs 164

7.5. Reconstructed bison scapula from the Lowton site 170

8.1. Stumpware examples from the East St. Louis Precinct of Greater Cahokia. 183

8.2. Distribution of all precontact features identified at the East St. Louis Precinct. 186

ILLUSTRATIONS

8.3. Portable X-ray fluorescence results 189

8.4. Experimental use of stumpware replica 190

8.5. Limestone bluffs and deposits in the American Bottom region
of Illinois 193

9.1. Map of the Greater Cahokia region and three major
urban precincts 197

9.2. Terminal Late Woodland communities at the East St. Louis site 199

9.3. Lohman phase communities defined for this study 201

9.4. Stirling phase communities defined for this study 213

TABLES

1.1. Quantification of Chipped Stones, Fire-Cracked Rocks, and
Nonknapped Rocks and Ground Stones at Site 914, by Raw
Material Type 22

1.2. Flotation-Derived Flora Analyzed by Kathryn Parker 31

1.3. Quantification of Quartzite Fire-Cracked Rocks Identified within
the Earth Oven Feature at Site 914, by Fragmentation Type 33

2.1. Frequencies of Plant Species Present in Discrete Pottery
Vessel Residues 47

2.2. Interior Carbonization/Cooking Residue Patterns on Pottery
Vessels from the Cloudman Site, by Component 49

2.3. Resource/Resource Combination and Cooking Mode by
Component 53

3.1. Woodland Plant Macroremains from the Finch Site. 68

3.2. Woodland Faunal Assemblage from the Finch Site 74

3.3. Ceramic Assemblage from the Finch Site 80

4.1. Ceramic Vessel Counts at Morton Village, Separated by
Cultural Tradition Style 98

5.1. Zooarchaeological Samples from Feature 224 by Zone. 113

5.2. Species Composition of Animal Remains from Feature 224,
for All Zones. 115

6.1. Summary of Macrobotanical Remains from Pit Features. 137

6.2. Summary Table of Macrobotanical Remains from Feature 224. 147

8.1. Results of Portable X-Ray Fluorescence Analysis of
Stumpware Samples from the East St. Louis Precinct. 188

9.1. Analyzed Lohmann and Stirling Phase Features by Area. 202

9.2. Summaries by Count of Floral and Faunal Assemblages from the
Lohmann Phase Communities. 206

9.3. Summaries by Count of Floral and Faunal Assemblages from
the Stirling Phase Communities. 214

Acknowledgments

This book is the sum of efforts of a wonderful cohort of archaeologists working in the Midwest and beyond. It began as a discussion among food-enthusiastic scholars at Michigan State University and blossomed into a region-wide symposium that welcomed and embraced a wide range of approaches and perspectives. The chapters of this book were first presented as papers in the Sponsored Symposium of the Midwest Archaeological Conference in 2021, which sparked deep interest and conversations about the topic, along with encouragement from colleagues to turn the session into an edited volume. Along the way, we received advice and wisdom from Lynne Goldstein, Ethan Watrall, Michael Conner and William Lovis. The book was compiled with support from Michigan State University Department of Anthropology and Southern Illinois University Edwardsville Department of Anthropology. Several contributors to this volume, including two of the editors, were mentored by Jim Skibo, who helped inspire our passions for pottery, food, and/or cooking. Several other contributors were Jim's friends, colleagues, and/or collaborators, so we honor his memory. Finally, we are grateful to the emotional support received by family, friends, and partners, especially Jeffrey M. Painter and Michael Mohr.

ANCIENT INDIGENOUS CUISINES

Introduction

Cuisine in the Ancient Midcontinent

SUSAN M. KOOIMAN, JODIE A. O'GORMAN,
AND AUTUMN M. PAINTER

An anthropology of food celebrates the adage "you are what you eat" and expands it with a caveat—you are also *how* you eat. The types of foods that we eat and the ways in which we prepare, cook, and consume those foods are strongly tied to our backgrounds, to our past and present selves and relationships, and to a specific time and place. These routines and rituals are encapsulated by the term "cuisine," which undoubtedly evokes a specific meaning to each reader. Archaeologists have become especially fond of the term for this very reason; it is imbued with cultural significance and therefore particularly useful in our endeavors to understand past cultures. Furthermore, new and/or improved methods of identifying foodstuffs, analyses of food processing tools, and the increasingly integrative application of these approaches allow for new insights and perspectives on past cooking and consumption. This volume features archaeological explorations of the cuisines of ancient Indigenous peoples of the Midcontinent of North America, examined through a range of cutting-edge methods and perspectives and exemplifying a wide range of questions and outcomes that demonstrate the versatility and strength of culinary studies.

FOOD STUDIES, FOODWAYS, AND CUISINE

For decades, cultural anthropologists around the world have been captivated by and engaged in subsistence studies. These studies focus on foods chosen by past and present societies and how foods are procured (Twiss 2012). From Audrey Richards's (1939) study of the food habits of the Bemba in Africa in the 1930s to work by some of the biggest names in the discipline, including Malinowski (1950), Lévi-Strauss (1969, 1997), Boas (1921), Mead (1964, 1997), and Bourdieu (1977), anthropological inquiries into the nature of food-related practices and food habits of contemporary societies have been integral components of ethnographic studies and theoretical engagements.

Archaeologists were likewise fascinated with food and subsistence of past societies. The earliest subsistence studies, often conducted from the cultural ecology or other environmentally deterministic perspectives, focused on modes of procurement and production, or how people reacted to and navigated their environments (Dirks and Hunter 2012; Trigger 1996). Later, the development of the fields of zooarchaeology and paleoethnobotany ushered in a new era of plant and animal identification (Pearsall 2015; Reitz and Wing 2008). These offered greater insight into the specific nature of "diet," or the ingredients and calories that people consumed (Hastorf 2017:71), and resource "exploitation," which refers to plant and animal species procured for consumption and other uses. These studies helped anthropologists and archaeologists understand human-environmental relationships, mobility, and adaptive decisions in the face of ecological pressures.

Yet the terms "subsistence" and "diet" can be narrow and restrictive and generally exclude considerations of the cultural and social meanings of food (Twiss 2012). Richard Wilk decried the "hegemony of subsistence" in anthropology and archaeology, which he claimed was at the expense of understanding preparation and consumption of food and their role in society (2016:274). "Exploitation" is a pragmatic term plagued by the same issues as "subsistence" and "diet." It carries the added semantic burden that is particularly problematic in the archaeology of North America as it suggests a negative, nonreciprocal relationship with the environment, which might be considered at odds with the ethos of Indigenous American heritage.

Food is not just about sustenance and survival, and food choice is not shaped solely by environment and availability. Food choice goes beyond the biological and caloric requirements; food is cultural, and specific foods are often selected (or rejected) based on how they function within the existing culinary and subsistence regimes in a society (Holly 2019; Wilkins and Nadeau 2015). Food and food traditions inhabit the space between the everyday domestic sphere and the broader social, political, and ideological spheres (Appadurai 1981; Atalay and Hastorf 2006; Cutright 2021; Hastorf 2017; Fischler 1988; Montanari 2006; Smith 2006; Twiss 2012). This fact is highlighted in the present, where food is often central to special events and holidays and is a key component to our daily rituals, so much that our lives are scheduled around food preparation and consumption. The need for daily consumption of food and the socially and culturally constructed rituals surrounding it means it is a potentially powerful means through which people may communicate their position within and perceptions of their natural and social worlds. Therefore, exploration of food habits and behaviors can potentially provide a vast array of information about past societies beyond standard interpretations of diet.

Terms like "foodways" and "cuisine" better capture the importance and meaning of food in societies past and present by moving us beyond the simple identification of ingredients and into the realm of the complex interactions among people and between people and things (Twiss 2012). John Honigman (1961) coined the term "foodways" in the title of his study of the Attawapiskat people of Ontario, a seeming combination of "lifeways" and "food habits," which he never defines in the text. Folklorists Jay Anderson and Don Yoder adopted the term in the 1970s, establishing foodways as an integral topic in folklore studies (Long 2004, 2009). Yoder (1972:325) defined it as "the total cookery complex, including attitudes, taboos and meal systems—the whole range of cookery and food habits in a society." Jay Anderson (1971:57) was more specific (and influential), defining foodways as the "whole interrelated system of food conceptualization and evaluation, procurement, distribution, preservation, preparation, consumption, and nutrition shared by all members of a society." Cultural anthropologists later adopted the term as well. Carol Counihan simplified Anderson's definition to "beliefs and behaviors surrounding the production, distribution, and consumption of food" (1999:2), and other anthropologists explored foodways from a wide variety of themes and perspectives (Albala 2013; Anderson 2014; Appadurai 1981; Belasco and Scranton 2002; Beoku-Betts 1995; Camp 1982; Counihan and van Esterik 1997; Fischler 1988; Mintz 1985, 1996; Mintz and DuBois 2002; Montanari 2006; Weller and Turkon 2015; Wilk 1999, 2012).

Foodways studies later gained popularity in archaeology, where the need to understand the centrality of food in various cultural and social spheres has been recognized, leading to a proliferation of archaeological studies and publications focused on foodways (Beaudry 2013; Fritz 2019; Hastorf and Johannessen 1994; Hastorf 2017; Holly 2019; Twiss 2007, 2012, 2019). This is an important perspective that led to an integral shift in the archaeology of food (for comprehensive summaries of archaeological food and foodways studies, see Smith 2006, Twiss 2012, and Graff 2018).

However, the broadness of foodways can be untenable for many archaeological studies, particularly those dealing with single sites or working in regions and time periods with no written records to aid analysis and interpretation.

The term we focus on in this volume, *cuisine*, is more specific, more personal, and more immediately accessible than the larger umbrella of foodways. It limits considerations of food production, procurement, and distribution to questions of how these activities affect cuisine, and primarily focuses on food selection and consumption—the choice of what is eaten and brought into the body. Cuisine is also closely connected to cooking, an act that some claim distinguishes humans from all other species (Lévi-Strauss 1969; Wrangham et al. 1999). As Hastorf (2017:68) puts it, cooking and cuisine can transform "material foodstuffs into cultural entities." In our estimation, cuisine is a narrower, more intimate perspective than foodways. It moves the target of interpretation past the broader connections between food and various sociopolitical systems and focuses on what is being consumed and cooked and the immediate sociocultural factors that shape these decisions.

Cultural anthropologists and other food studies scholars began to explore the concept of cuisine not long after foodways studies became more widespread. Among the first of these is Jack Goody's *Cooking, Cuisine, and Class: A Study in Comparative Sociology* (1982), in which he distinguishes cuisine (which he mainly associates with cooking) from the broader arena of foodways, although he acknowledges the firm links between production, distribution, and cuisine. He distinguishes between the "high" and "low" cuisines of the upper societal strata and lower classes, respectively, in stratified societies, and he argues that cuisine has long been used as a device for distinguishing those with political and economic power from those without. Sidney Mintz elaborates on the concept, maintaining that everyday cuisine is regional and "requires a population that eats that cuisine with sufficient frequency to consider themselves experts on it" (1996:96). Like Goody, he distinguishes this basic cuisine from "high" or *haute* cuisine, which is borne out of politics and social change. Many subsequent studies of cuisine have likewise focused on its role in economic, political (including colonial), and class negotiations and interactions (Appadurai 1988; Cheung 2005; Clark 2004; Goody 2006; Gvion 2006; Mintz 1996; Sohodleanu 2020; Thrush 2011). Many of these and additional studies address the close relationship between cuisine and identity (Apfelbaum 2001; Demgenski 2020; Peace 2011; Sengupta 2010).

Again, archaeologists have followed food studies trends and have begun their own examinations of cuisine, although some archaeologists have taken a more straightforward view of the concept. Fuller (2005:761) defines cuisine, or culinary practice, as "the combination of foodstuffs (i.e., species) and the methods for preparing them"—in short, preparation and cooking practices plus ingredients. It is commonly understood that ingredient choice varies by culture and that choice is shaped by many factors including symbolic meanings, social constraints, and spiritual traditions surrounding foods (Bourdieu 1977; Fischler 1988; Mintz 1985; Lévi-Strauss 1969, 1997; Smith 2006). Environment and resource availability are inherent constraints on food choice. Therefore, ingredients chosen for consumption reflect both culture and nature. However, ingredients alone do not a cuisine make. Two societies may choose the same species or ingredients for consumption but prepare them in vastly different ways and combinations. Food preparation and cooking turn ingredients into recipes, and these dishes make up the core of a society's cuisine.

However, early food studies demonstrate that there is more to cuisine than just ingredients and cooking style. Claude Fischler argues that the "food + cooking = cuisine" equation is too simple, instead defining cuisine as "not so much a matter of ingredients, transformed or not, as of classifications and rules ordering the world and giving it meaning" (1988:285). By identifying cuisine, we can understand which species and dishes people conceived of as food (which when consumed becomes part of the body) and what was not considered food, an important distinction that is not universal across cultures (Fischler 1988). Haute cuisine would be a little less "haute" were it consumed in a greasy-spoon diner; therefore, the rules and rituals surrounding food consumption *and* their contexts are also integral aspects of cuisine.

Others have incorporated these considerations into their definitions of cuisine. Counihan (1999:19) defines cuisine as "food elements used and the roles for their combination and preparation," whereas Hastorf (2017) expands the definition more broadly to include psychological and religious attitudes toward food and meals. Cutright's (2021:5) definition, "*cuisine* is the set of cultural rules, ideals, and behaviors that shape what is appropriate to eat, when, with whom, and in what preparations," encapsulates these ideas. Food choice, preparation, and consumption behaviors reflect and create how societies viewed themselves and ordered their world—in other words, these behaviors are rooted in identity. In clearer consideration of the positionality of cuisine *we define cuisine as the selection of food ingredients and methods of food preparation, cooking, and serving/consumption in relation to its social, cultural, and environmental contexts.*

Although narrower than "foodways," the term "cuisine" still incorporates the sociocultural aspects of food selection and consumption, and more specifically identity, or how individuals within a society view themselves (Ohnuki-Tierney 1993; Wilk 1999). Cuisine has been framed as a language, a code or system of symbols or rules that structures not only daily activities but how we view and understand the world (Anderson 2014; Counihan 1999; Cutright

2021; Hastorf 2017). It provides a message of solidarity, a shared grammar of food preparation and consumption (Douglas 1997; Lévi-Strauss 1969), and it can create a sense of shared place and/or experiences (Anderson 2014; Bell and Valentine 1997). Cuisine can also be used to separate, to create the "other"—those from a different nation, geographic region, ethnicity, religion, and/or socioeconomic class—by acting as a physical means of symbolizing the unfamiliar or the different (Anderson 2014; Long 2004). The position of cuisine to create and perpetuate differences in ethnicity, class, and even gender means it can be used as a powerful tool for both social integration and social distinction.

Cuisine can be particularly useful in archaeological studies because of its relationship to cooking. The study of food in archaeology has often been divorced from the study of cooking and implements used in food preparation and cooking (Beaudry 2013). Recent attention to cooking in the past decade (Graff 2018, 2020; Graff and Rodríguez-Alegría 2012) and methods for identifying methods of cooking and food processing, such as functional analysis of pottery (Skibo 2013), has made inquiries into cuisine more accessible. Moore keenly observed that "archaeologists have seldom managed to link evidence for individual foods or processing techniques to the study of cuisine . . . the combination of ingredients, flavors, and textures in meaningful combinations. Without this understanding, we offer only limited access to the shared social and symbolic values of those dishes" (2012:80). Identification of past cooking habits used alongside ever-advancing methods for foodstuffs identification, such as various types of food residues associated with food preparation tools, can make explorations of ancient cuisine more tenable and connect food behaviors with identity and associated core beliefs of ancient societies. It is these attempts to link food and cooking with cuisine that is at the core of this volume.

A more recent movement has encouraged an even more focused perspective on food consumption: the "meal." Hastorf defines a meal as "an eating occasion that takes place at a certain time and/or includes specific prepared food, usually a social event" (2017:59). Meals include a mixture of solid foods and liquid beverages, and when and how those foods and drinks are served and eaten (Douglas 1997). Beaudry points out that preparation of meals and participation in mealtimes evoke cultural and personal meaning, emotion, memory, and value (2013:185). Meals, as the experiential component of cuisine, are rooted in social and cultural contexts and therefore reflections of aspects of the past that archaeologists often seek. However, as the authors point out, an investigation of meals would require information about ingredients and preparation and consumption hardware plus written records, such as menus.

Hastorf (2017) acknowledges that in prehistoric contexts, meals are largely accessible through coprolites and preserved stomach contents of deceased individuals. Although very useful, the exploration of meals in precontact Indigenous societies of the Midcontinent may not be feasible, except in the case of identifiable feasting events (Bray 2003; Dietler and Hayden 2001), thus our focus on the broader, yet still meaningful, cuisine.

Others have proposed approaches for understanding the sociocultural contexts of food. Classical archaeologist Pitts (2015:95) outlined his "archaeology of consumption," or the study of the process of food acquisition (production to distribution), transformation (preparation to ingestion), and disposal (2015:95). Meanwhile, historical archaeologist Mary Beaudry called for a focus on menus, meals, and dining (2013:154), an approach she later named "gastronomic archaeology," an interdisciplinary examination of how people experience meals and mealtimes and the social, cultural, and sensory contexts of eating (2017). Although neither mentions cuisine, both approaches would gather data that could be used to infer cuisine; the former would be inclusive of data broader than cuisine, and the latter would require the use of written records.

We do not propose a unified approach of "culinary archaeology," because, as demonstrated by the studies in this volume, the ways in which archaeologists can explore cuisine are wide and varied. However, like Beaudry, we acknowledge that the pursuit of past culinary traditions often requires multiproxy and/or interdisciplinary approaches because of the complex nature of cuisine itself. Many previous studies of cuisine and those contained within this volume demonstrate the efficacy and power of these approaches.

CULINARY STUDIES IN ARCHAEOLOGY

This volume is not the first to address the issues of cuisine; archaeologists have been exploring the role of cuisine, explicitly or not, in past societies for the past two decades. These works investigate the role of food and cooking in identity and culture, although not all use the term "cuisine." Halstead and Barrett (2004), Fuller (2005), Atalay and Hastorf (2006), and Twiss (2012) were among the first to define and outline cuisine or cuisine-related concepts in the context of archaeology. Since then, other researchers have begun to explore the topic from a variety of perspectives, including the role of food selection and preference (Smith 2006) and the identification of the methods and meanings of cooking (Graff 2018, 2020; Graff and Rodríguez-Alegría 2012; Moore 2012).

As food and cuisine can be used to signal identity and is a strong symbol of cultural affinity, discussions of identity and ethnicity dominate the archaeological literature on food choice and cuisine (Bardolph 2014; Barrett et al. 2001; Cook and Schurr 2009; Egan-Bruhy 2014; Hastorf 2017; Jones and Richards 2003; Oras et al. 2018; O'Sullivan 2003; Painter and O'Gorman 2019; Scott 1996; Smith 2006). Studies focused on cooking and food preparation, oft-overlooked yet critical components of cuisine, have proliferated as methods for investigating cooking practices have improved (Arranz-Otaetui et al. 2018; Buonasera et al. 2019; Graff and Rodríguez-Alegría 2012; Moore 2012). One of the growing trends in archaeology is the investigation of cuisine by identifying the components of food residues associated with ceramic cooking pots (Briggs 2016; Dotzel 2021; Miller et al. 2020; Papakosta et al. 2019; Reber and Evershed 2004; Shoda et al. 2018; Taché and Craig 2015; Yoshida et al. 2013).

Although the word "cuisine" has appeared in archaeological publication titles in the past (e.g., Joyce and Henderson 2007; Saul et al. 2013), the trend has proliferated in the past five years (Brinkman 2019; Dunne at al. 2022; Hendy et al. 2018; Kooiman 2021; Liu and Reid 2020; Lundy et al. 2021; Popper 2019; Robson et al. 2019; Tsafou and García-Granero 2021). These studies encompass research across Europe, Asia, Africa, and North America, from ancient to historic time periods. This suggests a widespread disciplinary shift in perspective provided by both food and cooking for understanding past societies, perhaps prompted by advanced methods for identifying foodstuffs and analyzing cooking implements and techniques, and their ever-increasing tandem application to the study of past food habits. Whether this focus on cuisine is a trend or a more permanent corner turned, archaeological understandings of human society and food benefit from the research of this era. Studies focused on cuisine in the ancient Indigenous Midcontinent are no exception.

ARCHAEOLOGY OF FOOD IN THE MIDCONTINENT

In this volume, we follow the Midwest Archaeological Conference's usage of Midcontinental to refer to the Midwestern United States and neighboring areas, including the area "between the Appalachian Mountains and the Great Plains, [and] from the Boreal Forests to the Gulf of Mexico" (*Midcontinental Journal of Archaeology* Aims and Scope statement), though we exclude the far south from consideration. Archaeologists working in this region have largely followed the same broad disciplinary trends in subsistence studies, including the recent focus on foodways and cuisine. Midcontinental archaeological studies produce a wealth of information about subsistence and settlement adaptations that reflects the rich landscape of this region. Over thousands of years, the Midcontinent has had diverse cuisines tied to social and environmental variability. Plant and animal communities vary from prairie to forest to riverine, and great and small lacustrine settings.

In the Midcontinent, Native Americans created a vibrant social tapestry of which food and cuisine were central; the depth and breadth of subsistence studies reflect this richness. Birthplace of the Eastern Agricultural Complex (EAC), it is here that archaeologists discovered (Asch and Asch 1977, 1978; Struever 1962; Watson 1969, 1974;) and continue to trace the emergence and patterns of farming of native domesticates (Asch and Asch 1985; Fritz and Smith 1988; Gremillion 2004; Mueller 2017; Smith et al. 2007; Smith and Yarnell 2009; Watson and Kennedy 1991) and later adaptations incorporating nonlocal plants (Fritz 2019; Monaghan et al. 2014). Food choice and acquisition in the Midcontinent went beyond agricultural pursuits. In some areas, particularly among hunter-gatherers of the Upper Great Lakes and other northern climes, specific wild resources, such as fish and wild rice, provided ample bounty and became the focus of cuisine (Boyd et al. 2014; Cleland 1982; Dunham 2014; Smith 2004). As well, many societies within a wide range of environmental settings spanning thousands of years adapted semisedentary to sedentary lifestyles often including horticultural pursuits (Fritz 2019) along with local hunting and fishing traditions (Schroeder 2004).

Many of the foundational studies that uncovered this complex regional history of subsistence used traditional evidence for diet and subsistence, such as faunal and macrobotanical remains. While such important work continues, other approaches have emerged. Following in the footsteps of their colleagues working in southeastern North America (e.g., Peres 2017; Peres and Deter-Wolf 2018; Scarry and Reitz 2005; Welch and Scarry 1995), scholars in the Midcontinent began shifting their direction of inquiry from the identification of foodstuffs and the timing of their use or adoption toward more holistic interrogations of foodways and the role of food in ancient Indigenous cultures. Although a favorite approach among scholars studying Mississippian societies (Bardolph 2014; Buchanan 2018; VanDerwarker et al. 2013), it has also been used in a variety of temporal and geographic contexts across the Midcontinent (Kooiman 2016; McLeester and Schurr 2020; Neubauer 2017; O'Gorman 2016; Painter and O'Gorman 2019; Redmond et al. 2020; Watts et al. 2011).

Although there will always be a need and a place for subsistence and foodways studies, regional scholars have realized the value of understanding past culinary traditions. Archaeologists in the Midcontinent are now on the cutting edge of research focusing on cuisine. The studies in this volume represent some of the best examples of this research.

CUISINE: A MIDCONTINENTAL PERSPECTIVE

Several interrelated themes arise throughout the studies in this volume, including food choice, culinary practices, and the social contexts of cuisine. Methodologies vary within and between themes as well, and several chapters employ newer and innovative techniques such as experimental work on corn nixtamalization, identification of food residues, the use of cooking facilities, and use-wear of pottery. Using multiproxy holistic approaches that bring together what are traditionally separate analytical categories is another commonality among many of the studies here, representing a trend emphasizing multiple lines of evidence to bring about richer and stronger interpretations of past cuisine. Differences through time or between contemporary social groups also crosscut the themes. Like any aspect of culture, cuisine can change from generation to generation through creative agency, but culinary alterations may also be a result of new environmental pressures, either natural or social. The social aspects of food choice and cuisine are particularly important for understanding identity, including the use of cuisine to take on an identity, or to distinguish and define one's identity through specific culinary practices and food choice. These decisions often facilitated social negotiations in the past, as they still do today.

Recognizing selected plant and animal components that served as food is a central component to cuisine studies, and it is here that traditional methods of diet reconstruction or subsistence patterns are foundational. Studies within this volume incorporate traditional methods of identifying past diet but go beyond the identification of general consumption patterns to explore contextual distinctions and differences in cuisine across time and space. Two chapters, Martin's (chapter 5) faunal analysis and Nordine's (chapter 6) paleoethnobotanical study, examine a specific ritually related feature within the larger context of plant and animal use at the Morton Village site in the Central Illinois River Valley. Their studies illuminate the use of cuisine in social negotiations among local Mississippian and migrant Oneota residents. Diachronic trends in cuisine from Early through Late Woodland emerge in Haas's (chapter 3) contribution that brings together plant and animal data along with ceramic trends from southeastern Wisconsin. Farther south in the American Bottom, Schaefer, Simon, and King (chapter 9) use archaeobotanical assemblages to reveal shifts in multiple aspects of cuisine as it relates to

INTRODUCTION 11

changing social organization despite a remarkably stable selection of plants from Terminal Late Woodland through the height of Mississippian power at Cahokia. Culinary practices, including food processing, cooking, serving, and consumption, build on understandings of the array of food items selected by revealing the transformative process of turning plants and animals into cuisine. Neubauer (chapter 1) takes us to the Late Archaic period in the Great Lakes where she identifies earth ovens for baking. Cooking in ceramic pots developed in the Midwest shortly thereafter and chapters by Kooiman and Albert (chapter 2), and Painter and O'Gorman (chapter 4) examine use-wear on vessels to access specific cooking methods. Kooiman and Albert's (chapter 2) methodology couples use-alteration with food residue analysis to reveal regional culinary traditions from Middle to Late Woodland times. By looking at functional, stylistic, and spatial contexts of one particular vessel type, Painter and O'Gorman (chapter 4) examine the social role of cuisine in postmigration negotiations at the Morton Village site. The role of cuisine in community identity and the emergence of new traditions is also explored by Betzenhauser (chapter 8) in her chapter on the use of nixtamalization by Mississippians in the American Bottom, and Malainey (chapter 7) evaluates the introduction of maize and cultural connections in Manitoba. Experimental archaeology coupled with archaeometric analysis and contextual data on related pottery forms allows Betzenhauser (chapter 8) to bring the nixtamalization process to light. Malainey (chapter 7) draws on identifying the movement of a new cuisine into an area by recognizing not only the food components but also tools of production and processing. Two of the chapters (Malainey, chapter 7, and Schaefer, Simon, and King, chapter 9) emphasize major societal shifts and are particularly informative as they highlight the link to food choice in those shifts.

A HISTORY OF INDIGENOUS FOOD, SUBSISTENCE, AND COOKING IN THE MIDCONTINENT

As the chapters in this volume cover considerable amounts of time (3000 BC to AD 1400) and space (Figure I.1), we provide an introduction of the cultural developments from Paleoindian to Late Precontact periods within the Midcontinent for nonspecialists or those working outside the region. We suggest Gayle J. Fritz's (2019) book, *Feeding Cahokia: Early Agriculture in the North American Heartland,* for further reading as it provides an accessible and detailed account of the evidence for changing plant use patterns from Archaic through Mississippian periods in the Midwest.

12   SUSAN M. KOOIMAN, JODIE A. O'GORMAN, AND AUTUMN M. PAINTER

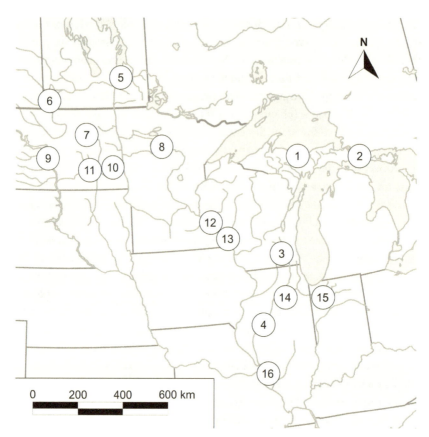

Figure I.1. Map of archaeological sites discussed in the book: 1. Site 914; 2. Cloudman Site; 3. Finch Site and Koshkonong Creek Village; 4. Morton Village; 5. Lockport; 6. Olson/DgMG-40c; 7. Devils Lake northeastern Plains village (NEPV) sites; 8. Bemidji; 9. Knife-Heart River area; 10. Shea; 11. James River NEPV sites; 12. Red Wing–Pepin locality; 13. Trempealeau–La Crosse area; 14. Zimmerman; 15. Greismer; and 16. Cahokia. (Base map by Kaldari and Halava, CC BY-SA 3.0. Additional rivers added by Autumn M. Painter using Affinity Designer.)

There are no chapters covering cuisine of the Paleoindian period (13,000–8000 BC); reframing Paleoindian subsistence to focus on cuisine would certainly be an interesting development. The Midcontinent was an entirely different landscape than today with incredible torrential rivers too dangerous for boat use (Morrow 2014) and fishing, with receding ice in the north leaving behind the Great Lakes. Little is known about Paleoindian subsistence beyond evidence of megafauna use and large cervid hunting (Carr 2012; Seeman et al. 2008); there is scant evidence for plant use (Gingerich and Kitchel 2014).

During the transition from Pleistocene to Holocene epochs, climatic changes created new environmental landscapes in the Midcontinent. Cultural shifts of the Early Archaic (9500–7000 BC) and Middle Archaic (7000–4000 BC) periods saw the introduction of new foods and cuisines that were transformational as well. Grassland and forest habitats formed, rivers stabilized and aquatic ecosystems formed, and the Great Lakes reached their current configurations (Styles and McMillan 2009). During this early Holocene period, greater differentiation in subregional environmental conditions emerged. People hunted bison in prairies of the western Midcontinent, while deer and smaller mammals, such as squirrels and rabbits, were the focus in other subregions. Other aquatic resources, especially in seasonally replenished backwaters, including waterfowl, fish, and freshwater bivalves, contributed to cuisines as well. Compared to the Pleistocene, cuisines of the Early and Middle Archaic periods expanded greatly not only because climatic and other environmental shifts changed floral and faunal communities, but also because people began tending their local landscapes to optimize food availability (Styles and McMillan 2009). Archaeological evidence for food choices included a wider array of animals and wild plants, such as nuts used for oil and nutmeats, and seedy and wetland plants (Fritz 2019; Simon 2009; Styles and McMillan 2009). By the Late Archaic (4000–1000 BC), people were baking in their earth ovens as studied by Neubauer (chapter 1), or cooking food in organic (nonceramic) containers, boiling the contents internally by adding heated stones (Neubauer 2018; Sassaman 1993; Skibo et al. 2009). Archaic communities were growing squash, sunflower, and marshelder and a bit later had added an array of other plants including chenopod, maygrass, erect knotweed, and little barley (Asch and Asch 1985; Fritz 2019; Simon 2009; Smith 2011). We know these cultigens as the Eastern Agricultural Complex (EAC). Archaic peoples returned often to camps located in areas with diverse and abundant resources, optimizing the use of locations where they could rely on good fishing, nut harvests, deer, and small mammals (Fritz 2019). Wetland resources appear to be particularly important as well (O'Gorman and Lovis 2006).

During the Early (1,000–300 BC) and Middle Woodland (300 BC to 400 AD) periods, foodways established by the Late Archaic continued, but there were important developments that would vastly change cuisine in the Midcontinent. By Early Woodland times the use of pottery vessels became widespread and signaled a major shift in cuisine. Initially thick-walled and grit-tempered, vessels were likely used for processing nut (Ozker 1982) and sunflower oils, as well as simmering of other foods (O'Gorman and Lovis 2006). However, along the northern margins of the region, particularly in the northern Great

Lakes, social groups who were likely exposed to pottery technology chose not to adopt it, instead carrying on with cooking traditions and technologies that continued to suit their highly mobile lifestyle (Brose and Hambacher 1999; Skibo et al. 2009). In some areas, subsistence efforts were more focused EAC cultigens, particularly in the more southern part of the Midcontinent, while in the north there seems to be more reliance on gathered foods and hunting/fishing, and likewise more mobility (O'Gorman and Lovis 2006). However, even in areas with greater emphasis on the cultigens, these foods remained supplementary to economies more focused on the foraging of wild plants (Wymer and Abrams 2003). Additionally, the increasing use of cultivated plants may have led to small shifts in hunting practices, particularly garden hunting (Wymer and Abrams 2003).

During the Middle Woodland period, a sphere of interaction and exchange referred to as Hopewell (Charles and Buikstra 2006; Carr 2005) connected local communities through the building and use of ceremonial centers and linked centers in Ohio, Illinois, and Michigan together. Interaction among those connected to the centers included an exchange of local and exotic items artfully made and imbued with symbolic meaning along with the flow of ideas and personal relationships (Bolnik and Smith 2007). Foods were likely exchanged within the sphere as well (Mueller 2013). Maize, developing into a food staple over much of the Midcontinent in later periods, is first introduced during the Middle Woodland likely as a novel food in the exchange network, a curiosity rather than a staple (Fritz 2019). In the north, communities engaged in trade relationships or down-the-line exchange with Hopewellian communities but eschewed adoption of distinctly Hopewell materials or burial practices. These groups adopted pottery by ca. 200 BC (Albert et al. 2018), manufacturing vessels in the style of the geographically expansive Laurel tradition and other related local traditions (Brose and Hambacher 1999). Chapters by Kooiman and Albert (chapter 2) and Haas (chapter 3) explore local changes in the upper Great Lakes and southeastern Wisconsin, respectively, to better understand cuisines of these earlier Woodland periods and the significant changes that develop during the succeeding Late Woodland period.

It is during the Late Woodland period (AD 400–900 or later) that we see a growing differentiation in the types of lifestyles practiced by groups in different subregions of the Midcontinent. Variability in subsistence pursuits was one aspect of cultural differentiation that included settlement patterns, stylistic and technological shifts in pottery, localized distinctions in ceremonial life that often incorporated variations on the use and building of mounds (McElrath et al. 2000; see Johannessen 1993 for foodways overview). Introduction of the bow and arrow along with other techniques leading to more efficient ways of hunting surely also affected cuisine. In the American Bottom, EAC farmers of the Terminal Late Woodland shifted to a focus on maize and helped give rise to the Cahokia phenomenon (Fritz 2019). Betzenhauser (chapter 8) and Schaefer, Simon, and King (chapter 9) begin their studies of the role of cuisine in the rise of Cahokia and Mississippian society in this period (AD 900–1050).

This was not the Late Woodland scenario in the rest of the Midcontinent. Farther north, groups maintained more of a mobile lifestyle but within increasingly restricted territories, leading to a focus on highly productive seasonal resources such as fish or wild rice, while sometimes adding maize and other cultigens as a supplement to their diets (Albert et al. 2108; Cleland 1982; Dunham 2014; Kooiman et al. 2022; Lovis et al. 2001; McHale Milner 1998; O'Shea and McHale Milner 2002; Schroeder 2004). In some areas, maize began to play a larger role, and Late Woodland groups gave rise to a number of Upper Mississippian groups who incorporated maize, bean, and squash agriculture into their more permanent villages without taking on the sociopolitically hierarchical nature of the Mississippians. By AD 1000, there was a patchwork of different societies in the Midcontinent with their own identities—cuisine is expected to have played a significant role in the formation and negotiations of those identities.

During the Late Precontact (AD 1000–1600 or later) period, an array of societies occupied the Midcontinent, including Mississippians, Upper Mississippians, and several groups with characteristics more similar to societies of the Plains. One way to understand the interactions of these groups is through their shifting culinary traditions. Malainey (chapter 7) considers the cultural implications of the spread of maize farming into the northern reaches of its distribution. All of these groups could be described as living in villages with subsistence linked to farming, but the extent to which maize played a role in their subsistence, along with sociopolitical and other cultural variables, produce important distinctions (see Schroeder 2004 for a detailed discussion). Our discussion focuses on Oneota and Mississippian traditions to provide context for the chapters in this volume.

Oneota groups were widespread in discontinuous areas of Wisconsin, Iowa, Illinois, Minnesota, and Michigan (see Schroeder 2004:Figure 3). Oneota sites are easily distinguished from Late Woodland or Mississippian sites by shell-tempered pottery bearing iconic Oneota motifs. The pottery of these three traditions is important as it reveals potential culinary distinctions. Late Woodland and Oneota pottery assemblages are predominantly jars, while

Mississippian assemblages include jars, bowls, plates, bottles, pans, beakers, and more (Schroeder 2004).

There is a great deal of variation within the Oneota tradition across time and space in terms of size and organization of village sites, but all share a lack of the type of hierarchical structure evident at Mississippian sites. Likewise, in subsistence patterns, there is a good deal of variability in the particular cultigens and wild plants and animals making up diet, but Oneota tended to focus more on the intensification through diversification model (Gallager and Arzigian 1994) than on intensification of maize agriculture or EAC crops found in Mississippian society (Egan-Bruhy 2014), although corn played a role in Oneota cuisine. Oneota typically grew corn, beans, and squash, and they used a wide range of fruits, wetland plants, nuts, and other foods in addition to selective use of EAC crops. Hunting and fishing also played a critical role in Oneota cuisine. Deer, sometimes elk, sometimes bison, small mammals, birds, and fish, seemingly anything available locally (or accessible during hunting forays), were all incorporated into Oneota subsistence patterns. Research to delimit variability in food choice and other aspects of cuisine within the Oneota tradition remains largely unexplored. Chapters 4 to 6 examine Oneota cuisine and its role in identity from a single village where local Mississippian and Oneota people that migrated into the area resided. Painter and O'Gorman (chapter 4) examine the adoption of a type of Mississippian serving vessel by Oneota cooks and its role in identity and other social negotiations. Martin (chapter 5) identifies quotidian and rare animal deposits within a special function context, and Nordine (chapter 6) provides insights into the nontypical plant remains from that context and offers a broader view of Oneota and Mississippian plant food choice and identity at the site.

The Mississippian tradition in the Midcontinent (AD 1000–1400) was located in the central Mississippi Valley, Ohio Valley, and Tennessee and Cumberland valleys (see Schroeder 2004:Figure 4). Mississippian societies also had a good deal of variation but shared a hierarchical social organization embedded in religion that involved large-scale mound building and intensive agriculture built on crops of the EAC and incorporation of maize, squash, and later beans. This hierarchical community structure also led to class-based differences in cuisine (Ambrose et al. 2003; Jackson and Scott 2003). In the American Bottom and other locations, settlement patterns include a hierarchy of sites from scattered small rural farmsteads to large political centers with large mounds. Cahokia was the largest of these centers with administrative and burial mounds, a large plaza, neighborhoods, and direct linkages to a larger landscape of supporting administrative and ceremonial centers.

For years, archaeological interpretations at Cahokia and supporting sites in the American Bottom have stressed the importance of intensive maize agriculture. Understanding the culinary history of maize at Cahokia is important, and Betzenhauser (chapter 8) explores how maize was processed and the role of certain ceramic forms in this process. Although maize became important to Mississippian subsistence and identity, it was not at the expense of traditional, locally domesticated plants. New studies recognize the importance of farming traditional and diverse crops, especially EAC cultigens (Fritz 2019; Simon and Parker 2006). Beginning in the Terminal Late Woodland, Schaefer, Simon, and King (chapter 9) take us through the height of Cahokia examining changes in foods and their procurement along with shifts in social organization.

Given their sedentary and large villages tied into a regional system, food from the uplands, such as nuts and game, came to the larger administrative ceremonial sites, such as Cahokia. Floodplain resources, such as backwater and river channel fish, and waterfowl were among food choices. Crops could be grown in the floodplains as well as uplands (Fritz 2019). Not only were diverse foods flowing into Cahokia from the hinterlands, so too, it seems, were diverse people. Isotopic data have revealed that the population at Cahokia was made up of people from different areas of the Midcontinent, making it a multicultural city. As Fritz (2019:89) observes, such cultural diversity has "significant implications for the way we think about all aspects of social and economic life, including farming and cuisine." In other words, there is still much to explore about the complexities of life and social negotiations at Cahokia, including its culinary traditions and innovations.

So, given this already rich history of Midcontinental diet and subsistence, why cuisine? Cuisine combines the baseline ingredients of traditional subsistence studies with new perspectives and holistic approaches, a recipe that emphasizes and affirms the centrality of food in human society. In this volume, in highlighting cuisine, we also emphasize methods employed by archaeologists working in the Midcontinent that connect food choice to cooking/processing and the insights these provide into the natural, social, and ideological environments of the past.

Although we focus on cuisine, we do not suggest that there is no place in archaeology for food studies of wider or more focused scopes. In fact, some of the chapters in this volume demonstrate that some ancient societies underwent significant social and behavioral changes to accommodate new culinary components and practices. Other studies incorporating broader bodies of data to look at foodways and even interregional food systems will continue to be useful for understanding food-related movements and social interaction on a regional scale. Work focused more narrowly on diet and subsistence provides critical information about societies in the past and has provided the foundation of culinary research; past, present, and future work will remain foundational to studies exploring cuisine, foodways, and food systems. The body of work in this volume offers examples of how culinary research in the Midcontinent has enriched archaeological knowledge of its Indigenous occupants across space and time and makes a significant contribution to the literature on the emerging international field of archaeological cuisine studies.

Chapter 1

Earth Oven Cuisine via Fire-Cracked Rock Cooking in the Midcontinent

FERNANDA NEUBAUER

Earth oven usage was common among hunter-gatherer and ancient populations in the Midcontinent and worldwide, yet these oven features are often mischaracterized as hearths (Black and Thoms 2014:204). An earth oven (Figure 1.1a), however, is a specific layered cooking arrangement of fire, heated rocks, and food items designed to bake foods for periods ranging from a few hours to several days (Black and Thoms 2014:205). This chapter focuses on the cooking technique where food is sealed in a pit or depression with moisture supplied by the food itself and the packing materials like leaves. It also discusses some of the varying ways in which earth ovens were constructed and used ethnographically and archaeologically. Prepared in this manner, foods cook from all sides via moist heat in an oxygen-reduced environment (Milburn et al. 2009:3).

Fire-cracked rocks (FCR) used in earth ovens represent the physical remains of these cooking facilities. On Grand Island, in Michigan's Upper Peninsula, FCR dominate the Late Archaic (c. 3000–1 BC) archaeological assemblage, but few studies investigate the roles that this ubiquitous class of artifact played in the everyday lives of ancient peoples (e.g., Benchley et al. 1988; Neubauer 2016, 2018a, 2019; Skibo et al. 2009; Skibo and Malainey 2013).

This chapter provides an example of an earth oven facility containing FCR and discusses its archaeological signatures as well as the results of FCR use-alteration analysis. A case study of earth oven function is drawn from a Late Archaic period feature dated to approximately 1000 BC at Site 914 (FS09-10-03-914/20AR387) on Grand Island (Figure 1.2). The analysis of earth oven feature morphology, soil characteristics, and associated materials at Site 914 is also discussed to contextualize cuisine and FCR use by Late Archaic people in the region.

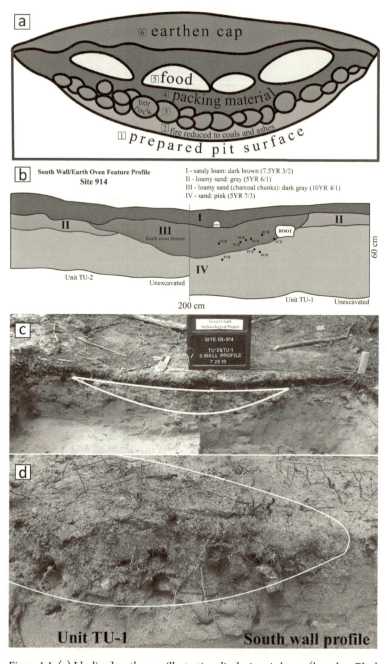

Figure 1.1. (a) Idealized earth oven illustration displaying six layers (based on Black and Thoms 2014:205): (1) prepared pit surface; (2) fire reduced to ashes and coals; (3) hot rocks; (4) packing material (e.g., leaves); (5) food; and (6) earthen cap. (b, c) South wall profiles of units TU-2 and TU-1 showing the profile of the earth oven feature at Site 914. (d) Close-up of the feature profile showing the disturbance of tree roots at the site. (Courtesy of Fernanda Neubauer.)

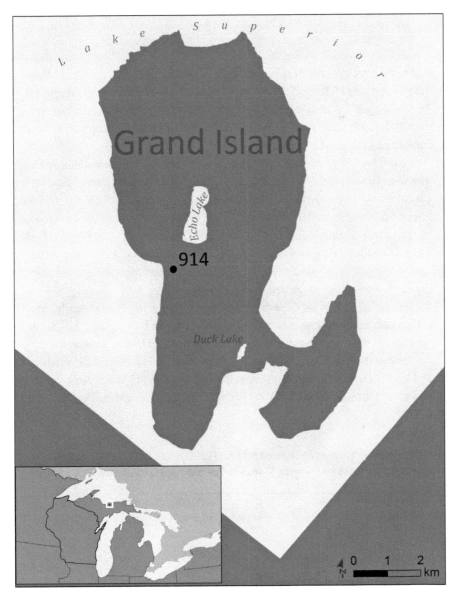

Figure 1.2. Location of Site 914 on Grand Island in Michigan's Upper Peninsula. (Base map from ArcGIS [ESRI]. Map courtesy of Fernanda Neubauer.)

SITE BACKGROUND

Site 914 is situated at an elevation of 192–95 m above mean sea level, with an estimated total site area of approximately 40,000 m². In 1991, the Leech Lake Tribal Council's Heritage Sites Program (LLHSP 1992) identified the site via 35 positive shovel tests containing high concentrations of FCR, often with over 100 pieces recovered in a single test pit. No Phase II excavations were conducted by LLHSP in 1991.

From July 17 to August 1, 2013, I codirected Phase II excavations at Site 914 with James M. Skibo and Eric C. Drake as part of the Grand Island Archaeological Program and in collaboration with local Anishinaabe and the US Forest Service (Neubauer 2013). We identified over 100 positive shovel tests, which predominantly contained FCR. Shovel testing pit 9–9.5 (Figure 1.3) was selected for further investigation because it contained a high concentration of 157 lithics, of which 149 were FCR. Four units measuring one square meter each were then excavated there according to true north (see Figure 1.3), on the southern portion of the site. Level one, a layer composed of sandy loam (O horizon, sod layer), was excavated by natural levels (see Figure 1.1b), while subsequent levels were excavated via arbitrary levels of five centimeters.

The units contained 7,028 lithics: 89% (n = 6,271) were FCR weighing 114 kg, 9% (n = 644) were chipped stone, and 2% (n = 113) were nonknapped rocks and ground stones (Table 1.1). The archaeological assemblage from the

Table 1.1. Quantification of Chipped Stones, Fire-Cracked Rocks (FCR), and Nonknapped Rocks and Ground Stones at Site 914, by Raw Material Type

Raw Material	Chipped Stone		FCR		Nonknapped Rock and Ground Stone		Total	
	n.	%	n.	%	n.	%	n.	%
Quartzite	398	61.80	5,126	81.74	91	80.54	5,615	79.90
Quartz	157	24.38	768	12.25	3	2.65	928	13.20
Chert	88	13.66					88	1.25
Sandstone	1	0.16	192	3.06	14	12.4	207	2.95
Basalt			50	0.80	1	0.88	51	0.73
Black shale					1	0.88	1	0.01
Other			135	2.15	3	2.65	138	1.96
Total	644	100	6,271	100	113	100	7,028	100

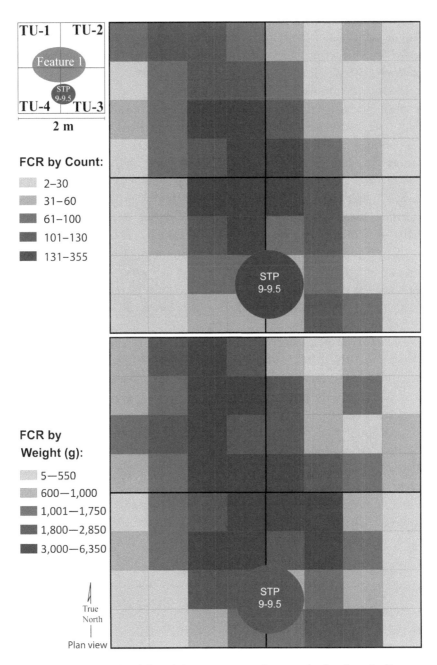

Figure 1.3. Fire-cracked rock (FCR) density at Site 914 by count (*top*) and weight (*bottom*), indicating a heavier concentration of FCR in and around the feature. STP = shovel test pit. (Illustration courtesy of Fernanda Neubauer.)

site is associated with an earth oven feature visible in all four units, measuring 1 m in diameter and 20 cm deep (see Figure 1.1b–d). A charcoal sample collected from the feature yielded an accelerator mass spectrometry (AMS) date of 2950 ± 30 ^{14}C BP (Beta-423705, wood charcoal, δ^{13}C = -25.5‰, cal BC 1260–1050; Neubauer 2018a:693). This sample was collected from unit TU-4 at 80 cm north, 49 cm east, and 12 cm below surface and was situated atop a FCR piece in charcoal-stained soil also containing charcoal pieces.

During experiments, Bellomo (1991) observed that, in general, natural fires create a hole in the substratum, while only human-controlled fires produce basin-shaped features in profile. The units at Site 914 were visibly disturbed by tree roots (see Figure 1.1c, d), but the basin-shaped morphology of its feature indicates that it was created through human activity (see Figure 1.1b). In addition, lining the bottom of the feature was a heavy concentration of FCR. Figure 1.3 shows the plan view distribution of FCR by count and weight. Both display a heavier concentration of FCR where the feature is situated, and a gradual decrease farther from the feature. FCR is piled up directly north of the feature, and to the south to a lesser degree.

I have discussed elsewhere the evidence for hunting, fishing, gathering, larger-scale food processing, and cooking at Late Archaic sites on Grand Island (Neubauer 2016, 2018a, 2018b). I suggested that the dense accumulations of FCR, associated with food processing tools and some traces of the foods themselves, were the primary by-products of communal culinary practices. I suggested that Grand Island represented an important place on the landscape for the Late Archaic peoples who repeatedly used the island for fall social and food-processing aggregations, while other seasons were characterized by the dispersal of smaller groups throughout the landscape. When comparing Late Archaic sites on the southern shore of Lake Superior in the Upper Peninsula with Late Archaic sites from Grand Island, I noted that Grand Island sites tend to be much larger in scale as a by-products of their repeated short-term reoccupation (Neubauer 2018b).

BACKGROUND INFORMATION ON EARTH OVEN CUISINE IN NORTH AMERICA

The oldest known earth oven facility in North America was identified at the Moose Creek site in Central Alaska and dates to around 8500 BC, while earth ovens in the Great Plains and northwest regions date to approximately 8000 BC (Walter and Schroeder 2023; Thoms 2009). The use of FCR is nearly ubiquitous throughout the Archaic period, but not during the preceding Paleoindian and subsequent Woodland periods (Hill 2007:299; Speth 2015:57; Thoms 2008a:121). By about 2000 BC, there is generally a marked increase in the number and diversity of hot-rock cooking features (Thoms 2009).

Thoms (1989, 2009) suggests that the intensification of hot-rock cooking technology, which was necessary for foods that required prolonged cooking, was a manifestation of land-use intensification. Prolonged cooking facilitated land-use intensification by affording greater use of nutrients across the available foods on a given landscape and by making some foods more palatable and digestible. Earth ovens are widely used in family and communal cookery, often to bake underground plant storage organs, such as tubers, bulbs, taproots, corms, and root nodes (Thoms 2015:199). For example, Lepofsky and Peacock (2004) suggest that the 453 post-2000 BC earth ovens that they identified and analyzed from the Canadian Plateau in southwest Canada were primarily used to process root foods.

Ethnohistoric and Ethnographic Descriptions

In February 1682, Robert Cavelier de La Salle, a French explorer, dined at Indigenous villages between the mouths of the Missouri and Ohio Rivers. In a letter published by Pierre Margry, La Salle described an earth oven used to cook a wild root called *macopin* that tasted like sweet onions and grew in nearby swamps (Thoms 2008b:445).

Although numerous foods were baked in earth ovens, including meat and various plants, some of the most commonly cooked foods using the technique were tubers and bulbs (Black and Thoms 2014:204; Ellis 1997:55). For example, ethnographic information provided by Buckelew (1911:72–73) describes the use of hot rocks in earth ovens by the Lipan Apache in Texas to cook sotol (*Dasylirion texanum*) for several days, where they dug large circular holes three to four feet deep and several feet in diameter.

Some earth ovens were made with small holes through which water could be poured to cook foods through steaming, known as steaming pits or steaming ovens (Thoms 2008b). Ethnographic accounts by Coues (1893:1012) report that the Chopunnish (Nez Perce) in the Pacific Northwest poured small amounts of water through a hole in their earth ovens. Moreover, in the 1930s, ethnographic data from Kalispel elders, hunter-gatherers living in forested montane regions of northeastern Washington and northern Idaho, attest to the use of wild plant foods, earth ovens, steaming and boiling pits, and hot-rock griddles during the 1800s (Thoms 2008b:443). Round (c. 2.4–3.1 m in diameter and 0.15 m deep) or elliptical earth oven pits (c. 2.1 x 1.5 x 0.15 m) were used by the Kalispel people to cook camas bulb (*Camassia quamash*; Thoms 2008b:449).

Unfortunately, though, ethnographic evidence for the use and construction of earth ovens is generally lacking from the Midcontinent (Wilson and VanDerwarker 2015:167). An exception are the accounts of Hough (1926:37) for the Ho-Chunk—also known as Winnebago—who lived in parts of Wisconsin, Minnesota, Iowa, and Illinois, and cooked maize in steaming ovens: "They dig a large circular pit 1 to 2 feet in depth, with flat smooth bottom, heaping the excavated earth in a ring around the border of the pit. A heap of new corn is piled near by and rocks are heated on a fire. Everything being in readiness, the hot rocks are piled in the middle of the pit and the corn heaped in, leaving a central hole down to the rocks. Earth is covered over the mass and water poured down on to the rocks, producing a tremendous volume of steam. The pit remains closed for several hours."

Variation

The case study discussed in this chapter is only one example of an earth oven feature, but there is considerable variation in earth oven size, construction method, and the amount of time used to cook foods (see Thoms et al. 2018). Furthermore, there are two predominant methods of heating: direct, when a fire is built inside a pit, and indirect, when heated rocks are placed on the ground surface or in a shallow pit for slow cooking (Wilson and VanDerwarker 2015:168). Generally, based on Wandsnider's (1997) cross-cultural ethnographic study, fires were built inside pits for direct heat in high-temperature cooking, while heated rocks covered with layers of vegetation for indirect heat were normally used to prepare foods requiring a moist cooking environment.

Earth ovens are a subclass of pit features used for cooking (Wilson and VanDerwarker 2015:166). Archaeological analyses of earth ovens, roasting pits, and pit features have contributed considerably to studies of late precontact cuisine in the Midcontinent (e.g., Bardolph 2014; Binford et al. 1970; DeBoer 1988; Fortier 1983; Harris 1996; Holt 1996; Kelly et al. 1987; Koldehoff and Galloy 2006; Stahl 1985; Wilson and VanDerwarker 2015). For example, Binford and colleagues (1970) provided one of the earliest and most detailed investigations of Late Woodland (AD 500–1000) and Mississippian (AD 1000–1400) earth ovens at the Hatchery West site in Illinois.

Some scholars (e.g., Barr 1979; Cremin 1980, 1996, 1999; Faulkner 1972; Parachini 1981; Spero 1979; Walz 1991) have also documented large numbers of roasting pits or pit features associated with Late Precontact Upper Mississippian sites in northwestern Indiana and southwestern Lower Michigan that exhibit a somewhat different morphology and construction technique from the feature from Site 914. These features, while of similar size as the Grand

Island feature, are deeper and lack the copious amounts of FCR, among other attributes. In contrast, roasting facilities associated with Late Woodland sites in the Upper Ohio Valley, similar to the one from Grand Island, have been examined by Espenshade (1999).

Therefore, there is potential variation in the construction of earth ovens geographically and/or temporally. This may suggest several important factors about how these facilities were constructed and used, ranging from different types of culinary practices through broader aspects of how people were organizing themselves across the cultural and natural landscapes.

LITHIC ANALYSIS AND EARTH OVEN COOKING TECHNOLOGY

All of the lithics used as hot rocks at Site 914 were beach cobbles, which are readily available along the shoreline of Grand Island. Of the total FCR assemblage, 82% (n = 5,126) were quartzite, 12% (n = 768) were quartz, 3% (n = 192) were sandstone, 2% (n = 135) were other raw material types (mostly granite, gneiss, and gabbro), and 1% (n = 50) were basalt (see Table 1.1). Because the feature was predominantly concentrated in levels two (c. 7 to 12 cm below surface) and three (c. 12 to 17 cm below surface), I selected the FCR from those levels for further analysis. The results of my analysis of 1,509 FCR weighing 42 kg is discussed below. Here, only rocks that completely fractured into two or more pieces (i.e., heat fracture) and that were identified in situ (i.e., not in the screen) make up the sum of 1,509 FCR, thus allowing for an analyses of their spatial distribution and fracture patterns. Of those, 1,319 consist of quartzite, all of which were beach cobbles.

FCR Use Alteration

Use alteration is defined as the chemical and physical changes that occur on the surface and/or subsurface of FCR as a direct or indirect result of use in a human fire-related activity. In contrast, nonuse alteration of FCR can be caused by a variety of natural processes, such as wildfires. The magnitude of use alteration is largely determined by the amount of time a rock remained heated, the intensity of heat to which the rocks are exposed, and the number of episodes in which they are heated (Jackson 1998).

Earth ovens can be subjected to intense heat of up to 900°C for a relatively brief time followed by a long cool-down period (Stark 2002a:13). Therefore, because of the amount of time they remained heated, rocks used in earth ovens should display a high degree of use alteration (see Neubauer [2018a] for a detailed description of various FCR use-alteration patterns). Indeed, this appears

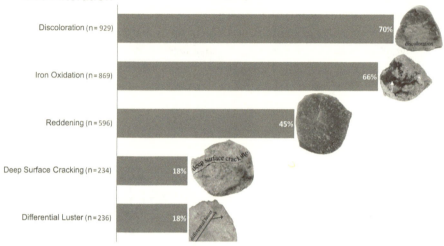
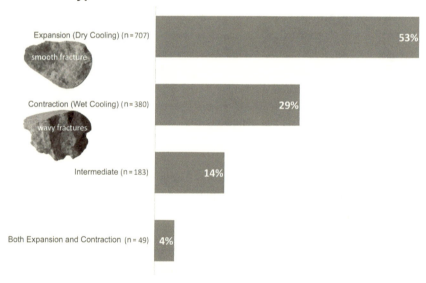

Figure 1.4. Quartzite fire-cracked rock (FCR) at Site 914: (*top*) fracture types indicating a predominance of expansion fracturing (dry cooling); (*bottom*) percentage and number of the most frequent use-alteration patterns, and examples of quartzite FCR fractured by contraction due to wet cooling and expansion during dry cooling. (Illustration courtesy of Fernanda Neubauer.)

to be the case at Site 914. Of the 1,319 quartzite FCR analyzed (Figure 1.4), 70% (n = 929) exhibited discoloration, 66% (n = 869) iron oxidation, 45% (n = 596) reddening, and 18% deep surface cracking (n = 234) and differential luster (n = 236).

FCR Fracture Patterns

Two distinct types of breakage patterns have been attributed to rocks cracked during dry or wet cooling, and these patterns are especially evident in quartzite (e.g., McDowell-Loudan 1983; McParland 1977; Taggart 1981; Zurel 1979), which comprises 82% of FCR at Site 914. Expansion-fractured FCR (dry cooling) display smooth fracturing (see Figure 1.4) and occur most frequently on rocks heated and cooled in a hearth, which causes the outside portion of the rock to heat and expand faster than the relatively cooler rock interior. In contrast, contraction-fractured FCR (wet cooling) exhibit crenulated (wavy, jagged) cracks over the fracture (see Figure 1.4) that are most frequently created during rapid cooling immersion in water (e.g., McDowell-Loudan 1983; McParland 1977; Taggart 1981; Zurel 1979). In contraction fracturing, the exterior of the rock cools quickly and contracts, setting up stress as a consequence of the shock response (Jackson 1998:39–41). Some FCR fracture types cannot be placed in either category and are referred to as intermediate type, while other FCR pieces exhibit both types of breakage and are denoted as both expansion and contraction fracture types.

At Site 914, 53% (n = 707) of the quartzite FCR exhibit expansion fractures (dry cooling) and 29% (n = 380) display contraction fractures (wet cooling), while 14% (n = 183) represent the intermediate type and 4% (n = 49) display both expansion and contraction fractures (see Figure 1.4). The high percentage of expansion fracture breakage pattern indicates that the rocks were slowly cooling in a relatively dry environment. Combined with the feature's size and morphology, the FCR characteristics further support an interpretation that the feature is the remnant of an earth oven used to bake foods.

Packing Material Moisture Content

Driver and Massey (1957:233) describe an earth oven as "a hole in the ground into which hot stones and food were placed. It was covered with the earth from the hole so that the heat and steam would be confined long enough to cook the food, normally overnight. The food was usually wrapped in leaves, bark, and other handy materials to keep it clean." The layer of vegetation is important to protect foods from the hot rocks and to provide moisture during the cooking process (Leach et al. 2005:202). High temperatures in the thermal elements (i.e., hot rocks), which reach around 900°C, and water in the packing material are necessary to maintain prolonged food temperatures near 100°C. The moisture in the packing material ensures an environment where steam permeates the food layer and cooks as convective heat, effectively preventing the food from burning (Stark 2002b:12).

The packing material adds moisture to the oven, which might explain why 29% of the quartzite FCR exhibit contraction fracturing or wet cooling (see Figure 1.4). Furthermore, the contraction fracturing suggests that Late Archaic peoples at Site 914 used an indirect heating method for slow cooking in a moist environment. This high percentage of contraction fracturing also indicates that an earthen cap closed the pit, trapping moisture and heat inside, as opposed to an open pit that would be expected to produce an even higher percentage of expansion-fractured FCR (Neubauer 2018a).

Earthen Cap

The earthen cap (see Figure 1.1a) is an important heat trap because as soon as a fire dies, any uncovered rocks rapidly begin to lose heat to the surrounding environment. Insulating the heating element in a pit with an earthen cap delays this conductive heat loss (Black and Thoms 2014:208).

In their experiments, Leach and colleagues (1998) found that a moderate-sized oven, about a meter in diameter like at Site 914, requires almost half a cubic meter of material (equivalent to 490 kg of sandy loam) to adequately seal it. This is a significant amount of material, so much so that the earth excavated to create the pit is not enough to seal an oven by itself during its first use, and therefore, it is necessary to add nearby earth. In subsequent firings it is possible to reuse earth, although the authors noted that each time an earthen cap was dismantled, the earth was widely scattered. Leach and collaborators (1998) caution that the process of borrowing earth to cover ovens has important implications for the understanding of site formation processes. It is possible that the collection of earth to construct and rebuild ovens would have incorporated artifacts from elsewhere on the site that are unrelated to the oven in cases where earthen caps were used.

Wood Fuel

Earth ovens are characterized by dark carbon-rich soils (Black and Thoms 2014:217). Sealed ovens create an oxygen-reduced atmosphere coating soil in soot, causing fuel beneath hot rocks to turn into charcoal. The fuel of open-air fire is usually more fully combusted and reduced to ashes (Black and Thoms 2014:217–18). Charcoal can break down through time via bioturbation and chemical weathering, however, while carbon-stained sediments often persist (see Figure 1.1d). The intensity of carbon staining can reflect a feature's age and soil characteristics, or the number of baking episodes (Black and Thoms 2014:218). The feature at Site 914 contained charcoal and charcoal-stained soils inside and around its proximity, indicating that fire was lit in situ.

Building and using earth ovens about one to two meters in diameter produces copious amounts of smoke, charcoal, FCR, and carbon-stained sediments. Accordingly, these cooking activities are unlikely to be conducted within or in close proximity to residential structures (Thoms 2008b:455). Thus, the construction and utilization of earth ovens by ancient peoples required longer timescales in both preparation and cook time, necessitating significant participation, cooperation, and energy input from members of the community to amass the resources to operate them (Backhouse 2008:123). Jackson (1998:115), for example, observed that, during earth oven replication experiments conducted in the northern Rocky Mountains, at least 200 pounds of Ponderosa pine and oak were needed for fuel, resulting in a maximum sustained temperature of 600–700°C.

At Site 914 on Grand Island, Kathryn Parker analyzed the flotation-derived botanical remains from two liters of soil samples collected from the feature and surrounding soils. Parker identified spruce, red oak, and conifer, which represent some of the wood types used as fuel for the earth oven (Table 1.2). No food remains were identified. The lack of food remains is consistent

Table 1.2. Flotation-Derived Flora Analyzed by Kathryn Parker

Botanic Information	Total Number
Total Wood	60
Total Weight (g)	0.67
Breakdown by Taxon	
Picea sp. (spruce)	1
Quercus sp., subgenus Erythrobalanus	
(red oak subgroup)	3
Conifer	14
Ring porous	3
Unidentifiable	7
Total Miscellaneous Botanical Materials	7
Dicotyledon stem	2
Gracile tendril	5

Note: These were collected from two liters of soil samples from the earth oven feature and its surroundings.

with expectations for identifying earth ovens in some regions based on ethnographic observations (Peacock 2002). These accounts indicate that sometimes the only plant materials that come in direct contact with fire are those used as heating elements in the hot-rock pavement area, so archaeobotanical assemblages of earth ovens should be generally dominated by the carbonized remains of the species of wood used as fuel (Peacock 2002:49–50).

The paucity of plant remains in the earth oven at Site 914 supports the ethnographic model predicting that plant-based foods may not always be preserved through charring because they could have been buffered from the heat by layers of foliage to protect them from burning, and thus preventing them from entering the archaeological record (Peacock 2002:50, 57). There are archaeological examples in the Midcontinent of botanical remains preserved within Mississippian/Woodland earth ovens (e.g., Cremin 1980; Frederick et al. 2019; Wilson and VanDerwarker 2015), possibly a result of differing regional cooking methods in which less or no buffer was used to shield food from the heating elements.

EARTH OVEN EXPERIMENTS

Scholars have used experiments to seek for identifiable ways that certain cooking and food preparation techniques might be visible archaeologically (e.g., Bentsen and Wurz 2019; Neubauer 2019; Thoms et al. 2018). Wilson and DeLyria (1999) conducted three earth oven experiments that were fired several months apart to cook camas. They selected 266 cobbles (135 kg) of andesite/basalt and quartzite weighing an average of 508 g. They placed rocks in a basin-shaped earth oven measuring 1 meter in diameter and 40 cm deep. This is the same shape and size of the oven at Site 914, except that the experimental pit was twice as deep. In all three actualistic experiments, the same 166 rocks were consecutively used in the base of the pit and 100 others on the top hot-rock layer. The base rocks were heated for 1.5 hours to a temperature of 350°C. A layer of sediment was placed on top of the lower heating element, followed by a layer of leaves, a layer containing food, and another layer of leaves. Over those layers more sediment and wood for the capping rock (the heating element) were placed, which were added to the fire and burned for 1.5 hours at a temperature of 300°C. After 1.5 hours, the pile of charcoal and rocks were covered with sediments to form an earthen cap 29 cm above the ground surface. The oven was opened 21 hours after its completion and the top heating element rocks continued to be approximately 50°C. According to ethnographic and archaeological records, earth oven pits around 1 meter in diameter, like the experimental oven and the one at Site 914 on Grand Island, were typically used for 24 hours or less (Thoms 2009:588).

Wilson and DeLyria (1999) determined that a low percentage of the quartzite rocks by weight remained whole: 1% in the upper heating element and 13% in the lower after the second oven experiment. During all three successive firing experiments, several rocks exploded within the first hour. They also exhibited a high number of deep surface cracks, which facilitates fracturing when rocks are used again in heating contexts. Most damage to the rock occurred during the initial firing, but damage continued with each successive firing. Rocks in the oven were fractured by spalling off thin flat potlids or by breaking into block-like chunks, with block breakage more common to quartzite than to igneous rocks.

During the three experiments, nearly 62% of the quartzite cobbles of the top layer and 40% of the bottom layer were fractured into block/core-like fragments (heat fractures that broke the core of the rock), and between 37% in the upper layer and 52% in the lower layer of the quartzite rocks by count were fractured into spall/flake-like fragments (small FCR pieces and roughly the size of flakes; Wilson and DeLyria 1999). The quartzite FCR recovered from within the earth oven feature at Site 914 on Grand Island was calculated for comparison with the results of Wilson and DeLyria's (1999) experiment (Table 1.3). The quartzite FCR recovered inside the feature in level 2 was compared with the results obtained for the top FCR layer of the experimental ovens, and level 3 with the bottom FCR layer. Note, however, that this is only for comparison purposes to estimate whether the studied oven could have been used/fired once or multiple times. This does not necessarily mean that the oven at Site 914 was constructed the same way as the experimental ovens, such as with two layers of hot rocks instead of one. The top layer (level 2) contained 86% (n = 107) spall/flake-like fragments and 14% (n = 17) block/

Table 1.3. Quantification of Quartzite Fire-Cracked Rocks Identified within the Earth Oven Feature at Site 914, by Fragmentation Type

| | Earth-Oven Feature | | | | | |
| | Level 2 | | Level 3 | | Total | |
Fragment Type	n.	%	n.	%	n.	%
Spall/flake-like	107	86	316	81	423	82
Block/core-like	17	14	74	19	91	18
Total	**124**	**100**	**390**	**100**	**514**	**100**

core-like fragments, and 81% (n = 316) and 19% (n = 74) in the bottom layer (level 3), respectively (see Table 1.3).

Likewise, among all raw material types at Site 914, 79% (n = 1,171) of the FCR comprised spall/flake-like fragments, while 21% (n = 338) were block/core-like fragments. The higher number of spall fragments in comparison to the lower number of block-like fragments, combined with the evidence regarding the large numbers of FCR inside and surrounding the feature, suggest that the oven at Site 914 had been used multiple times.

CUISINE AND LIPID RESIDUE ANALYSIS

The FCR may hold the key to investigating how food was processed and cooked by ancient peoples, especially in areas where organic remains are poorly preserved, as in the case of Site 914. One of the latest and most promising methodologies employed to address FCR utilization is through the extraction of ancient fatty acids preserved within the rock. Studies have demonstrated that lipid residues are readily absorbed into the micro-fractures that open when rocks are heated in cooking contexts (e.g., Quigg 2003; Quigg et al. 2001). Lipid residues are also present on the surface of pottery and ground stones, and within soil samples collected from hearth features (e.g., Haas, chapter 3; Kooiman and Albert, chapter 2; Kooiman 2021; Malainey and Figol 2014; Smith et al. 2015; Quigg 2003; Quigg et al. 2001). Incredibly, researchers have extracted fatty acids from 14,000-year-old hearth soil samples from Alaskan sites (Kedrowski et al. 2009).

On Grand Island, food residue studies have been conducted by Skibo and colleagues (2009). They selected three FCR samples recovered from the Late Archaic component at Site 754 for lipid residue analysis using gas chromatography as well as six ceramic sherds of the subsequent Initial Woodland period (AD 1–600) occupations from Sites 754 and 929. They noted that "the presence of plant sterols, very high levels of $C18:1$ isomers, low levels of $C18:0$, and only traces of triacylglycerols in these residues are consistent with their identification as nut oils" (Skibo and Malainey 2013:176), indicating that these FCR and ceramics were used to process and cook nuts. As a control, a local nonthermally altered quartzite cobble was tested for lipids and none were found. The Late Archaic component at Site 754 yielded a conventional radiocarbon age of 2950 ± 70 BP (Beta-201135; 1390–940 BC, 2-sigma; Skibo et al. 2009:48), indicating that the site is contemporaneous with Site 914 (2950 ± 30 BP).

Acorns, beechnuts, and hazelnuts are native to Grand Island (Ball 1993).

They are highly nutritious and provide an ample source of calories, fats, carbohydrates, fiber, and protein (Messner 2011:15). Acorns are naturally inedible without special preparation because of the presence of toxic tannic acids; therefore, cooking made some food resources, which were previously underutilized or not utilized because they were indigestible without processing, edible and more palatable. Hough (1926:36–37) describes an example of the use of earth ovens to cook acorns in which the "Pomos of California made a fire and put in stones to heat. When they were hot half of them were taken out and the remainder pushed together to form a layer, and were covered with a layer of oak and iris leaves. Acorn meal was then put on this layer, then a layer of leaves, and finally the remaining hot stones. Six inches of earth was piled on top and the heap was left to cook for six or eight hours."

Nuts have been identified at archaeological sites nearby Grand Island. Acorns and hazelnuts, along with large quantities of maize, were recovered from flotation samples collected from an earth oven feature at C. W. Cooper, an early Mississippian (AD 1150–200) site in west-central Illinois (Wilson and VanDerwarker 2015). Nuts (including acorn, hickory, hazelnut, and walnut) have also been identified in several cooking pits at Finch (47JE0902), a Woodland site spanning ca. 100 BC to AD 1200 in southeastern Wisconsin, via flotation and ceramic lipid residue analysis (see Haas, chapter 3). Similarly, small quantities of beechnut and acorn were recovered through flotation of 2,019 liters of soil samples collected from dozens of roasting pits at Schwerdt (20AE127), a fifteenth-century Upper Mississippian site located in the Lower Kalamazoo River Valley, in southwest Lower Michigan (Cremin 1980:287). Faunal remains and some edible berries were also identified at the Schwerdt site, but the most important plant remains identified were the aquatic tuber of the American lotus (*Nelumbo lutea*). Furthermore, Frederick and colleagues (2019) reported a single Early Late Woodland (median ^{14}C age of cal AD 783) circular pit feature at the Green site in southern Lower Michigan. The feature measured 130 cm in diameter, lacked FCR, and consisted of a 20 cm deep burned layer of hundreds of carbonized acorns and oak wood. Frederick and collaborators (2019) hypothesized that the Green site feature was an acorn cooking pit used for drying and charring acorns during the fall to prolong their shelf life, before subterranean caching for consumption in later seasons.

It is likely that the earth oven at Site 914 was used to cook plants. Even though dense edible plant remains are absent at the Grand Island sites due to their acidic soils, the residues of nut processing on Late Archaic FCR at Site 754 (contemporaneous in age to Site 914) and on Woodland ceramic sherds at Sites 754 and 929 on the island (Skibo et al. 2009) make it probable that fall nut collecting was an important activity and source of food to the hunter-gatherer groups of the Late Archaic period and to the subsequent hunter-gatherer pottery makers of the Woodland period there.

Thoms (2003) suggests that there are greater numbers of FCR found in areas where there are more plant foods per capita in comparison to the amount of game meat per capita. Furthermore, the most likely explanation for the massive amounts of FCR evidenced in Late Archaic sites on Grand Island (e.g., Benchley et al. 1988; Dunham and Anderton 1999; Neubauer 2016, 2018a), as compared with the smaller quantities observed in Woodland sites, is that cooking with ceramic vessels replaced hot rocks during the latter period, a trend noticed by Thoms (2003) across North America. Thoms suggests that, in general, when ceramic use increases, FCR use decreases. With the adoption of ceramics, the potential for a more controlled range of temperatures and cooking durations became feasible (Messner 2011:71; Skibo et al. 2009).

CONCLUSION

One of the principal means for understanding ancient culinary practices and domestic life is through the analysis of cuisine, which includes the methods for preparing food (see definition of cuisine in Kooiman et al., Introduction). Food processing incorporates a wide range of activities associated with preparation for storage or immediate consumption, including threshing, winnowing, milling, grinding, baking, boiling, steaming, roasting, and toasting (Hastorf 1988:125). The documentation of the presence and extent of food-processing activities at archaeological sites can be crucial in interpreting site function (VanDerwarker et al. 2016). In this regard, FCR provide powerful insights because they are produced as by-products of the systematic use of hot rocks in various cooking and heating facilities, therefore retaining important traces of information related to the activities of ancient domestic life.

This chapter adds information to an underdeveloped research and literature base (see Koenig and Miller 2023) but also has broader implications for the identification, classification, and interpretation of a particular type of highly variable cooking feature that occurs throughout the region and across much of North America for millennia. The methods for the analysis and identification of earth oven features outlined in this case study can be applied to other regions of North America to assist in understanding past cuisine choices and preferences.

As a case study, I used converging lines of evidence to argue that the majority of FCR at Site 914 resulted from the baking of foods in an earth oven facility that had been used multiple times. Earth ovens that were heavily and repeatedly used can be distinguished by higher frequencies of small-fragment FCR associated with charcoal and evidence of in situ burning (Petraglia et al. 2002:11–14). The single feature's size (1 m in diameter), depth (20 cm), basin-shaped morphology, FCR characteristics, and the presence of charcoal and charcoal-stained soils indicate that it functioned as an enclosed earth oven for baking foods.

The archaeological signatures of the earth oven discussed here may only be applicable to features containing FCR. The feature at Site 914 fits well with Thoms's (2008b:457) expected archaeological signatures of earth ovens with FCR: basin-shaped pit (often one to three m in diameter and 0.1–0.3 m deep); sometimes containing rock lining and always with a lens of heating elements (i.e., FCR) underlain by and intermixed with thermally altered sediments (oxidized, carbon stained); FCR (small to large in size) typically sooted and varying considerably in size; scattered FCR in the immediate vicinity of remains of earth ovens; and flakes and tools expected therein as discard from routine clean-up activities.

The earth oven at Site 914 can be seen as the result of the passing of essential knowledge and understanding of cooking activities related to the oven's construction, stone selection, the process of maintaining heat using hot rocks, and the acquisition and preparation of food resources (Neubauer 2018b:25). People interacted with earth ovens by creating; excavating into the ground; carrying rocks, fuel, and plant or animal foods to that location; cooking; and either abandoning or returning to and reusing these ovens. Earth ovens could have been influenced by several agentive factors. For example, people may have selected locations for ovens due to their physical proximity to food resources, considered soil properties, wind direction, distance to residence and food cache, and availability of preferred wood fuel and cooking stones (Carney et al. 2022:4).

It is hypothesized that the Late Archaic inhabitants of Grand Island practiced intensive nut (Skibo et al. 2009) and fall-spawning fish processing (Benchley et al. 1988; Neubauer 2016; Frederick et al. 2019) to produce surpluses that could have been stored for the winter, with resultant changes in community size and organization, land-use intensification, activity scheduling, and the like (Neubauer 2018b). Fall sites in Michigan's Upper Peninsula during the Late Archaic tend to be located in areas with abundant resources, such as nuts and fall-spawning fish species in the case of Grand Island. Therefore, sites in prime locations tended to be repeatedly occupied for the replenishing of tools (e.g., Lac LaBelle and the Duck Lake site on the mainland) and for large-scale food processing (e.g., Grand Island sites), to stock winter food supplies.

The evidence for the development of larger-scale food processing and production on Grand Island during fall social aggregations, likely for storage for winter consumption, signifies increased labor and cooperative requirements during the Late Archaic (Neubauer 2018b). This could have resulted in a gradual shift in social organization toward greater intergroup cooperation through the strengthening of affinal relationships, and group definition and identity, leading to increased socioeconomic complexity and organization when compared with the preceding Middle Archaic period (Neubauer 2018b).

Although this chapter focuses on the Midcontinent, this research has implications for other regions as it may contribute to the identification and analysis of earth ovens containing FCR at archaeological sites worldwide. Like ceramic cooking vessels, stone exposed to heat displays visible and recognizable use-alteration patterns (see Neubauer 2018a). As remnants of ancient cuisine, the analyses of the fracture and use-alteration patterns of FCR associated with earth oven features, as discussed here, provide important insights into earth oven usage in cooking and food preparation.

Chapter 2

Indigenous Cuisine in the Northern Great Lakes

SUSAN M. KOOIMAN AND REBECCA K. ALBERT

The complexities of cuisine can be difficult to capture archaeologically, but an approach using multifaceted analysis of adhered food residues on pottery contextualized with ethnographic and ethnohistoric data offers a rich and unique view of past food choice and cooking methods. In the northern Great Lakes region, this approach reveals diachronic variation in the selection of important plant resources and changing styles of food preparation over time, along with the long-term maintenance of other culinary traditions of the Indigenous occupants of this region. Both culinary change and continuity can be connected to evolving natural environments, social relationships, and identities.

This approach combines inferring modes of cooking from the patterning of carbonized food residues on interior pottery surfaces with the identification of phytoliths and starches present in carbonized food residues on pottery, which provide evidence of specific plant species processed in ceramic cooking vessels. These data from the Cloudman site and other sites dating to AD 1–1500 in the Upper Peninsula of Michigan are assessed in context with ethnographic and ethnohistoric information to identify recipes and dishes prepared by ancient Indigenous cooks. The cumulative results reveal insights into regional culinary traditions and their connection to natural and social environments, providing a model for reconstructing past cuisine in a variety of archaeological contexts.

CUISINE, IDENTITY, TRANSMISSION, RECIPES, AND DISHES

Cuisine includes food choice, food processing, food combinations, and cooking technology. It has been referred to as "food culture" because it also reflects broader social customs, interactions, relationships, and identities (Fischler 1988; Montanari 2006). Contemporary discussions of cuisine often evoke ethnicity—a group of people with a shared history and/or identity—and their traditions of using particular ingredients and cooking styles. Culinary traditions are often rooted in specific geographic regions because they reflect ingredient availability, which varies based on the local environment (Bell and Valentine 1997). Yet, even when groups have access to the same resources, they may develop vastly different cuisines that are influenced by technology, social interactions, and unique culture histories.

The two base components of cuisine, ingredients and cooking, can be conceptualized in two ways: the *recipe*, or the formula of a specific combination of ingredients and the methods of preparation and cooking; and the *dish*, or the recognizable outcome of a recipe, which is consumed. Modern diners might be more concerned with the dish, a familiar or identifiable culinary entity associated with ingredients and cooking methods, one they can select from a menu, while avid cooks may be more concerned with the recipe, or the cumulative food preparation processes and components that result in the perfect meal. For example, the dish we call pizza requires the cook to follow a general recipe: making a dough and topping it with tomatoes, cheese, and other ingredients, followed by baking and several preparatory steps along the way. One may know, consume, and enjoy a dish without knowing the recipe. Recipes convey a sense of tradition and conferred knowledge, a formula passed down from one generation to another, or knowledge shared among contemporaries. Dishes, the end products of recipes, instantly evoke a mélange of ingredients, flavors, and textures as well as their associations with identity, be they ethnic, regional, familial, or other. Dishes are known and enjoyed by everyone in a particular community or population, not just the cooks.

Tracing the sharing and spread of recipes and dishes can reveal much about past social interactions and cultural transmission (or lack thereof) as well as their role in marking social belonging and distinctions. The cultural information that is carried with recipes and dishes could be critical for deeper understandings of past societies, including their long-held traditions and internal and external impetuses for change. Yet without written records of recipes or firsthand descriptions of dishes, archaeologists must often use modern and historical accounts of food traditions and trust they carry information about past iterations of cuisine. How to identify recipes and dishes in the past directly through the archaeological record has proven a challenge, but carbonized food residues adhered to pottery provide a pathway to understanding some of the important subtleties of cuisine.

THE RESIDUES OF CUISINE

Since cuisine is defined by ingredients plus food preparation and cooking methods (Counihan 1999; Fuller 2005; Hastorf 2017; see Introduction of this volume), identification of both the specific items cooked together and the method of cooking can provide evidence for ancient cuisine. Food residues, both absorbed and adhered, provide a direct association between ancient ceramic cooking vessels and the foods cooked within them. Absorbed residues, including lipids and other organic compounds that are absorbed into the fabric of an unglazed ceramic cooking vessel, also provide this direct link between food and cooking implement. They are chemically extracted and analyzed, a destructive technique that is nonetheless very useful for identifying certain types or categories of foods once processed within a vessel (Malainey 2011). Adhered residues constitute visible carbonized food remains located on either the interior or exterior of a cooking pot. These can be scraped from the surface of the pottery vessel without incurring damage and analyzed through a variety of techniques, including chemical methods (i.e., stable isotope analysis and lipid or organic residue analysis) and the identification of microbotanical remains preserved in the physical food residues. The most common microbotanical remains identified through adhered residue analysis are phytoliths and starches.

Phytoliths are inorganic silica bodies that form in between plant cells as a result of regular water uptake (Piperno 2009). As a result of their formation process, phytoliths can have distinctive and diagnostic morphologies depending on the plant species from which they originate. In contrast to inorganic phytoliths, starches are organic sugar molecules created by plants during photosynthesis. The most common starch created by plants are transitory starches, which are small (> 5 microns) and typically undiagnostic (Torrance 2006; Gott et al. 2006). Some plant species, especially those that have been domesticated, produce large "storage" starches with a distinctive morphology—these storage starches are the most important starch type for microbotanical analysis. Not all plants produce phytoliths or starches that are diagnostic; however, many plants that are important in North American agriculture, such as maize, beans, and squash, produce distinctively shaped starches and/or phytoliths.

Additionally, adhered food residue, one of several "use-alteration traces," is particularly useful for determining vessel function, or how a pottery vessel was used in the past. Use-alteration traces indicate specific uses from throughout the life history of a pottery vessel (Skibo 1992, 2013). The presence of carbonized food residue distinguishes a vessel as a cooking pot used over a fire from those used for serving or storage. The location and distribution of carbonized residue along the interior surface of a cooking vessel can also be related to specific modes or methods of cooking, based on ethnographic and experimental observations (Kobayashi 1994; Skibo 1994).

Previously, the inferred relationship between cooking method and foodstuff would have been tentative, as it was difficult to distinguish whether absorbed or adhered residues on pottery were from accumulated past cooking events, the final cooking event in the life history of a pottery vessel, or a combination of both. However, an experimental study by Miller and colleagues (2020) found that adhered carbonized residue found on pottery represents the last cooking event or events in the life history of a vessel, while absorbed residues constitute an amalgam of foods from past cooking events that are little altered by the final cooking event. Because cooking methods are inferred from the patterning of interior carbonized residue, the resources identified in these same carbonized food remains can be directly tied to the mode of cooking and, therefore, cuisine. Additionally, if adhered residue represents the final cooking event, then multiple distinct foodstuffs identified in these residues may have been cooked together, providing further clues about recipes and dishes.

Adhered carbonized food residues can be explored through a variety of proxies for ancient diet. Chemical analyses can identify a wide array of signatures representing plants and animals, but often these identifications are limited to broad food categories (e.g., fatty plants, aquatic resources, large herbivores). Analysis of microscopic plant remains, although limited to a handful of plants that produce identifiable starches and phytoliths, allows identification at the level of species, and therefore an exact component of a food residue—an ingredient. Determining specific plant species present, the degree to which they co-occur in adhered pottery residues, and residue patterns associated with specific cooking methods can provide strong evidence for specific dishes and food preparation traditions of past societies.

THE CLOUDMAN SITE: A CASE STUDY IN CUISINE

Data from the pottery assemblage from the multicomponent Cloudman site in the northern Great Lakes provides a case study for tandem application of use-alteration trace analysis and microbotanical analysis of carbonized food remains adhered to pottery. The Cloudman site is located on Drummond Island, in Lake Huron, off the coast of the eastern Upper Peninsula of Michigan (Figure 2.1). It lies on the northern bank of the Potagannissing River, occupying a series of river terraces close to the mouth of the river at Lake Huron. Ideally

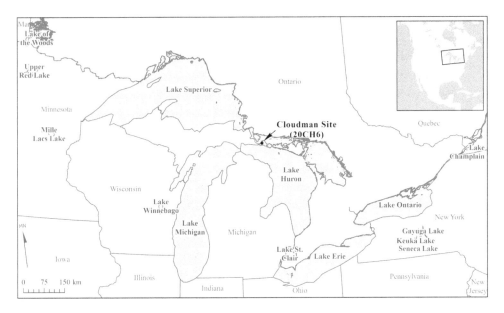

Figure 2.1. Map of the Cloudman site and surrounding northern Great Lakes region. (Base map from ArcGIS [ESRI]. Map courtesy of Adriana Martinez.)

situated near riverine, lacustrine, and terrestrial resources, the site was repeatedly occupied by Indigenous peoples over the span of 1,500 years.

The Cloudman site was excavated between 1992 and 1994 by Michigan State University, and pottery vessel identification and taxonomic analysis were conducted by Branstner (1995). A combination stylistic pottery analysis and radiocarbon dating of carbonized food residues on pottery revealed that the site was occupied by pottery-producing Indigenous groups between AD 50 and AD 1530 (Kooiman 2021; Kooiman and Walder 2019; Kooiman et al. 2019). Within this period, four distinct components yielding pottery have been identified: Middle Woodland (cal AD 50–200), Early Late Woodland (cal AD 900–1000), Late Woodland (cal AD 1200–1300), and Late Prehistoric (cal AD 130–1530) (Branstner 1995; Kooiman and Walder 2019; Kooiman et al. 2019). This long history of occupation at a single locale makes it an exemplary site through which to examine diachronic culinary tradition and change.

Macrofloral and faunal remains from limited contexts provided some preliminary information about diet at the Cloudman site. Cloudman occupants ate a variety of fruits (including strawberry, raspberry, elderberry, and wild plum), nuts (such as hazelnuts, walnuts, and acorns), and seeds/cultigens such as chenopod, maize, and wild rice (Egan-Bruhy 2007). Faunal remains from only two features associated with the later occupations were analyzed, yielding remains from small and large mammals, waterfowl, turtle, and both spring- and fall-spawning fish (Cooper 1996). These data identify the plant and animal species that were likely selected for consumption, but macroscopic food remains are difficult to tie directly to cooking vessels, cooking methods, and recipes/dishes because they are usually not found in direct context with cooking technologies.

Over 200 distinct pottery vessels were identified within the Cloudman site pottery assemblage (Branstner 1995). Regional (Laurel and Blackduck) and local (Juntunen sequence) wares characterize the majority of vessels from the three earliest components. The Late Precontact (post–AD 1300) component is more complex, consisting of what appears to be a series of short-term occupations over a 200-year time span, characterized by distinct, nonlocal Woodland and Iroquoian-style pottery types. Taxonomic classifications of pottery vessels from the Cloudman site have been outlined elsewhere (Branstner 1995; Kooiman 2018, 2021), as have the relationships between the physical characteristics of vessels, cooking patterns, and chemical signatures of foods cooked (Kooiman 2018, 2021; Kooiman et al. 2022). The goal of this chapter is to closely examine the relationship between specific ingredients (as could only be identified by starches and phytoliths) and cooking methods, which can allow us to explore potential recipes and dishes prepared by the past occupants of the Cloudman site.

METHODS

Use-Alteration Analysis

All 202 identifiable vessels from the Cloudman site were assessed for use-alteration traces. The vessels were distinguished by unique rim sherds or partial vessels; there were no complete vessels in the assemblage. A total of 106 distinct vessels had interior carbonization, 45 of which displayed characterizable patterns. Three primary patterns were identified: Pattern 1—boiling, which was characterized by a ring of residue at or just below the rim; Pattern 2—stewing, which was characterized by solid carbonization down the length of the rim sherd (and/or by carbonization on associated body sherds); and Pattern 3—boiling plus stewing, which was characterized by a ring of thick carbonization at or just below the rim, with a thinner layer of carbonization continuing below the rim onto the neck/body (see Kooiman 2021 or Kooiman et al. 2022 for photos and diagrams).

Phytolith and Starch Analysis

Of the vessels with visible carbonized food residues, 52 vessels were selected for microbotanical analysis. These were chosen to reflect a variety of time periods and taxonomic classifications. A new disposable scalpel was used to gently scrape carbonized residues from the ceramic sherds onto a piece of weighing paper. This piece of weighing paper was then used to funnel the carbonized residue into a 15-mL centrifuge tube. After transferring the sample into the centrifuge tube, the weighing paper was discarded, and the sample was ready for chemical processing.

Although there are several methods for extracting microbotanical remains from residues, such as chemical flotation, chemical digestion of excess carbon with a solution of potassium chlorate and nitric acid was selected for this sample type, as it has been successfully used to isolate microbotanical remains from carbonized residues from ceramic sherds from other sites in the region (Raviele 2010; Albert et al. 2018). For a more detailed explanation of the chemical digestion procedure used in this study, see Raviele (2010) or Kooiman et al. (2022).

After samples were chemically digested, samples were mounted onto microscope slides using Permount and analyzed under a compound microscope. Diagnostic starches and phytoliths from North American agricultural crops were identified by noting diagnostic morphology and metrics from reference materials. Reference materials used for this research include the use of a comparative collection of maize phytoliths and starches made available by Maria Raviele and various published texts on phytoliths and starches from plants commonly identified as an aspect of North American cuisine (Burchill and Boyd 2015; Piperno 2006; Raviele 2010; Yost and Blinnikov 2011). Diagnostic phytoliths and starches were photographed for future reference.

RESULTS

Ultimately, residues from 29 of the 52 sampled vessels yielded identifiable phytoliths and starches. Of these vessels, 21 had residue patterns that could be associated with a specific mode of cooking, allowing comparisons between specific ingredients and cooking methods among this subset. The aim of this chapter is to identify aspects of ancient recipes, which restricts the scope to vessels yielding both identifiable food species (phytoliths and starches) and clues to cooking method (interior carbonization patterns). Although it was a small sample size, it still serves as a useful proxy for the broader patterns of food behaviors at the Cloudman site.

Ingredients

Analysis of phytoliths and starches derived from adhered carbonized residues collected from the interior surfaces of pottery from the Cloudman site revealed the early presence of maize, wild rice, and squash (Figure 2.2), all of which are associated with vessel residues dating as early as cal AD 50–200, and which continue to be used throughout all periods of occupation (Kooiman 2021; Kooiman et al. 2019). Macroscopic remains of both maize and wild rice were also identified at the site despite the overall poor preservation conditions resulting from acidic soil at the site, providing further evidence of the importance of these two foods for Cloudman site occupants (Egan-Bruhy 2007). The fluctuating frequencies of microscopic remains of these foods during subsequent occupations have been discussed at length elsewhere (Kooiman 2021; Kooiman et al. 2022), so are only reviewed and summarized here with a discussion of new insights.

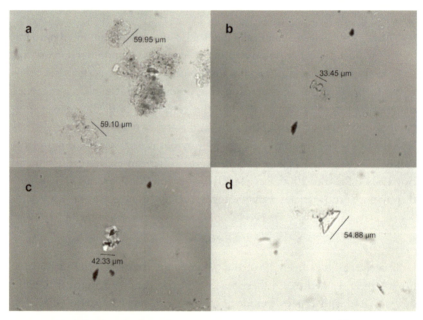

Figure 2.2 Microbotanical remains from Cloudman site pottery residues: (a) two *Cucurbita* phytoliths; (b) *Zizania palustris* phytolith; (c) two *Zea mays* starches; (d) *Zea mays* rondel phytolith. (Reproduced from Susan M. Kooiman, Rebecca K. Albert, and Mary E. Malainey. Multiproxy Analysis of Adhered and Absorbed Food Residues Associated with Pottery. *Journal of Archaeological Method and Theory* 29[3]:795–830, 2022; figure 6. Springer Nature.)

NORTHERN GREAT LAKES

Table 2.1. Frequencies of Plant Species Present in Discrete Pottery Vessel Residues

Resource	Middle Woodland (AD 50-200)		Early Late Woodland (AD 900-1000)		Late Late Woodland (AD 1200-1300)		Late Precontact (AD 1300-1500)	
	n	%	n	%	n	%	n	%
Maize (phytolith)	1	-	1	-	1	-	2	-
Maize (starch)	4	-	6	-	1	-	0	-
Maize (all[a])	5	41.6	6	31.6	2	25	2	22.2
Wild Rice	2	16.7	1	5.3	5	62.5	6	66.7
Squash	2	16.7	3	15.8	1	12.5	4	44.4
Total Vessels	12	-	19	-	8	-	9	-

[a]Includes number of distinct vessels with residues yielding maize phytoliths and/or starches; one Early Late Woodland vessel yielded both a maize starch grain and phytolith.

Maize phytoliths are present in a larger proportion of Middle Woodland vessel residues than in residues associated with any of the later occupations, and frequencies of residues containing maize phytoliths decrease steadily through time (Table 2.1). This is an unexpected trend given that maize is not a major component of diet for most societies in the Midwest until after AD 900 (Emerson et al. 2020).

The proportion of vessel residues containing wild rice is higher among Late Late Woodland and Late Precontact vessels than in pottery used before AD 1200, corroborating observations made by Dunham (2014) that wild rice appears more common during these time periods. Squash is present in only a small proportion of residues associated with the earliest three occupations of the site and spikes in frequency among Late Precontact, or post–AD 1300, residues (44.4%). The occupants of the Cloudman site consumed many of the same ingredients for over a thousand years, yet the culinary components that were most highly favored varied through time.

Cooking Methods

Ethnographic and experimental observations of cooking in ceramic pots have demonstrated that different modes of cooking can leave behind discernible patterns of carbonized food residues on the interior surface of a cooking pot. Stewing, a long-term water reduction process, can leave a solid, relatively consistent layer of carbonization along the interior surface. Parching and roasting can also leave solid residues, although in a patchy distribution (Skibo 1992,

2013). Boiling and simmering, methods that maintain an aqueous cooking environment for the foodstuffs in a vessel, result in a ring of carbonized residue above the water line, which can be anywhere from the shoulder of the vessel to the rim (Skibo 1992, 2013). In the northern Great Lakes, cooks routinely filled their vessels, whether for boiling or stewing, to the very top (Kooiman 2016, 2021; Kooiman et al. 2022).

Previous investigations of pottery assemblages from several other Middle and Late Woodland sites in the Northern Great Lakes region demonstrated a preference among Middle Woodland cooks for stewing or parching (Albert et al. 2018; Kooiman 2012, 2016). A pattern indicative of boiling or simmering was more prevalent among cooking vessels associated with Late Woodland sites (Kooiman 2012, 2016).

This same trend of changing cooking styles between the Middle and Late Woodland periods was observed among the Cloudman site assemblage (Figure 2.3, Table 2.2). The stewing/parching carbonization pattern was more common among the Middle Woodland vessels, while boiling became the predominant cooking mode observed among vessels from the early Late Woodland component and all subsequent occupations. The timing of this apparent change in cooking styles does not correspond with any of the aforementioned changes in the frequencies of maize, wild rice, and squash microbotanical remains.

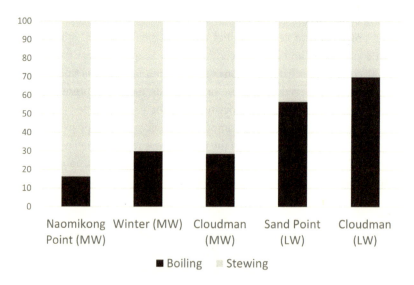

Figure 2.3. Frequencies of boiling and stewing interior carbonization patterns on cooking vessels from sites and site components in the northern Great Lakes. MW = Middle Woodland. LW = Late Woodland. (Courtesy of Susan M. Kooiman.)

Table 2.2. Interior Carbonization/Cooking Residue Patterns on Pottery Vessels from the Cloudman Site, by Component

Cooking Residue Pattern	Middle Woodland (AD 50-200)		Early Late Woodland (AD 900-1000)		Late Late Woodland (AD 1200-1300)		Late Precontact (AD 1300-1500)	
	n	%	n	%	n	%	n	%
Boiling	2	29	8	50	6	50	4	40
Stewing	5	71	4	25	2	17	2	20
Boiling + Stewing	0	0	4	25	4	33	4	40
Total	7	100	16	100	12	100	10	100

A new cooking pattern was also observed among the Cloudman pottery assemblage, one in which a thinner layer of residue covering the interior surface of the pot could be observed in addition to a thicker ring or residue near the top of the vessel (Kooiman 2021). This "boiling plus stewing" pattern was also more common among vessels from the later three occupations, and most common during the Late Precontact occupation (Kooiman 2021; Kooiman et al. 2022).

Food Combinations and Recipes

Comparing resources present in cooking residues, as identified by starches and phytoliths, against corresponding interior carbonization patterns among the Cloudman site pottery vessels provides some possible clues into local recipes. There were 29 total vessels with residues yielding identifiable microbotanical remains (Figure 2.4). In over 65% of these samples, maize, squash, and wild rice appear to have been cooked separately from each other. Whether they were cooked completely alone is another matter, as there are many foodstuffs uncaptured through microremains. Maize was most frequently cooked independently from wild rice and squash (n = 8), although squash (n = 6) and wild rice (n = 6) were also cooked separately in multiple vessels. Wild rice and maize appear to be the most common combination and were cooked together throughout all occupations of the Cloudman site, co-occurring in 21% (n = 6) of samples. Combinations of wild rice and squash were rarer (n = 2, 7%) while maize was never cooked exclusively with squash.

Resource combinations also change through time. In the earliest two occupations (AD 50–1000), maize and squash are usually cooked independently from the other identifiable plant foods, while wild rice is only cooked with maize (Figure 2.5). In the latter two occupations (AD 1200–1500), these resources are more often cooked together. Wild rice was most likely to be cooked separately from the other foods, perhaps because it required different cooking methods, but maize is never cooked separately. All three resources co-occur only in vessels associated with the post–AD 1300 (Late Precontact) component of the site.

Comparisons between resources and cooking mode reveal other possible interesting trends (Figure 2.6). Wild rice, either when cooked separately from or in combination with either of the other two resources, was processed in a variety of ways (both boiling and stewing or a combination). Squash, when cooked with maize or wild rice, is never associated with interior carbonization patterns associated with stewing, despite the fact that slow-cooked squash breaks down and creates a thick, creamy consistency for soups and stews. This may not have been the desired consistency for squash; instead, the objective in cooking it on its own may have been to get it to the point of being edible, or to

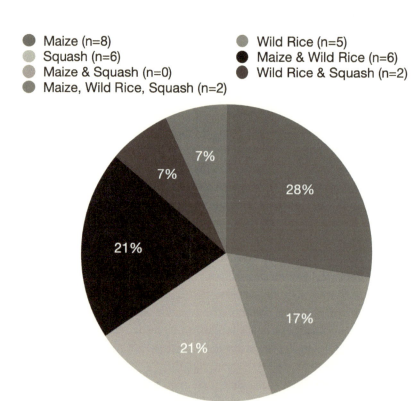

Figure 2.4. Frequencies of resources found alone or together in adhered carbonized residues from discrete pottery vessels at the Cloudman site. (Courtesy of Susan M. Kooiman.)

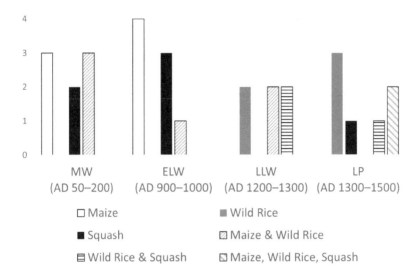

Figure 2.5. Number of discrete pottery residues containing resources and resource combinations by component (from a total of 29 vessels). MW = Middle Woodland. ELW = Early Late Woodland. LLW = Late Late Woodland. LP = Late Prehistoric. (Courtesy of Susan M. Kooiman.)

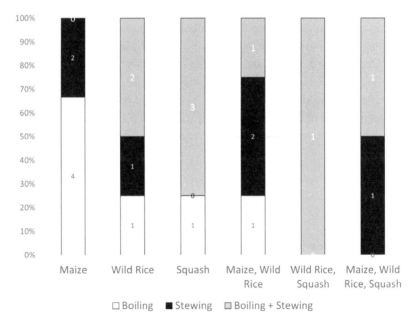

Figure 2.6. Frequencies of resources and resource combinations by associated cooking style. (Courtesy of Susan M. Kooiman.)

rehydrate stored, dehydrated pieces. Alternatively, squash may have been only one component of a recipe that was boiled. Both squash and wild rice, cooked either separately or together, were most commonly associated with boiling plus stewing, possibly reflecting the need to boil these foods initially to start the cooking process and the subsequent reduction of heat to allow for "low and slow" cooking, which would complete the absorption process by the starches, reaching the desired consistency.

The most striking pattern emerges from a diachronic comparison of maize with cooking mode (Table 2.3). Carbonized residues on Middle Woodland pottery containing maize microbotanicals are exclusively found in the pattern associated with stewing. However, in the Early Late Woodland period (AD 900–1000), maize is often cooked separately from rice and squash and is boiled or simmered. This pattern may indicate a change in the processing of maize and may have also contributed to the overall change in cooking styles through time.

Finally, boiling plus stewing becomes the predominant cooking mode for processing all three of the primary plant resources after AD 900. This suggests that cooks commonly used both methods for cooking, perhaps even as part of the same cooking event, a habit observed in many historic and contemporary cooking techniques.

The patterns revealed from the microbotanical and interior carbonization patterning highlight trends that may be key to understanding Indigenous recipes, dishes, and cuisine in the ancient northern Great Lakes. Despite these insights, there remain many unknowns, including other specific foods not captured or apparent in preserved food residues and specific food preparation techniques. Ethnographic and ethnohistoric accounts can provide analogical information that allows further insight into food combinations, recipes, and dishes.

ETHNOGRAPHIC AND ETHNOHISTORIC DATA

Ethnographic observations of the culinary traditions of historic Indigenous groups occupying the northern Great Lakes can be used to infer possible food preparations in the past. The general passage of time, the effects of colonialism, and technological change (such as the replacement of ceramic cooking vessels with metal pots) prevent our assumptions that practices observed in the past century are accurate portrayals of culinary practices in the centuries and millennia prior, but they can still provide valuable insights into the knowledge and techniques that ancient Indigenous groups may have employed in their food selection and preparation practices. For this study, ethnographic accounts of

NORTHERN GREAT LAKES

Table 2.3. Resource/Resource Combination and Cooking Mode by Component

Component	Cooking Mode	Resource(s)
MW[a]	Stewing	Maize
MW	Stewing	Maize
MW	Stewing	Maize, Wild Rice
MW	Boiling	Squash
ELW[b]	Stewing	Maize, Wild Rice
ELW	Boiling + Stewing	Squash
ELW	Boiling + Stewing	Squash
ELW	**Boiling**	**Maize**
ELW	**Boiling**	**Maize**
ELW	**Boiling**	**Maize**
ELW	**Boiling**	**Maize**
LLW[c]	Stewing	Wild Rice
LLW	Boiling	Maize, Wild Rice
LLW	Boiling + Stewing	Maize, Wild Rice
LP[d]	Boiling	Wild Rice
LP	Stewing	Maize, Wild Rice, Squash
LP	Boiling + Stewing	Maize, Wild Rice, Squash
LP	Boiling + Stewing	Squash
LP	Boiling + Stewing	Wild Rice
LP	Boiling + Stewing	Wild Rice, Squash
LP	Boiling + Stewing	Wild Rice

Note: Maize in the Early Late Woodland (ELW) is emphasized.
[a]MW = Middle Woodland.
[b]ELW = Early Late Woodland.
[c]LLW = Late Late Woodland.
[d]LP = Late Precontact.

Ojibwe people in northern Wisconsin and Minnesota (Densmore 1979, 2005; Hilger 1959; Vennum 1988) and Iroquoian groups from Ontario and New York (Waugh 1973), and ethnohistoric data from the Wendat of southeastern Ontario (Tooker 1991) were used to understand the culinary practices employed and the dishes consumed by the occupants of the Cloudman site.

Cooking Squash, Wild Rice, and Maize

The Ojibwe ate pumpkins and squash fresh, or they dried them for use later in the winter (Densmore 1979, 2005; Hilger 1959). When consumed fresh, they were generally baked in coals (Hilger 1959:144). There are no ethnographic accounts among those observed for this study that mention stewing squash, which is consistent with the findings at the Cloudman site. Squash was cut into strips to dry, and dried squash and pumpkin were boiled with meat or maple sugar (Densmore 2005:319; Hilger 1959:144). If dried squash were boiled long enough, it could gradually break down and act as a thickening agent, potentially resulting in the dual boiling/stewing interior carbonization patterns associated with squash phytoliths in Cloudman cooking vessels.

Wild rice, or *manoomin*, has long been a primary dietary staple of Ojibwe groups of the northern Great Lakes. An ideologically and ceremonially important food, it has transformed into a marker of Ojibwe identity (Vennum 1988) and has even been used to distinguish their cuisine from those of neighboring Odawa groups (Scott 1996). Densmore (1979, 2005), Hilger (1959), and Vennum (1988) all identify wild rice as the primary staple of Ojibwe diet. Following harvest, wild rice was dried either by air/fire drying or parching (Densmore 1979; Hilger 1959). To prepare it for consumption, wild rice was boiled in water or broth (Densmore 1979:39) or boiled in soups (Hilger 1959:148). It was also boiled in water and eaten "with or without maple sugar" or boiled with meat (Densmore 2005:319).

Some accounts record contact-period groups preparing wild rice in the form of a gruel, which required a greater liquid-to-rice ratio than nonglutinous (fluffy) rice (Vennum 1988:47). Rice was also used to "thicken broths including venison, bear, fish, and wildfowl," cooked into a bread-like paste, or pounded into flour (Vennum 1988:48). Wild rice is cited by Vennum (1988) as being incorporated into a variety of stews with venison, small game, duck, and other plant foods—culinary components that are missed by starch and phytolith analysis.

By the historic era, the Ojibwe considered maize a primary food staple. While fresh or green maize was roasted in the husk, it was also "cut before it was fully ripe" (i.e., green) then shelled and dried by spreading it on sheets of birchbark, after which it was boiled and seasoned with maple sugar (Densmore 1979:39; Densmore 2005:319). Maize was also boiled in its shucks before ripening, then braided, and hung to dry. The dried maize was then ground into meal and used primarily for thickening soups (Hilger 1959:145). These two examples show there were a variety of preparations for green corn. The Ojibwe also made hominy by boiling fully ripened and dried maize in hardwood ashes, one method of nixtamalization (Densmore 2005:319). *Nixtamalization* is a process of boiling dried maize in an alkali solution to remove the outer coating (pericarp), leaving the more nutritious starchy core, or *hominy* (Fitzgerald 2001; Katz et al. 1974; Lovis et al. 2011).

Iroquoian groups are famous for their maize-based agricultural practices, and the crop figures strongly into their cuisine. Over 40 methods of corn preparation were recorded in a single ethnographic source, a hint at the rich cuisine formed around this single species (Waugh 1973). The Wendat preferred boiling maize to roasting it and commonly used it as the primary ingredient in soups, which constituted many of their meals (Tooker 1991:68). Maize was usually nixtamalized, rinsed, and hulled before being incorporated into dishes as hominy or pounded into a flour (Waugh 1973:84). Iroquoian groups also prepared green corn on the cob for immediate consumption, boiling the cobs while still in their husks (Waugh 1973:95). *Succotash*, a dish that is familiar with modern diners, was made with "unripe corn and beans in the same state, boiled with bears' flesh" (Waugh 1973:96).

Cooking Methods

As detailed, boiling was a common method of cooking a variety of foods in historic Indigenous cuisine. Rogers (1962:C53), who discusses cooking minimally, even points out that among the Round Lake Ojibwe of Ontario "all food is prepared basically in one of two ways, either boiling or roasted on a spit beside a fire; boiling is more common and practically all species of mammal, bird, and fish are cooked in this way." Among the Iroquois, "a very large proportion of . . . foods [was] evidently of liquid nature—numerous references to soups and broths made from ripe and unripe corn, beans, squashes, meats, and other materials" (Waugh 1973:79). Corn soup was particularly common, and modern iterations tend to be rather aqueous. There are reports of "great kettles of Indian corn soup, or thin hominy, with . . . fish boiled in it" (Waugh 1973:136). The ubiquity of boiling, or making aqueous dishes such as soups (which may also be simmered, creating a similar carbonization pattern), as a cooking practice among postcontact Ojibwe and Iroquoian groups appears rooted in cooking traditions extending much further back in time, based on evidence from Cloudman and other sites in the northern Great Lakes where similar patterns have been observed (Albert et al. 2018; Kooiman 2016).

"Stewing" was only specifically mentioned as a cooking technique by Vennum (1988) in his discussion of wild rice preparations. Several other sources mention adding ingredients such as acorn flour, pumpkin blossoms, and corn silk to soups as "thickening agents," which may have also resulted in soups with a less aqueous and a thicker, more stew-like viscosity and texture (Densmore

1979; Hilger 1959; Waugh 1973). Stewing was practiced at the Cloudman site throughout its history, but it was most commonly employed during the earliest Middle Woodland occupation, as well as at other sites in the northern Great Lakes, 2,000 years before these ethnographic observations.

Dishes

The ethnographic sources surveyed only name a few specific dishes. The Ojibwe commonly cooked *tassimanonny*, a dish of boiled wild rice, corn, and fish (Vennum 1988:49), similar to the aforementioned Iroquoian succotash, which uses beans instead of wild rice. *Sagamité* is a Wendat/Iroquoian dish in which ground hominy meal was first boiled, then other foods, such as squash/pumpkin and pounded fish, were added, which would thicken the soup (Tooker 1991:68). *Sagamité* preparation could result in the combined interior carbonization pattern (Pattern #3) indicative of both boiling and stewing, a cooking technique most prevalent in the Late Precontact component of the Cloudman site, which is characterized by the presence of Iroquoian-style cooking vessels.

DISCUSSION

Carbonized food residues on pottery, or the visible, physical remains of cooked foods, can capture a recipe from the past. Containing information on both the "how" and the "what" of cooking, adhered food residues provide good evidence for inferring past culinary decisions and practices. Alongside ethnographic analogy, archaeologists can use these residues to reconstruct ancient cuisine, including specific recipes and dishes. Data from the Cloudman site pottery assemblage exemplify what can be distilled from these proxies.

Cooking, Recipes, and Dishes at the Cloudman Site

In 65% percent of Cloudman site vessel residue samples, there was only evidence of one of the plants species identified from phytoliths and starches (maize, wild rice, and squash). It appears these three foods were frequently cooked independently of each other, whether alone or in combination with foods uncaptured in microbotanical remains, such as animal proteins. Wild rice, when cooked apart from squash or maize, was boiled, stewed, and boiled plus stewed at the Cloudman site (see Figure 2.6). The Ojibwe boiled wild rice and also boiled and steamed it or produced gruels with it, each of which would produce a different interior carbonization pattern. Squash was either roasted (outside of cooking vessels) or boiled but never stewed, which is generally consistent with how it was cooked at the Cloudman site.

Among pottery residues containing evidence for more than one of these plant foods, maize and wild rice were the most frequent combination. Maize is a great source of carbohydrates, and wild rice contributes some protein, making the two foods nutritionally complementary. Wild rice, maize, and squash are only found together in food residues associated with the Late Precontact (AD 1300–1500) occupation of the site. All three resources had been components, to varying degrees, of local cuisine for over a thousand years. A cuisine consisting of specific recipes for preparing dishes including all three of these foods appears to have developed by this late period.

The exact nature of these recipes and dishes is unknown, but both the food residue patterning and ethnographic information provide insight into some possibilities. Among both the Iroquois and Ojibwe, stewing was a less popular cooking method than boiling or boiling then simmering foods to a thicker consistency, which reflects the diachronic trends observed at the Cloudman site and other northern Great Lakes sites. A dish made and consumed by the Ojibwe is *tassimanonny*, in which wild rice, maize, and fish are boiled together. Wild rice and maize, as mentioned, were a common combination in the Cloudman pottery residues. The site's lakeshore locale means that abundant fish were likely eaten at the site, and, in fact, stable isotope analysis of the adhered residues from the Cloudman site revealed that most residues contained signatures for aquatic resources (Kooiman et al. 2022). Residues containing both maize and wild rice microbotanical remains were adhered to vessels in patterns suggesting processing via both stewing and boiling/boiling plus stewing, so early versions of this dish may have appeared as long ago as two thousand years. There is no evidence that maize and squash were ever cooked in exclusive combination at the Cloudman site, so dishes like the Wendat *sagamité* are absent from the Cloudman culinary repertoire, based on the evidence presented here. However, *sagamité* includes hominy meal, and hominy, made from dried and nixtamalized maize, is less likely to be visible in the microbotanical record (Raviele 2010). Therefore, the inclusion of hominy in these ancient recipes may be archaeologically invisible.

Diachronic Culinary Change

Two patterns observed by previous research in the northern Great Lakes involve diachronic changes in both cooking methods (Albert et al. 2018; Kooiman 2016, 2021) and in the use of maize as a food source (Dunham 2014; Kooiman 2021; Kooiman et al. 2022). Stewing is replaced by boiling as the most frequent cooking style by at least AD 900 (Kooiman 2021; Kooiman et al. 2022). The timing of the change in cooking style does not correspond with any conspicuous changes in food selection (based on adhered pottery residues) but may instead be connected to a change in the way maize is processed.

The apparent decrease in the processing of maize in pottery vessels over time at the Cloudman site is a trend counter to those observed in societies to the south, where maize became a common culinary component only after AD 900 (Emerson et al. 2020; Schroeder 2004). Its early presence (ca. AD 100) at the Cloudman site may seem odd given its northerly location, but maize phytoliths and starches have been consistently encountered at Middle Woodland sites along the Great Lakes, from Minnesota to Ontario to upstate New York (Albert et al. 2018; Boyd and Surette 2010; Burchill and Boyd 2015; Hart et al. 2007; Raviele 2010; St-Pierre and Thompson 2015). This early adoption of maize by Middle Woodland groups in the Upper Great Lakes, who were still highly mobile, may represent opportunistic adoption of a new resource into an existing broad spectrum subsistence strategy. Maize may have been grown in small garden plots, left until the seasonal round allowed groups to return to these plots, and then consumed when the crops were successful, creating a bonus supplemental food during good growing years. Alternatively, maize may have been acquired by northern Great Lakes communities through down-the-line trade, although the origins of this potential trade good are unclear (Raviele 2010).

The decline in microbotanical evidence for maize over time at the Cloudman site may be the result of its decreasing importance in lieu of other locally abundant resources (such as wild rice, and acorns; see Dunham 2014), but culinary practices and taphonomy may also play roles. Raviele's (2010, 2011) experimental work showed that dried maize is unlikely to deposit phytoliths in carbonized residues. Instead, green, fresh maize cooked on the cob or recently scraped off the cob will deposit proportionally higher amounts of phytoliths into residues, since it is the cob rather than the kernel that contains identifiable phytoliths. As Dotzel (2021) emphasizes, culinary traditions that focus on cooking and consumption of fresh, green corn are more likely to be visible in food residues than those traditions that favor ripened and dried maize that must be nixtamalized before consumption. This differential phytolith deposition and preservation may account for the temporal gap between maize phytoliths and maize macroremains observed across much of eastern North America (Dotzel 2021). A total of nine maize kernels were identified from contexts associated with the post–AD 1200 occupations of the Cloudman site, demonstrating the juxtaposition between micro- and macrobotanical frequencies (Dunham 2014; Egan-Bruhy 2007).

However, taphonomy does not fully explain observations at the Cloudman site. Dunham (2014) found that maize macroremains, while present, were not as ubiquitous as wild rice and acorn remains at post–AD 1200 sites across the eastern Upper Peninsula of Michigan, including the Cloudman site. Both maize macroremains and phytoliths were present in post–AD 1200 components of the Cloudman site, and so its occupants were likely cooking and eating maize green upon initial ripening in addition to drying maize for storage, and nixtamalizing it before consumption. The ethnographic and ethnohistoric observations from both Anishinaabe and Iroquoian culinary habits show that groups around the Great Lakes practiced both nixtamalization of dried corn and the cooking and consumption of green corn.

The transition of the emphasis from stewing to boiling sometime between AD 200 and AD 900 was observed at multiple sites across the Upper Peninsula of Michigan (Albert et al. 2018; Kooiman 2016; Kooiman 2018). The practice of nixtamalization emerged in eastern North America after AD 800 (Myers 2006) and is credited with making maize a more viable crop for societies that became more dependent on it, such as the Mississippians post–AD 900. The new culinary technique of nixtamalization, which requires extensive boiling, may have been passed along to groups in the northern Great Lakes and could be one reason why boiling or simmering becomes more prevalent in the early Late Woodland, but it is likely not the sole driver of this change. Instead, we must look at the broader picture of pottery function and cuisine.

Before the adoption of pottery, northern Great Lakes groups likely cooked in organic containers, either by placing hot rocks into the vessels to heat contents from the inside, or by placing these vessels directly over the fire and keeping them full, as was practiced historically (Densmore 1979; Holman and Egan 1985; Speth 2015; Wallis and Wallis 1955; Waugh 1973). Either method would have made temperature control difficult, and the contents would have boiled quickly. Although northern Great Lakes groups chose not to involve themselves in the manufacture of pottery for 800 years after groups to the south adopted the technology, by 200 BC, some advantages in pottery manufacture became apparent. This may have been the ability to better control cooking temperature, primarily by maintaining lower and more even temperatures and allowing long-term stewing or simmering (Skibo et al. 2009). Stewing has many advantages for cooking meat; longer exposure to moist heat promotes the process of hydrolysis, wherein connective tissues are turned into gelatin, which makes meat more tender; and lipid hydrolysis, which makes meat for flavorful, tender, and digestible (Wandsnider 1997). As opposed to spit roasting, cooking meat in a container captures and retains valuable fats essential to hunter-gatherer survival. Boiling promotes starch gelatinization and pasting, which makes starches more digestible and therefore more nutritious (Wandsnider 1997:6).

In addition to the nutritional advantages of cooking with pottery, the ability to leave a pot unattended for long periods of time may have been seen as an advantage for the women in charge of cooking, allowing them time to attend to other tasks. Changes in social obligations and mobility or access to certain resources can affect women's decisions regarding how to invest their time, and at some point, the energy required to manufacture pottery became a worthwhile seasonal investment, allowing women more time flexibility on a daily basis (Whelan et al. 2013). Although Laurel pottery is relatively thin, the earliest pottery in lower Michigan and Illinois, Schultz and Marion Thick types, are thick wares that would not be ideal for boiling or rapid cooking (Garland and Beld 1999; Ozker 1982). Therefore, the early adoption of pottery across the Midwest may be rooted in the novelty of stewing or long-term simmering/cooking. By the Late Woodland period, that novelty may have worn off, and pottery was used for all modes of cooking, including boiling.

Cuisine, Interaction, and Identity

Social interactions and identities also play a part in culinary change. Nixtamalization may have arrived as part of the wider maize culinary package that spread across eastern North America, possibly in connection to certain ideologies associated with maize (Hastorf and Johannessen 1994; see Betzenhauser in this volume). Maize arrived and was a regular component of the diets of people across the northern Great Lakes during the Middle Woodland period, while it remained unimportant among groups to the south, many of whom were engaged in the Hopewell sphere of interaction and exchange to some degree. Societies in the northern Great Lakes participated minimally in Hopewell and did not appear to have adopted Eastern Agricultural Complex crops native to the southern Midcontinent, instead readily adopting the foreign, tropical maize. Then, as maize became a staple crop for those in the south, likely because of the nutritional advantages of nixtamalization, people in the northern Great Lakes may have adopted the new processing technique but did not increase their reliance on the crop. Groups in the northern Great Lakes continually maintained a cuisine distinct from their southern neighbors.

Wild rice is considered a sacred food of historic and modern Ojibwe, important both ceremonially and as a dietary staple. As such wild rice is closely tied to Ojibwe identity (Densmore 1979, 2005; Scott 1996; Vennum 1988). The increasing importance of wild rice at the Cloudman site (and other Great Lakes sites) after AD 1200 may signal the origins of its role as a central component of cuisine and identity among Indigenous groups in the Upper Great Lakes (Dunham 2014; Kooiman 2021).

Comparisons between food residues (components and patterning) and pottery typologies may provide further insight into culinary identities and/or differential pottery function. The Late Precontact occupation of the site is characterized by Traverse Ware, a scalloped Woodland variety, and Iroquoian-style pottery resembling types common in southeastern Ontario. The accelerator mass spectrometry (AMS) dates from residues associated with these two distinct ceramic styles are also statistically distinct (Kooiman and Walder 2019), suggesting a series of brief occupations from AD 1300 to 1500. Some have conjectured that proto-Odawa traders acting as middlemen between the Ontario Iroquois to the east and Woodland groups to the west may have occupied the Cloudman site throughout this period (Branstner 1995; Cleland 1999). Rather than manufacturing their own pottery, they may have used pottery from diverse trade partners. However, distinct combinations of foods were present among the Traverse versus Iroquoian-style pottery (Kooiman 2021). This could be evidence of groups with distinct identities, cuisines, and pottery styles occasionally occupying the site. Alternatively, if all Late Precontact occupants of the Cloudman site were proto-Odawa, the differences in plant species associated with distinct pottery types might be related to pottery function. Each stylistic type may have been preferred for different cooking tasks based on their physical properties (such as thickness or size). The sample sizes of the Cloudman site pottery assemblage is too small to investigate this relationship between technology and cuisine, but it provides a good example of how this approach might be used to investigate the relationships between cuisine and identity and/or special vessel function.

CONCLUSION

The Cloudman assemblage overall is too small to make sweeping conclusions about cuisine and culinary change across the Woodland northern Great Lakes and represents but a microcosm of the cuisine at the Cloudman site itself. The methods employed in this study are time-consuming and expensive and require intact adhered or preserved absorbed residue, which limits vessels that can be sampled. Many foods are being excluded from consideration by our focus on microbotanical remains; stable isotope analysis of these same adhered food residues suggests that these plant remains were likely cooked alongside aquatic resources (Kooiman 2021; Kooiman et al. 2022), while lipid residue analysis of absorbed residues suggest a much broader array of both plants and animals had been processed in the Cloudman vessels before their final use (Kooiman et al. 2022). Organic residue analysis could be applied to adhered residues to provide additional information about the faunal components of these final dishes cooked at the site.

However, the information presented here can serve as a starting point from which to explore other regional sites to fully investigate the nature of ancient Indigenous cuisine and to understand the environmental, social, and even ideological contexts surrounding food choice and preparation behaviors. The application of use-alteration trace analysis and microbotanical analysis of food residues from pottery can reveal much about past culinary practices, particularly when considered in the context of ethnographic information. This approach holds great potential for future research in the Midcontinent, across North America, and in other regions of the world, allowing archaeologists to continue to delve deeper into ancient cuisine.

Chapter 3

Woodland Tradition Cuisines in Southeastern Wisconsin

JENNIFER R. HAAS

The study of cooking and food preparation practices has demonstrated great potential to reveal social information about past and contemporary populations by identifying the ways in which everyday practices relate to political, economic, religious, and social realms (Graff 2018; Hastorf 2017; Hastorf and Weismantel 2007). Recent archaeological research has contextualized social aspects of food, examining the types of foods commonly consumed as well as the styles of cooking and preparation activities that occurred in particular contexts to develop a more complete picture of past foodways and cuisine (Graff 2018; Graff and Rodríguez-Alegría 2012; Hastorf 2017; Kassabaum 2019; VanDerwarker et al. 2016). Foodway data from the Finch site (47JE0902), a domestic habitation in southeastern Wisconsin, are used to examine Woodland people's relationship with and use of plant and animal resources over the course of a millennia (circa 100 BC to AD 1200). Multiple material data sources from the Finch site, including traditional plant macrobotanical studies, faunal analyses, ceramic morphological and use-wear analyses, and absorbed chemical residue analyses, along with ethnographic documentation, are used to interpret cuisines of Woodland groups. Containing spatially discrete Early, Middle, and Late Woodland occupations, good preservation of plant and animal remains, and secure radiocarbon dates, the site provides an unprecedented examination of Woodland peoples' relationship with and use of plant and animal resources.

REGIONAL CONTEXT AND THE FINCH SITE

A full understanding of Woodland tradition lifeways in southeastern Wisconsin is currently lacking, especially with regard to the Early and Middle Woodland periods (Benchley et al. 1997; Goldstein 1992; Haas 2019b; Jeske 2006; Jeske and Kaufman 2000; Rusch 1988). The limited dataset, coupled with trends from adjacent regions, suggests that people occupying southeastern Wisconsin during the Early and Middle Woodland were seasonally mobile foragers largely relying on a variety of wild plants and fauna, with some evidence for seed cultivation and domesticates (Arzigian 1987; Goldstein 1992; Haas in press, 2019a; 2019b; Jeske 2006; Salkin 1986; Salzer 1965, n.d.; Stencil 2015; Stevenson et al. 1997; Wiersum 1968; Zalucha 1988). Early Woodland has been conventionally dated from 500 BC to AD 100, Middle Woodland from AD 100 to 400, and Late Woodland from AD 600 to 1200 (Stevenson et al. 1997). However, recent direct dates on diagnostic materials from the Finch site, coupled with a synthetic review of previously reported regional radiocarbon dates, indicate a temporal overlap between the Early and Middle Woodland periods (Haas 2019a, 2019b). This overlap hints at underlying social complexities not fully elucidated by current taxonomic classifications (Haas 2019a; Stoltman 1990, 2005, 2006).

The conventional model for Late Woodland groups in southeastern Wisconsin encompasses two distinct phases, Horicon and Kekoskee, differentiated by mound use, ceramic styles, and subsistence patterns (Salkin 2000). The Horicon phase (AD 700 to 1050) is associated with effigy mounds, Madison ware ceramics, and subsistence regimes focused on mammal procurement, especially deer, supplemented with fish, birds, reptiles, wild plants, and limited maize use (Gartner 1999; Salkin 2000; Simon 2000). Kekoskee-phase (AD 800 to 1300) sites tend to be large, nearly year-round habitation areas. Subsistence regimes involved cultivation of plant crops (maize [*Zea mays*], squash [*Cucurbita pepo*], goosefoot [*Chenopodium* sp.], maygrass [*Phalaris caroliana*], and sunflower [*Helianthus* spp.]) (Arzigian 1993; Meinholz and Kolb 1997; Picard 2013; Richards 1992).

Finch Site

The Finch site is located on a locally prominent hill and small terrace adjacent to a marsh and inland from Lake Koshkonong (Rock River). Large-scale excavations (2009 to 2012) yielded high quantities of ceramics, well-preserved ecofacts (faunal remains and plant macroremains), chipped stone artifacts, ground stone, and fire-cracked rock as well as a high feature density (Haas 2019b). As a small, seasonally occupied open-air habitation locale, the site harbors spatially discrete Early, Middle, and Late Woodland occupations, offering an accounting of a domestic/household habitation (Haas 2019a, 2019b). Several AMS dates were obtained for the Finch site indicating Woodland occupations (calibrated) from 166 BC to AD 1258 (2060 ± 25 to 830 ± 25 radiocarbon years before present [RCYBP]) (Haas 2019b). The Early Woodland component dates to AD 21 to 129 (1930 ± 25 RCYBP), the Middle Woodland to 166 BC to AD 325 (2060 ± 25 to 1790 ± 20 RCYBP), and the Late Woodland from AD 907 to 1258 (1040 ± 25 to 830 ± 25) (Haas 2019b).

The Early Woodland component represents a seasonal fall domestic and resource processing campsite defined by diagnostic lithics (Kramer, Waubesa, and Robbins) and ceramic vessels (Incised Over Cord-Marked [IOCM], Dane Punched, and Prairie ware). The primary activity area is in the southern portion of the site where a small, oval-shaped house and several cooking pits were once located (Haas 2019b:Figure 17.2). The cooking pits are recognized as locales where food resources were being processed but lack the formal structure of earth ovens (see Neubauer, chapter 1). The cooking pits near the house contained copious amounts of grit-tempered pottery, nutshell fragments (identified as walnut [Juglandaceae], black walnut [*Juglans nigra*], and acorn [*Quercus* sp.]), with low amounts of charred faunal remains. Although most faunal material is unidentifiable, fish taxa are present. South of the house and associated cooking pits is a second Early Woodland activity area that abuts the edge of a larger midden or disposal locale (Haas 2019b). Here, tasks focused on intensive resource processing for white-tailed deer (*Odocoileus virginianus*) and other medium/large mammals (Haas 2019a, 2019b). Cooking pits in the midden area typically contained animal bone with good representation of medium/large mammals, especially white-tailed deer, as well as fish and turtle; two cooking pits yielded butchery evidence in the form of cut marks on the lower leg portions of white-tailed deer (*Odocoileus virginianus*). Cooking pit contents and butchery patterns strongly suggest bone grease rendering, an observation further supported by the herbivore biomarker identified in several pots. Moreover, the fatty acid signature for one Early Woodland jar indicates a fat depleted animal, a likely occurrence during mid-late winter (January–February). This occurrence further supports bone grease rendering as well as season of site occupation (Haas 2019a; Malainey and Figol 2017, 2019).

Seasonality of occupation and site activities for the Middle Woodland component are broadly similar to the Early Woodland. The Middle Woodland component marks a domestic and resource processing campsite intermittently occupied during the late summer through fall (possibly winter) months. Diagnostic material culture consists of Rock ware (Kegonsa Stamped, Shorewood Cord Roughened), locally produced Havana wares (Naples Stamped, Sister Creeks Punctate), transitional forms (Deer Creek Incised and Douglass

Net Marked), as well as Snyders and Steuben projectile points/knives (Haas 2019a, 2019b).

Two primary activity areas define the Middle Woodland occupation (Haas 2019a:Figure 18.2). The more northerly locale consists of a small circular house flanked by cooking pits, refuse/multifunctional pits, and dense debris scatters. One artifact scatter consists of a nearly complete Shorewood Cord Roughened vessel, a possible precursor to the container caches associated with the later Late Woodland component. Cooking tasks near the house primarily involved the processing of nuts given the ubiquitous presence of hickory (*Carya* sp.), hazelnut (*Corylus* sp.), and acorn (*Quercus* sp.). Squash (*Cucurbita* sp.) rind is also present suggesting use for cooking and/or serving tasks. The southerly activity area delineates a space where intensive animal resource processing took place. Many of the cooking pits in this area may have been habitually cleaned out and reused either for another cooking episode or for other purposes (such as refuse). Based on material content, two types of cooking activities occurred, one involving nuts/nutmeats and animal resources and the other focused on medium/large mammals (including white-tailed deer), birds, fish, and turtles. Cut marks are present on the lower limb and foot elements of several white-tailed deer and large mammal fragments consistent with bone grease rendering.

The Late Woodland component represents a seasonal, late spring through fall occupation. Diagnostic material culture consists of both Madison and collared (Point Sauble, Aztalan, Starved Rock, Pseudo) wares, as well as Madison Triangular, Honey Creek Corner notched, and Cahokia projectile points/ knives (Haas 2019b). A single expansive activity area is associated with the Late Woodland component in the northern portion of the site. Four domestic structures were identified, including larger rectangular and smaller circular forms, with some exhibiting internal posts (Haas 2019b). Numerous cooking pits and hearths were identified in proximity to the houses. Foods from the cooking pits include squash (*Cucurbita* sp.), maize (*Zea mays*), nutshell (hickory, walnut, black walnut, and acorn), wild rice (*Zizania aquatica*), fruits (*Prunus* sp., Rosaceae, Solanaceae), fish, and mammal bone. Associated with the Late Woodland component are several container cooking/cache pits where cooking containers were intentionally cached and/or stored (Haas 2019b).

MATERIALS AND METHODS

The Finch site Woodland tradition cuisines are identified by way of multiple material datasets consisting of the plant macroremains, faunal remains, and ceramic vessels. The plant macroremains and zooarchaeological assemblage are derived from feature and unit contexts and were recovered via flotation, 1/4-inch dry screening, and 1/8-inch water-screening (Haas 2019a, 2019b). All charred plant materials ≥ 2.0 mm were identified, inventoried, and analyzed; the material in the < 2.0 mm sample was scanned under a binocular microscope (10X–30X). All charred seeds and seed fragments from the < 2.0 mm size grade were removed, identified, and tabulated. Identifications were made with the aid of standard manuals and in reference to comparative specimens in the Archaeological Research Laboratory Center at the University of Wisconsin–Milwaukee (Delorit 1970; Martin and Barkley 1961; Montgomery 1977; USDA 2017) (Haas 2019a, 2019b). The plant macroremain assemblage is characterized through a variety of qualitative and quantitative measures, including density (d), ubiquity (U), and plant food ratios (q) (Kintigh 1984, 1989; Marston 2014; Pearsall 2015; VanDerwarker and Peres 2010; Popper 1988). The plant food ratio represents the value of a plant taxon divided by the total plant food weight, thus reducing biases due to preservation and/or population/household size differences.

The Finch site zooarchaeological assemblage, largely composed of vertebrate faunal remains, was identified and preliminary analysis conducted as part of a master's thesis project (Stencil 2015). For this chapter, new quantitative analyses were conducted on the zooarchaeological assemblage. Identifications, completed by Stencil (2015), used comparative collections from the University of Wisconsin–Milwaukee Department of Anthropology, the University of Wisconsin–Madison Zoology Museum, and comparative texts by Becker (1983), Gilbert (1990), and Gilbert et. al. (1996). Specimens were identified to the most specific taxonomic level possible. Specimens that could not be identified to species-level were, if possible, identified to taxonomic class (mammal, bird, fish, reptile, amphibian, and bivalve) (Beisaw 2013; Davis 1987; Lyman 1994; Reitz and Wing 2008; Wheeler and Jones 1989). Bone weight, number of identified specimens (NISP), and mammal size classification are employed to characterize the assemblage composition. Abundance is measured through descriptive statistics based on NISP and bone weight. Frequency of use is examined through ubiquity.

The ceramic assemblage includes 137 total vessels, including Early Woodland (n = 27), Middle Woodland (n = 45), and Late Woodland (n = 65) vessels (Haas 2019a, 2019b). Most vessels are delineated largely based on body/upper body and rim elements; few lower body sherds are associated with the Finch vessels and no basal sherds could be confidently assigned to individual vessels (Haas 2019a, 2019b; Picard and Haas 2019). Attribute data were recorded for

68 JENNIFER R. HAAS

all vessels; however, the functional analysis included only the more complete vessels (12 Early Woodland vessels and 22 Middle Woodland vessels) to minimize bias resulting from the absence of data (versus the absence of a particular trait) (Haas 2019a).

MATERIAL CULTURE ANALYSES

Plant Food Macroremain Assemblage

The Early Woodland plant food assemblage is characterized by very high amounts of nutshell and very low quantities of squash rind and wild seeds (Table 3.1). Four taxa are present in the plant food assemblage, consisting of two nut varieties, squash rind (*Cucurbita* sp.), and one wild fruit seed identifiable only to the nightshade (Solanaceae) family. The nut taxa represented in the assemblage include black walnut (*Juglans nigra*) and acorn (*Quercus* sp.). In addition, several nutshell fragments identifiable only to the walnut (Juglandaceae) family are present as are unidentified nutshell fragments.

Table 3.1. Woodland Plant Macroremains from the Finch Site

Type	Count	Weight (g)	Plant Food Ratio		
			(q) Count: Total Plant Weight	Density (d)	Ubiquity (U)
Early Woodland					
Wood Charcoal	397	12.221	–	1.46	53
Plant Food					
Nuts	65	0.949	67.15	0.69	39
Black walnut (*Juglans nigra*)	24	0.554	24.79	–	17
Walnut (Jugladaceae)	25	0.257	25.83	0.69	17
Acorn (*Quercus* sp.)	17	0.05	17.56	–	6
Seed (Wild)	2	0.002	2.07	0.06	6
Squash (*Cucurbita* sp.)	2	0.017	2.07	–	11
Total Early Woodland Plant Food	69	0.968	71.28	0.74	39
Plant Diversity: H'a=0.847 V'=0.611					
Middle Woodland					
Wood Charcoal	975	31.077	–	18.18	81

SOUTHEASTERN WISCONSIN

Plant Food					
Nuts	138	1.655	74.03	3.74	67
Hickory (*Carya* sp.)	82	1.134	70.57	26.26	43
Bitternut hickory (*Carya cordiformis*)	2	0.052	3.24	0.1	5
Walnut (Juglandaceae)	8	0.181	11.26	0.1	1
Hazelnut (*Corylus* sp.)	3	0.031	1.93	0.15	1
Acorn (*Quercus* sp.)	36	0.209	13.01	0.61	24
Seed (Wild)	17	0.019	9.12	0.71	1
Squash (*Cucurbita* sp.)	14	0.19	7.51	0.05	19
Total Middle Woodland Plant Food	169	1.864	90.67	4.49	71
Plant Diversity: H'=1.272 V'=0.578					
Late Woodland					
Wood Charcoal	11509	444.192	–	74.93	93
Plant Food					
Nuts	3477	47.32	67.98	12.35	57
Hickory (*Carya* sp.)	2611	41.19	51.05	0.74	48
Shagbark hickory (*Carya ovata* sp.)	16	1.4	0.31	–	3
Walnut (Juglandaceae)	53	0.45	1.04	0.04	7
Hazelnut (*Corylus* sp.)	6	0.13	0.12	0.00	4
Black walnut (*Juglans nigra*)	6	0.27	0.12	0.01	4
Acorn (*Quercus* sp.)	579	2.51	11.32	0.39	28
Unidentified	192	1.23	3.75	0.06	16
Nutmeat	14	0.14	0.27	–	1
Seed (Wild)	64	0.851	1.25	0.41	36
Squash (*Cucurbita* sp.)	7	0.453	0.14	0.06	6
Maize/corn (*Zea mays*)	257	2.524	5.02	1.77	45
Total Late Woodland Plant Food	3805	51.148	74.39	1.46	68
Plant Diversity: H'=0.899 V'=0.311					

Note: Counts and weights include plant macroremains recovered from flotation and non-flotation methods. Density data based on flotation sample data and measures count per ten liters. See Haas 2019b for complete inventory. Ubiquity is limited to feature context specimens.

H' = Shannon Weaver Diversity Index; V' = equitability.

The importance of nuts to the Early Woodland plant food assemblage is demonstrated by their relative frequency, density (d = 0.69), and ubiquity (U = 0.39) (see Table 3.1). The high plant food ratio (q = 67.15) further underscores the substantial contribution of nuts, as compared with wild seeds (d = 0.06; U = 6.00; q = 2.07) and squash (U = 11.00; q = 2.07), in the Early Woodland plant food assemblage. Of the nut resources, walnut family (Juglandaceae) nuts and black walnut (*Juglans nigra*) are more abundant than acorn (*Quercus* sp.) (Figure 3.1). Notably absent from the Early Woodland nut resources is hickory (*Carya* sp.). Seeds and squash, although present, have very low frequencies, densities, and ubiquities. The presence of squash (*Cucurbita* sp.) rind associates this domesticate with the Early Woodland component.

The plant food assemblage associated with the Middle Woodland component consists of high quantities of nutshell and low to moderate amounts of wild seeds and squash (see Table 3.1). A total of nine taxa are represented including four nut taxa (hickory [*Carya* sp.], bitternut hickory [*Carya cordiformis*], hazelnut [*Corylus* sp.], and acorn [*Quercus* sp.]), three wild seed varieties, and squash. Seeds consist of two weed seed taxa (spurge [*Euphorbia* sp.] and bedstraw [*Galium* sp.]) and one grain/oil seeds and greens taxa (wild knotweed [*Polygonum* sp.]). Seeds and squash, although present, have very low frequencies, densities, and ubiquities. Squash rind is one of two domesticates associated with the Middle Woodland occupation at the Finch site. The other domesticate is a nonfood type, tobacco (*Nicotiania* sp.).

The importance of nuts to the Middle Woodland plant food assemblage is demonstrated by their overall density (d = 3.74), ubiquity (U = 67.00), and high plant food ratio (q = 74.03) (see Table 3.1). The nut taxa consist of hickory (*Carya* sp.), acorn (*Quercus* sp.), bitternut hickory (*Carya cordiformis*), and hazelnut (*Corylus* sp.). Of the nuts, hickory (*Carya* sp.) is most abundant; however, moderate amounts of acorn (*Quercus* sp.) and very low quantities of bitternut hickory (*Carya cordiformis*) and hazelnut (*Corylus* sp.) are present (see Table 3.1 and Figure 3.1). The plant food ratio further underscores the higher importance of hickory (q = 70.57) relative to other nut resource varieties (plant food densities range from 1.93 to 13.01) (see Table 3.1). Also present in the assemblage are several fragments only identifiable to the walnut (Juglandaceae) family, unidentifiable taxa, and nutmeats.

The Late Woodland plant food assemblage is characterized by high amounts of nutshell, moderate quantities of tropical domesticates, and low amounts of squash rind, wild rice, and other wild seeds (grain/oil/greens, fruit, and other) (see Table 3.1). Notable newcomers to the Late Woodland food assemblage are maize (*Zea mays*) and wild rice (*Zizania aquatica*). Represented

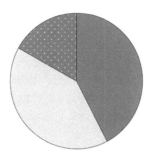

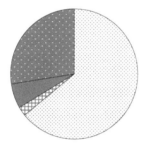

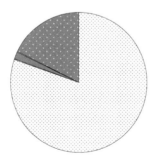

Figure 3.1. Nutshell composition (relative frequency) by component. (© Jennifer R. Haas.)

plant taxa include 19 types, consisting of five nutshell varieties, 12 wild seed types, squash, and tropical cultigens (*Zea mays*). Represented wild seeds consist of grain/oil/greens (chenopod [*Chenopodium* sp.], wild rice [*Zizania acquatica*]), fruits (Rose family [Rosaceae], nightshade family [Solanaceae], grape [*Vitis* sp.], plum/cherry [*Prunus* sp.]), and other seed types (dogwood family [Cornaceae], spurge [*Euphorbia* sp.], bedstraw [*Galium* sp.], wax myrtle [*Myrica* sp.], grass family [Poaceae], and violet [*Viola* sp.]). Nutshell and maize are the most ubiquitous plant food types. All of the identified maize is of the eight row variety with *kernel:cupule* ratios suggesting the storage of shelled maize at the site (Haas 2019b).

Similar to the preceding components, the overall importance of nuts to the Late Woodland plant food assemblage is indicated by their overall density ($d = 12.35$), ubiquity ($U = 57.00$), and high plant food ratio ($q = 67.98$) (see Table 3.1). Nut taxa represented in the Late Woodland assemblage include hickory (*Carya* sp.), shagbark hickory (*Carya ovata* sp.), walnut family (Juglandaceae), hazelnut (*Corylus* sp.), black walnut (*Juglans nigra*), and acorn (*Quercus* sp.). The most abundant nut taxa are hickory (*Carya* sp.) and acorn (*Quercus* sp.) (see Table 3.1 and Figure 3.1).

Comparison of plant food macroremain assemblages among the Early, Middle, and Late Woodland components is accomplished using two abundance metrics, including plant food ratio (q) and ubiquity (U), grouped by major plant category (nuts, wild seeds, and domesticates) and diversity indices (see Table 3.1). These metrics reveal differences between the components, highlighting significant changes in plant foodways. The plant food ratio and ubiquity values both indicate an uptick in the importance of nuts from the Early to the Middle Woodland (see Table 3.1). The plant food ratios rise slightly, but the ubiquity values indicate a 72% increase, suggesting much more widespread use of nuts by the Middle Woodland site occupants. Nut use appears to decrease slightly by the Late Woodland, corresponding with an increase in domesticate use. Diversity indices reveal that the Middle Woodland assemblages have a higher species diversity than the Early or Late Woodland assemblage, and that plant diversity trends toward less even distributions through time (see Table 3.1).

The composition of nut assemblages further illustrates significant differences among the Early, Middle, and Late Woodland assemblages (see Figure 3.1). Relative frequencies of nut taxa indicate that the Early Woodland site occupants favored black walnut (*Juglans nigra*) and walnuts (Juglandaceae) with modest use of acorns (*Quercus* sp.). By the Middle Woodland, hickory nut (*Carya* sp.) appears and predominates. Acorn (*Quercus* sp.) follows hickory in abundancy, and hazelnuts (*Corylus* sp.) are present for the first time. The occurrence of hazelnuts may indicate horticultural land clearing activities during the Middle Woodland (Simon and Parker 2006). From the Middle to Late Woodland, hickory (*Carya* sp.) nut use intensifies with hickory nuts representing over 80% of Late Woodland nut assemblage. Similar to the Middle Woodland assemblage, acorns (*Quercus* sp.) follow hickory (*Carya* sp.) in abundance for the Late Woodland. Hazelnut (*Corylus* sp.), black walnut (*Juglans nigra*), and walnut (Juglandaceae) are also represented in the Late Woodland nut assemblage in low frequencies.

In addition to differences in nut use and composition, more dramatic changes occur within the overall plant food assemblages from the Middle to the Late Woodland periods. During the Late Woodland, tropical domesticates and wild rice make their appearance. Plant food ratios indicate maize (*Zea mays*) as representing a small proportion of the plant foods (based on plant food ratios) but are ubiquitous, occurring in nearly half of Late Woodland features. Although Indigenous cultigens are present in the Early and Middle Woodland assemblages, represented by squash (*Curcurbita* sp.), the plant food ratios and ubiquity measures demonstrate that domesticated plants were of relatively lower importance as compared to nuts. In the Late Woodland, with the appearance of maize, there is a moderate decrease in nut abundance as compared with in the preceding Middle Woodland component. Examining the types of nuts represented in the Late Woodland assemblage, the high proportion of hickory (*Carya* sp.) nuts reflects continuity with the Middle Woodland component and the continued relative importance of hickory nuts within the plant food diet.

Faunal Assemblage

The Early, Middle, and Late Woodland zooarchaeological assemblages contain amphibian, bird, fish, mammal, and reptile taxa, indicating local procurement of resources from the ecological zones surrounding the Finch site (Table 3.2) (Haas 2019b; Stencil 2015). Overall, the Woodland assemblages contained an abundance of animal bone; however, comparatively few specimens are identifiable to taxon and species attributable, in part, to the high degree of fragmentation observed for the assemblage (Haas 2019a; Stencil 2015).

A total of five species are identifiable in the Early Woodland assemblage. Species identification is limited to the mammal and reptile taxa; none of the faunal remains classified as bird or fish are identifiable to species. Mammal species include even-toed ungulate (Artiodactyl), wolf/coyote/dog (*Canis* sp.), elk (*Cervus canadensis*), and white- tailed deer (*Odocoileus virginianus*). Specimens typed as Artiodactyl most likely represent white-tailed deer (*Odocoileus*

Table 3.2. Woodland Faunal Assemblage from the Finch Site

Taxon	Species	NISP[a]	Weight (g)	Percent NISP	Percent Weight	Ubiquity (U)
Early Woodland						
Bird	Unidentified	2	0.69	0.28	0.29	2
Fish	Unidentified	37	0.87	5.1	0.37	6
Mammal				89.94	97.79	59
	Even-toed ungulate (Artiodactyl)	2	1.83	<0.01	0.01	4
	Wolf/coyote/dog (*Canis* sp.)	2	2.82	<0.01	0.01	2
	Elk (*Cervus canadensis*)	2	0.86	<0.01	<0.01	2
	White-tailed deer (*Odocoileus virginianus*)	9	42.37	0.01	0.18	11
	Unidentified	638	183.67	0.88	0.78	57
Reptile	Turtle (Testudines)	343.67		4.68	1.55	19
Total		726	236.78			
Animal Diversity: H'b = 1.309 V'c = 0.673						
Middle Woodland						
Bird	Unidentified	2	0.29	0.16	0.05	3
Fish				2.33	0.1	7
	Channel catfish (*Ictalurus punctatus*)	1	0.2	<0.01	<0.01	2
	Unidentified	28	0.41	0.02	<0.01	7
Mammal				96.38	99.48	44
	Even-toed ungulate (Artiodactyl)	3	5.18	<0.01	0.01	2
	Striped skunk (*Mephitis mephitis*)	1	0.9	<0.01	<0.01	2
	Muskrat (*Ondatra zibethicus*)	1	1.29	<0.01	<0.01	2
	Raccoon (*Procyon lotor*)	2	2.28	<0.01	<0.01	3
	White-tailed deer (*Odocoileus virginianus*)	34	93.38	0.03	0.16	10
	Unidentified	1,158	482.03	0.93	0.82	43
Reptile	Turtle (Testudines)	14	2.18	1.13	0.37	10
Total		1,244	588.14			
Animal Diversity: H' = 1.218 V' = 0.586						

Late Woodland

Amphibian	Unidentified	1	0.02	0.04	<0.01	--
Bivalve	--	33	1.82	1.48	0.35	9
Bird		28	2.1	1.26	0.40	6
	Mallard (*Anas platyrhynchos*)	1	0.1	0.04	0.02	--
	Greater prairie chicken (*Tympanuchus cupido*)	1	1.49	0.04	0.29	--
	Unidentified	26	0.51	1.17	0.10	6
Fish		888	13.72	39.82	2.64	29
	Freshwater drum (*Aplodinotus grunniens*)	2	0.1	0.09	0.02	1
	White sucker (*Catostomus commersonii*)	1	0.18	0.04	0.03	1
	Channel catfish (*Ictalurus punctatus*)	1	0.5	0.04	0.10	1
	Walleye (*Sander vitreus*)	6	0.29	0.27	0.06	3
	Unidentified	878	12.65	39.37	2.43	26
Mammal		116	231.6	5.20	44.57	26
	Coyote (*Canis latrans*)	1	1.08	0.04	0.21	--
	Elk (*Cervus canadensis*)	1	188.96	0.04	36.37	1
	Bobcat (*Lynx rufus*)	1	3.99	0.04	0.77	--
	White-tailed deer (*Odocoileus virginianus*)	4	6.4	0.18	1.23	4
	Deer mouse (*Peromyscus maniculatus*)	1	0.01	0.04	0.00	--
	Raccoon (*Procyon lotor*)	2	1.68	0.09	0.32	--
	Unidentified	106	29.48	4.75	5.67	25
Reptile		49	10.54	2.20	2.03	7
	Turtle (Testudines)	44	10.31	1.97	1.98	6
	Unidentified	5	0.23	0.22	0.04	1
Total		2,230	519.6			
Animal Diversity: H '= 1.362 V '= 0.531						

Note: Ubiquity is limited to feature context specimens. See Haas 2019b for complete inventory.

[a]NISP = number of identified specimens.

[b]H' is Shannon Weaver Diversity Index.

[c]V' is equitability.<end file>

virginianus) (Stencil 2015). All reptiles are turtle (Testudines). The identifiable assemblage has very high frequencies of mammal remains, low to moderate amounts of fish and reptiles, and very low quantities of birds. The size-identified mammal assemblage is dominated by medium/large mammals and large mammals (Figure 3.2). Ubiquity values indicate that mammals are the most abundant taxa, followed by turtle; least ubiquitous are fish and bird.

A total of eight species are represented in the Middle Woodland assemblage including channel catfish (*Ictalurus punctatus*), even-toed ungulate (Artiodactyl), striped skunk (*Mephitis mephitis*), muskrat (*Ondatra zibethicus*), raccoon (*Procyon lotor*), white-tailed deer (*Odocoileus virginianus*), and turtle (Testudines). The even-toed ungulate (Artiodactyl) may represent white-tailed deer (Stencil 2015). The identifiable assemblage is characterized by very high frequencies of mammal remains and very low quantities of reptiles, fish, and bird. The size-identified mammal assemblage is dominated by medium/large mammals and large mammals (see Figure 3.2). Mammals are the most ubiquitous taxa, followed by turtle. Least ubiquitous are fish and bird.

The Late Woodland faunal assemblage consists of very high quantities of fish remains, moderate to low amounts of mammals, and low quantities of amphibians, bivalves, birds, and reptiles. Represented animal taxa include four fish species (freshwater drum [*Aplodinotus grunniens*], white sucker [*Catostomus commersonii*], channel catfish [*Ictalurus punctatus*], and walleye [*Sander vitreus*]); six mammal species (coyote [*Canis latrans*], elk (*Cervus canadensis*], bobcat [*Lynx rufus*], white-tailed deer [*Odocoileus virginianus*], deer mouse [*Peromyscus maniculatus*], raccoon [*Procyon lotor*]); two bird species (mallard [*Anas platyrhynchos*], greater prairie chicken [*Tympanuchus cupido*]); one amphibian species (unidentified); and one reptile species (Testundines). Based on NISP and ubiquity measures, fish are the most abundant taxon, followed by unidentified mammal species. Amphibian, bivalve, bird, and reptile occur in low amounts. The size-identified mammal assemblage indicates that small-sized mammals have the highest frequency, with similar, but lower, quantities of medium and large mammals (see Figure 3.2). Ubiquity values underscore the frequent use of fish, a taxa present in about one-third of Late Woodland features.

Comparing the faunal assemblages across all components shows some distinct differences regarding taxa composition; however, species diversity and evenness remain constant (see Table 3.2). The taxa composition of the Early and Middle Woodland faunal assemblages are very similar. Both have abundant mammal remains, especially white-tailed deer (as well as even-toed ungulates and medium/large mammals, that may represent white-tailed deer). Less represented within both the Early and Middle Woodland assemblages are fish,

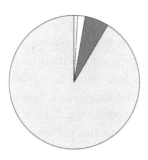

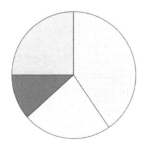

Figure 3.2. Relative frequency of mammal sizes (number of identified specimens) by component. (© Jennifer R. Haas.)

reptile (turtle), and bird. The taxa composition of the Late Woodland component is very different from the preceding Early and Middle Woodland. The Late Woodland assemblage has a greater quantity and wider variety of fish species. Although more mammal species are identified in the Late Woodland assemblage, mammal abundancy is less than in preceding time periods. Moreover, during the Late Woodland, the emphasis shifts from medium/large and large mammals to small mammals (see Figure 3.2). NISP percentages reveal medium/large and large mammals account for over 90% of the Early and Middle Woodland unidentified mammal bone assemblage. By the Late Woodland, medium/large and large mammals constitute only about one-third of the unidentified mammal bone assemblage.

The NISP percentages, based on counts, and ubiquity values for the fish and mammals, the better represented taxa for each component, provide a way to compare the assemblage compositions. Both measures reflect the significance of mammals, most identified as medium/large and large, for the Early and Middle components. Mammals are represented in 59% of all Early Woodland features and 44% of Middle Woodland features. The NISP percentages for the Early Woodland component show mammals representing 90% of the assemblage and, for the Middle Woodland, 96% of the faunal assemblage. For the Late Woodland features, mammals are present in about one-third (29%) of all Late Woodland features and have a NISP percentage of 5%.

The fish taxon reveals a trend of increasing use through time. Both NISP percentages and ubiquity indicate infrequent use of fish for both the Early and Middle Woodland components. Fish are present in only 6% of Early Woodland features and 7% of Middle Woodland features. By NISP, fish account for 5% of the Early Woodland assemblage and 2% of the Middle Woodland assemblage. By the Late Woodland, fish occur in 29% of all Late Woodland features and compose 40% of the assemblage (by NISP).

CERAMIC ASSEMBLAGE

The final dataset examined to assess Woodland tradition cuisines is the ceramic assemblage (Table 3.3). Woodland vessels from the Finch site are presumed to have a food-related function, likely involving cooking and/or storage, given that nearly all are identified as jars in the context of a domestic habitation site type (Braun 1983; Haas 2019b; Hally 1983; Rice 1987; Skibo 2013; Smith 1988). Early Woodland vessels are small- to medium-sized grit-tempered globular (globe-shaped) jars, with some conoidal (cone-shaped) forms, with direct or slightly everted rims, plain interiors, cord-marked exteriors, and moderately thick walls (average 7.72 mm). Middle Woodland vessels tend to be larger conoidal jars (grit-tempered) with more variability of rim stances (direct, everted, and inverted), plain or smoothed interiors, cord-marked exteriors, and thicker walled (average 8.51 mm). Although Middle Woodland vessels tend to be thicker than Early Woodland jars, the increased thickness may relate to the size of the vessel (Haas 2019a). Late Woodland vessels are all grit-tempered, large globular, thin-walled (average 6.00 mm) jars with direct or everted rims.

Intended vessel use is inferred from morphological attributes of form, orifice diameter (overall size), thickness, and rim stance. Based on these attributes, the Early and Middle Woodland vessels were designed to be used in different ways. Early Woodland vessels are smaller in size and include globular forms better suited for rapid heating or boiling with rim stances allowing easy access to the pot during cooking or serving. These globular forms are not well represented in the Middle Woodland assemblage. Middle Woodland vessels are typically larger, conoidal-shaped vessels designed for longer-term heating at lower temperatures with easy access to vessel contents. Late Woodland vessels are globular and thin walled, suggesting intended use for rapid heating and/or sustained boiling (Braun 1983; Skibo and Schiffer 1987; Skibo 2013).

The reconstruction of intended function may not directly correlate with the actual use (Skibo 2013, 2015). Actual function, or use alteration, relates patterns of exterior sooting, interior carbonization, and attrition to cooking and processing techniques (Skibo 2015). Chemical residue analysis further addresses actual use by identifying remnants of plants and animals preserved in the ceramic fabric (Malainey et al. 1999, 2001; Skibo et al. 2016). For this study, the analysis of actual use is limited to the Early and Middle Woodland vessels (Haas 2019a).

Exterior sooting, exterior carbonization, and interior carbonization are common on the Early and Middle Woodland vessels, implicating their use within (or in proximity) to fire (Haas 2019a) (see Table 3.3). Exterior sooting and carbonization are present on just over one-half of the Early and Middle Woodland vessels but more prevalent on the Early Woodland vessels. Sooting on Early Woodland vessels typically occurs on the upper and mid-body vessel portions with exterior carbonization present, in lower relative frequencies, on the rim/lip and the rim/ upper body. Middle Woodland vessels have the highest relative frequency of exterior carbonization on the rim/lip with sooting also present, in slightly lower frequencies, on the rim/upper body and body. The differential patterning of exterior soot on Early and Middle Woodland vessels suggests different techniques for positioning in, on, and/or over the fire. Early Woodland vessels, with higher frequencies of exterior sooting on the body, tended to be placed directly in a fire, while Middle Woodland vessels, exhibiting higher frequencies of exterior carbonization on the rim and lip, were more commonly placed on coals. This observation is consistent with results of intended function, finding an association of some of the Early Woodland jars with globular forms, designed for rapid heating that allowed placement directly in a fire. Middle Woodland vessels are thicker-walled conoidal forms, indicating longer-term cooking with lower heat. Some of the Early and Middle Woodland vessels also exhibited exterior carbonization near the rim/lip, possibly caused by spillovers and/or splatter.

Table 3.3. Ceramic Assemblage from the Finch Site

	Early Woodland	Middle Woodland	Late Woodland
Attribute Analysis			
Jar Form			
Sample size	27	43	65
Conoidal	30% (6)	87% (38)	–
Globular	26% (7)	9% (4)	92% (60)
Tecomate	–	2% (1)	--
Indeterminate	44% (12)	–	8% (5)
Vessel Size			
Sample size	18	32	31
Orifice Diameter Average (cm)	18.33	22.69	28
Orifice Diameter Range (cm)	10–30	10–46	10-6
Wall Thickness			
Sample size	27	42	46
Thickness Average (mm)	7.72	8.51	6
Thickness Range (mm)	4.04-13.26	6.17-11.47	3.59-10.5
Rim Stance			
Sample size	27	45	65
Direct	59% (16)	44% (20)	66% (43)
Everted	41% (11)	31% (14)	32% (21)
Inverted	–	24% (11)	–
Indeterminate	–	–	2% (1)
Use-Wear Analysis			
Sample size	12	22	–

Exterior Soot Present	58% (7)	50% (11)	-
Rim/lip	29% (2)	45% (5)	-
Upper body and/or body	57% (4)	27% (3)	-
Rim and upper body	14% (1)	27% (3)	-
Interior Carbonization Present	67% (8)	59% (13)	-
Carbonization band on rim	13% (1)	38% (5)	-
Patches on body	38% (3)	31% (4)	-
Isolated patches on rim	13% (1)	15% (2)	-
Patches on body and rim	38% (3)	15% (2)	-
Lipid Category - Biomarker			
Sample sizer	5	8	-
Decomposed Nut Oil & Plant	-	1 (conifer)	—
Herbivore & Plant	2 (conifer -1)	6 (conifer - 2)	—
Herbivore Only	1	-	—
Medium Fat Animal & Plant	1 (conifer)	-	—
Plant Only		1	—
Indeterminate	1	-	—

Note: Numbers in parentheses indicate number of vessels. See Richards 1992 for jar form definitions.

Food residue burned into the interior vessel surface provides direct evidence of pot use for cooking and resource processing (Kooiman 2016, 2019; Skibo 2013). Interior carbonization is present on the majority of the Early and Middle Woodland vessels. For both components, interior carbonization is patchy, suggesting dry-mode cooking. The patchy characteristics may also result from taphonomic processes breaking down the residue in spots. Few vessels exhibit interior carbonization bands, demarcating the water/scum line of the pot and indicative of wet-mode cooking (Haas 2019a; Skibo 1992, 2013; Kooiman 2018).

The patterning of carbonization and chemical composition of lipids preserved in the vessel fabric are integral components for the reconstruction of cooking activities and food selection habits (Kooiman 2018). Chemical residue analysis was completed for a small sample of the Early and Middle Woodland vessels, confirming their use for food preparation tasks involving animals, especially large herbivores, as well as plants. The identified chemical residue profiles are grouped into five different categories consisting of decomposed nut oil and plant, herbivore and plant, herbivore only, medium fat animal (fish?) and plant, and plant only (see Table 3.3). Most Early and Middle Woodland vessels yielded evidence of both herbivore and plant products. For these vessels, large herbivores were concurrently prepared along with plant foods, or plant foods were prepared in the same pots that were also used to cook large herbivores (Malainey and Figol 2017, 2019). The other categories (herbivore only, decomposed nut oil and plant, medium fat content animal and plant, low-fat content plants, medium-low-fat content plant, and plant only) are each represented by a single vessel. A lone Middle Woodland vessel yielded the only evidence of nut oil. The conifer biomarker was identified in five vessels, including two Early Woodland jars and three Middle Woodland vessels; pine resin may have been applied to the interior of the vessel to reduce permeability, as known from precontact pottery and among contemporary pottery-producing societies using low-fire, unglazed wares (Kobayashi 1994; Kooiman 2018; Skibo 2013). Finally, the plant roots, low-fat plant, and medium-fat content plants detected by the lipid residue analysis lack a clear correlate in the plant macroremain assemblage, emphasizing the limitations of the archaeological record in that not all resources used by past site occupants are represented by macrobotanical data.

DISCUSSION

Finch Site Woodland Tradition Cuisines

Based on the ceramic data, plant macroremains, and zooarchaeological remains, it is possible to develop an accounting of cuisines associated with the Woodland occupations at the Finch site. The foodway data allow for the identification of key trends that can be compared to and contextualized within the regional dataset.

The Finch site data reveal that Early Woodland cuisines involved the heavy use of nuts, medium/large mammals (mostly white-tailed deer and other even-toed ungulates), and turtle, with limited use of squash, fish, and birds. Favored nut resources were walnut (family), black walnut, and acorn. Ceramic vessels included globular forms, designed for more rapid heating and boiling, and conoidal forms better suited to heating at lower temperature and for longer periods of time. Patterns of exterior sooting and interior carbonization indicate dry-mode cooking techniques were favored over boiling/simmering (wet-mode) techniques. Exterior soot patterns suggest that the ceramic cookpots tended to be placed over a fire during cooking and, based on overall jar shape and lip stance, were designed for easy access to the vessel contents during cooking or serving. Lipid residue signatures reveal that herbivores, medium fat content animals, and plants were processed in the pots. Corroborating faunal data suggest that these animals may have included white-tailed deer, elk, and, possibly fish. Although nuts are the most abundant plant food category (based on macroremains), the lipid residue analysis did not identify nut residue within the Early Woodland vessels. Pots do not appear to have been used exclusively for plant foods, and at least one pot evidences only herbivore residue, suggesting white-tailed deer processing/cooking. This herbivore-only cookpot exhibits a use-wear pattern representative of lower-temperature simmering/stewing, a technique consistent with bone marrow/grease extraction. The butchery evidence and animal bone fragmentation patterns further suggest that white-tailed deer and other medium mammal processing activities (bone grease/marrow extraction and roasting) were occurring on site.

Middle Woodland cuisines involved the heavy use of nuts, squash, medium/large mammals (mostly white-tailed deer and other even-toed ungulates), and turtle with limited use of fish and birds. Favored nut resources were hickory and acorn, although bitternut hickory, hazelnut, and walnuts are also represented. There is evidence for more intensive use of nuts, with a heavy focus on hickory nuts, and more use of domesticates (squash), as compared to the Early Woodland. Most Middle Woodland ceramic vessels were designed to be used for longer-term heating at lower temperatures. The ceramic cookpots evidence multiple cooking methods, with direct, wet-mode stewing or boiling the favored techniques. Dry-mode roasting and wet-mode simmering/stewing methods were likely also used, however, to a lesser extent. Cookpots, designed for easy access to the vessel contents during cooking or serving, tended to be placed over coals during cooking, and many vessels show evidence of heavy use. Lipid residue signatures, combined with the plant macroremain and zooarchaeological data, suggest that nuts, herbivores (likely white-tailed deer), plant roots, and low-fat content plants were processed in the cookpots. Similar to the Early Woodland occupation, the butchery evidence and animal bone fragmentation patterns indicate that white-tailed deer (and possibly other medium/large mammals) bone marrow/grease extraction was a frequent site activity.

Late Woodland cuisines involved the heavy use of nuts, especially hickory and acorn, fish, and smaller sized mammals. By the time of the Late Woodland, site occupants are using maize on a regular basis and there is the first evidence of wild rice. Mammals, including white-tailed deer, are also of some importance. Grains/greens and fruits, squash, birds, and turtles are part of the Late Woodland foodways in a more limited way. Late Woodland vessels, relatively large and thin-walled globular pots, were designed for rapid and effective heating and boiling. Use-alteration of Late Woodland vessels is a future research topic.

Ranking the ubiquity values of the plant and animal taxa further illustrates the changing foodways at the Finch site. For the Early Woodland, the top five ranked foods are unidentified mammals (59%), reptile (Testudines, 19%), walnut (Jugladaceae, 17%), and black walnut (*Juglans nigra,* 17%). White-tailed deer and squash are at fifth place (both at 11%). For the Middle Woodland, the top five ranked foods are unidentified mammals (44%), hickory nut (43%), acorn nut (24%), and squash (19%). White-tailed deer and turtle are tied for the fifth place at 10%. Last, the top five ranked foods for the Late Woodland are hickory nut (48%), maize (45%), acorn (28%), fish (29%), and unidentified mammal (25%). The ranked ubiquities reveal key trends including the importance of mammals to Early and Middle Woodland site occupants, the importance of black walnut and walnut for the Early Woodland component, the appearance and favor toward hickory nuts during the Middle Woodland (and sustained importance during the Late Woodland), as well as the appearance and use of maize in the Late Woodland, accompanied by an increase use in fish and decreased importance of mammals.

A Regional Perspective of Woodland Tradition Foodways

Based on the foodway data and their archaeological context, the Early and Middle Woodland components reflect an overall continuity in lifeways, especially relative to cooking, foodways and organization of living space. Both components reflect a long-standing seasonal (fall) occupation where a variety of living, cooking, and animal resource processing activities occurred. These activities included nut processing as well as marrow extraction/bone grease rendering of medium/large mammals, especially white-tailed deer. Living and work spaces were organized in a similar manner. Domestic spaces for the Early and Middle Woodland components are defined by a singular small house surrounded by cooking pits delineating an area of domestic and household activities. Spatially separated from the house are intensive resource processing and discard areas, containing cooking facilities that functioned differently than those in closer proximity to the houses. Activities in the intensive resource processing area were more focused on animals; some tasks involved deer processing and bone marrow/grease rendering. Faunal data reveal that Early and Middle Woodland animal exploitation strategies were similar, focusing on large game, in particular medium/large mammals and even-toed ungulates (including white-tailed deer). Lipid residue signatures confirm that at least some Early and Middle Woodland pots were used to process/cook both herbivores (white-tailed deer) and plants. As Middle Woodland is understood as an Indigenous development, continuation of large game hunting from the Early Woodland aligns with expectations.

The Late Woodland component evidences a different use of space than the preceding periods. People were coming to the site on a seasonal basis but occupying the site for longer periods of time, perhaps arriving at the site earlier in the year, in late spring/early summer and living at the locale through fall. During the Late Woodland, activities occurred across a singular expansive area that harbored four houses. Surrounding the houses were cooking pits and hearths, and ceramic cooking pots were intentionally cached at the site. In contrast to earlier occupations, a spatially discrete intensive resource processing and discard area was not identified for the Late Woodland component. This may relate, in part, to the significant shift in animal exploitation from large game to smaller-sized mammals and fish.

The Early and Middle Woodland components reflect a reliance on wild plant resources, especially nuts, large game hunting (mostly white-tailed deer and other even-toed ungulates) with ceramics heavily used for processing a variety of plant and animal resources. However, a close examination of the material record reveals changing cuisines. The most compelling evidence is derived from the plant food assemblage and ceramic use-wear analysis that reflects an intensification of nut harvesting and the development of new processing techniques during the Middle Woodland. The data further suggest some evidence for an increased reliance on gardening. Nut preferences shift from black walnut to hickory, and nuts become a much more substantial part of the plant food diet. The larger and thicker Middle Woodland pots were being used for longer-term simmering. Pouring and/or serving often resulted in splattering, allowing food to adhere to the lip/rim and char. Ubiquity measures and plant food ratios, as well as greater plant diversity, suggest that cultigens were used more frequently and were a more important food resource during the Middle Woodland period.

The habitat and attributes of the most abundant nut taxa (black walnut and hickory), as well as their processing and use, as inferred from ethnohistoric data, elucidate the close connection between shifts in cuisines and changing lifeways. Walnut and hickory trees have distinct habitats that correlate with different harvesting/collection strategies and foraging territories. Notably, walnut trees are more dispersed and rarely present in pure stands. Walnut roots produce juglone, a substance toxic to other vegetation (including other walnuts), inhibiting seedling development near mature trees (Scarry 2003). Hickory trees, in contrast, typically grow in groves with heavy crop yields every two to three years. In good years, masts may be exceptionally locally abundant, allowing for the harvest of large quantities of nuts with relatively little search and travel time (Scarry 2003). Comparing walnut and hickory nut harvesting activities, collection of hickories would have been more expedient and likely to have occurred in closer proximity to a campsite within a more restricted foraging area.

Hickory and walnuts also have distinct processing requirements. Walnut processing most likely involved hand picking. Although walnuts have hard shells that are difficult to crack, the large nutmeats are readily separated from the shell once split. Walnuts may also have been parched but were likely not boiled as this technique produces an unpalatable, tannin-laden oil (Scarry 2003; Talalay et al. 1984). In contrast, hand picking is an unsuitable technique for hickories as the nutmeats are not readily separated (Scarry 2003). Ethnohistoric and experimental methods describe much more expedient methods for processing hickories that involve cracking, followed by pounding/pulverizing and immersion in liquid to extract the oil (Gardner 1997; Scarry 2003; Swanton 1946; Talalay et al. 1984). Pulverizing the hickory nuts and placing them in slowly boiling water results in the nutmeat oil rising to the surface where it is skimmed off (Talalay et al. 1984). What remains of the nutmeats, mostly protein, dissolves into a milky emulsion in the water, and by pouring the fluid through a strainer, the shells are removed (Fritz et al. 2001; Scarry 2003; Talalay et al. 1984). Based on ethnographic data, the oil was used as a beverage, a stock for soup, and/or as a cooking ingredient (Speck 1909; Swanton 1946; Talalay et al. 1984).

The differences in processing activities reflected in the ceramic use-wear analysis may partially relate to particular types of plant and animal resources. The appearance of conoidal pots in the Middle Woodland is consistent with the intensification of hickory nut harvesting and extraction of nut oil. The thicker-walled conoidal pots, designed for longer-term simmering, would have been better suited for nut oil extraction. Although the chemical residue profiles reveal that, in general, both herbivores and plants were prepared in the Early and Middle Woodland cookpots, the Middle Woodland vessels yielded the only evidence of nut oil. Burning activities involving wood charcoal were more intensive and frequent for the Middle Woodland occupation that also may relate to an intensification of hickory nut processing (Haas 2019a).

Changing food preferences from the Early to Middle Woodland period are reflected in the Finch site data. Based on ethnographies, bone grease and hickory nut oil/milk were key ingredients in soups and broths (Dunsenberry 1960:61; Manne 2012:177; Wilson 1924:182; Fritz et al. 2001; Scarry 2003: Swanton 1946). As bone grease/marrow activities are associated with both the Early and Middle Woodland components, the appearance and intensive use of hickory during the Middle Woodland may suggest that people increasingly favored nut oil as a key culinary ingredient. If the Early Woodland Finch site occupants used bone grease in soups, the shift to hickory nuts and hickory nut oil/milk during the Middle Woodland may represent a new recipe and way of cooking.

The changing plant food preferences and processing techniques observed in the Early and Middle Woodland data further reflect changing social dynamics. The intensification of hickory nut use represents a novel way of acquiring nutrient-dense resources in a more efficient manner, allowing people to stay closer to the campsite. Viewed from this perspective, the shifts in cuisines link to deliberate choices by household groups involving labor and resource trade-offs. Moreover, as ethnographies suggest that women performed most of the food collecting, processing, and cooking activities for daily consumption, and manufactured ceramics at the household level, these decisions were mostly likely made by, or minimally largely shaped by, women (Crown 2000; Fritz et al. 2001; Goody 1982; Graff 2018; Hastorf 1991; Montón Subías 2002; Skibo et al. 1997). In various regions of the Eastern Woodlands, the Middle Woodland period coincides with the initial appearance of horticulture economies (Arzigian 1987), dramatic increases in the use of starchy seeds, squash, and hazelnuts (Fortier 2006), and intensive harvesting of deer and anadromous fish (Brashler et al. 2006; Streuver 1968). Collectively, the Finch site data associate the Early and Middle Woodland transition as a dynamic period marked by changing cuisines, an increased commitment to plant resources (including cultigens), a constriction of foraging areas tethering groups closer to residential sites, and further marked by the consumption of different plant foods and new ways of cooking.

The trends of an increasing commitment to plant resources and decreasing mobility continue into the Late Woodland, along with evidence of larger social groups. The decreasing mobility is inferred from the intensification of gardening and cultivating activities, as well as the greater number of houses. Ceramic vessel volume increases, suggesting larger social groups, and some pots were intentionally cached at the site. The Late Woodland seasonality data indicate that people were coming to the site earlier in the year and staying at the site for longer periods of time. By the Late Woodland, site occupants are regularly growing and consuming maize with the first evidence of wild rice. Of note, nut processing activities are not supplanted by the appearance and use of tropical cultigens. Hickory nut processing, initiated in the Middle Woodland, continues as a favored resource during the Late Woodland. The appearance and widespread use of maize are, however, correlated with a dramatic change in the use of wild animal foods, shifting from a near reliance on medium/large mammals, including white-tailed deer, to frequent use of fish and smaller-sized mammals.

The near absence of Eastern Agricultural Complex taxa, the occurrence of eight-row maize, and evidence of a mixed economy (good representation of nuts, squash, and wild seeds, in addition to maize) suggest Late Woodland cuisines at the Finch site align better with eastern groups than with populations to the south (Egan-Bruhy 2014; King 1999; Parker 1996; Simon 1998). The dramatic shift in animal taxa, from a focus on mammal procurement during the Early and Middle Woodland periods to heavy dependence of fish resources and small mammals, may further accord with eastern Algonquin foodways. The Late Woodland foodways at the Finch site compare well with those at the nearby site of Aztalan (47JE0001) where the Late Woodland component yielded an abundance of hickory nutshell, maize, squash, acorn, hazelnut, mammal, fish, and bird remains (Picard 2013). The Mississippian component is associated with an increase in fish use (Warwick 2002).

The Finch site ceramic assemblage shows distinctive changes throughout the Woodland continuum, some of which are clearly linked to changes in cuisines. As noted, the differences in Early and Middle Woodland jar morphology correlates with the plant macroremain data that indicates a shift to intensive hickory nut processing. Comparing Middle Woodland with Late Woodland, ceramic vessels become thinner, larger, and predominantly globular in form. This pattern suggests that new types of foods, or combinations of foods, were being processed in novel ways by the Late Woodland people. The plant and animal evidence shows shifts from the Middle to Late Woodland, with new foods (maize and wild rice) and changing animal preferences from medium/large mammals to smaller mammals and fish. Hickory nuts continued to be of importance, so were those resources also processed in the Late Woodland pots? The ceramic use-wear completed for the Early and Middle Woodland vessels found that most ceramic vessels were used for the cooking of both plant and animal resources. Does this hold true for the Late Woodland vessels? A ceramic use-wear study, including assessment of actual use through lipid residues, is needed for the Late Woodland component to further address these questions.

In sum, the foodway data from the Finch site demonstrate a shift in cuisines from the Early to Middle Woodland period involving an intensification of hickory nut harvesting, an increased emphasis on gardening, and development of innovative food-processing technologies. The trends of an increasing commitment to plant resources and decreasing mobility continue into the Late Woodland, along with evidence of larger social groups. The appearance and widespread use of maize at the Finch site is correlated with a dramatic change in the use of wild animal foods, shifting from a near reliance on medium/large mammals, including white-tailed deer, to frequent use of fish and smaller-sized mammals. The rich dataset resulting from the complementary nature of these diverse methods reveals a wealth of information about social processes, underscoring the potential application of such an analytic approach to long-standing problems in other archaeological contexts worldwide. The results underscore the importance of using multiple datasets to assess foodways and identify cuisines.

Chapter 4

Plates, Cuisine, and Community at the Morton Site

JEFFREY M. PAINTER AND JODIE A. O'GORMAN

The movement of Oneota peoples into the Mississippian-occupied central Illinois River Valley (CIRV) of west-central Illinois at about AD 1300 is associated with social and cultural shifts in the region, including both small-scale warfare and cooperative interactions between migrants and locals (Bengtson and O'Gorman 2016; Hatch 2015; Milner 1999; Milner et al. 1991; O'Gorman et al. 2020; O'Gorman and Conner 2023; Steadman 2008). Recent research focuses on these postmigration interactions to better understand how they affected the lived experiences of those in the region and associated shifts in practices and traditions. An important theme of this research focuses on how cuisine may have been used to negotiate a path toward cooperation and even coalescence between the groups, or the role it played in deflecting such major integrative changes. Here, we define coalescence as an adaptive process of cultural transformation through which different groups form an integrated community that helps the new community succeed within a particular historic context. Within this ongoing process, many changes may occur, while some elements of the precoalescent group identities remain (Clark et al. 2019; Kowalewski 2006).

In this chapter, we consider one type of pottery vessel, broad-rimmed plates, to explore how associated culinary practices were used to negotiate identity and community in a postmigration setting. To do so, we take a multimethod approach incorporating functional, stylistic, and spatial analyses and draw on hybridity theory (Alt 2006, 2018a; Deagan 2013; Liebmann 2015; Silliman 2013; Stockhammer 2012, 2013) to conceptualize how these wares and their associated foodstuffs were actively engaged in social practices in the process of coalescence and community formation. Morton Village, a well-documented multiethnic community formed during a postmigration period, serves as a case study.

THE ROLE OF CUISINE AND HYBRIDITY IN COALESCENCE

Hybridity, as used here, refers to blended objects or traits as well as a transformational process through which groups from different backgrounds could negotiate differences and redefine social relationships. Although most often used to elucidate the tendrils of power and its resistance in postcolonial settings, its use can go beyond cases with such disparate power differentials (Deagan 2013; Liebmann 2015). For example, Alt (2006) and Clark and colleagues (2019) draw on hybridity and "third space" to illuminate practices entangled in cultural change in precolumbian North America. At its core, hybridity denotes a sense of in-betweenness, ambiguity, and fluidity in contexts of culture contact and change, creating "third spaces" within which people could act creatively to rethink social roles and meanings (Bhabha 1990; 1994). Such creativity is capable of generating altered behaviors, beliefs, and material traits that were part of this negotiation process. It emphasizes innovation, creativity, and the ability of actors to shape larger social processes occurring around them. Unlike many other approaches to culture contact, hybridity emphasizes that all parties are involved in these processes and are therefore also affected by their outcomes.

While this approach can be used to study many aspects of the past, cuisine lends itself well to the lens of hybridity. Particularly in postmigration situations, where groups must solve basic issues of sharing food resources and are exposed to each other's practices of preparing, cooking, serving, and eating in new proximity to one another, multiple third-space contexts seem likely. Because cooking and consumption happen daily throughout the community, cuisine is also an effective platform for social negotiation. Especially in situations of culture contact, cuisines can become a focus of continuity or change, in either case serving as a critical point of interaction (Hastorf 2017; Twiss 2012).

It is possible, even likely, that many aspects of cuisine changed in the postmigration context of Morton Village, but the adoption and use of plates by Oneota migrants are the most visible archaeological markers. Here, the Mississippian plate form and its associated culinary entanglements were adapted by Oneota migrants for use in their social negotiation of a new cultural landscape. Following a brief introduction to the site, we discuss the use of plates in Mississippian and Oneota traditions before providing our analysis.

MORTON VILLAGE: AN ONEOTA AND
MISSISSIPPIAN COMMUNITY

One of five known villages with an Oneota presence in the CIRV, Morton Village is the most thoroughly investigated (Figure 4.1). Excavations in the 1980s associated with road realignment included complete excavation of the associated Norris Farms cemetery and limited village excavations (Santure et al. 1990). This, together with more recent excavations conducted from 2008 through 2017, provides a view of the 9-ha village composed of 146 possible structures and hundreds of pit features, 329 of which have been excavated. About a third of the structures have been subject to test excavations and include both wall trench (traditionally Mississippian) and single-post (traditionally Oneota) domestic and special function buildings. Several lines of evidence, including radiocarbon dates and the distribution of diagnostic ceramics within structures and pit features, support synchronous occupation of the site by the two groups (O'Gorman and Conner 2023). Spatial layout of the village, adaptation of ceremonial practices, sharing of symbols (Bengtson and O'Gorman 2016), and shifts in culinary practices (Painter 2021) suggest community involvement in the coalescence process, although that process appears incomplete. Negotiations between the two groups indicative of creative hybridity have been observed in village community structure, the creation of ritual space near the center of the site, and shifts in sociopolitical organization for both groups (O'Gorman and Conner 2023). Additionally, earlier research on cooking suggests some aspects of cuisine emphasize distinct identities, while evidence from plates indicate Oneota adoption of specific local customs (Painter 2021; Painter and O'Gorman 2019).

Other culinary studies at Morton Village, such as Nordine's paleoethnobotanical analysis (2020, and see chapter 6, this volume) and Autumn M. Painter's (2022) archaeozoological analysis indicate that the food components in the respective cuisines display only nuanced distinctions. Food choices do not seem to be habitually circumscribed due to concerns over violence, and the location of the village allowed access to diverse resource zones and animals within 10 km of the site (Painter 2022). Cuisines of the groups incorporated deer, elk, fish, an array of smaller animals and birds, maize and other cultivars, and wild plants. Slight differences in food preferences between groups, such as an Oneota preference for thick hickory and *Chenopodium* (Nordine 2020) and perhaps preferences for kinds of fish (Painter 2022) were observed. At the regional level, carbon isotopic analysis by Tubbs (2013) indicates that Mississippian individuals from the slightly earlier Orendorf site consumed a diet more focused on maize than the Oneota interred at Norris Farms 36 cemetery. However, due

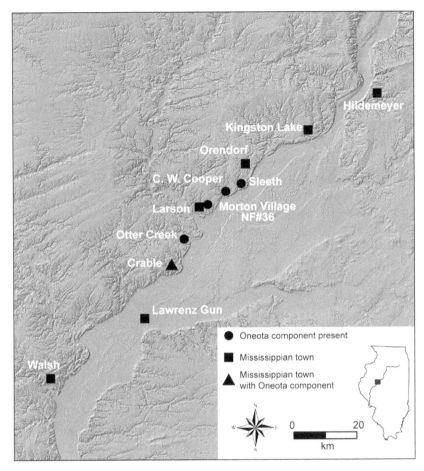

Figure 4.1. Map showing Morton Village site along with major Oneota and Mississippian sites in the Central Illinois River Valley. (Base relief map from Illinois Geospatial Data Clearinghouse with additional Manifold GIS and Adobe Illustrator by Michael Conner. Reproduced from Jodie A. O'Gorman and Michael D. Conner, Making Community: Implications of Hybridity and Coalescence at Morton Village. *American Antiquity* 88(1):79–98, 2023; Figure 1. CC BY-4.0.)

to a lack of Mississippian human remains that can be directly associated with Morton Village, it is impossible to determine whether the Mississippians living at Morton Village continued that culinary focus. Tubbs's (2013) study also reminds us that intragroup cuisine may have internal variability as well. Males in her Norris Farms 36 sample consumed more meat, while females consumed more maize, a pattern Tubbs (2013) suggests may have to do with differential food access for men on hunting forays.

As raw ingredients are malleable and can be transformed into a number of different dishes, investigations into cooking methods in addition to food choice can reveal greater distinctions in cuisine (Rodríguez-Alegría and Graff 2012; Graff 2018; Hastorf 2017). At Morton Village, a use-wear analysis of jars (Painter 2021), the primary cooking vessels used at the site, indicated that the ways Mississippian-style and Oneota-style jars were used were statistically similar. However, some minor differences, such as a higher rate of roasting or frying in Mississippian-style jars, were present. When the function of jars from Morton Village was compared with that of those from the Mississippian Larson site and the Oneota Tremaine Complex, similarities and differences between the assemblages were apparent. Similarities among jars with the same traditional ceramic styles (for example, Mississippian-style jars from Morton Village and Larson) suggest that some past aspects of cooking traditions were being maintained among the residents at Morton Village, while shifts between these groups, such as a marked difference in the rate of boiling or simmering between Oneota-style jars from Morton Village and those from the Tremaine Complex, also indicate that some cooking preferences were evolving at the site. Painter (2021) argues that these patterns indicate that the hybridization of tastes and cooking practices was occurring at Morton Village, leading to greater similarities in cuisine choices at the site. While shifts were underway, they had not yet completely reshaped the cuisines of residents.

Investigations of cooking and food choice have provided a greater understanding of the negotiations occurring during coalescence at Morton Village, but other aspects of cuisine can be considered. Serving and consumption practices also play a role in a community's foodways traditions and should be included to gain a more holistic perspective regarding the role of cuisine in coalescence. At Morton Village, and in the Midcontinent in general, broad-rimmed plates are thought to have been used as serving vessels whose decorations linked them to larger ceremonial or religious practices (Hilgeman 2000). They are also one of the most visible markers of postmigration change in the CIRV (Esarey and Conrad 1998; Lieto and O'Gorman 2014; Santure et al. 1990). As such, investigations of plate use at Morton Village may reveal further insights into negotiations regarding cuisine and ongoing coalescence.

BROAD-RIMMED PLATES CONTEXTUALIZED

To understand the Oneota adoption of broad-rimmed plate use at Morton Village, we first provide historical context for the use of this form in the Mississippian world and note its relative lack of use among Oneota peoples. As noted, plates with their highly visible decorative motifs and unrestricted shape (Figure 4.2) are typically interpreted as serving vessels, and they are often recovered in ceremonial settings. In the American Bottom, at Cahokia and other related

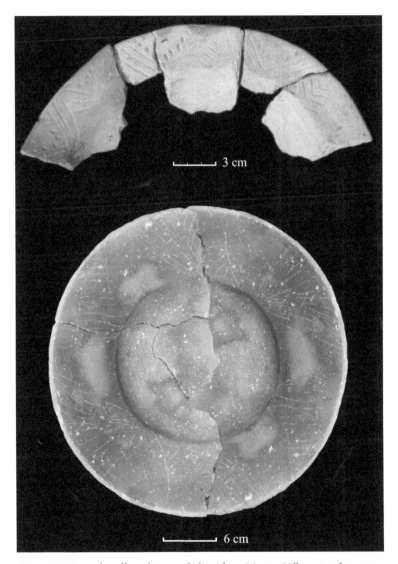

Figure 4.2. Examples of broad-rimmed plates from Morton Village: *top*, fragments of an Oneota-style plate. (Photograph courtesy of Jodie O'Gorman.); *bottom*, one-half of Mississippian-style plate (left side). A mirror image has been created and flipped to demonstrate how the whole plate would have appeared. (Photograph by Joshua Lieto. Courtesy of Jodie A. O'Gorman.)

sites, the Wells Incised plate form appears as Ramey Incised jars disappear from assemblages during the Moorehead phase in the early AD 1200s (Emerson 1997a; Pauketat 2004). At the same time, in the lower Ohio Valley, similar plates occur at Mississippian sites where their decorations are more commonly painted but also incised (Hilgeman 2000). This change in dish production and its culinary and ideological linkages are entangled in far-reaching ideological shifts in Cahokian cosmological narratives. Ramey Incised vessel form and iconography, incorporating both Upper and Under World symbols, were part of a narrative of access to those powers (Pauketat and Emerson 1991). Wells Incised plates, however, invoke powers of the Upper World through sun symbolism (Emerson 1997b; Hilgeman 2000) and/or avian symbols (Buchanan 2020). Their presence in assemblages in the Cahokia area, including both domestic and ceremonial contexts, makes up a small portion (less than 15%) of vessels (Buchanan 2020). Later, as the power of Cahokia waned and migrants moved out of the American Bottom, plates appear to take on new importance as witnessed at the Common Field Site at AD 1200–1350 in east central Missouri where plates make up over 30% of the assemblage. There, a sharp increase in the use of plates is tied to their use in ceremonies related to social stress, threat of violence, and small-scale warfare (Buchanan 2015, 2020).

In the central Illinois River Valley, Ramey vessels are present from the beginning of the Mississippian presence in the CIRV (1050 AD), although local adaptations of symbolism reveal a selective use reflecting local sociopolitical developments and views (Friberg 2018). Similar to patterns in the American Bottom, Ramey vessels disappear from CIRV assemblages as plates are introduced from 1150 to 1250 (Conrad 1991). The percentage of plates in assemblages on CIRV Mississippian sites is likewise similar to that observed in the American Bottom. At the CIRV Mississippian temple mound sites, plates make up less than 15% of the assemblages, and this is also the case at Morton Village when the total number of all vessels from the site is considered (Figure 4.3; Table 4.1).

What is interesting at Morton Village is the relative number of plates in the Oneota-style versus Mississippian-style subassemblages. Plates appear to be less important in Oneota cuisine. At the site, plates decorated with Oneota motifs make up 6.9% of all identified Oneota-style vessels, while Mississippian-style plates are 33% of all identified Mississippian-style vessels (see Table 4.1). This frequency may suggest a heightened response to violence and increased ceremonialism involving plates, such as that proposed by Buchanan (2015, 2020) at the Common Field site. However, a large number of jars at Morton Village cannot be assigned to Mississippian- or Oneota-style assemblages, and

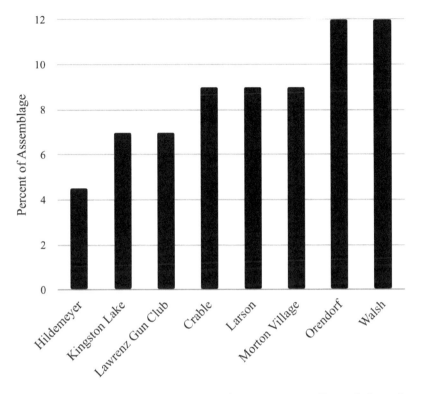

Figure 4.3. Bar chart comparing the percentage of plates at Morton Village with those of other Mississippian assemblages in the Central Illinois River Valley. Data from other sites from Harn 1994, Table 3, and Zelin and Emerson 2016, Table 7.4. (Chart courtesy of Jodie O'Gorman.)

it is likely that a considerable number of these are Mississippian-style jars that have smoothed shoulders with cord-marked bases. If even half of these vessels are Mississippian style (a conservative estimate), then the 33% frequency is reduced by half. Given this constraint, we do not argue that plate frequency at Morton Village is significantly greater than observations at CIRV Mississippian sites. Additionally, Oneota-style plates are less common at the site than Mississippian-style plates.

Motifs on Mississippian-style plates in the CIRV also are similar to those from the American Bottom and other regions, with the use of sunburst symbolism and other Upper World symbols, such as line-filled nested triangles, becoming more common over time (Conrad 1991). Mississippian-style plates at Morton Village are no exception (Figure 4.4). Oneota symbolism, primarily

Table 4.1. Ceramic Vessel Counts at Morton Village, Separated by Cultural Tradition Style

Vessel Style	Jars	Bowls	Plates	Other
Mississippian	90	14	53	3
Oneota	257	75	25	4
Indeterminate	308	189	12	19
Total	**655**	**278**	**90**	**26**

expressed on jar shoulders across the Oneota world, appears to have always been closely tied to avian Upper World symbols (see Benn 1989). Oneota plate use outside the CIRV is rare overall but does occur in Bold Counselor sites in the American Bottom (Jackson 1999). At Morton Village, nested chevrons and concentric arcs with or without punctates depict tail feathers and wings, common elements of hawk-men symbolism (see Figure 4.4). Buchanan (2015, 2020) suggests that the sunburst Mississippian motifs, rather than depicting the sun, instead represent this same hawk-falcon-Thunderer symbolism as part of a social landscape dominated by warfare and related ceremonies. Whether the traditional interpretation of sunburst or avian symbolism is supported, the shared Upper World symbolism, and worldview of which it is part, may have provided a common referent in the negotiation and formation of new postmigration identity and emerging coalescence at the Morton Village site. At the same time, such a shared reference would allow the Oneota to creatively express their own identity within the sacred or profane practice in which the plates played a symbolic and culinary role.

Were Oneota migrants adopting this vessel form to emulate or take part in Mississippian events? To indicate social parity? Were they using the plates in the same way as their Mississippian neighbors, or adapting the form for their own purposes? Or even using the form in a subversive manner? Hybridity theory suggests that we should consider such options. First though, we need to better understand how these vessels may have been used in the past, and we turn to functional and spatial analyses to do so.

INVESTIGATING PLATE FUNCTION

To examine how plates were used at Morton Village, functional and spatial analyses were conducted. To conduct the functional analysis, use-alteration,

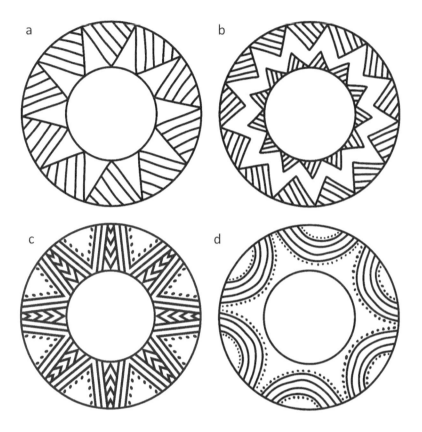

Figure 4.4 Stylized plate designs from Morton Village: (a and b) Mississippian style and (c and d) Oneota style. (Adapted from O'Gorman and Conner 2023, Figure 9.)

morphological, and surface treatment data were examined. In particular, use-alteration analysis is one of the only techniques that can be used to recover direct evidence of vessel function, such as the cooking and processing methods for which a vessel was used (Skibo 2013). As vessel use does not occur in isolation, combining functional data with analyses of spatial patterning can contextualize vessel function and uncover more information about past behaviors and traditions (Blitz 1993; Kooiman 2016).

Analysis of Vessel Function

When ceramics are used for different tasks, traces of those activities are left on the vessel. Depending on the activity performed, patches of carbonization, sooting, pitting, scratches, and other signs of damage can develop on a vessel's interior and exterior. Many of these traces are created in a consistent manner through predictable processes, making it possible to use this evidence to help infer how a vessel was used in the past (Hally 1986; Skibo 2013). These inferences are somewhat limited by the nature of the data. Since these analyses look at large-scale patterns of use-wear, they are only able to infer function at a general level, such as cooking with a lot of liquid compared with cooking with little liquid. Patterns of use-wear also develop over time through an accretional process (Kobayashi 1994), so patterns of use reflect how a vessel was used throughout its life, not necessarily how it was used during individual events or cooking episodes. Despite these limitations, use-alteration analysis is an effective method for investigating plate function, as it is able to differentiate between cooking and serving vessels and inform our understanding of how plates were used.

To conduct a use-alteration analysis of plates from Morton Village, plate fragments that composed at least half of the vessel profile, including both rim and basin sections, were selected for analysis. These vessels were visually examined for any evidence of use, including sooting, carbonization, scratches, or pitting. Based on the location of use-alteration evidence on their interiors, vessels could be placed into a number of functional categories, which include serving/storage, wet-mode cooking, dry-mode cooking, multipurpose cooking, and unknown. These functional categories are based on the results of past ethnoarchaeological, experimental, and archaeological research on jars, which found particular patterns of use-wear that correlate to specific cooking methods (Hally 1986; Kooiman 2018, 2021; Miller 2015; Skibo 2013). For example, vessels used for serving or storage may have scratching or other evidence of manipulation, but they will not have any evidence of being used over a fire, such as soot on their exterior or carbonization on their interior. Vessels used for wet- or dry-mode cooking will have sooting on the exterior and carbonization on the interior, but interior carbonization patterns are located in different areas. For wet-mode vessels, carbonization and charred residues will be located in a band on the interior rim, with none on the base, while dry-mode vessels will have interior carbonization on the base of the vessel only. Multipurpose vessels will have soot on the exterior and areas of carbonization on rim and base with clean zone between. Unknown vessels will have soot on exterior but no interior carbonization or anomalous interior carbonization pattern that does not fit the other categories.

Differences in function between the two ceramic stylistic groups at the site were also explored. To examine differences between ceramic styles, the plates analyzed for use-wear were subdivided into Mississippian-style and Oneota-style categories based on decorative style and motif. Mississippian-style decorations are typically composed of incised line-filled triangles, often in a sunburst pattern, while Oneota-style decorations are composed of thicker trailed lines and punctates done in a wet paste. After vessels in each subassemblage were placed into one of the five functional categories, the two stylistic groups were compared statistically. For the comparison, visualizations were first created to look for similarities and differences in the rates of the functional categories. Plate function was then lumped into "serving" and "cooking" categories, and the two subassemblages were compared using a Fisher's Exact test (Hess and Hess 2017; Nelson 2020). This test was used to support or reject the null hypothesis that the stylistic subassemblages possessed similar proportions of cooking and serving vessels, with a probability rejection threshold of 0.05 or lower. Lumping of data was necessary to ensure that functional categories with no vessels did not skew the results.

In addition to the use-alteration analysis, information regarding surface treatments and vessel morphology was also examined to explore functional differences between the two subassemblages. While surface treatments are often applied for aesthetic reasons, they also provide clues about the intended function of a vessel. For example, carbon coatings applied to vessels through smudging do not survive exposure to fire (Hally 1986), so vessels that have such surface treatments were not used over a fire and likely were not intended to be cooking vessels. To gather information on surface treatments, the treatments applied to interior and exterior surfaces were recorded at the same time vessels were examined for use-wear.

Vessel morphology can also be used to better understand a vessel's intended function, as certain vessel shapes are better for different tasks (Henrickson and McDonald 1983; Smith 1988). As vessels were examined, several morphological measurements were collected, including rim diameter, rim length, rim angle, rim thickness, lip thickness, and base thickness. These measures were first examined and compared using descriptive statistics (including mean, median, standard deviation, box-and-whisker plots, and histograms). Means between the assemblages were then compared statistically using a Welch's Two-Sample T-Test (Delacre et al. 2017; Ruxton 2006). This particular type of T-Test was used to account for the presence of unequal variances and unequal sample sizes between the two subassemblages. It was performed to test the null hypothesis that the means of the two groups were equal, with a rejection threshold of 0.05.

Spatial Analysis

To explore the contexts in which plates were used at Morton Village, provenience information was examined. While some vessels were piece plotted during excavation, most provenience information was collected at the feature or structure level. Since specific point data was unavailable for every plate, vessels were placed into one of three general spatial zones to better understand their distribution in different activity areas. These three spatial zones are inside a structure, within four meters of the edge of a structure, and farther than four meters from the edge of a structure. These zones are used as proxies for the use of a vessel inside of a structure, within a household's immediate activity area, and in open areas, such as outdoor communal spaces. We assume for the purpose of this analysis that a vessel was deposited near its location of use, as ethnographic and ethnoarchaeological research demonstrate that "economy of effort" commonly guides the disposal of unwanted items (Beck 2006; Deal 1985; Hayden and Cannon 1983:154) but acknowledge that this may not always be the case.

Unlike in the use-alteration analysis, all plates from Morton Village with adequate provenience information were included in the analysis. Plates were placed into one of the three spatial zones based on their recovery location. Plates recovered from within a feature were categorized based on the location of the feature; for example, plates from features found more than four meters from the wall of a structure were placed into the "farther than four meters from a structure" zone. If a feature intersected a structure wall, excavation notes were consulted to determine the temporal relationship between the feature and structure. If created before or after the construction of a structure, a feature was determined to be outside of that structure and its distance from other nearby structures was measured. A similar process was used for plates recovered from test units or excavation blocks. If a test unit was not associated with a structure, plates from that test unit were categorized based on the distance between the edge of the test unit and any adjacent structure walls. If a test unit was excavated to investigate a structure, then excavation notes were consulted to gather further provenience information. If a plate was found on the floor of a structure, it was placed into the "within a structure" category. If it was from basin fill, then the plate was assumed to have been deposited as trash during or after the abandonment of the structure (Deal 1985; LaMotta and Schiffer 1999) and was not used within that structure. Instead, its distance from other adjacent structures was measured to determine whether it was deposited within or farther than four meters from another structure. For four vessels from Structure 13, which were marked only with a structure number and lacked field notes, we were unable to further differentiate their depositional history. As they are marked as coming from a structure, we placed them into the "within a structure" category, but this may be misleading. Fortunately, only four vessels had this issue, and other plates from the same structure are labeled as coming from basin fill, so it is possible that the lack of "fill" label with these four plates indicates they are from contexts associated with the use of Structure 13 and not secondary contexts.

After the plates were placed into one of the three spatial categories, spatial patterns were examined at the site level. Similar to the use-alteration analysis, the spatial data were then divided into Oneota-style and Mississippian-style groups and compared to see whether any meaningful variability was apparent that might reflect different patterns of use. Statistical comparisons were made using a Chi-square test, which evaluated the null hypothesis that both styles of plates were distributed in similar proportions at the site. A rejection threshold of 0.05 or lower was needed to reject the null hypothesis.

As a final exploration of plate spatial patterning, plate provenience was examined in more detail, including evaluating their presence in known ritual versus domestic contexts and their association with domestic cooking vessels, such as jars. Excavation coverage of the ritual structures is more complete than that of the domestic structures.

This spatial analysis is limited by the recent strategy used to test multiple structures across the site, and the confines of right-of-way and other limitations during the 1980s. While the recent strategy provided broad coverage of the site, with 38 structures explored, only one domestic structure and two ritual structures were excavated in their entirety. The investigations in the 1980s completely excavated 6 of 12 structures identified. Given that plates are relatively uncommon at the site and most households were only tested with less than a third of their area excavated, chances of finding plates within households are exceedingly low. Even when structures are entirely excavated, the chances of finding a plate fragment are low. To illustrate, at Orendorf, where 28 burned structures were excavated in their entirety, only eight of the structures contained at least a fragment of a plate (less than 30% of structures) (Evans et al. 2019).

RESULTS

For the use-alteration analysis, a sample of 45 plates was examined, including Mississippian-style, Oneota-style, and indeterminate vessels. Overall, the use-alteration analysis results confirm that plates were generally used for noncooking purposes at the site, as 73.3% of the overall sample did not possess evidence of carbonization or sooting. While noncooking functions, like serving, may have been their primary function, a small percentage of plates were also used over a fire, possibly for cooking or food processing. Out of the 45 vessels, 11.1% were used for wet-mode cooking, 2.2% appear to have been used multiple ways, and 13.3% had indeterminate use-wear patterns. These patterns suggest that when plates were used for cooking or other processing purposes, water or other liquids were regularly involved, and burning or roasting was rare. A residue analysis pilot study conducted by O'Gorman (2016) that tested two plates found that both plates possessed lipids corresponding to a mix of herbivore (such as deer or elk) and low-to-medium fat content plants (such as greens, roots, berries, and corn). These results indicate that plates, when they were used for food processing, may have been used to process common food ingredients instead of specialty or ceremonial goods. That being stated, these ingredients could have taken on greater significance through plates, as the act of cooking, warming, or serving food in these vessels may have imbued common ingredients with special meaning.

When divided by decorative style, some statistically significant differences in the use of plates became evident. Within the plate sample, 31 plates could be categorized as Mississippian style, while 11 were categorized as Oneota style. Among the Mississippian-style plates, 80.6% were used for noncooking functions while 19.4% were used over a fire, with most of these possessing anomalous carbonization patterns. This observed rate is similar to how Painter (2021) found plates were used at Larson, a temporally earlier Mississippian mound center just to the south of Morton Village. For the 11 Oneota-style plates analyzed, only 45.5% were used for noncooking purposes, while 36.4% were used for wet-mode cooking. When compared statistically using a Fisher's Exact test, the differences between these rates were found to be statistically significant, with a resulting p-value of 0.04909. In general, it appears that at Morton Village, Mississippian-style plates were used primarily for noncooking purposes, while Oneota-style plates were more flexible and could be used equally for cooking and noncooking tasks.

Morphological analyses indicate that plate shape may also correlate with plate function in interesting ways. At Morton Village, a wide variety of plate rim angles were present (n = 24), ranging from 15 to 75 degrees. When compared to vessel function, 73% of plates with flatter profiles (those that have rim angles of 40 degrees or less) were used for noncooking purposes, similar to the functional rates of the overall assemblage. Only 54% of plates with more bowl-like profiles (rim angles of 40 degrees or more) were used for noncooking purposes, while 46% were used over a fire. These data indicate that flatter plates were more commonly used as serving vessels, while more bowl-like plates were used in a flexible fashion. This morphological difference suggests that some plates may have been designed with flexibility in mind, as a more bowl-like shape would aid in cooking while still providing easy access to the contents of the vessel and ensuring the visibility of the symbols and motifs decorating the rim. When compared between the two stylistic subgroups, both possess the same trend in plate rim angle and function, although the sample sizes are small. Additionally, comparisons of other morphological measurements between the two stylistic groups found no clear statistical differences in plate shape, although the small sample size for Oneota plates may limit the potential of these comparisons.

Beyond use-wear, differences in surface treatment were also present between the two stylistic groups, further providing insight into the choices made by potters and cooks. Among the Mississippian-style vessels, 35.5% were smudged and burnished, leaving a black carbon coating on the surface that would have burned away if the vessel was put over a fire. A small number of other Mississippian-style plates were just burnished, while about half were only smoothed. Only one Oneota-style vessel was smudged, while the rest were smoothed. Given that smudging is a surface treatment that will not survive cooking over a fire, these numbers suggest that many Mississippian-style plates were produced exclusively as serving vessels, while the potters who made Oneota-style plates at Morton Village may have designed them with a more flexible, multipurpose function in mind. Additionally, or alternatively, the groups may have been engaging with different traditions of color symbolism that affected the production and use of plates at the site.

Spatial analyses indicate that plates were used in a variety of contexts at the site, with most being found in general refuse contexts. In total, 87 plates from Morton Village possessed enough provenience information to be included in the spatial analysis, divided into 52 Mississippian-style, 23 Oneota-style, and 12 indeterminate plates. These plates were distributed relatively evenly throughout the three spatial zones, with 27.6% found inside a structure, 36.8% found within four meters of the edge of a structure, 29.9% found farther than four meters from the edge of a structure, and 5.7% found in ambiguous contexts at the edge of a structure. Similar outcomes were found when plates were divided by decorative style, with both Oneota-style and Mississippian-style plates found spread across the three spatial zones. This similar distribution was confirmed by a Chi-square test, which returned a result that is not statistically significant $(X^2[2, N = 75] = 0.63, p = 0.7312)$.

Distributions were also similar between the stylistic groups when function was considered. Within the sample of 42 Mississippian- or Oneota-style plates that had functional data, about 50% of the plates used for serving were found within a structure, while 50% were found outside of one. For those that were used for cooking or food processing, 66.7% of Oneota-style plates and 75% of Mississippian-style plates were found outside of a structure, while a minority were found in interior contexts.

Interrogating the spatial data more closely, it appears that small fragments of plates show up across the site in midden or domestic refuse deposits but also in ritual or ceremonial contexts. Each of the four ritual contexts at Morton Village that have been sufficiently excavated have at least one plate present in association with it. Structure 34, a partially excavated large (approximately 100 m^2) circular enclosure with a center post similar to other Mississippian structures in the CIRV and American Bottom (Conrad 1991; O'Gorman and Conner 2023; Wilson and Melton 2019), has two small plate fragments recovered from wall trenches. No plates were found within Structure 16, a unique and completely excavated single-post construction interpreted as an integrative ritual facility (O'Gorman and Conner 2023), but a sizable rim section from a large plate (diameter of 37 cm) was recovered from F175, a pit feature immediately outside of Structure 16. Structure 20, a fully excavated sweat lodge, contained almost half a plate used for serving or some other noncooking function. Residue analysis of this plate indicated that it was likely used to serve a stew made of deer or elk and greens or berries and probably corn (O'Gorman 2016). F224, a unique pit feature located in the corner of Structure 25, contained fragments of four plates, one of which was half the vessel. It also held an astonishing amount of animal remains and remarkable artifacts within clearly demarcated zones and has been interpreted as the remains of a multiphased feasting event (O'Gorman and Conner 2023, and see chapters 5 and 6 this volume). While the three small plate fragments may have ended up in the pit as incidental inclusions, the larger segment was clearly part of the feasting deposit, and use-wear indicates that it was used for cooking in multiple ways. Jars from this feasting deposit were not used in this multifunctional way but reveal that dry, wet, and stewing methods were also used. The other fragment for which use-wear could be determined indicated its use as a serving plate. Another matter of interest with the plate used for cooking is that it does not follow the typical style/manufacturing distinctions. Rather, it was decorated with incising while the clay was still soft, perhaps indicating some experimentation with production. These contexts, together with plate use-wear data, indicate that, indeed, sometimes plates were used for serving in highly visible "public" contexts but also in much smaller, intimate ceremonial settings.

While there appears to be some direct evidence of the use of plates in ceremonial or ritual contexts, we also wanted to examine whether or not they were used alongside jars, bowls, and water bottles during the preparation, storage, or consumption of foods within domestic structures. A closer look at plates associated with structures indicates that most were found in basin fill, while others were recovered in architectural contexts, such as wall trenches or post molds, within internal pit features, or in excavation levels that were at the intersection of basin fill and floor. No plates have been found on the floor of the numerous structures tested in recent excavations, although work in the 1980s recovered a single small fragment from the floors of two structures. Within the one wall trench structure that we excavated in full, numerous jars (including Mississippian and Oneota styles) and one bowl were found, but there were no plates present on the floor. However, twelve small fragments of plates were found in the basin fill. As is clear from sheer numbers (660 recorded jars versus 90 plates), plates were made and used in smaller numbers. And, as noted, very few structures at Morton Village have been excavated in their entirety. Curation of these vessels over time by residents of Morton Village may have also contributed to their lower numbers and infrequent deposition.

DISCUSSION AND CONCLUSION

Despite some lingering questions, it is clear that plates were an important accoutrement in Morton Village cuisine. While our analysis generally confirms the common interpretation that plates were typically serving vessels, it also demonstrates that plate function was more complex and closely tied to ongoing coalescence and social transformation at the site. Some plates at Morton Village were used over a fire, presumably for cooking, while some differences in plate function between Mississippian-style and Oneota-style plates were apparent.

In general, functional analysis shows that Mississippians appear to have continued using the familiar plate form decorated in Mississippian fashion—mostly serving and occasionally over a fire. Oneota potters and cooks adopted the form. Decorating their plates in traditional designs, Oneota may have used plates in traditional Mississippian practices and settings but also expanded the ways in which the plates were used in cooking and serving to fit their own cuisine. Prior analyses show that Oneota jars and bowls at the site were used as flexible tools that served multiple functions, including different types of cooking and storage (Painter 2021). Likewise, Oneota-style plates were also used for multiple purposes. Analyses of plate morphology and surface treatment suggest that Oneota-style plates may have been designed with this multipurpose function in mind, as potters chose not to smudge their vessels and to make some plates that had more bowl-like shapes.

Our spatial analysis indicates that both Oneota and Mississippians were using plates in similar and varied settings, including communal or ceremonial contexts and domestic spaces, and that they were used for both serving and cooking in these contexts. While many plate fragments were found in general midden or domestic refuse deposits, they were also found within each of the special-use contexts excavated at the site. As such, it appears that plates were important for special activities or communal action, but their presence in domestic refuse and other contexts also suggests that plates, their symbolism, and perhaps the food dishes they held, were also important in private meals or rituals. No plates were found directly in contact with a structure floor though, so more work is needed to understand their role in domestic spaces or why they are commonly disposed of in domestic refuse.

Based on the available data, it appears that Oneota potters and cooks adopted the plate vessel form to take part in interhousehold events and activities with their new neighbors. Partaking in these events and the performative use of plates may have helped Oneota migrants to build ties with their Mississippian neighbors and develop shared practices and a shared cuisine, aiding the coalescence process and the creation of a new community identity. While migrants adopted a Mississippian vessel form and worked toward a new community identity, they also continued to decorate plates with traditional Oneota designs and symbolism and expanded the way they were used, signaling the maintenance of some of their own traditions and unique identity within Morton Village life. In the postmigration world of social negotiation, not only *what* was eaten, but the culinary performances involved in *how* it was eaten, could help to bring people of different backgrounds together, while also keeping some traditional aspects of past identities alive.

As it is generally argued that women were the primary potters and cooks within Native American communities in the Eastern Woodlands (Briggs 2015; Skibo and Schiffer 1995; Swanton 1946), the use of plates may also provide a glimpse into the intersection of gender and social transformation within postmigration settings. At Morton Village, changes to cuisine and culinary instruments are but one of a suite of avenues that may have played a role in ongoing hybridity and coalescence. Shifts in mortuary practices and the construction of integrative facilities are also apparent and aided the coalescence process (Bengtson and O'Gorman 2016; O'Gorman and Conner 2023), while other changes may have occurred that are not as archaeologically visible. At this time of negotiation and dynamic community relationships, many individuals and groups within the community may have been seeking their own way to influence, gain power through, or stop the process of coalescence. Cuisine and pottery, common and very visible aspects of life that was under the control of women within the community, may have been avenues through which women were able to exercise power and influence over social negotiations. Plates specifically appear to have been a symbolically charged and important aspect of interhousehold activities through which Mississippian and Oneota women could have promoted community cohesion while also claiming space for their own unique identities within Morton Village. In this way, cuisine provides a glimpse into the coalescence process and can be used in tandem with other lines of evidence to explore the actions of different actors within these communities.

This analysis, focused on the use and spatial context of one ceramic ware in the culinary repertoire at Morton Village, provides new insights on cuisine hybridization practices in postmigration settings. The methods employed can easily be used at other sites to more closely interrogate the use of this ware type in other settings to gauge culinary patterns across space and time in the CIRV and elsewhere. As for lingering questions, a better understanding of what foodstuffs were served on these plates and the variability of those foods for different occasions and in different social settings would certainly enhance our ability to examine this aspect of cuisine. Further use of lipid analysis coupled with microbotanical identifications, such as starches and phytoliths (see Kooiman and Albert, chapter 2), are promising. Of particular interest in this regard are any potential differences in those items that are served without heating on the plate versus those that are cooked or warmed within, and the contexts that may associate with possible distinctions. Finally, we plan to expand our own analysis to include bowl forms, which are more ubiquitous at sites, in the hope that their patterns of use in serving and cooking may reveal other ways cuisine is involved in the negotiation of identity and community.

Chapter 5

Ceremonial Feasting and Culinary Practices in the Central Illinois River Valley

A Zooarchaeological Perspective

TERRANCE J. MARTIN

Excavations at the Morton Village site (11F2), a fourteenth-century coalescent society in the central Illinois River Valley (CIRV), revealed part of a structure that contained multiple internal pit features representing activities of local Mississippian and Oneota residents. Feature 224 was unique among these pits in having a high density of domestic refuse that included thousands of faunal remains representing dozens of animal species. Although important for revealing food choice, culinary practices, and possible environmental constraints, this pit feature must be understood in its special social context. When cuisine is envisioned as food selection and preparation within a specific cultural context, the contents of Feature 224 can also be perceived as expressions of religious, economic, and political life that together played a significant role in group interactions (Graff 2020:339, 341). Instead of food consumption by a single household group, the large faunal assemblage appears to mark the culmination of a specific ritually related community event. Comparison to special deposits at other sites in the Midcontinent illustrates how ceremonial contexts can contribute to a better understanding of past cuisines on a regional scale.

The discovery in 2012 of six refuse pits within a burned wall trench structure at the Morton Village site was especially exciting in that the pit designated Feature 224 contained thousands of well-preserved animal remains along with pieces of Mississippian and Oneota pottery representing at least 29 vessels. This deposit by itself promised to improve our understanding of animal use by the Bold Counselor phase population that resided at a minimum of five sites in the

CIRV during the early fourteenth century (Esarey and Conrad 1998; Esarey and Santure 1990). These communities were especially significant in that they were inhabited by local Mississippian residents and recent Oneota migrants.

In addition to providing insights on former natural habitats, the zooarchaeological data from across Morton Village can reveal how diet and cuisine were similar to or different from those in contemporary Mississippian sites in the CIRV, and whether diet at Morton Village was similar to or different from our idea of Oneota diet in other regions of the Midwest. As Jodie O'Gorman (2016:1) explained, "A foodways perspective uses multiple lines of evidence in order to contribute to a more comprehensive interpretation of the social interplay Oneota and Mississippian peoples engaged in, surrounding their use of food . . . [including] social negotiations of peacemaking and warfare." The role of cuisine is important at Morton Village as a way of expressing a new coalescent identity in the CIRV as viewed through the more limited focus on food selection and consumption in the special social context of Feature 224.

FEATURE 224 AT THE MORTON VILLAGE SITE

Feature 224 was located in the southwestern portion of Structure 25 and was about 125 cm in diameter and 65 cm deep (Figure 5.1). Excavations revealed four distinct zones of fill within Feature 224. Two accelerator mass spectrometry (AMS) radiocarbon dates from Zones 3 and 4 indicate that the refuse pit was filled during the mid-1300s AD. Analysis of ceramic vessel rims found throughout the pit fill indicate the presence of at least 29 vessels. Oneota-style pottery sherds were confined to the top two zones and include one large vessel that was found at the very top of the pit (O'Gorman and Conner 2023). Although most of the items from the pit are characteristic of domestic refuse, special artifacts include a 3.3-kg slab of iron ore (hematite and limonite) in Zone 4, and Zone 3 was the source of a celt, deer-ulna awl, small carved deer antler tip, modified turtle plastron, and a tool made from an incised antler with an imbedded beaver incisor (Figure 5.2). The pit also contained more than 16,000 animal remains consisting mostly of bone fragments and isolated teeth that were recovered by ¼-inch mesh screen and flotation. Identifications were made by me at the Illinois State Museum's Research and Collections Center using the zoology section's osteology reference collection. Standard zooarchaeology methods follow those described by Martin and Parker (2017:305–7; also see McConaughy 1993:12–13 and Reitz and Wing 2008) including estimates of minimum numbers of individuals (MNI) and biomass derived from allometric scaling (Reitz et al. 1987) calculated for each zone. A minimum of 350

Figure 5.1. Plan of Structure 25 and Feature 224 profile. (Reproduced from Jodie A. O'Gorman and Michael D. Conner, Making Community: Implications of Hybridity and Coalescence at Morton Village. *American Antiquity* 88[1]:79–98, 2023; Figure 1.)

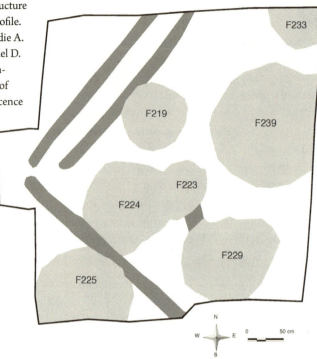
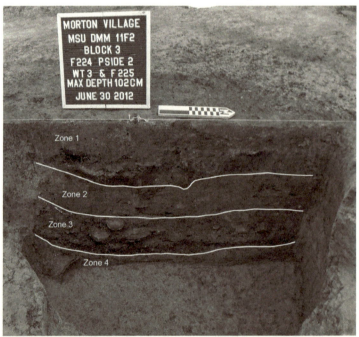

individuals are represented in all four zones of Feature 224, but Zone 3 furnished 77% of the feature's faunal assemblage by number of specimens (NSP) (Table 5.1). Except for Zone 1, less than 3% of the animal remains in Feature 224, by specimen count or by specimen weight, were altered by fire. No interzone cross-mends of animal bones were found, but cross-matched portions of five ceramic vessels support contemporaneity of the upper and lower deposits (O'Gorman and Conner 2023). Despite extensive flotation sampling, plant remains were surprisingly sparse throughout the pit (see Nordine, chapter 6).

Table 5.1. Zooarchaeological Samples from Feature 224 by Zone

	Macrorecovery		Flotation			Biomass
	NSP[a]	NSP Wt (g)	NSP	NSP Wt (g)	MNI[b]	(kg)
Zone 1	221	104.6	357	26.9	33	2.340
Zone 2	1,871	1,055.6	1,083	92.3	94	15.954
Zone 3	6,506	4,043.6	5,867	708.1	206	56.872
Zone 4	142	40.1	-	-	17	.857
Profile	16	4.0	-	-	-	.106
Totals	8,756	5,247.9	7,307	827.3	350	76.129
Zone 1	Burned: 38	25.3	37	11.8		
	Calcined: 7	2.0	4	0.3		
	Total heat-altered: 45	27.3	41	12.1		
	% Heat-altered: 20.4	26.1	11.5	45.0		
Zone 2	Burned: 18	24.2	1	0.1		
	Calcined: 8	3.0	3	0.6		
	Total heat-altered: 26	27.2	4	0.7		
	% Heat-altered: 1.4	2.6	0.4	0.8		
Zone 3	Burned: 12	15.2	19	9.5		
	Calcined: 8	1.8	16	0.4		
	Total heat-altered: 20	17.0	33	9.9		
	% Heat-altered: 0.3	0.4	0.6	1.4		
Zone 4	Burned/calcined: 0	0.0	0	0.0		
Profile	Burned/calcined: 0	0.0	0	0.0		
Totals	Burned: 68	64.7	55	21.4		
	Calcined: 23	6.8	23	1.3		
	Total heat-altered: 91	71.5	78	22.7		
	% Heat-altered: 0.1	1.4	1.1	2.7		

[a]NSP = number of specimens.
[b]MNI = minimum number of individuals.

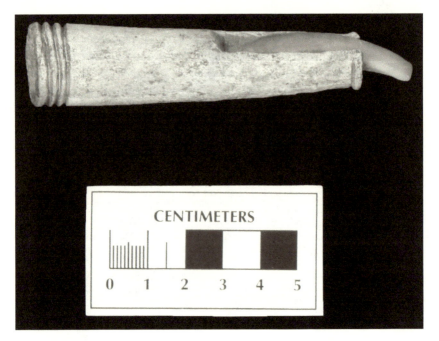

Figure 5.2. Deer antler tool with embedded beaver incisor found in Feature 224, Zone 3. (Photograph by Michael D. Conner. Courtesy of the Illinois State Museum.)

There are more than 4,800 specimens that could be identified below class (i.e., number of identified specimens [NISP]), and these represent at least forty animal taxa (Table 5.2). White-tailed deer are most abundant among mammal remains with a minimum of 13 individuals. Three bones from deer fawns (all in Zone 3) indicate late summer kills. In terms of estimated biomass, deer provided the greatest quantity (nearly 50%) with secondary sources coming from wapiti (represented by at least three individuals) and beavers. Despite multiple avian species, birds seem to be underrepresented as items of cuisine in Feature 224. There are a minimum of ten individual ducks, but only one Canada goose and no swans or cranes. In addition to great blue heron and American coot, the most plentiful avian species is double-crested cormorant with at least five individuals represented by bones in Zones 1, 3, and 4. Wild turkeys are the most numerous terrestrial bird (at least three individuals). Three bald eagle bones were found, probably representing two individuals, consisting of a cranial bone (quadrate) in Zone 1 and a humerus and rib in Zone 3. All of the turtles are aquatic species; no terrestrial box turtles (*Terrapene* spp.) were encountered. Many small fragments of carapace and plastron could not

Table 5.2. Species Composition of Animal Remains from Feature 224, for All Zones

	Macrorecovery		Flotation			
	NISP[a]	NISP Wt (g)	NISP	NISP Wt (g)	MNI[b]	Biomass (kg)[c]
CLASS: MAMMALIA						
Eastern Mole, *Scalopus aquaticus*	4	.4	1	.2	2	-
Eastern Cottontail, *Sylvilagus floridanus*	6	3.2	5	1.8	1	.112
Franklin's Ground Squirrel, *Poliocitellus franklinii*	1	.2	-	-	1	.006
Eastern Gray Squirrel, *Sciurus carolinensis*	1	.4	1	.2	2	.018
Eastern Fox Squirrel, *Sciurus niger*	3	1.5	-	-	1	.038
Tree Squirrel, *Sciurus* sp.	2	1.2	-	-	1	.031
Beaver, *Castor canadensis*	110	328.7	20	22.2	5	5.449
Muskrat, *Ondatra zibethicus*	13	11.1	1	.8	3	.261
Raccoon, *Procyon lotor*	27	60.2	3	2.4	4	1.174
Wapiti, *Cervus elaphus canadensis*	37	456.3	8	13.6	5	6.904
White-tailed Deer, *Odocoileus virginianus*	329	2,026.7	40	110.4	13	27.317
Wapiti/deer, Family Cervidae	1	.4	-	-	-	.012
Subtotals, Identified Mammals	534	2,890.3	79	151.6	38	41.322
Unidentified large mammal	447	554.2	130	107.5	-	9.920
Unidentified medium-sized/large mammal	564	185.2	190	53.7	-	3.964
Unidentified medium-sized mammal	68	31.8	11	4.1	-	.702
Unidentified small/medium-sized mammal	2	.4	-	-	-	.012
Unidentified small mammal	3	.2	1	.1	1	.009
Subtotals, Unidentified Mammals	1,084	771.8	332	165.4	-	14.607
CLASS: AVES						
Double-crested Cormorant, *Phalacrocorax auritus*	26	45.3	2	2.7	5	.719
Great Blue Heron, *Ardea herodias*	1	2.5	-	-	1	.047
Canada Goose, *Branta canadensis*	1	2.1	-	-	1	.040
Large duck spp., Subfamily Anatinae	15	10.5	4	2.2	4	.221
Medium-sized duck spp., Subfamily Anatinae	12	4.8	4	<.1	4	.091

	Macrorecovery		Flotation			
	NISP[a]	NISP Wt (g)	NISP	NISP Wt (g)	MNI[b]	Biomass (kg)[c]
Small duck spp., Subfamily Anatinae	4	1.3	2	.2	2	.031
Bald Eagle, *Haliaeetus leucocephalus*	2	2.0	1	.1	2	.041
Wild Turkey, *Meleagris gallopavo*	25	56.0	3	.6	3	.854
American Coot, *Fulica americana*	3	.9	-	-	1	.019
Subtotals, Identified Birds	**89**	**125.4**	**16**	**5.8**	**23**	**2.063**
Unidentified large bird	57	26.8	5	1.2	-	.451
Unidentified medium-sized/large bird	47	14.3	2	.4	-	.243
Unidentified medium-sized bird	8	1.4	20	4.1	-	.100
Unidentified small/medium-sized bird	2	.2	-	-	-	.005
Subtotals, Unidentified Birds	**114**	**42.7**	**27**	**5.7**	**-**	**.799**
CLASS: REPTILIA						
Snapping Turtle, *Chelydra serpentina*	22	75.4	8	5.4	5	.780
Spiny Softshell Turtle, *Apalone spinifera*	1	4.9	-	-	1	.092
Painted Turtle, *Chrysemys picta*	18	28.8	4	5.9	3	.355
Common Slider, *Trachemys scripta*	19	54.7	5	11.9	4	.719
cf. Common Slider, *Trachemys scripta*	-	-	4	.3	1	.014
Common Map Turtle, *Graptemys geographica*	1	.7	-	-	1	.025
Slider/Map Turtle, *Trachemys/ Graptemys*	-	-	1	.3	1	.014
Pond Turtles, Family Emydidae	46	16.2	5	1.7	2	.301
Unidentified Turtle	9	5.3	1	.2	-	.128
Subtotals, Identified Reptiles	**116**	**186.0**	**28**	**25.7**	**18**	**2.428**
CLASS: AMPHIBIA						
Frog sp., *Lithobates* sp.	2	.1	-	-	1	-
CLASS: OSTEICHTHYES						
Gar sp., *Lepisosteus* sp.	67	16.2	92	3.9	16	.400
Bowfin, *Amia calva*	1,935	496.4	741	137.0	85	5.753

	Macrorecovery		Flotation			
	NISP[a]	NISP Wt (g)	NISP	NISP Wt (g)	MNI[b]	Biomass (kg)[c]
Pike/Pickerel, *Esox* spp.	161	52.8	53	13.4	18	.955
Stoneroller sp., *Campostoma* sp.	1	<.1	-	-	1	-
Smallmouth/Black Buffalo, *Ictiobus bubalus/niger*	17	8.4	1	.3	[7]	.180
Buffalo sp., *Ictiobus* sp.	30	10.8	36	8.5	22	.349
Carpsucker sp., *Carpoides* sp.	3	.6	-	-	1	.020
Buffalo/Carpsucker, *Ictiobus/ Carpoides*	2	.7	1	.1	-	.025
Sucker spp., Family Catostomidae	4	1.6	16	.7	1	.067
Black Bullhead, *Ameiurus melas*	9	1.1	3	.3	5	.028
Yellow Bullhead, *Ameiurus natalis*	10	1.5	10	1.6	4	.058
Brown Bullhead, *Ameiurus nebulosus*	44	7.7	31	2.5	15	.188
Black/Brown Bullhead, *Ameiurus melas/nebulosus*	-	-	1	<.1	1	-
Bullhead spp., *Ameiurus* spp.	58	5.7	55	1.3	15 [22]	.131
Channel Catfish, *Ictalurus punctatus*	29	21.4	10	4.3	15	.457
Blue/Channel Catfish, *Ictalurus* sp.	2	5.6	-	-	1	.105
Flathead Catfish, *Pylodictis olivaris*	1	1.4	-	-	1	.027
Bullhead/Catfishes, Family Ictaluridae	8	1.4	17	1.8	-	.060
Black Bass, *Micropterus* spp.	151	47.1	39	8.6	21	.861
cf. Green Sunfish, *Lepomis* cf. *cyanellus*			3	.2	3	.007
Bluegill, *Lepomis macrochirus*	19	.8	-	-	9	.025
Sunfish spp., *Lepomis* spp.	48	4.1	88	4.2	20 [24]	.166
Rock Bass, *Ambloplites rupestris*	3	.5	2	<.1	4	.017
Black Crappie, *Pomoxis nigromaculatus*	-	-	1	<.1	1	-
Crappie spp., *Pomoxis* spp.	10	2.1	6	.4	3	.063
Sunfish spp., Family Centrarchidae	78	4.4	71	2.3	1 [31]	.147
Walleye/Sauger, *Sander* sp.	-	-	2	<.1	2	-
Freshwater Drum, *Aplodinotus grunniens*	6	3.1	3	<.1	5	.101
Subtotals, Identified Fish	2,696	695.4	1,282	191.4	270	10.190

	Macrorecovery		Flotation			
	NISP[a]	NISP Wt (g)	NISP	NISP Wt (g)	MNI[b]	Biomass (kg)[c]
Unidentified Fish	2,751	313.9	2,809	139.2	-	4.720
UNIDENTIFIED VERTEBRATA	1,297	123.2	2,730	142.3	-	-
CLASS: BIVALVIA						
Spike, *Elliptio dilatata*	2	25.3	-	-	1	-
Hickorynut, *Obovaria olivaria*	1	5.0	-	-	1	-
Subtotals, Identified Mussels	3	30.3	-	-	2	-
Unidentified Mussels	70	68.8	4	.2	3	-
Grand Totals	8,756	5,247.9	7,307	827.3	356	76.129
Totals, Identified below class	3,440	3,927.5	1,405	374.5	352	56.003
Percentage identified below class	39.3	74.8	19.2	45.3		73.6

[a]NIP = number of identified specimens.
[b]MNI = minimum number of individuals, maximum distinction approach (i.e., sum of MNI calculated separately for each zone). Numbers in brackets are the MNI for that particular species or taxon but are not used in calculating the total MNI for the animal class.
[c]Biomass calculated for vertebrae taxa within each zone using allometry formulae presented by Reitz and Wing (2008:68) and then totaled for entire feature.

be identified more precisely than the pond turtle family (Emydidae). Somewhat of a surprise given the abundance of aquatic turtles, musk turtles (i.e., stinkpots [*Sternotherus odoratus*]) are absent altogether.

Fishes contributed 82% of the identified specimens from macrorecovery and flotation and include more than 18 taxa with 76% of all identified fish specimens coming from Zone 3. Bowfins dominate all fishes with a minimum of 85 individuals and is the most abundant fish species in each zone, ranging from 55% of the NISP in Zone 1 to 70% in Zone 3. The family Centrarchidae consists of black bass (most probably being largemouth bass) and various sunfishes such as rock bass, crappies, and bluegills. Catfishes (family Ictaluridae) include all three bullhead species as well as channel catfish and flathead catfish. Suckers (family Catostomidae) consist mostly of buffalo fish, but there are also several carpsuckers. Most of the gars are probably shortnose gar, and 67% of all gar specimens are ganoid scales (more than 100). Although gar appear most plentiful in Zone 1, 76% of the specimens in that zone are scales. Other fish include freshwater drums, walleyes or saugers, and a small stoneroller from the minnow family (Cyprinidae).

ANIMAL COMPONENTS OF CUISINE IN THE CIRV

Beyond a previous analysis of animal remains that were recovered from 20 features at Morton Village (Styles and King 1990), Autumn Painter (2022) analyzed faunal samples from more than 60 refuse deposits across Morton Village to determine what impact immigrant Oneota families had on hunting and fishing patterns by resident Mississippians. Kelsey Nordine's study of plant use at Morton Village (see chapter 6) also focuses on trying to determine subtle differences in cuisine by Mississippian and Oneota groups that inhabited the CIRV. To provide a broader perspective on the faunal collection from Feature 224 and how it contributes to our understanding of a Bold Counselor phase cuisine, I take a comparative approach to assess what is known from other relevant sites in the CIRV. I then focus on Feature 224, the animal species present, seasonality of procurement, and details of skeletal portions and butchering patterns. The occasion of a family or community feast would have been influenced by the social meaning of particular animals, their accessibility, and seasonal availability, as well as how specific animals are transported, disarticulated, certain portions shared or distributed (in the case of large animals), and prepared for consumption at a special event. Then, was the refuse routinely discarded or were prescribed rituals followed? Unfortunately, most behavioral aspects of food procurement, preparation, and consumption during special occasions may not easily be perceived when viewing only animal remains in refuse deposits. If we knew who prepared the various foodstuffs that are represented in Feature 224, we might better understand how particular Bold Counselor individuals operated within their households as well as within the greater community (Graff 2020:341). People of different cultural traditions who come to inhabit the same area will have access to the same natural resources, but how each group incorporates these various items into a CIRV version of Oneota or Mississippian cuisine is of special interest. And the ways that special occasions, rituals, or ceremonies prescribe how these animals and plants are to be consumed add additional challenges.

Analysis of faunal collections from the Lamb site, located just downstream in Schuyler County, provides a snapshot of Early Eveland phase Mississippian animal procurement for a hamlet that was occupied year-round (Bardolf and VanDerwarker 2015:227) during the early twelfth century where "residents practiced a broad-based faunal exploitation strategy in which fish and white-tailed deer were the primary prey" (Bardolph and Wilson 2015:144; Kuehn and VanDerwarker 2015), and maize was the major crop and dietary staple (Bardolph and VanDerwarker 2015:229). Thus, the Lamb site represents a baseline from which local Late Woodland and Early Mississippian communal subsistence practices can be compared with those of Morton Village to find differences from fourteenth-century Bold Counselor phase foodways and cuisine as well as the possible impact of increased regional hostilities (VanDerwarker and Wilson 2016). Of primary interest for the CIRV, does the faunal assemblage from Feature 224 provide an example of everyday coalescent foodways and cuisine, or does it signify a special late summer ceremonial event? Occurring within Structure 25, the Feature 224 faunal collection would seem to represent food consumed by a single household, but due to the immense amount of short-term refuse, the deposit more likely indicates some kind of a special event. The disposal of this much refuse in a single pit inside of a structure seems remarkable and may indicate that Structure 25 was a special-use building, a discrete location for staging a special event (Graff 2020:344). Our focus now shifts to attempting to determine whether Feature 224 was the result of everyday domestic consumption of foodstuffs or whether it was the scene of ritual feasting during a larger community event.

Species composition tables by Painter (2022) for the multiple Morton Village contexts show totals of 3,642 identified vertebrate specimens making up a minimum of 518 individual mammals, birds, reptiles, and fishes, which greatly enhances, but is generally consistent with, the initial study by Styles that resulted in 263 identified specimens representing at least 43 individuals and 19 taxa (Styles and King 1990:58). The faunal assemblage from the Lamb site consists of 1,218 identified vertebrate specimens from at least 158 individuals (Kuehn and VanDerwarker 2015:239–40). Both Lamb and Morton Village are located near bluff edge settings above broad floodplains on the west side of the Illinois River. The bottomlands consist of "many relict marshes, sloughs, and meander scar lakes. Historically, the flood plain near the Morton site was a maze of large lakes and meandering channels" (King 1990:4).

A significant difference among the three faunal collections is the relative scarcity of freshwater mussels at Morton Village. Only three mussel shells from two species were identified from among the mostly small shell fragments in Feature 224 (0.5% of specimens from all animal remains; i.e., number of specimens). Whereas 30 identified shells from eleven species were recovered from the general Morton Village features, this is still a small proportion of all faunal remains (0.2% of all specimens) (Painter 2022). In contrast, 18 species of mussels are represented among the 174 identified shells from the Lamb site, where mussel shells make up 10.5% of all specimens. Despite this difference, the prevalence of fish remains (exceeding 54% of the NISP) in all three faunal collections attests to the importance of aquatic resources, especially when also considering the abundance of birds, reptiles, and mammals that were procured from local aquatic habitats (Figure 5.3).

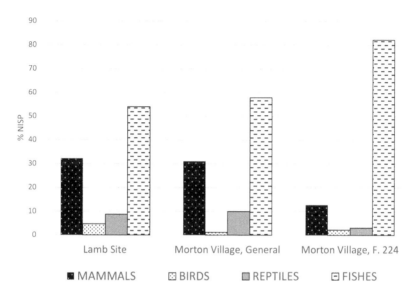

Figure 5.3. Morton Village site and Lamb site vertebrate faunal collections, comparison by class, percentage number of identified specimens (% NISP). (Graph courtesy of Terrance J. Martin. Data also from Painter [2022] and Kuehn and VanDerwarker [2015].)

Waterfowl, especially various ducks, are prevalent among avian remains in all three collections but are especially dominant for the Lamb site (Figure 5.4). Six additional species of aquatic birds were also identified, but most distinctive are double-crested cormorants, which are present only in Feature 224. Before European settlement, cormorants were spring and fall migrants in central Illinois with some pairs probably nesting in colonies in favorable habitats during April and May in the CIRV (Bohlen 1989:9). Bald eagles are also present at Lamb and in Feature 224, and the large raptors most commonly occur along major rivers and lakes where they feed on fish, ducks, geese, small mammals, and carrion (Bohlen 1989:44–45; Tekiela 1999:47). Wild turkey bones are more numerous in the Morton Village's general collection and in Feature 224 and suggest that Bold Counselor hunters also focused on heavily wooded habitats (Bohlen 1989:57).

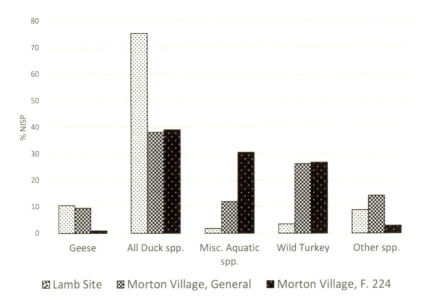

Figure 5.4. Morton Village site and Lamb site avian faunal collections, percentage number of identified specimens (% NISP). (Graph courtesy of Terrance J. Martin. Data also from Painter [2022] and Kuehn and VanDerwarker [2015].)

Unless the residents of Lamb and Morton Village preferred different varieties of fishes, the species identified more likely suggest that fishes were obtained from different kinds of wetland habitats. This was not an exclusive choice by the inhabitants of the respective sites but most likely reflects species availability in wetland habitats closest to the respective site. As noted by Styles (1981:93), "procurement probably focused on a water body rather than a particular species." Whereas bullheads and catfishes are most plentiful at Lamb, followed by northern pikes, Morton Village fishes—in the general assemblage and in Feature 224—are dominated by bowfin (Figure 5.5). When biomass is calculated, suckers (predominantly large buffalos) and catfish dominate the Lamb site in contrast to bowfins at Morton Village (Figure 5.6). Although all of the catfish and bullhead species occur in large rivers, bullheads prefer quiet pools and backwaters having soft substrates (Metzke et al. 2022:225–27). Northern pikes inhabit clear pools of rivers where there is vegetation, and smaller grass pickerels can be found in marshes and backwaters (Metzke et al. 2022:241–42). Bowfins are also common near vegetation in low gradient backwaters (Metzke et al. 2022:69), and their "lung-like air bladder" allows

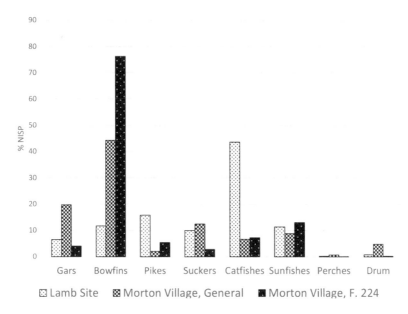

Figure 5.5. Morton Village site and Lamb site identified fishes, percentage number of identified specimens (% NISP). (Graph courtesy of Terrance J. Martin. Data also from Painter [2022], Kuehn and VanDerwarker [2015].)

Figure 5.6. Morton Village site and Lamb site identified fishes, % biomass. (Graph courtesy of Terrance J. Martin. Data also from Painter [2022], Kuehn and VanDerwarker [2015].)

bowfins and gars to be the last fishes to survive in remnant sloughs where the shallow stagnant water is low in oxygen (Pflieger 1975:66; Sutton 2000:161). Although not currently regarded as a food fish because of its strong taste, bowfin can be split dorsally along the vertebrae, sun-dried, and salted. If not prepared soon after capture, the flesh of bowfins will turn soft and mushy. When bowfins are eaten by contemporary consumers, they are usually rendered into "fishballs, jambalaya, and gumbo" (Sutton 2000:165).

Unsurprisingly, white-tailed deer is the prevalent mammal species in all three assemblages, but deer are especially dominant at the Lamb site where they compose 85.8% of the mammal NISP, 43.5% of the mammal MNI, and 93.3% of the biomass from mammals. Otherwise, tree squirrels and cottontails were distant secondary resources. Secondary mammals at Morton Village are wapiti and beavers. Although the large aquatic rodents are more conspicuous in Feature 224 in terms of NISP, wapiti contributed much more to the overall biomass. Morton Village shows a greater diversity in mammal prey overall than the Lamb site, and the general faunal assemblage exclusive of Feature 224 includes the only mustelids (i.e., mink, badger, otter, and striped skunk), bobcat, as well as the largest number of canid remains (probably domestic dogs; seven specimens and at least three individuals). Unknown, of course, is how these various small- and medium-sized mammals contributed to an overall Bold Counselor phase cuisine or whether they were equally important for their hides.

Essential for understanding how white-tailed deer were used by the people who were responsible for various faunal collections, attention was given to tabulating deer specimens by skeletal portion following the format used by Kuehn and VanDerwarker (2015:241). Values for the Morton Village general faunal assemblage were derived from Painter (2022:Figure 6). Faunal assemblages for Lamb, Morton Village at large, and Morton Village Feature 224 consistently show abundant bones from the lower legs instead of the high meat-bearing portions of the upper fore- and hindlimbs (Figure 5.7). This suggests an emphasis in all three collections on extracting marrow from metacarpals and metatarsals, and possibly "bone grease processing" and/or "stewing and soup making" (Morin and Soulier 2017:97). These activities would normally be carried out at base camps or main villages. When deer skeletal portions from Lamb and Morton Village Feature 224 are tabulated as food utility indices, we still see a broadly similar pattern (Figure 5.8). Although less than the total proportion of low-utility deer specimens, the Lamb site exhibits only slightly higher proportions of mid- and high-utility deer portions than found in Feature 224 at Morton Village. The compositions of skeletal portions and food utility indices for wapiti remains from Feature 224 are similar to those for deer.

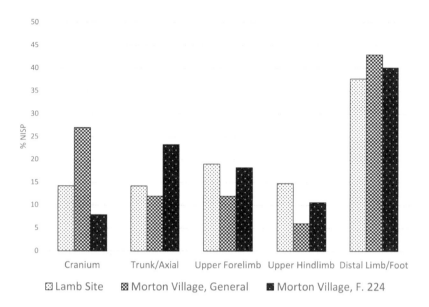

Figure 5.7. Morton Village site and Lamb site deer skeletal portions, percentage number of identified specimens (% NISP). (Graph courtesy of Terrance J. Martin. Data also from Painter [2022], Kuehn and VanDerwarker [2015].)

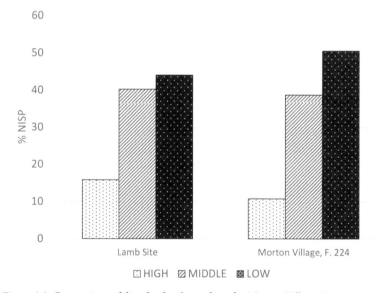

Figure 5.8. Comparison of deer food utility indices for Morton Village Feature 224 and the Lamb site, percentage number of identified specimens (% NISP). (Graph courtesy of Terrance J. Martin. Data also from Kuehn and VanDerwarker [2015].)

VanDerwarker and Wilson (2016:90–93) compared preliminary data from four CIRV sites, including Lamb, for microfaunal remains from flotation samples to portray "a clear decrease in fish and a corresponding increase in mammals throughout the region's occupation" from 1100 through 1300 AD (2016:91). This trend is attributed to a reduction in time devoted to travel from bluff top villages to productive fishing locations in the bottoms as a consequence of increased hostilities and fear of raids after 1200 AD. The later emphasis on mammals may be a result of the necessity for increased garden hunting closer to main habitation sites. Whereas "extremely bellicose conditions" (VanDerwarker and Wilson 2016:97) may have influenced alterations in daily situations and foodways, resulting in changes to traditional cuisines, examination of subsistence remains from various Morton Village contexts has not revealed the predicted pattern that would be consistent with food insecurity due to structural violence (Painter 2022:Chapter 4). Perhaps the inhabitants of Morton Village during the Bold Counselor phase found ways to maintain access to valued local faunal and botanical components of their cuisine while living with conditions of periodic short-term violence.

EVERYDAY OR SPECIAL CUISINE?

Whereas ceramics and refuse reflect food preparation, serving, and consumption in the Bold Counselor phase, the amount and diversity of artifacts and animal remains that were rapidly deposited in Feature 224 indicate an event unlike everyday domestic subsistence practices. However, other than interior location, special artifacts, and the massive quantity of animal remains, most other aspects of Feature 224 do not seem to correspond to a special feasting situation, at least not a "fabulous feast" (Hayden 2001:23) of an extravagant ritual nature. As Wallis and Blessing (2015:5) observed, "Large pit features that are often associated with mounds at Mississippian sites offer more convincing evidence of feasting. These contexts tend to exhibit skewed element proportions among large mammals, low taxonomic diversity, occasional presence of rare taxa, and association with ritual paraphernalia, all within depositional contexts that indicate a high degree of contemporaneity."

Large mammals in Feature 224 consist of white-tailed deer and wapiti. Feasting activities are expected to be indicated by greater proportions of high meat bearing body portions from these large mammals, mainly upper forelimbs and upper hindlimbs (Jackson and Scott 1995:112; Kassabaum 2018:26, 2019:264; Kelly 2001:347; Knight 2004; Pauketat et al. 2002:264; VanDerwarker 1999:31), but this is not the pattern for Feature 224. Proportions of bone fragments from the upper forelimb, upper hindlimb, and axial portions (vertebrae and ribs) in Feature 224 are greater than those from Morton Village's general collections, but that seems to be due to the greater numbers of cranial fragments and isolated teeth in those general collections.

The faunal assemblage is also characterized by a high diversity of animals (at least 41 vertebrate taxa), although dogs that were ritually killed and eaten to mark special occasions elsewhere are absent altogether (Jackson and Scott 1995:106; Wallis and Blessing 2015:9). Kuehn (2023:224) notes that dogs and indeterminate canids were abundant in both Terminal Late Woodland II and Lohmann phase Mississippian assemblages, but most were intentional burials except for two individuals in the later occupation having been sacrificed during ceremonial activities. Remains of black bears, which were believed to possess immense spiritual power (Kassabaum 2018:26; 2019:624–26; Peles and Kassabaum 2020; Wallis and Blessing 2015:9), are also missing from Feature 224.

Feature 224 is the only context at Morton Village that contains the remains of bald eagles and double-crested cormorants. One bald eagle bone was found at the Lamb site, a radius from a wing that had been modified for an unknown function (Kuehn and VanDerwarker 2015:243). Eagles were symbols of authority among Mississippian societies (Fishel 2017; Hall 1991:29–30), and a bald eagle was buried at the Norris Farms 36 Cemetery (Santure and Esarey 1990:93). Native Americans in the Southeast displayed eagle feathers and tails when a group was at war, as well as when that group was seeking peace, and they believed that eagles have special powers, such as curing illnesses or ensuring success in fishing. If an eagle was killed, it must be shown proper respect through rituals (Krech 2009:107–13, 121, 157). Eagle bone whistles and feathers were also used to decorate calumet pipes in the Great Plains and Midwest (Hall 1997:50). The significance of raptor bodies (bald eagles, hawks, and vultures) and interactions between Middle Missouri and Middle Mississippian traditions are illustrated by Feature 8 at the Phipps site in northwestern Iowa where more than 400 lower leg and foot bones from raptors were found in one deposit along with red-slipped sherds and other trading-related items (Fishel 1997). Raptors were also present at sites in the East St. Louis Precinct of the Greater Cahokia complex, especially during the Stirling phase of the Mississippian period when lower leg bones from owls, hawks, and falcons were apparently used as ritual paraphernalia (Kuehn 2023:195).

Double-crested cormorants are noteworthy in that they feed on fishes and other aquatic animals by diving as deep as 25 feet and being capable of staying underwater for as long as 70 seconds (IDNR 2021; Tekiela 1999:19).

Cormorants were present among over fifty other species of birds that were commonly consumed along the Southeastern Coastal Plain by Indigenous populations (Krech 2009:37). Paul Parmalee noted that cormorant remains were found at several precontact Arikara sites in South Dakota, but "they appear to have been of only minor interest or value to those people living along the Missouri River" (1977:200). Parmalee also identified double-crested cormorant (among 64 avian species) from refuse deposits at the Cahokia Mounds. Other than commenting that cormorants (along with American coots and sandhill cranes) were most likely obtained during the birds' spring and fall migrations, Parmalee did not suggest any other special significance (Parmalee 1957:1975). Similarly, only one cormorant bone was identified from Terminal Late Woodland II contexts at the nearby East St. Louis Precinct, and two bones were found in Lohmann phase contexts (Kuehn 2023). Despite large collections of bird remains from early Late Woodland and late Late Woodland/ Mississippian deposits at the Rench site (11P4), only one cormorant bone was identified from the earlier Weaver phase assemblage (Martin and Masulis 1993:284). Did the coalescent Bold Counselor phase people responsible for Feature 224 have a special reverence for cormorants and their ability to transverse from the "Beneath World" to the "Middle World" and to the "Above World" (Reilly 2004)? The rarity of bald eagles and cormorants in faunal assemblages at most other late precontact sites in the region may indicate that neither were part of the normal local cuisine.

In contrast to the Morton Village where no swan bones have been identified, bones from swan were the most abundant avian taxon found in Cahokia's Sub-Mound 51 borrow pit. Four 3-x-3 m units were excavated by cultural strata in 1967 and 1968, and the late eleventh-century Lohmann phase deposits were hypothesized to have been refilled as part of continuous central platform and plaza construction and plaza rituals as part of conspicuous consumption during a large-scale, socially integrative feasting event (Kelly 2001; Pauketat et al. 2002). Kelly noted that no swan wing bones were present and suggested that swans were acquired and processed for their wings and feathers instead of for their meat. Consistent with this pattern, more than sixty swan specimens were recovered from Terminal Late Woodland II through Moorehead phase Mississippian occupations in the East St. Louis Precinct, a dozen of which had been modified into various kinds of tools (Kuehn 2023).

At least 85 individual bowfins may suggest an "easily amassed resource" (Kassabaum 2018) from productive backwater pools and ponds near Morton Village. However, could the abundance of bowfins reflect a "defensive strategy" (VanDerwarker and Wilson 2016:83) that restricted fishing locations to less visible, more secluded marshes and backwater ponds? Feature 224 had shells from only three individual freshwater mussels, whereas freshwater bivalves, from numerous riverine habitats, were more plentiful and diverse when found in refuse deposits elsewhere at Morton Village. Thus, the nature of the social gathering or ritual that resulted in the rapid accumulation of materials in Feature 224 remains unknown, but it is unlike feasting activities that have been reported for Cahokia Mounds or other Mississippian communities to the south.

Megan Kassabaum (2019) proposed a way of classifying "eating events" based on two characteristics, "group size" and "level of sociopolitical competition," resulting in a typology of feasting that allows for occasions in which "feasts in more egalitarian communities likely reinforced group cohesion and equality" (2019:616), similar to "potluck feasts" in Hastorf's typology (2017:198–99). This dual-dimensional model avoids "confusing large, competitive feasting practices with the kinds of practices that differentiate feasts in general from everyday consumption" (Kassabaum 2019:627). Similarly, Logan (2022) proposed that large roasting pits used by Late Woodland hunter-gatherer-gardeners at sites in the lower Missouri River region of northeastern Kansas were part of feasts that were held "to foster a sense of community among scattered families, to forge a social network that promoted reciprocity rather than competitiveness" (2022:39). Thus, the events that resulted in Morton Village's Feature 224 may be perceived as a feasting event in which many everyday resources were amassed by a moderate-sized group of participants and consumed near or within Structure 25 for an occasion of community-building and solidarity through rituals that were carried out for the purpose of "establishing and maintaining relationships between participants" instead of "rituals associated with status negotiation" (Kassabaum 2019:626). The reason for the ritual or ceremony is unknown, as is the nature of the ritual, the number of the participants, and the relationship of the participants. To date, there is no evidence of communal storage facilities at Morton Village, so household storage pits seem to have been part of household-scale production instead of communal storage. Seen in this context, regular or periodic feasts by extended family groups would have been important to maintain mutual obligations and strengthen social and economic bonds (Edwards 2020:204–5).

Another example is the Locus B "ash heap" at the site of Parchman Place (22C0511) in the Yazoo Basin in northwestern Mississippi. This seems to represent a fourteenth-century AD household feasting event that was associated with an annual harvest renewal ceremony. Although the "animals and plants represented are entirely within the realm of mundane foodstuffs," the "high degree of burning and calcination . . . point[s] to practices involving purposeful deposition [that] may have analogues in the offering of 'first fruits'" as part of a maize harvest ceremony (Nelson et al. 2023:169). The late summer seasonality indicators for Morton Village's Feature 224 may also coincide with some form of harvest ceremony, although plant remains—especially maize—were not abundant in the pit fill (see Nordine, chapter 6), and a fire-renewal ceremony is not indicated, since only a very small proportion of the animal remains were burned or calcined (see Table 5.1).

Morton Village's Feature 224 faunal assemblage is consistent with a diverse pattern of terrestrial and aquatic animal procurement that is characteristic of most other refuse deposits at Morton Village (Painter 2022). Even if the result of an egalitarian style of extended family feasting occasion, Feature 224 presents an accurate record of local culinary practices for a Bold Counselor phase community in the CIRV with the addition of some possible ritual elements (double-crested cormorants and bald eagles) that were not part of regular everyday foodways (also see Nordine, chapter 6).

ANALYTICAL CHALLENGES AND CONCLUSIONS

Long-term, multidisciplinary investigations of large and complicated archaeological sites are common, but rarely are results of detailed, specialized studies fully combined as part of a final product. Reitz and colleagues (1996:12–14) point out that although environmental archaeologists must balance the demands of various methodological and procedural concerns, the primary objective should be to integrate the results of these findings to address broader anthropological issues. More recently, various case studies emphasizing cuisines and food archaeology were presented with the objective of finding social meanings and implications of food choices (Hastorf 2017:13), and these face similar challenges in that studies of plant and animal remains, ceramics, and organic residues must be incorporated if comprehensive and meaningful conclusions can be attained.

By focusing on understanding everyday as well as special event parts of the animal components of cuisine, I illuminate the lived experience of some inhabitants of Morton Village during the Bold Counselor phase as an alternative for examining special deposits in isolation. A more complete understanding of Morton Village's Feature 224 awaits a comprehensive synthesis of information from plants, including seasonality indicators (see Nordine, chapter 6), artifact studies, and organic residue analyses of stable isotopes and lipids (e.g., Briggs 2016; Edwards 2020; Eusebio et al. 2022; Hadden et al. 2022; Kooiman 2016,

2021; Kooiman et al. 2022; Painter and O'Gorman:Chapter 4; Yerkes 2005). Despite advances in many residue analyses, other analytical challenges include complications and ambiguous results that can arise due to complex mixtures of substances having different chemical components, impacts of various kinds of human processing in the past, and alterations caused by deposition in soils (Graff 2020:345–46). Also, residue signatures "typically represent an amalgam of foods from past cooking events rather than the most recent cooking episodes" (Kooiman 2021:56, citing results of experiments by Miller et al. 2020), and organic residue analyses are often not fine-grained enough for detailed resolution of the precise roles that animals and plants played in ancient cuisines. Until advances in these various techniques are capable of addressing these issues, zooarchaeology and archaeobotany will still have important roles to play by providing detailed information on the specific animals and plants that were available and procured by past societies. Together, the applications of these approaches will enhance our ability to better understand ancient diet and cuisine in particular settings.

Chapter 6

Exploring Identity through Cuisine and Ritual at the Morton Village Site, West-Central Illinois

KELSEY NORDINE

The Morton Village site (11F2), a multiethnic site in the central Illinois River Valley (CIRV), was home to people identified archaeologically as Bold Counselor Oneota and Mississippian from approximately AD 1300 to 1400. Material remains at Morton Village represent active social negotiations that were required for Oneota and Mississippian people to coexist. In this study, the results of paleoethnobotanical analysis of pit features at Morton Village, including plant remains recovered from a feasting context, are examined through the lens of cuisine to explore how this multiethnic community managed the pressures and opportunities of Oneota and Mississippian interaction following Oneota migration into the CIRV. Special attention is focused specifically on a plant not known for being a food source, but one that was likely a powerful component of this feasting context.

Cuisine is one of the more salient aspects of social and cultural identity, relevant to both the physical and social person (Atalay and Hastorf 2006). Examining plant use from the perspective of cuisine provides important insights into identity and group belonging, which is critical to understanding the social changes occurring at the Morton Village site. As Graff (2020:34) explains, "cuisine and identity are intrinsically linked because categories of belonging are attached to choices about preparing, serving, and consuming food," In other words, the rules of cuisine are learned, inherited, and part of a suite of knowledge that also serves as an expression of social values and norms (Atalay and Hastorf 2006).

CUISINE AND SOCIAL IDENTITY

Food studies in anthropology and archaeology often frame food as one of the most prominent aspects of social identity and as an important mode by which people signal values, beliefs, affiliations, and norms (e.g., Douglas 1966; Graff 2020; Hastorf 2017; Kassabaum 2019; Twiss 2007b). Beliefs and traditions surrounding food can be viewed as "condensed social facts that reflect a group's disposition and values" (Hastorf 2017:223). Both quotidian and special meals, such as feasts, work to create and reflect social beliefs within and among groups, playing active roles in negotiation and maintenance of social identities (Dietler 2001; Dietler and Hayden 2001; Hastorf 2017; Kassabaum 2019; Twiss 2007b, 2008). Food traditions are especially relevant to archaeologists in that they are material representations of group values and identities. The multicultural configuration of Morton Village makes this site an ideal place to understand the role of food and cuisine in the creation and maintenance of new community norms and traditions visible elsewhere in Morton Village through changing burial practices and ceramic traditions (Bengtson and O'Gorman 2016; Lieto and O'Gorman 2014; Painter and O'Gorman 2019). Both daily and special, ritual interactions with food at Morton Village provide important data that speak to the ways in which archaeologists can understand food as a means of negotiating new community traditions and as a reflection of cultural identity. This is particularly important when understood within the context of group migration into a new region, in this case, the Bold Counselor movement into the CIRV.

Discussions of migration often become discussions of coalescence, hybridity, or creolization of culture (e.g., Bengtson and O'Gorman 2017; Clark et al. 2013; Clark et al. 2019; Deagan 2013; Kowalewski 2006; O'Gorman and Conner 2023; and Painter and O'Gorman 2019), making the role of cuisine in contexts of migration or coalescence an important factor in understanding how these processes of movement and change affect the systems and traditions that sustain people. Hybridity is well-defined by Deagan (2013:261) as "creation, through interaction and negotiation, of new transcultural forms," which are created within spaces of multicultural engagement (Deagan 2013). These new forms are integral to processes of coalescence, a series of historically contingent processes and attributes involving the interactions and complex entanglements of distinct groups that result in "transformation or reshaping of social, political, ideological, and economic nature of the larger group, but subgroups retain elements of their respective cultural identities" (O'Gorman and Conner 2023:80). Similarly, creolization is conceptualized here as a set of historical and cultural processes involving the varying, historically specific, and complex ways in which people choose to absorb or intermix various cultural elements in multicultural contexts (see Deagan 1983). Cuisine, while often conservative and slow to change (Egan-Bruhy 2014; Graff 2020) as a local phenomenon is thus very likely to undergo processes of creolization when new groups migrate into a region or community, absorbing some aspects of the local cuisine while also introducing new foods and methods of preparing, cooking, and serving these foods (Dawdy 2010).

ONEOTA AND MORTON VILLAGE BACKGROUND

Oneota is a widespread archaeological manifestation located primarily throughout the Prairie Peninsula of the midwestern United States following the Late Woodland occupation of the same region and into the Contact period (ca. AD 900–1700) (Benn 1989; Brown and Sasso 2001). Oneota settlements are often found in ecotonal regions, near the confluence of upland and floodplain forests, river systems, and prairie ecosystems, often on terraces along major rivers or near lakes and swamps (Gibbon 2012; Schroeder 2004:316). Schroeder (2004) also describes seasonal resettlement of Oneota groups for the purposes of hunting and fishing. This choice in settlement area is reflected in the characterization of Oneota subsistence as "flexibly adapted" to a variety of food preferences and procurement strategies (Parker 1992:485; see also Gallagher and Arzigian 1994; Henning 1970; King 1990). Large, dispersed settlements are common and house size varies within the Oneota tradition (Hollinger 1995).

The Morton Village site (see Figure 4.1, this volume) was occupied contemporaneously by Bold Counselor and Mississippian groups between approximately AD 1300 and AD 1400 (Esarey and Conrad 1998; Painter and O'Gorman 2019; Santure et al. 1990). Painter and O'Gorman (chapter 4, this volume) discuss the background of the Morton Village in more detail, as well as evidence for the multicultural configuration of the site.

Although structures and pit features were designated by the primary investigators as Oneota, Mississippian, or mixed material (containing both Oneota and Mississippian ceramics) based on their ceramic content or construction style, importantly, these divisions based on group affiliation inferred from material culture do not indicate separate systems of lifeways at Morton Village. Understanding the landscape of interaction at Morton Village requires a view of the material culture as both a mode of maintaining some aspects of cultural or ethnic identity while acknowledging that social boundaries at Morton Village during this time were likely shifting as they were being actively negotiated by both groups. From this perspective, the very existence of Bold Counselor Oneota material assemblages must be understood with respect to Mississippian lifeways (Esarey and Conrad 1998). The active negotiation of social boundaries within this community makes Morton Village an ideal landscape for examining cuisine and its role in negotiating social identity among this newly multicultural community.

METHODS

Botanical samples from Morton Village were floated between 2009 and 2014 during field seasons at Morton Village. For this analysis, flotation samples from 25 features with diagnostic pottery sherds were analyzed: 12 Oneota, 4 mixed Oneota/Mississippian, and 9 Mississippian, totaling 59 individual samples and 528 liters of floated soil. Samples were divided into light and heavy fractions during flotation, heavy fractions were passed through 1/16th-inch window screen and stored and sorted separately. Light fractions were caught in fabric cloth and dried. Light and heavy fractions are not physically combined but sorted according to the same protocol. All flotation samples were analyzed in the Paleoethnobotany Laboratory at Washington University in St. Louis. Samples were sorted under a low-power binocular microscope (7–45X). Each light fraction and heavy fraction was size graded before sorting under the microscope by passing it through USDA geological sieves. Samples were sorted completely at the 2.0-mm mesh size and greater, and all charred plant remains were either given a taxonomic determination or classed based on material type (e.g., wood, bark, stem). All recognizable cultigens (e.g., maize components, squash, beans, tobacco, and Eastern Agricultural Complex crops), as well as acorn shell and other seeds, were identified at 1.4 mm and greater, and only seeds were pulled from mesh sizes less than 1.4 mm.

All flotation samples from Mississippian (n = 9 features and 185 liters of floated soil) and Oneota pits (n = 12 and 264 liters of floated soil) and mixed material pits (n = 4 and 89 liters of floated soil) were sorted completely. Recovered macroremains were recorded in the following way: wood was weighed but not counted, all nutshell fragments with the exception of acorn were counted and weighed down to the 2.0-mm sieve size, all cultigens and acorn nutshell were counted and weighed down to the 1.4-mm sieve size, and all seeds from the greater than 2.0-mm screens were counted but not weighed. Seed number estimates (SNE) were calculated as a possible measure of control for fragmentation in seeds. The SNE is approximated by using anatomical parts of seeds (and whole seeds), providing an estimation of the minimum number of seeds present in a sample (Lopinot et al. 2015:215). Identifications of plant matter were made to the lowest possible taxonomic determination based on the comparative reference collection at Washington University in St. Louis.

RESULTS OF PIT FEATURE AND FEASTING CONTEXT BOTANICAL ANALYSIS

Two primary objectives of our study were to examine whether plant use differs between Oneota, Mississippian, and mixed features and to explore the implications of these differences through the lens of cuisine choices, particularly as they relate to maintaining or negotiating social identity within a multicultural community. This section provides results from the analyzed pit features as well as the contents of Feature 224, a likely feasting deposit (see also Martin, chapter 5, this volume), and the subsequent section discusses the plants recovered in terms of cuisine, identity, and community, and the ways in which cuisine may have been used as a powerful mode of negotiating or maintaining group identity at the site.

Contents of Pit Features

Oneota pit features yielded a total of 51.7 grams of wood charcoal, which is approximately 0.20 grams of wood charcoal per liter of floated soil. Raw data from all analyzed features are summarized in Table 6.1.

Nutshell and tropical cultigens were abundant in Oneota pits, while Eastern Agricultural Complex (EAC) crops, discussed subsequently, and fruits made up a much smaller portion of recovered macroremains. Miscellaneous taxa, including seeds from some plants that produce edible leafy greens, disturbance taxa, and tobacco were also recovered. The majority of taxa present in Oneota pits were recovered from two large features, 213 and 214.

Mississippian pits contained a total of 49.95 grams of wood charcoal (0.27 grams/liter of floated soil). Nutshell and tropical cultigens were also common in Mississippian samples, although they appear in differing quantities, densities, and ubiquity from some Oneota and mixed material pits. Most material recovered from Mississippian pits came from three pit features (Features 152, 174, and 209), and Mississippian features yielded similar taxa to those recovered from Oneota pits, with slightly fewer taxa present. Maize was ubiquitous in all Oneota, Mississippian, and mixed material features, and nutshell was ubiquitous in all mixed materials and Mississippian features, with a lower ubiquity value for nutshell recovered from Oneota pits.

Mixed material pits contained 92.92 grams of wood charcoal, or 1.04

Table 6.1. Summary of Macrobotanical Remains from Pit Features

	Oneota External Pits		Mississippian External Pits		Mixed External Pits	
Number of samples	29		19		10	
Number of features	12		9		4	
Total liters of floated soil	264		185		89	
Category/taxon	Raw count	Weight (g)	Raw count	Weight (g)	Raw count	Weight (g)
Wood weight (g)	—	51.7	—	49.95	—	92.92
Nutshell (total)	**548**	**8.35**	**909**	**3.45**	**892**	**3.3**
Thick hickory (*Carya* sp.)	413	6.96	78	1.11	76	1.3
Thin hickory (*Carya* sp.)	8	0.3	6	0.09	0	0
Hazelnut (*Corylus* sp.)	14	0.16	11	0.19	5	0.06
Acorn (*Quercus* spp.)	51	0.31	812	2.03	802	1.84
Juglans cf. *nigra*	0	0	0	0	3	0.05
Juglans cf. *cinerea*	1	0.02	0	0	0	0
Juglandaceae	61	0.6	2	0.03	1	0.02
Tropical cultigen (total)	**1,283**	**9.76**	**472**	**3.38**	**669**	**4.58**
Maize kernel/embryo (*Zea mays*)	1,078	7.85	331	2.3	579	3.76
Maize cupule/glume (*Zea mays*)	194	1.67	140	1.07	85	0.68
Common bean (*Phaseolus vulgaris*)	11	0.24	1	0.01	5	0.14
EAC[a] cultigen (total)	**29**	**—**	**21**	**—**	**38**	**—**
Squash rind (*Cucurbita pepo* ssp. *ovifera*)	1	0.01	19	0.09	6	0.04
Maygrass (*Phalaris caroliniana*)	1	—	0	—	0	0
Little barley (*Hordeum pusillum*)	0	0	1	—	1	—
Chenopodium berlandieri ssp. *jonesianum*	22	—	0	0	21	—
Sunflower pericarp fragments (*Helianthus annuus*)	15	—	0	0	9	—
Sunflower kernel (*Helianthus annuus*)	1	—	0	0	0	0
Sumpweed (*Iva annua*)	0	0	1	—	1	—
Other cultigen (total)	**5**	**—**	**0**	**—**	**0**	**—**

	Oneota External Pits		Mississippian External Pits		Mixed External Pits	
Tobacco (*Nicotiana* sp.)	**5**	—	**0**	0	**0**	0
Fruits (total)	**19**	—	**0**	—	**1**	—
Persimmon (*Diospyros virginiana*)	2	0.01	0	0	0	0
Grape (*Vitis* sp.)	2	—	0	0	1	—
Sumac (*Rhus* sp.)	3	—	0	0	0	0
Prunus sp.	12	0.14	0	0	0	0
Other Seed Taxa (total)	**504**	—	**191**	—	**120**	—
Purslane (*Portulaca oleracea*)	307	—	68	—	47	—
Mollugo sp.	0	0	1	—	0	0
Wild chenopod (*Chenopodium* sp.)	55	—	25	—	6	—
Cheno-am	2	—	4	—	2	—
Spurge (*Euphorbia* sp.)	1	—	0	0	1	—
Verbena (*Verbena* sp.)	4	—	6	—	7	—
Caryophyllaceae Family	1	—	2	—	0	0
Poaceae (grass family)	35	—	19	—	21	—
Cyperaceae (sedge)	6	—	20	—	1	—
Eleusine indica	2	—	0	0	0	0
Amaranth (*Amaranthus* sp.)	11	—	2	—	0	0
Solanum sp.	9	—	1	—	0	0
Rumex sp.	0	0	1	—	0	0
Solanaceae	0	0	3	—	0	0
Solanum ptychanthum	9	—	4	—	1	—
Nelumbo lutea (American lotus)	1	0.01	0	0	1	0.02
Convolvulaceae (morning glory)	1	—	0	0	0	0
cf. Asteraceae	0	0	1	—	0	0
Unidentified seeds	22	—	16	—	12	—
Unidentifiable seed fragments	38	—	18	—	21	—

[a]EAC = Eastern Agricultural Complex.

grams of charcoal/liter of floated soil. Taxa recovered from mixed material pits are similar to those recovered from Oneota and Mississippian pits, including nutshell, tropical and EAC cultigens, miscellaneous/disturbance taxa, and edible leafy greens. The volume of floated soil for mixed material pits analyzed for this study is lower than Oneota and Mississippian pits but provides an important point of comparison. Examining Morton Village as a multicultural community, and envisioning food choices as part of a suite of foods that make up cuisine choices, requires analysis of similarities and differences between Oneota and Mississippian-designated features and structures, but mixed material pits may indicate ways in which cooperative processes related to plant use and food production played out at the site, or perhaps communal refuse or storage areas used by both Mississippian and Oneota households.

Nutshell

Oneota and Mississippian pit features yielded both thin and thick varieties of hickory nutshell (*Carya* spp.) as well as acorn (*Quercus* sp.), hazelnut (*Corylus* sp.), and walnut (*Juglans* spp.). Thick hickory and hazelnut were ubiquitous in mixed material and Mississippian features, whereas Oneota features yielded lower ubiquity values for nutshell. Thick hickory was the dominant nut taxon recovered from Oneota samples, representing 77% of recovered nutshell by count (n = 413 fragments), but the presence of thin-shelled hickory fragments in both Mississippian and Oneota pits indicates that Morton Village residents were either making use of several species of *Carya*, or there is significant variation in the shell thickness of one single species. Thick hickory was present in Mississippian and mixed material pits, but making up only 9% of the total nutshell assemblage in both sets of samples. Hickory is an oily, nutritious nut containing high amounts of fat, and ethnoarchaeological evidence suggests that the nuts may have been pounded in large batches to release oils and fats and then formed into balls that could be stored for later consumption (Fritz et al. 2001). Inedible parts of thick hickory may also have been used as fuel (Bardolph and VanDerwarker 2015).

Acorn was also present in Oneota pit features but only made up approximately 9% of recovered nutshell. Conversely, Mississippian and mixed material pits showed much higher concentrations of acorn, which composes 89% of the total nutshell assemblage for both feature types. In contrast, in other sites in the CIRV region (e.g., the early Mississippian component of C. W. Cooper and the Eveland Phase at the Lamb site), acorn tends to occur less frequently in those sites than thick hickory, possibly due to acorn not preserving as well as thick hickory (Bardolph and VanDerwarker 2015:222; Wilson and VanDerwarker

2015). Acorns are high in tannins, which taste bitter and may be toxic if consumed in large quantity, requiring them to be leached before they can be consumed. Acorns can then be used to prepare food, such as flours for breads, stews, or other items (Scarry 2003). A small amount of acorn nutmeat was recovered from two Oneota features. No nutmeat was recovered from Mississippian pits. Francis King's (1990) study, part of salvage excavations at Morton Village in the 1980s, indicated significant quantities of acorn nutmeat from one analyzed feature designated as Oneota at Morton Village, indicating that acorn nutmeat may have been an important ingredient in food and cuisine at Morton Village. The differences in the acorn assemblage collected from Mississippian and Oneota pits may represent differing processing habits or responsibilities at the site.

Hazelnut was recovered in small quantities from Oneota pits, making up only 3% of the nutshell assemblage. Mississippian and mixed material pits contain similarly low quantities of hazelnut shell: approximately 1% of the nutshell assemblage for both sets of features. Hazelnuts were likely processed for the nutmeat rather than oil extraction because of the high fat content of the nutmeat (Biwer and VanDerwarker 2015:94).

Juglandaceae nutshell, either *Carya* or *Juglans*, was also recovered from Oneota pit features, making up 11% of total nutshell, and was identified to family only, except for a single fragment of *Juglans cinerea*, or butternut. Mississippian samples contain a very small quantity (n = 2) of Juglandaceae nutshell. Mixed material samples yielded similarly low quantities of Juglandaceae (n = 4), three of which are identified as *Juglans nigra*, or black walnut.

Some researchers have suggested that extracting nutmeats from hazelnut and walnut may have required less processing time than creating flours or oils from hickories and acorns, though it is also possible that the opposite is true, with batch processing of hickories and acorns producing larger amounts of edible material through less total work time (Biwer and VanDerwarker 2015).

Tropical Cultigens

Tropical cultigens, including maize (*Zea mays*) and the common bean (*Phaseolus vulgaris*), were by far the most common taxa identified in all analyzed features. Oneota pits yielded a density of 4.82 fragments of maize per liter of floated soil and made up approximately 55% of all recovered maize macroremains from external pits. Mississippian samples contain a lower density of maize fragments (2.55 fragments per liter of floated soil), and maize kernels, cupules, glumes, and embryos represent 30% of the total macrobotanical assemblage from Mississippian pit features. Mixed material samples yielded the highest density of maize fragments, containing 7.46 fragments of maize/liter of soil, and maize fragments make up 39% of the total plant assemblage in these features. Evidence of common bean cultivation is present in Oneota contexts in the form of carbonized cotyledons (n = 11 fragments), with a SNE of 8. Mississippian samples yielded a single bean cotyledon, and mixed material samples yielded 5 cotyledon fragments (SNE = 3). The common bean did not become a significant dietary component anywhere in eastern North America until after AD 1200 (Hart and Scarry 1999; Monaghan et al. 2014). Monaghan and colleagues (2014) suggest that the spread of the common bean during the thirteenth century closely mirrors interactions and movements of Plains, Oneota, and Northern Late Woodland people. Early dates on beans in the CIRV cluster between AD 1250 and AD 1350, which, significantly, is coincident with Oneota migrations into the region. The introduction of the common bean is a vital aspect of "Three Sisters" agricultural systems, making its presence at Morton Village an important component to understanding potential shifts in cultivation strategies (Monaghan et al. 2014). It is possible that the introduction of beans into the CIRV was one mode by which cuisine evolved in the region, particularly when considered alongside the appearance of Oneota migrants.

Eastern Agricultural Complex Crops

The EAC is a sophisticated suite of small, starchy and oily seeded crops that predates maize farming in eastern North America. The complex includes squash (*Cucurbita pepo* ssp. *ovifera*), bottle gourd (*Lagenaria siceraria*), goosefoot or lamb's quarters (*Chenopodium berlandieri* ssp. *jonesianum*), maygrass (*Phalaris caroliniana*), little barley (*Hordeum pusillum*), sumpweed or marshelder (*Iva annua* var. *macrocarpa*), sunflower (*Helianthus annuus* var. *macrocarpus*), and knotweed (*Polygonum erectum* ssp. *watsoniae*). Premaize agricultural systems were variable throughout the Midwest, and the process of maize supplanting EAC cultigen use in the Late Precontact period likely looks different from region to region (Fritz 1990). Seeds, achenes, fruits, and rinds from EAC crops appear in lower quantities at Morton Village sample than do nutshell and maize, which may be a function of reduced use or because EAC botanical material recovered from archaeological contexts is typically something that is mostly edible parts of the plant, and thus produces less visible processing waste than a taxonomic category like nutshell or maize (VanDerwarker and Wilson 2016).

The most common EAC crop recovered from all features was *Chenopodium berlandieri* (n = 43). *Chenopodium berlandieri* ssp. *jonesianum* is a now-extinct, formerly domesticated subspecies of chenopod cultivated in ENA and shows evidence of domestication through its reduced testa thickness, truncate margins related to increased volume of starchy interior contents, and a smooth-textured seed coat. These traits appear at approximately 1700 BC, with cultivation likely occurring for many years before the earliest appearance of this domesticated subspecies (Fritz and Smith 1988a; Gremillion 1993; Langlie et al. 2014; Mueller et al. 2017; Smith and Yarnell 2009). Evidence of chenopod cultivation in ENA is highly complex, involving a spectrum of wild, weedy, and cultigen morphs and some overlap in morphometric evaluations of archaeological *Chenopodium* seeds. Thin-testa (less than 20 μm) morphs do occur naturally, with some research claiming that these morphs may represent about 5% of weedy chenopod seeds in modern populations, but thin-testa morphs compose a much higher percentage of archaeological chenopod seeds (up to 100%) (Gremillion 1993). Gremillion (1993) suggests a crop/weed pairing of chenopod types may be responsible for variation of testa thickness and seed coat texture in archaeological assemblages, but the role of developmental plasticity in morphological features has yet to be fully explored with this plant.

The chenopods recovered from Morton Village pit features are currently identified as *C. berlandieri*, but without scanning electron microscopy of testa thickness, I do not identify the chenopods from Morton Village as *C. berlandieri* ssp. *jonesianum*. There appear to be at least two morphs of chenopod present at the site, including smooth-testa and reticulate-testa morphs, some with truncate margins and an overlapping embryo forming a "beak." This dimorphic chenopod assemblage may represent a crop/weed relationship, and the form of what is likely cultigen chenopod, despite a reticulate pattern on the seed coat, may be representative of changing farming practices, selective pressures, or hybridization processes (Gremillion 1993), all of which would have had important implications for Morton Villagers as they considered the role of EAC crops alongside the "Three Sisters" and shifts in what was considered good food.

Fragments of sunflower (*Helianthus annuus*) pericarp were also recovered from Oneota (n = 15 fragments) and mixed material features (n = 9) and were not present in Mississippian pits. Based on the highly fragmentary state of these pericarp fragments, a SNE is unavailable for this taxon. One sunflower kernel was recovered from an Oneota feature and measured 3.8 millimeters in length and 1.5 millimeters in width, which places it outside the range of domesticated sunflower kernel size (Smith 2006; Wright 2008). Sumpweed, or marshelder, is present at Morton Village in Mississippian and mixed material pits (n = 1 for each feature classification). The *Iva* achenes from Mississippian and mixed material pits both measure 3.7 millimeters in length and 2.3 millimeters in width, indicating that they are within the size range of the domesticated variety, *Iva annua* var. *macrocarpa* (Yarnell 1972). However, others (e.g., Wagner and Carrington 2014) suggest achene lengths below 4.0 mm to be outside the range of domesticated sumpweed. The sumpweed recovered appears to be smaller than average for a domesticated variety and larger than wild populations. Sunflower and sumpweed were likely excellent sources of oil (Yarnell 1972).

A single maygrass (*Phalaris caroliniana*) seed was recovered from Oneota pits. Mississippian and mixed material pits do not contain maygrass. Little barley (*Hordeum pusillum*) is present in mixed material (n = 1) and Mississippian pits (n = 1) and is absent from Oneota pits. Like maygrass, little barley is an early fruiting grass, typically ready for harvest in springtime, and would have been an important source of sustenance coming out of the winter months (Adams 2014).

Fruits

Fruit seeds make up a very small percentage (less than 1%) of the botanical assemblage from Oneota features. The taxa recovered include persimmon (*Diospyros virginiana*) (n = 2 fragments), grape (*Vitis* sp.) (n = 2 fragments), and a *Prunus* species (n = 12 fragments), likely North American plum (*Prunus americana*) or cherry (*P. serotina*). Sumac (*Rhus* sp.) was also recovered (n = 3 seeds). Mixed material pits yielded one grape seed fragment, and Mississippian pits did not contain any fruits.

Other Seeds

American lotus (*Nelumbo lutea*) seed fragments (n = 2) were recovered from mixed material and Oneota pits but were absent from Mississippian pits. Oneota Feature 288 contained a single *Ipomoea* sp. seed. Both *Nelumbo lutea* and *Ipomoea* sp. are starchy food sources. American lotus is native to eastern North America and produces edible, starchy tubers often added to hominy or stews as well as small nut-like seeds that can be roasted or cracked open and eaten (Moerman 1998). Specific to seeds, *Ipomoea* sp. seeds are identified by Parker and Simon (2018) as part of a suite of "magic plants" because some species are known to be used in ceremonial or ritual contexts.

Miscellaneous Taxa

A variety of other taxa, including seeds of edible leafy greens and disturbance taxa, made up approximately 20% of all recovered macrobotanical remains from Oneota pits. Mississippian and mixed material pits contained fewer of these taxa, accounting for 11% and 6% of recovered taxa, respectively. The most prevalent taxon in this group was *Portulaca oleracea,* or purslane (n = 307 in Oneota samples, n = 68 in Mississippian samples, and n = 47 in mixed material samples), which grows easily in disturbed areas and is well known for its edible, green leaves, although it is difficult to tell based on context whether this plant was being used for food or if it appears in the archaeological record because it was growing in freshly cleared areas at the site. A variety of grass seeds and sedges was also recovered from all contexts, but these seeds and sedges were not identified to genus (see Table 6.1). Other miscellaneous taxa are also reported in Table 6.1.

Two taxa from the Solanaceae were recovered from Mississippian, mixed, and Oneota pits family, including *Solanum* sp. and, more commonly, *Solanum ptychanthum,* or eastern black nightshade. Oneota pits contained the highest number of *S. ptychanthum* seeds (n = 9), but it was also present in Mississippian (n = 4) and mixed material pits (n = 1). Eastern black nightshade has the reputation of being poisonous, but ripened berries are edible and sometimes incorporated into cuisines (Defelice 2003). Eastern black nightshade is discussed in more detail in the results of the Feature 224 analysis, below.

Five tobacco seeds (*Nicotiana* sp.) (Figure 6.1) were found in Oneota Features 213 and 214, both of which contained much of the recovered botanical material. Tobacco has been identified in both the archaeological and ethnohistoric record as a plant of significant importance that continues to be used by Indigenous groups today in daily and ritual or ceremonial contexts (Adair 2000; Bollwerk and Tushingham 2016; Creese 2016; Hedden 2016; Wagner 2000; Winter 2000). Tobacco is noted in ethnohistoric accounts as being a mode of mediation between two groups as well as between humans and supernatural beings, although the spread of Calumet ceremonialism into the Eastern Woodlands remains a subject of much debate (Blakeslee 1981; Brown 1989; Haberman 1984). Although not a food plant, the sacredness of the tobacco plant to Indigenous communities throughout eastern North America and the potential for it being a means of mediation between groups imply that tobacco may have had a role in special commensal eating occasions as a way to mark the occasion as something beyond an ordinary meal.

Again, there are several important distinctions between the botanical assemblages of Oneota, Mississippian, and mixed material pits. Acorn appears in much higher quantity and density in Mississippian and mixed material pits, whereas acorn nutmeat only appears in Oneota pits. There is also a conspicuous absence of *Chenopodium* in Mississippian samples. Little barley appeared only in Mississippian and mixed material pits. Tobacco was recovered only in Oneota pits, and sunflower was absent from Mississippian pits as well. Maize

Figure 6.1. *Nicotiana* sp. recovered from external pit feature. (Photograph courtesy of Kelsey Nordine.)

was by far the most commonly recovered botanical material recovered from all pits, with the highest quantity coming from mixed material pits. Beans were also more common in Oneota pits than Mississippian pits. I return to these differences and similarities in the discussion to explore the ways in which these differences and similarities in the botanical composition of analyzed samples reflect choices in cuisine, shifting beliefs regarding the social meanings and values embedded within cuisine, and the role of cuisine in social identity negotiation at Morton Village.

FEATURE 224 AND FEASTING AT MORTON VILLAGE

The contents of Feature 224, which likely represent a feasting deposit because of the high volume of animal bone and ceramic materials discarded in what appears to be a single deposition along with a number of remarkable artifacts and the pit's location within a structure (O'Gorman and Conner 2023; Martin, chapter 5, this volume), are particularly salient to understanding cuisine in the past. Remains from a feasting deposit represent cooked, shared meals that would have been prepared with a variety of ingredients to create a special meal, which Twiss (2008:419) explains as a mode of "recapitulating and expanding upon the structure of the domestic meal, and thus drawing participants into a world of food symbolism." In addition to the preparation and consumption of larger-than-usual amounts of food, feasting also contributes significantly "to the negotiation and maintenance of the status quo, and to processes of profound social change" (Twiss 2008:418), which is significant considering the recent migration of Oneota villagers into Morton Village. It is probable that these commensal eating events were critical components of negotiating a new community configuration involving both Mississippian residents and their Oneota neighbors.

The following section briefly reviews the structure of Feature 224 and provides raw data from this feature but focuses primarily on one specific plant present in an unusual context: *Solanum ptychanthum,* or eastern black nightshade. Its presence in samples from an in situ smoldering episode associated with a large fragment of an Oneota jar and a sandstone pipe on top of the Feature 224 feasting deposit may suggest that this plant had some amount of ritual power within the community, particularly for Oneota residents.

Structure of Feature 224

Feature 224 is a pit feature inside of Structure 25 at Morton Village (see Figure 5.1, this volume). The feature consists of four primary zones: Zone 4 consisted of "relatively clean B horizon" (Conner and O'Gorman 2012). This was not analyzed for plant remains. Zone 3 is the main artifact-bearing zone in the feature, which contained a large quantity of animal bone, Mississippian ceramic sherds, and stone, totaling 19.6 kg. Vessel analysis indicated that at least 29 ceramic vessels were present in Feature 224 (O'Gorman and Conner 2023). Zone 2 was likely a capping layer over Zone 3. Zone 1 contained a small area with what appears to be an in situ smoldering episode and yielded a large fragment of an Oneota jar and a small, Oneota sandstone pipe. The area of smoldering was then covered with debris or soil.

Flotation samples from Feature 224 yielded a surprising dearth of plant matter given the abundance of faunal remains (see Martin, chapter 5, for discussion on the Feature 224 faunal remains). All recovered taxa are listed in Table 6.2.

Table 6.2. Summary Table of Macrobotanical Remains from Feature 224

	Zone 1		Zone 2		Zone 3	
Number of samples	4		1		5	
Total liters of floated soil	33		10		50	
Category/taxon	Count	Weight (g)	Count	Weight (g)	Count	Weight (g)
Wood charcoal	—	77.54	—	11.61	—	22.71
Stem	3	0.03	0	0	0	0
Nutshell (total)	**159**	**0.87**	**0**	**0**	**20**	**0.33**
Carya sp. (thick hickory)	30	0.34	0	0	6	0.16
Juglans sp. (walnut)	1	0.02	0	0	2	0.02
Juglandaceae	0	0	0	0	2	0.05
Quercus sp. (acorn)	107	0.38	0	0	8	0.08
Corylus sp. (hazelnut)	18	0.10	0	0	2	0.02
Unidentified nutshell	3	0.03	0	0	0	0
Tropical cultigen (total)	**54**	**0.37**	**3**	**0.03**	**32**	**0.20**
Zea mays (maize kernel)	38	0.25	1	0.01	13	0.09
Zea mays (maize embryo)	0	0	0	0	1	0.01
Zea mays (maize cupule)	11	0.09	1	0.01	12	0.06
Zea mays (maize glume)	5	0.03	1	0.01	6	0.04
EAC[a] cultigen (total)	**54**	**—**	**1**	**—**	**4**	**—**
Lagenaria siceraria rind (bottle gourd)	0	0	0	0	2	0.02
Cucurbita sp. rind (squash)	0	0	0	0	1	0.01
Chenopodium berlandieri ssp. *jonesianum* (cultigen chenopod)	14	—	1	—	1	—
Chenopod perisperm	35	—	0	0	0	0
Helianthus annuus (sunflower pericarp fragments)	4	—	0	0	0	0
Phalaris caroliniana (maygrass)	1	—	0	0	0	0
Fruits (total)	**56**	**—**	**0**	**0**	**0**	**0**
Vitis sp. (grape)	2	—	0	0	0	0
Solanum sp.	6	—	0	0	0	0

	Zone 1		Zone 2		Zone 3	
Solanum cf. *ptychanthum* (eastern black nightshade)	48	—	0	0	0	0
Other Seed Taxa (total)	**85**	—	**2**	—	**2**	—
Verbena sp. (Verbena)	0	0	0	0	1	—
Chenopodium sp. (wild chenopod)	3	—	0	0	0	0
Cyperaceae	1	—	0	0	1	—
Mollugo verticillata (carpetweed)	2	—	0	0	0	0
Grass spikelet	1	—	0	0	0	0
Poaceae	62	—	2	—	0	0
Portulaca oleracea (purslane)	16	—	0	0	8	—
Unidentified:						
Unidentifiable seed fragments	11	—	0	0	7	—
Unidentified seeds	10	—	0	0	6	—

[a]EAC = Eastern Agricultural Complex.

Feature 224 represents ritualized consumption behavior consistent with feasting, but there are significant differences in the botanical composition of Zone 1 and the main artifact zone, Zone 3. The differences in ceramic types recovered from Zone 1 and Zone 3 may indicate that, although Oneota and Mississippian groups were likely participating in this event together, they may have had different roles in this ritual performance. As discussed by O'Gorman and O'Conner (2023:89–90), Oneota ceramics were "confined to the top two zones and include only one large vessel . . . vessel analysis also identified cross-matched portions of five vessels that support the contemporaneity of the upper and lower deposits."

Samples from Zone 3 of Feature 224 came from two different levels of excavated matrix but are combined here, as they represent a single cultural context. Samples from this zone were taken from the profile of the excavation unit and from matrix within the excavation unit and totaled 50 liters of floated soil. Zone 3 yielded maize, nutshell (thick hickory, walnut, acorn, and hazelnut), squash and bottle gourd rind, one *Chenopodium* seed, verbena, and purslane, all in relatively small quantities.

The botanical assemblage in Zone 1 is significantly different from that in Zone 3, containing a higher density of plant matter and more diversity, as well as evidence of in situ smoldering. Zone 1 flotation samples totaled 33 liters of floated soil and contained a total of 77.54 grams of wood charcoal, or 2.35 grams per liter of soil floated. The density of wood charcoal is much higher in Zone 1 than Zone 3, and it is likely that although some of the wood was probably charred as a result of smoldering, wood from the structural elements of Structure 25 probably entered the Zone 1 samples when the structure was burned. This is supported by the presence of three pieces of stem (0.03 grams), which may represent the remains of building material such as thatch for siding or roofs.

Nutshell was present in higher quantities in Zone 1 than Zone 3, as well. The species present in this zone are the same as in Zone 3 (thick hickory, acorn, hazelnut, and walnut). Acorn shell makes up 67% of recovered nutshell in this level. Maize was also recovered in higher quantity in Zone 1 than in Zone 3, but, interestingly, cupules and glumes make up 30% of the maize assemblage, which could be considered unusual as these are the inedible parts of maize that are removed during processing for consumption. Beans, squash, and bottle gourd were absent from this Zone. The EAC crops were present in higher quantities than in Zone 3. Zone 1 yielded 14 cultigen *Chenopodium* seeds and 35 perisperms, which may be evidence of thin testa morphs that could have lost their testas through cooking or processing. One fragment of maygrass was also recovered from Zone 1. Grape (SNE = 2) was also recovered from Zone 1. Two other types of fruits recovered from Zone 1 were *Solanum* sp. and *Solanum ptychanthum*, or eastern black nightshade. Forty-eight *S. ptychanthum* seeds were recovered from Zone 1, and six seeds were identified only to the genus *Solanum*.

Grass seeds (Poaceae family) were recovered in Zone 1 (n = 62) in much higher quantity than Zone 2, and no grass seeds were present in Zone 3. The presence of grasses in Zone 1 is likely the result of the structure being burned, depositing grass seeds that were probably present in thatching material used in building construction. The absence of grasses in Zone 3 and the low quantity in Zone 2 are evidence that the Zone 3 matrix accumulated was capped by Zone 2 relatively quickly.

The presence of only Mississippian ceramic remains in the main artifact zone (Zone 3) means that it is uncertain whether Oneota villagers were also present during the commensal event that produced Zone 3. However, the Zone 1 deposit is positioned directly on top of the capping layer above Zone 3, and this uppermost zone contained a section of an Oneota jar, a small, sandstone pipe, and *S. ptychanthum* seeds. O'Gorman and Conner (2023:91) also note cross-matching of 5 ceramic sherds between upper and lower levels, supporting their interpretation of the pit as the result of a "multiphased feasting event." All indications suggest that Oneota villagers did participate in this event in a significant way, although the length of time between deposition events remains unclear. The combination of a sandstone pipe fragment and nightshades, likely recovered from an in situ burning episode, suggests a deliberate contribution of these items to the deposit.

DISCUSSION

Cuisine is often considered to be conservative (Egan-Bruhy 2014; Graff 2020), which makes it an ideal lens for interpreting the various modes of community building at Morton Village, where Oneota and Mississippian residents likely held on to some of their beliefs about how to prepare and eat food and what is considered food. As cuisine likely shifted with the arrival of Oneota migrants, this shifting could have included new ideas about what is food, novel modes of preparing and cooking, sharing recipes, and sharing knowledge of new ways to use plants. Cuisine has the capacity to "mediate and transform social relations" (Graff 2020:340), which makes the lens of cuisine particularly salient in the context of a growing multicultural community.

This analysis produced several interesting patterns in plant use at Morton Village. In the context of domestic spaces (pit features), there appear to be several points of interest in the macrobotanical assemblage. Several taxa that were recovered from Oneota-associated pits, including *Chenopodium* and sunflower, were absent from Mississippian pits. Conversely, Mississippian pits appeared to contain a much higher quantity of acorn shell than do Oneota pits, whereas Oneota pits contained a higher quantity of thick hickory nutshell. This may be related to knowledge of aforementioned nut-processing strategies. However, because of the high density of acorn shell in mixed material pits, and the majority of acorn shell being recovered from only a single Mississippian pit, it seems plausible that these differences represent a shared responsibility between Mississippian and Oneota villagers for nut processing, or some other form of labor division, and not necessarily preference, which in itself could be construed as a shift in cuisine practices. Acorn nutmeats were present in Oneota samples, along with other food remains, suggesting that Oneota villagers were consuming acorn, if not processing it in large quantity.

Mississippian samples appear to have less diversity than Oneota samples, which do appear to be more diverse with beans, eastern black nightshade, tobacco, sunflower, and some fruits absent from Mississippian pits. These subtle differences in the plant assemblages of pit features suggest that Oneota residents of Morton Village likely arrived with different traditions related to cuisine, although drawing on the same basic ingredients, making the task of identifying separate cuisines archaeologically difficult. Integrated studies that draw on faunal, botanical, and ceramic evidence together to understand cuisine are better suited to identifying these subtle nuances in cuisine shifts in a multicultural community. This may be the result of simple preference for one plant over another, or more broadly, variable cultural values surrounding food, cooking, and consuming food. Coupled with evidence of changing ceramic forms at Morton Village (Painter and O'Gorman 2019; chapter 4, this volume), it is reasonable to expect some form of creolization of cuisines at Morton Village. There is also evidence at Morton Village that the importance of EAC crops was waning in comparison to maize, which is a significant shift in cuisine. It is possible that the differences in the EAC assemblages between Oneota and Mississippian pits represent Oneota residents continuing to farm, harvest, cook, and eat *Chenopodium,* but perhaps with reduced selection pressures. Interestingly, cultigen *Chenopodium berlandieri* and maygrass were present only in Oneota-associated external pits. The presence of these taxa in the zone of Feature 224 associated with an Oneota jar suggests the association of *Chenopodium berlandieri* and maygrass with Oneota villagers may be a pattern related to preference and cuisine, rather than an anomaly at the site. Because absence of evidence is not evidence of absence, it is equally possible that Mississippian villagers were consuming *Chenopodium* as well, but it may not have made up a significant portion of their diet or failed to appear in the archaeological record for a number of reasons. Another possible explanation for the differences in botanical remains between Oneota and Mississippian pits is that the community engaged in some kind of shared labor practice for producing food for the village, which I argue also constitutes an important aspect of cuisine. Who prepares food, grows food, and processes food are all culturally constructed and often along lines of gender and age. By conceptualizing cuisine in the archaeological past, we are able to consider the daily and ritual lives of past people in greater detail than studies of subsistence, nutrition, and diet. Cuisine would have been a critical component of Oneota and Mississippian identity negotiation at Morton Village, as cuisine is capable of mediating social relationships.

There is one taxon from Feature 224 deposit that warrants further attention: eastern black nightshade (*Solanum ptychanthum*). This is typically not considered a food plant today because it contains solanine, which is a highly toxic steroidal alkaloid that appears in the highest concentrations in young plant tissue and reduces as the plant matures (Parker and Simon 2018). Ingestion of eastern black nightshade in high quantity can cause a variety of symptoms, including "nausea, vomiting, diarrhea or constipation, excess salivation, drowsiness, reduced circulatory or respiratory effectiveness, loss of consciousness, and, in high, untreated doses, death" (Parker and Simon 2018:138). However, when ripe berries of *S. ptychanthum* are available, they can be used to make pies and preserves. Okiek groups in Kenya are known to consume the greens of wild *Solanum* (Defelice 2003; Heiser 1969; Marshall 2001). Ethnobotanical literature on medicinal uses of *S. ptychanthum* describes uses for this plant as an emetic, helminthic, sedative, and treatment for eye problems (Parker and Simon 2018). Given the potential toxicity of this plant at early stages of its growth and ethnobotanical evidence for its use in medicine and ceremony, at the very least, eastern black nightshade was likely a plant that was approached and used with some degree of caution by Morton villagers.

The use of eastern black nightshade for medicinal or ceremonial purposes likely has deep roots among Indigenous communities in the Midcontinent. Nightshade seeds are commonly recovered from Late Woodland contexts in the American Bottom alongside domestic refuse, which Parker and Simon (2018) interpreted as evidence that this plant was intentionally cultivated or encouraged and used purposefully as a food, medicine, or conduit to achieve a spiritual or religious outcome.

Solanum ptychanthum was also recovered from the Dixon site in Iowa (Bush 2019), which was occupied roughly contemporaneously with Morton Village and may therefore be a powerful plant to the Oneota migrants at Morton Village. *Solanum americanum* seeds have been recovered from several sites in the upper Midwest, including three *S. americanum* seeds from the OT site in southwestern Wisconsin (Hunter and Umlauf 1989), and *S. americanum* seeds have been recovered from Koshkonong Locality Oneota contexts (Jeske 2020).

Eastern black nightshade in Mississippian contexts in the American Bottom implicates this plant in group ceremonies or religious behavior centered on elite groups, as it is commonly found in special archaeological contexts such as ritually used structures, and there appears to be some degree of continuity in use of *S. ptychanthum* from the Late Woodland into the Mississippian period (Parker and Simon 2018). Parker and Simon (2018:122) classify *S. ptychanthum* as a "magic plant," which is defined as a plant that has chemical properties that make it special or uniquely useful, is associated with special objects, places, or archaeological contexts, is listed in ethnobotanical literature as having ritual properties, or has no other apparent uses as a food, fuel, or construction material. Its presence in samples from an in situ smoldering episode on top of a feasting deposit may suggest that this plant had some amount of ritual power within the community, particularly for Oneota residents. While generally not considered a contemporary food source (although published literature on this plant may not entirely account for the vast Indigenous ethnobotanical knowledge on food-related uses), this plant was likely significant in some way. I argue that these noncomestible plants should also be considered when exploring cuisines of the past; plants with significant ritual power may be used to imbue feasts or special meals with special significance.

CONCLUSION

The paleoethnobotanical analysis presented in this chapter indicates that Oneota and Mississippian villagers, while maintaining some of their traditions pertaining to food, cuisine, and ceramic production, were possibly sharing labor responsibilities for farming, gathering, processing, and consuming food, at both household and community levels, as well as shifting beliefs about food and cuisine. It is critical to understand Morton Village as a community in flux, building new traditions while maintaining some old ones, and to envision a settlement where distinctions between Oneota and Mississippian material culture do not necessarily indicate two separate lifeways. Rather, the material evidence of daily practice and ritually charged behavior likely represents the ways in which Morton villagers mediated conflict and integrated both groups as part of a community whole, while still maintaining some aspects of separate Oneota and Mississippian cultural beliefs and norms. The study of cuisine, as a critical part of daily life and ceremonial events, is a means by which archaeologists can begin to consider the meaning and cultural value of food, and how these beliefs can change through migration, coalescence, and identity negotiation at the community level.

Integrated analyses involving ceramic, faunal, and botanical data are likely to yield the most robust results when considering cuisine in the past. Further comparative work between Morton Village and Developmental Oneota sites to the west in Iowa as well as southern Wisconsin may provide more nuance and detail to what foodstuffs were favored, revered, stored, consumed, gathered, or hunted. Future work with lipid and residue analyses to provide important information about combinations of food consumed may help archaeologists better understand cuisine and continue examining the role of food and cuisine in community building, shifting beliefs around food, and hybridity and coalescent societies. Cuisine is more than simply food; it is also the beliefs, values, tastes, recipes, food serving traditions, and the importance of shared meals; therefore, the archaeological study of cuisine will be most meaningful when all these aspects of cuisine are examined through different archaeological methodologies.

Chapter 7

Bison Hoes and Bird Tails

Reconsidering the Introduction of Maize Farming into Manitoba

MARY E. MALAINEY

Archaeologists in the 1950s thought that precontact Indigenous maize farming in Manitoba seemed improbable, which delayed its formal recognition for decades. There is solid evidence for its presence north of Winnipeg between AD 1250 and 1450 at the Lockport site (EaLf-1). The recent discovery of bison scapula hoes at the Olson site (DgMg-167) in the extreme southwest corner of the province offers clues as to the subsequent movement of the farmers. Hundreds of kilometers separate these sites from horticultural villages of the Midwest and Northern Plains. Questions remain as to how and why maize cultivation was introduced, from where, and by whom.

The Lockport area was inhabited by hunter-gatherers with easy access to wild rice; the introduction of maize farming into Manitoba went beyond simply adding another starchy plant food to the menu. The production and use of maize were complex processes involving both practical (hoe construction, preparing ground, sowing, tending, harvesting, processing, storage pit construction, crop storage, and cooking practices) and spiritual aspects. Jelliffe (1967) defines cultural superfoods as those whose production and preparation occupies a major part of the community's agricultural and domestic work. Because of their importance, cultural superfoods may have a semidivine status and be woven into the group's religion, mythology, and history (Jelliffe 1967). Maize can be considered a cultural superfood among Indigenous groups practicing horticulture. The adoption of maize farming by the inhabitants of the Lockport area, and resulting changes in cuisine, is evidence that they had close contact with people with extensive experience in all aspects of its production and use.

Rogers (1995) proposed that relative advantage, compatibility, complexity, trialability, and observability affect the voluntary adoption of innovations. Archaeological evidence suggests these factors may have played a role in the acceptance of maize cultivation by precontact hunter-gatherers in Manitoba and, by proxy, innovation in cuisine. In this chapter, issues relating to how and why precontact Indigenous farming appeared in Manitoba are considered. The adoption of maize cultivation suggests the hunter-gatherers recognized advantages in doing so and/or that the practice was compatible with their lifeways. The presence of knowledgeable farmers from the southeast may have facilitated the introduction by providing demonstrations or hands-on learning opportunities. Archaeological evidence of precontact Indigenous horticulture in Manitoba is reviewed. Hypotheses regarding the introduction of maize are considered with respect to finds from the northeastern Plains and Upper Mississippi River Valley. Practical, technological, and ritual aspects of maize cultivation are assessed. Comparisons of pottery decorations identified as "tail of the raptor or Thunderbird" at sites located in Manitoba, the northeastern Plains of North Dakota, and Upper Mississippi Valley of Minnesota and Wisconsin are used to assess possible similarities in ceremonialism. Archaeological evidence of horticulture is considered within the environmental and cultural contexts of the sites. Differences in technology are evaluated through the occurrence and morphology of bison scapula hoes. These data are then used to evaluate hypotheses regarding the introduction of maize farming. Evidence shows strong connections with horticultural groups from the Red Wing–Pepin area of Minnesota and Wisconsin and suggests a route of entry along the parkland-tallgrass prairie border. This is contrary to the suggestion that maize horticulture was introduced from the south along the Red River by groups in eastern North Dakota.

PRECONTACT INDIGENOUS FARMING IN MANITOBA

Maize phytoliths and/or starch granules have been identified in the carbonized residues of Indigenous pottery at several Manitoba sites, possibly dating as early as AD 500 (Boyd et al. 2006, 2008, 2014; Boyd and Surette 2010; Deck and Shay 1992; Lints 2012); however, only the Lockport site north of Winnipeg and Pierson Wildlife Management Area (WMA) sites in the southwest corner of the province have concrete evidence of horticulture (Figure 7.1). Lockport is a multicomponent site about 26 km north of the confluence of the Red and Assiniboine Rivers, bearing the name of the town in which it is located. The site is in the aspen parkland or fertile belt, close to the northern

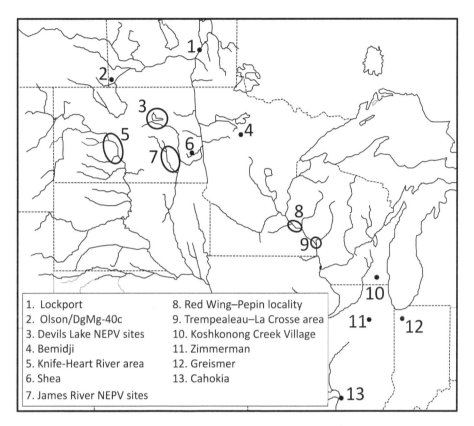

Figure 7.1. Map showing locations of sites discussed in this chapter. (Base map from Google Maps, traced in Microsoft PowerPoint.) (Map courtesy of Mary E. Malainey.)

edge of the tallgrass prairie (Hind 1971; Malainey and Sherriff 1996; Palliser 1968; Shay 1980). Alexander Mackenzie (1927) visited this part of the Red River in the late 1700s and remarked that the west side was covered with herds of bison and elk and the east side abounded with fallow deer, beaver, moose, bear, fish, fowl, and wild rice. Indigenous groups could obtain Selkirk chert for flaked stone tools from a bedrock exposure at the southern end of the Lockport site. The limestone outcrop created a set of rapids, which made the area particularly good for fishing but impassable to boats, so a lock and dam were constructed in 1910 (MacNeish 1958; Government of Canada 2021). Cultural deposits extending over 300 m north and over 2 m below the surface show the area was occupied 10 to 15 different times over the last 3,300 years (Buchner 1986, 1988; Flynn 2002; MacNeish 1958; Syms and Halwas 2019). Both natural and cultural disturbance processes have affected the site. Settlers began opening nearby burial mounds in the 1860s. Several archaeologists visited the site in the first half of the twentieth century and conducted limited excavations (Capes 1963; MacNeish 1958; Syms and Halwas 2019). A major flood in 1950 resulted in the loss of 15 m (50 ft.) of the east lower terrace where cultural deposits had been 2.4 m (8 ft.) deep (MacNeish 1958). Ongoing riverbank erosion since then has almost completely removed the lower terrace.

Richard S. MacNeish (1958), who excavated the site in the early 1950s, focused on its use as a fishing camp. He did not recognize the occurrence of precontact Indigenous maize cultivation at the Lockport site. Given the abundance of wild plant and animal resources in the area, he likely did not consider its presence. MacNeish (1958) suggested that the bell-shaped pits were similar to food storage pits used by Cree and Saulteaux and that the hunter-gatherers had used bison scapula hoes to excavate them. No attempt was made to identify the charred seeds frequently found in the large storage pits (MacNeish 1958).

Manitoba Historic Resources Branch (HRB) excavated 98 m² at the Lockport site under the direction of A. P. Buchner (1984–86) and David Hems (1987–88) (Buchner 1988; Flynn 2002). Ten complete or nearly complete scapula hoes and the fragments of nine other hoes were recovered (Roberts 1991). Five deep and nine shallow bell-shaped storage pits and nine hearths were intercepted during HRB excavations (Hems 1997). The deep storage pits generally extended 1.5 m below their level of origin; the shallow storage pits ranged from 15 cm to 1 m in depth (Hems 1997). Charred Eastern Complex eight-row variety maize, also known as Maize de Ocho or Northern Flint corn, was recovered in samples collected from storage pits, hearths, and the occupation layer (Deck and Shay 1992).

Buchner (1988:27) suggested a "horticultural interlude" occurred within a more extensive Blackduck occupation at the site. Radiocarbon dates indicated the Blackduck occupation began around AD 855 or 945 and spanned Beds C, D, and E. Horticultural materials appeared in the middle of Bed E more than 75 cm depth below surface (dbs) and continued until the interface between Beds B and C 40–50 cm below surface (Buchner 1986, 1988). An initial date of about AD 1200 was suggested for the appearance of horticultural materials. Both the Blackduck and horticultural occupations ended around AD 1480 (Buchner 1986, 1988). Buchner (1986:73) saw this as evidence of "an intrusive subcomponent whose origin undeniably lies to the south." Hems (1997) and Flynn (2002) instead argued that the intrusive horticultural occupation was restricted to Bed B/C, situated between and separate from the Selkirk and Blackduck occupations. The Bed B/C organic layer was a 10-cm-thick organic stratum that occurred 40 to 50 cm dbs (Flynn 2002; Hems 1997). Flynn (2002) dismissed early radiocarbon dates and suggested that horticultural activities lasted only a few decades in the mid-1300s to mid-1400s. In support of Buchner's (1988) chronology, Halwas and colleagues (2019) presented a combination of conventional radiocarbon dates on charcoal and accelerator mass spectrometry (AMS) dates on bison scapula hoes and maize that show the horticultural occupation at the Lockport site occurred from about AD 1250 to 1450. Buchner's (1988) interpretation of site chronology and stratigraphy is consistent with sedimentation rates based on data on at least five major floods between AD 1825 and 1997 (Province of Manitoba n.d.).

Concrete evidence of horticulture has been found at sites within the Pierson WMA in the southwest corner of Manitoba as well. The dense concentration of earthworks in the area indicated a high degree of sedentism, and mortuary goods suggested connections with Mississippian agriculturalists (Capes 1963; Montgomery 1908; Syms 1978, 1979); however, evidence of Indigenous cultivation remained elusive for decades. No cultigens were recovered during investigations of shallow depressions on the prairie level near the confluence of Gainsborough Creek and the Souris River. Syms (1974) suggested that the Protohistoric cylindrical pit at site DgMg-15 was a storage pit later used for smudges and refuse disposal. Hamilton et al. (2007) later employed geophysical techniques at DgMg-15 and adjacent DgMg-17 to locate other possible crop storage features, but their efforts were unsuccessful. A prairie-level surface depression at DgMg-162 marked a large oval roasting pit from the historic period that contained fragments of European china (Nicholson and Malainey 1994).

Tangible evidence of Indigenous farming emerged in September 2018, when Eric Olson found a bison scapula hoe (Figure 7.2 and Figure 7.3) on the banks of Gainsborough Creek in the Pierson WMA, about 1 km south of DgMg-162 and another in a debris pile about 20 m downstream of the first. Archaeological investigations of the adjacent floodplain, known as Olson site (DgMg-167), in 2019–21 encountered remains of a bone tool workshop. In situ remains included fragments of a modified bison scapula with perforated blade and several modified ribs in the same 1 × 1 m unit. A modified deer scapula was found 10 m north. Dates obtained on bone and charcoal from the workshop paleosol indicate the horticultural occupation began in the late 1400s/early 1500s and lasted over 200 years (Malainey 2020a-b, 2021a-e). Crops may have been grown in a large patch of mixed grass prairie in the valley. Indigenous farmers established residences on the prairie both west (DgMg-40c) and east

(DgMg-168) of the valley. Twenty-nine subsurface anomalies were detected at DgMg-40c using ground-penetrating radar. Testing of two closely spaced anomalies uncovered a knapping station consisting of 300 flakes of material visually similar to Knife River flint in one 1×1 m unit and almost 50 sherds of a thin-walled, globular vessel with a cord-roughened exterior in another. A small (6–7 cm diameter, 10 cm deep) tapering hole containing intentionally (probably ritually) buried fragments of a highly decorated vessel was found near a substantial hearth at DgMg-168. Residential debris was concentrated in Levels 3–4 (10–20 cm dbs) on both sides of Gainsborough Creek.

Both the Lockport and Pierson WMA sites are near burial mounds. Before construction of the Red River floodway, the Fidler Mounds (EaLf-3) were located about 300 m northeast of Lockport. Salvage excavations recovered 46 individuals from discrete burials and skeletal elements of another 17 from mound fill (Hewitt et al. 2008; Province of Manitoba 1963; Saylor 1976). One uncalibrated date of 380 ± 80 radiocarbon years BP on charcoal (Rutherford et al. 1984) suggested that the mounds were recently constructed. However, recent AMS radiocarbon age estimates on eight individuals clearly show the mounds were originally constructed during the Middle Woodland and then used repeatedly during the Late Woodland (Hewitt et al. 2008).

The Pierson WMA is near the confluence of the Souris River with its tributaries, Gainsborough Creek and the Antler River, an area noted for its high concentration of precontact Indigenous earthworks. About 90 mounds exist, and they have been the subject of archaeological research for over 110 years (Capes 1963; Montgomery 1908; Syms 1978, 1979). Nickerson's Mound H (Capes 1963), designated DgMg-40a, is located about 160 m south of the DgMg-40c residential debris. Syms (1979) included mounds from Saskatchewan, Manitoba, and North Dakota in his definition of the Devils Lake–Sourisford Burial Complex. While emphasizing connections to the Mississippian Southeastern Ceremonial Complex, Syms (1979) admitted dates of AD 900 suggest that some mounds may have been constructed by Sonota and/or Besant groups. There is no consensus among archaeologists as to whether Sonota and Besant represent distinct or related groups (Kooyman 2000; Neuman 1975; Peck 2011; Steuber 2018; Syms 1977; Walde et al. 1995). Their materials are associated with a period of transition among Northern Plains bison hunters marked by the appearance of pottery, bow and arrow technology, mound building, and flaked stone tools made predominantly from Knife River flint.

Evidence of a Besant/Sonota occupation at DgMg-40c includes a Besant projectile point from a rodent backdirt pile 40 m to the southeast of the residential debris and vertically oriented bison mandible and scapulae fragments

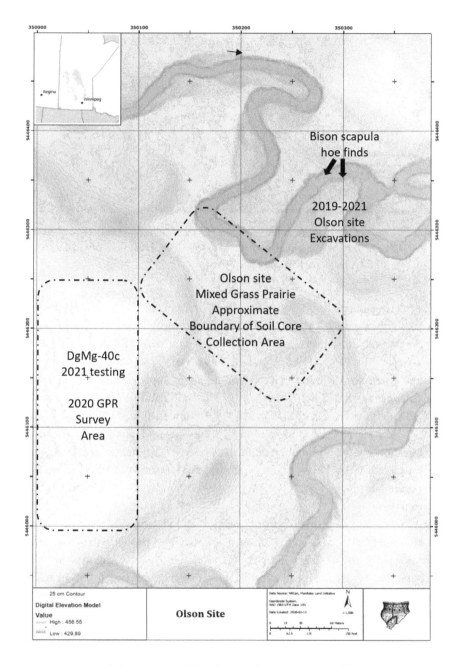

Figure 7.2. Digital elevation map of the Olson site/DgMg-40c locale. (Base map from NRCan, Manitoba Land Initiative; Coordinate System: NAD 1983 UTM Zone 14N. Map by Dan Szot. Courtesy of Mary E. Malainey.)

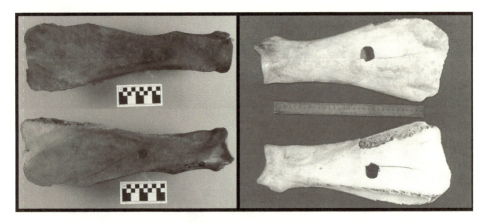

Figure 7.3. Bison scapula hoe from the Olson site (*left*) and Lockport (*right*). (Left photograph by Mary E. Malainey. Right photograph from Roberts [1991: Figure 7]. Used with permission of the Manitoba Archaeological Society.)

in a tapering pit between Levels 6 and 10 (25–50 cm dbs) directly beneath the pottery concentration (Malainey 2021d-e). Bone uprights are known to occur at Besant and/or Sonota and some Blackduck sites dating 2,500–1,000 years ago (Graham and Ives 2019). Graham and Ives (2019) identified a bone feature within Nickerson's Mound H as an upright shim, implying a Besant/Sonota association. Stemmed points similar to Early Woodland Adena, Kramer, and Waubesau types (Boszhardt 2002, 2003) are found in and north of the Melita area. These identifications were confirmed by William Lovis (personal communication, 2021) and demonstrate the presence of other mound-building groups. As with Lockport/Fidler Mounds, later Pierson WMA horticulturalists settled in an area with mounds constructed hundreds of years earlier and reused them.

Archaeological recoveries from Lockport and Pierson WMA sites are best positioned to shed light on the lifeways of Indigenous people associated with farming along the northern limit of precontact North American agricultural production. While microbotanical evidence of cultigens was found in residue adhering to precontact Indigenous pottery from other sites in southwest Manitoba (Boyd et al. 2006, 2008, 2014; Boyd and Surette 2010; Lints 2012), the case for precontact cultivation outlined by Nicholson (1990, 1991, 1994) and expanded elsewhere (Nicholson et al. 2006, 2008, 2011) remains circumstantial. Hunting and gathering groups are known to have traveled hundreds of kilometers to trade for maize during the historic period (Ray 1974). Its occurrence in cooking residues indicates use, not maize farming. Maize cultivation indicates a significant shift in cuisine, food patterns, and degree of group mobility.

EVIDENCE OF POSSIBLE ROUTES OF ENTRY AND EXTRAREGIONAL CONNECTIONS

Several lines of evidence must be considered when assessing the introduction of maize farming into Manitoba. First, differences in depictions of pottery motifs identified as "tail of the raptor" or Thunderbird are presented. Following this, archaeological indications of horticulture in eastern North Dakota and Upper Mississippi River Valley are reviewed along with the physical, cultural and temporal settings of sites. Finally, the occurrence and morphology of scapula hoes and possible digging tools from sites on the Northern Plains and Midwest are considered.

TAIL OF THE RAPTOR OR THUNDERBIRD MOTIFS ON POTTERY

Most Indigenous pottery vessels found at sites on the Northern Plains and parkland was used in food preparation, and pottery decoration has played a central role in attributions of cultural connections between Lockport farmers and other groups. MacNeish (1958), Buchner (1988), and Flynn (2002) all recognized influences from the south or southeast in the pottery from the Lockport site. MacNeish (1958:26) regarded sherds with wide-line incising "such as is found on Cambria Type B sherds of southern Minnesota" as evidence of trade. Buchner (1988) described the unusual pottery as Initial Variant Middle Missouri Tradition. Due in part to reports of "tail of the Thunderbird motifs," Flynn (2002) proposed the horticultural occupation at Lockport resulted from Northeastern Plains Village (NEPV) complex people moving north into Manitoba along the Red River. While admitting similarities existed, Flynn (2002:198) stated, "It should be made clear however, that the pottery from the horticultural occupation at EaLf-1 Sites is NOT Oneota." Oneota-like decorations on Lockport pottery was possible evidence that groups along the southern portion of the Red River may have been trying to "escape [Oneota] political coercion" and seek safe havens elsewhere (Flynn 2002:409–10).

The Thunderbird is a very powerful spirit associated with the Native Algonquin (Cree, Anishinaabe [Ojibwe], Blackfoot, Atsina, etc.) and Haudenasaunee (Iroquois) of northeastern North America (Benn 1989; Betts 2000; Fox 2004; Lenik 2010, 2012). It is a spirit of the sky that causes lightning, thunder, and wind that protects humans from its enemy, the Great Horned Serpent of the underworld. Depictions of complete thunderbirds appear in Precambrian Shield pictograph (rock painting) sites in Manitoba (Steinbring 1998) and incised on miniature (6.9–9 cm in height) vessels recovered from the Horizon site in southern Saskatchewan, the Reston site in southwest Manitoba, and site 32LM104 in southeast North Dakota (Swenson and Gregg 1988; Syms 1979). On these vessels, the head in profile is placed on the lower rim/neck area and the tip of the bifurcated tail (and sometimes outstretched wings) extends below the shoulder and approaches the base (Figure 7.4a). These vessels and a winged effigy pot from Hendrickson III are mortuary vessels associated with the Devils Lake–Sourisford Burial Complex (Schneider 1982; Syms 1979; Toom 2004).

When depicted on full-size, globular vessels from sites in the Midwest and Northeast Plains, motifs identified as the Thunderbird (or Thunderer) are represented only by the tail (Carpiaux 2018; Flynn 2002; Koncur 2018; Toom 2004). The motif appears between the neck and shoulder angles of vessels with straight, vertical, or slightly outflaring rims. Linear elements are executed as wide incised or narrow trailed lines combined with several vertically

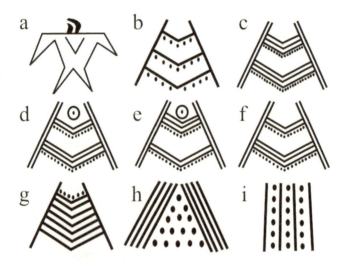

Figure 7.4. Examples of Thunderbird (a) and "tail of the raptor or Thunderbird" motifs (b–i) on pottery: (a) miniature mortuary vessel from Horizon site, (b) Lockport site, (c) McClelland site, (d) Mero, (e) Bartron, (f) Burnside School, (g) Koshkonong Creek, (h) Naze, and (i) Ituhu. (Illustration courtesy of Mary E. Malainey.)

oriented oval or trianguloid stamps or punctates. On Lockport site pottery, each of three chevrons is underlined by vertically oriented oval stamps/shallow punctates and flanked by oblique lines (see Figure 7.4b). The motif occurs directly underneath a decorated lip tab. Both the tab and motif represent quartering (depicted on the vessel four times to represent the cardinal directions).

Similar motifs occur on vessels from the Red Wing area of Minnesota (see Figure 7.4c–f) (Betts 2000; Koncur 2018; Rodell 1997). At the McClelland site (21GD258), the bird tail representing the Thunderer motif consists of nested chevrons underlined by vertically oriented oval punctates flanked by two oblique lines. Variations appear at Bartron (21GD02), Mero (21PI02), Burnside School (21GD159), and Adams (47PI12) (Koncur 2018). Rodell (1997) noted that punctation was rare on Diamond Bluff Complex pottery but used to border a line element on one grit and three shell-tempered rim shoulders. The depiction of sherd B/304 (Rodell 1997:Appendix H) appears to be a fragment of the McClelland site motif (see Figure 7.4c).

Carpiaux (2018:48) reports that the "thunderbird punctates and nested chevrons" motif are common at the Koshkonong Creek Village site (47JE0379) in Wisconsin, which dates to about AD 1000–1100. On shoulder sherd S0036, vertically oriented shallow oval punctates appear above the first of six or seven nested chevrons. The motif is flanked by oblique lines (see Figure 7.4g).

When occurring at Brice Prairie Oneota sites in the La Crosse, Wisconsin, area, vessels with similar motifs are called "Perrot Punctate" and date to AD 1300–1400 (Arzigian et al. 1994; Betts 2000; Boszhardt 1994), a type originally defined by Hall (1962).

Toom (2004) reported that sherds exhibiting stylized raptor or thunderbird motifs appear in 13 of 15 NEPV sites from eastern North Dakota dating AD 1200–1600. On one vessel from the Naze site (32SN246), the motif consists of a triangular cluster of elongated tool impressions flanked by at least four left oblique narrow trailed lines on the right (see Figure 7.4h). On another example from the Ituhu site (32SN110), three vertical columns of elongated tool impressions are separated and flaked by oblique narrow trailed lines (see Figure 7.4i). This is similar to a shoulder variant of Perrot Punctate described by Boszhardt (2004) as having single columns of punctates that border vertical tool trails. There is no mention of chevrons underlined by oval punctates at NEPV sites.

Evidence of Horticulture at Northeastern Plains Village Complex Sites

At the time of European contact, the portion of eastern North Dakota and western Minnesota through which the Red River flows was native tallgrass prairie (Fierer et al. 2013). Early twentieth-century archaeological research focused on the Arvilla burial mounds constructed on Glacial Lake Agassiz beach ridges located 24 to 32 km (15 to 20 miles) on either side of the Red River (Michlovic 1983, 1988; Teller and Clayton 1984); however, Michlovic (1983) noted that Late Precontact habitation sites were concentrated along the Red River itself and its tributaries. Dakota Sioux and "Chippewa" inhabitants of the woodlands of northern Minnesota used the area (Michlovic 1983; Toom 2004). Highly mobile inhabitants of eastern North Dakota played an important role in the movement of Knife River flint and obsidian to the Midwest (Michlovic 1983). Boszhardt (1998) suggested prearranged exchange existed between Besant/Sonota groups and Hopewell traders. The Cheyenne were the former inhabitants of Biesterfeldt, a postcontact Coalescent fortified horticultural village dating to about AD 1700 (Toom 2004; Wood 1971). The period from about AD 1200 to 1400 is most relevant to this discussion. Henning and Toom (2003) and Toom (2004) suggest that the area was occupied by the ancestors of the Hidatsa, whose archaeological remains represent the NEPV complex at that time.

Schneider (2002) argued that occurrences of scapula hoes, maize, and cache pits at sites in eastern North Dakota were evidence of maize horticulture. Toom (2004) included most of these sites in the NEPV complex. According to Toom (2004:283), NEPV groups were semisedentary "villagers without villages" who appeared in eastern North Dakota around AD 1200. Most NEPV sites were open campsites representing warm-weather occupations along the James River and around Devils Lake (Toom 2004). Gregg (1994) indicated bison was the mainstay of the NEPV complex diet, and there was no evidence the groups depended on horticultural surpluses for subsistence. Gregg (1994), Schneider (2002), and Toom (2004) have all suggested the presence of cultigens, including maize kernels, cupules, and and/or cobs fragments, and indicated that NEPV groups may have practiced some gardening for food.

While the occurrence of maize is widespread, evidence for gardening is tenuous, and the possibility that the cultigens they consumed were obtained by trade must be considered. The significance of maize at the Naze site (32SN246), a Middle NEPV site located along the James River, is disputed (Benz 1987; Gregg 1987; Schneider 2002; Toom 2004). While Schneider (2002) considered the occurrence of maize and possibly squash and beans as evidence of horticulture, Benz (1987) suggested that the near absence of cob fragments at Naze and other upper James River sites, such as Hendrickson III, indicate that maize may have been brought in from outside the valley. Gregg (1987:448) acknowledged that the degree of reliance on maize has not been determined; unless garden products made up at least half of all food resources, "a Late Plains Woodland classification might be more appropriate." Cache pits occur at only three of the 12 eastern North Dakota sites with maize: Naze, Hendrickson III (32SN403), and Shea (32CS101) (Schneider 2002). Schneider (2002) reported the occurrence of scapula hoes at three sites in southeast North Dakota: Shea, Hendrickson III, and Larson (32SN106). These identifications are discussed later in this chapter. There was no evidence of gardening at the NEPV sites near Devils Lake (Toom 2004).

Henning and Toom (2003) and Toom (2004) suggest that NEPV complex groups may be connected to the former inhabitants of Cambria sites in southwestern Minnesota. Henning and Toom (2003) argue that Cambria sites, occupied from AD 950 to 1300, were distinct from Initial Middle Missouri Great Oasis, Mill Creek, and Over complex sites in that evidence of Cambria-Mississippian interaction is limited or virtually absent. Cambria complex groups are believed to have moved northwest from the upper Minnesota River into the Red River and upper James River drainages ca. AD 1200 and formed the NEPV complex (Henning and Toom 2003; Toom 2004). Around AD 1400, NEPV groups moved west and settled around the confluence of the Knife and Missouri Rivers in west-central North Dakota where they adopted a sedentary, horticultural way of life known archaeologically as the Scattered Village complex. Their descendants are known historically as the Hidatsa (Henning and Toom 2003; Toom 2004).

EVIDENCE OF HORTICULTURE IN THE UPPER MISSISSIPPI VALLEY

Pre-European vegetation of the Upper Mississippi Valley was a prairie-forest ecotone consisting of prairie, oak savanna, and patches of hardwood and softwood forests, which supported a diverse array of floral and faunal resources from terrestrial and aquatic environments (Rodell 1997; Theler and Boszhardt 2000). Theler and Boszhardt (2000) suggest a gradual transition from a Late Woodland hunting and gathering economy to maize horticulture. There is no consensus with respect to mechanisms of change; however, groups became more sedentary and less reliant on wild resources over time (Schroeder 2003; Theler and Boszhardt 2000). The importance of native domesticates, such as marsh elder, goosefoot, and knotweed, decreased while production of maize, squash, and gourds intensified (Schroeder 2003). Mississippian influence increased with the establishment of outposts in a buffer zone between different Late Woodland Effigy mound cultures, first at the Fisher Mounds

Site Complex then shortly after at Trempealeau (Boszhardt 2004; Boszhardt and Goetz 2000; Pauketat et al. 2015, 2017). While the motivation for the founding of these northern settlements 920 river kilometers north of Cahokia (Green and Rodell 1994) and others at Aztalan in southeast Wisconsin and the Spoon River area in northwest Illinois is debatable, Pauketat and colleagues (2015) describe their occupants as missionaries or pilgrims. The cluster of related Mississippian sites in the Trempealeau locality is associated with the early Lohmann phase (AD 1000–1050) (Boszhardt 2004; Green and Rodell 1994). The Little Bluff Platform Mound Complex (47TR32), consisting of a large platform mound surrounded by smaller mounds or terraces connected by ramps or causeways, may have been built by Cahokians (Green and Rodell 1994; Pauketat et al. 2015, 2017). Neither of the Mississippian colonies were fortified with palisades, and there is no evidence of conflict. There is little archaeological evidence of interaction with Effigy Mound groups.

Around AD 1050–1100, evidence of Mississippian interaction moved to new or previously established communities on the north and south edges of effigy mound distributions (Boszhardt and Stoltman 2016; Green and Rodell 1994; Theler and Boszhardt 2006). Because of its relative proximity to Manitoba, the Red Wing occupation, located about 120 km upriver (north) of Trempealeau, is more relevant to this investigation. Ramey Incised pottery and short-nosed god masquette were found at Red Wing, which is associated with the Late Woodland Lewis phase (Boszhardt and Stoltman 2016; Green and Rodell 1994; Rodell 1997). Substantial farming villages, mound building, and American Bottom–derived symbolism appear (Rodell 1997). The Diamond Bluff site complex, located on a terrace in the Mississippi River valley in the Red Wing–Pepin locality, includes two village sites, about 500 earthen mounds, and smaller occupations covering 89 hectares (Rodell 1997). In his review of previous excavations, Rodell (1997) reports the recovery of at least 38 bison scapula hoes from the Bryan site assemblage with others found at 47PI2, Bartron, and Silvernale (21GD03). The majority of the 57 excavated pit features from 47PI2 are believed to have been used for storage. The deepest were cylindrical, hourglass, and bell-shaped pits that extended to a maximum depth of 99 cm dbs.

The Iva site may provide insights into cultural interactions between Late Woodland Lewis groups and Middle Mississippians during the Ramey horizon, ca. AD 1100–1150 (Boszhardt 2004; Boszhardt and Stoltman 2016). Boszhardt and Stoltman (2016) interpret the Late Woodland–Middle Mississippian component of the site, located almost 150 km south of Red Wing, as evidence of peaceful, direct interaction that included a feasting event. Locally manufactured Late Woodland vessels co-occur with imported Middle Mississippian vessels, and hybrids of the two traditions support assertions by Pauketat and Emerson (1991) that adoption of the Middle Mississippian worldview through ritual ceremonies may have included the exchange of pottery. It also provides evidence that Mississippian "missionaries" conducted outreach activities in areas far from their settlements. Boszhardt and Stoltman (2016:119) suggest that the Late Woodland peoples' acceptance of some ideological concepts, materials, and ritual ceremonies associated with the Middle Mississippian worldview resulted in the population becoming "creolized." Mississippian influence is less evident at communities known archaeologically as Oneota at La Crosse, which were established ca. AD 1300 when the Red Wing area was abandoned (Arzigian et al. 1994; Boszhardt 1994; Rodell 1997; Theler and Boszhardt 2000).

Scapula Hoe Morphology

Fundamental differences in bison scapula hoe design may be related to the cultural connections of the Manitoba farmers. Bison scapula hoes were used in ground-breaking and spring maize-planting ceremonies (Holland 1998; Weltfish 1965). Scapula hoes were retained and used for ceremonial purposes by the Hidatsa and Arikara after they had been replaced by metal hoes for agricultural use (Smith 1972).

The first bison scapula hoe found at the Olson site (DgMg-167) is the best-preserved and is 46.6 cm long (see Figure 7.3). Modifications include careful removal of the anterior and part of the posterior borders. Striations parallel to the base of the spine indicate it was scored then snapped off. A circular hole measuring about two centimeters in diameter occurs in the blade, about 20 cm from the glenoid cavity. The edges of the hole are polished, probably by a rope used to anchor the hoe blade to a handle. The medial border, which forms the bit or working edge of the hoe, is beveled and striations are present (Malainey 2019, 2020a–b, 2021a–e; Malainey and Olson 2018). The second bison scapula hoe is similar in form.

Hoes recovered from the Olson and Lockport sites are identical. Roberts (1991) noted that ten of the Lockport hoes are complete or nearly complete, and all have the dorsal spine removed. Nine of the 10 hoes have a distinctive mid-body perforation 14.5 to 20.0 cm from the edge of the glenoid. None of the anterior or posterior borders are side-notched. Reports of scapula hoes with perforated blades come from the Zimmerman site in Illinois and the Greismer site in Indiana (Brown 1961; Faulkner 1970). All eight bison scapula hoes from the historic period Zimmerman site had "central perforations with worn edges that presumably were the means for hafting" (Brown 1961:57). Faulkner (1970:150) identified precontact and early postcontact elk and bison scapula hoes found at Upper Mississippian sites in the Prairie Peninsula as digging implements, and the hole punched through the thin blade was "considered an element for hafting." Three elk scapula hoes, each with a circular hole in the blade, were recently found near Bemidji, Minnesota, by Grant Goltz (Kevin Brownlee, personal communication, 2021).

Circumstantial evidence of horticulture has been reported at other sites in Manitoba (Nicholson 1990, 1991, 1994; Schneider 2002). Nicholson (1990) reported a "bifurcated scapula hoe" from the Lovstrom site (DjLx-1). It was originally reconstructed in a "V" or forked configuration from fragments recovered from different 1 × 1 m excavation units in Block E (Nicholson 1990). As shown in Figure 7.5, it was later modified and now resembles the possible digging tool from the Larson site (32SN106) described by Gregg and colleagues (1987). The Lovstrom site scapula lacks evidence of wear (i.e., striations, polish) that one would expect from use as a digging tool. The asymmetrical groundstone tools from Lowton and Jonas sites were hafted so that the working edge was perpendicular to the shaft, but the coarse bit wear suggest that they were adzes, not stone hoes. The only Manitoba sites with bona fide bison scapula hoes are Lockport and Olson.

Scapula hoes typical of the La Crosse area Oneota after AD 1300 are somewhat different (Arzigian et al. 1994; Theler 2021). Common features include use of bison and elk bone and removal of the scapular spine and posterior ridge of the blade. The spine was removed by scoring along the base then snapping it off (Theler 2021), which is similar to the Manitoba hoes, but hoe

Figure 7.5. Reconstructed bison scapula from the Lowton site. (Photograph courtesy of Mary E. Malainey.)

blades are not perforated. A shallow notch centrally located on the costal margin of the glenoid cavity may be a function of the method of hafting used in the La Crosse area (Arzigian et al. 1994; Theler 2021). Theler (2021) suggests that the channel represents wear that developed from organic material, such as wood, used to steady the hoe when the bindings around the neck loosened. Theler (2021) reports approximate equal numbers of hoes were made from the scapula of males and females. Bison scapula from bulls are favored on the plains (Wilson 1987). Arzigian and colleagues (1994) indicate that the role of bison as an Oneota food source at the Gundersen site was unclear because unmodified bison bones are scarce, but bison scapula hoes are the most common bone tool.

The NPV complex sites occupied about the same time as Lockport generally lack intact, formal scapula hoes. Michlovic and Schneider (1993) reported three bison scapula hoe fragments at the Shea site (32CS101), a fortified village site on the Maple River, a tributary of the Sheyenne River (Michlovic and Schneider 1993). The average calibrated age on six samples was AD 1448, with a range between AD 1400 and 1642. One bison scapula hoe was reported at the Hendrickson III site, but no description or image of it was provided (Schneider 1982, 2002). Hendrickson III is a small, fortified earth-lodge village with an average corrected date of AD 1401 ± 55 and ranges between AD 1365 and 1525 (Schneider 1982). A possible bison scapula digging tool was found at Larson (32SN106), located along the James River about 5 km from Hendrickson III (Gregg et al. 1987; Schneider 2002). Gregg and colleagues (1987) refit and glued four fragments of a large mammal (probably bison) scapula from an excavation unit. A chopping tool was used to remove the dorsal spine, acromion process, glenoid cavity, and neck. The chop marks on the blade were smoothed and rounded (Gregg et al. 1987). Gregg and colleagues (1987) suggested the occurrence of light striations and polish toward the distal end indicated the scapula was a hoe or digging tool. No radiocarbon date was provided, but it was recovered from a Plains Village cultural layer (Gregg et al. 1987). Toom (2004) did not include Larson (32SN106) in his definition of the NEPV complex, but both Shea and Hendrickson III are identified as Middle period NPV complex sites.

Haury (1994) and Gregg (1994) provided contradictory reports about Horner-Kane (32RY77). Haury (1994) identified two fragments of large mammal scapulae from the site as manufacturing debris; however, Gregg (1994) suggested that Horner-Kane occupants had scapula digging tools similar to those used for gardening. No cultigens (maize, squash, sunflower, or beans) were recovered, but several different wild seeds and berries were used as food.

The primary purpose of the site appeared to be bison processing, including bone grease rendering (Gregg 1994). Schneider (2002) did not include Horner-Kane in his review of sites with evidence of horticulture. Toom (2004) considers it both an Early and a Late period NEPV site.

Toom (2004) argues that after AD 1400, NEPV complex groups abandoned sites in eastern North Dakota and moved to the confluence of the Knife and Missouri Rivers in the west central part of the state. Toom (2004) suggests that these Knife River archaeological sites represent the Scattered Village complex and tentatively associated them with the Hidatsa. The Scattered Village site (32M031) at the confluence of the Heart and Missouri Rivers is believed to have been occupied by the Hidatsa (Ahler 2002). Scapula hoes recovered from horticultural sites in the region are rarely perforated, and less finesse was used to remove the spine and ridge. None of the 177 scapula hoes and fragments from the Scattered Village site (32M031) described by Ahler and Falk (2002) had perforated blades; instead, notches were cut in either lateral edge of the blade to secure a cord or binding. Spine removal process was quite different. The presence of elongated gouges indicated a narrow-bitted stone punch hafted like a pickaxe was used "to fracture off the spine of the scapula and flatten the scar where the spine was removed" (Ahler and Falk 2002:13.9). Nine of the scapula hoes bore evidence that a metal tool was used to chop away bone mass (Ahler and Falk 2002). Perforated blades were uncommon on bone hoes examined by Griffitts (2006) from Bendish (32M02), Cross Ranch (320L14), Tony Glas (32EM3), Larson (32BL9), and Deapolis (32ME5). Holes occurred in two of the 35 scapula tools. Two holes were punched through the blade of one from Bendish, and one Tony Glas site scapula had a large, irregular oval hole between the ridges of the blade, but Griffitts (2006) made no mention of wear.

No holes typically occur in the blades of bison scapula hoes found at other sites along the Missouri River drainage from North Dakota south into Nebraska, Kansas, and Oklahoma. Circular scars, deep grooves, and holes in the neck of some hoes may relate to hafting (Bell 1980; Brown 1966; Holland 1998). Scapulae with deep notches or large perforations in the blade are found elsewhere, but they appear to have been used for processing pliable material, such as bark and hide, rather than as hoes (Bell 1971; Hofman 1980).

While the use of bison or elk scapula hoes was ubiquitous, regional variations in morphology shows more than one solution was reached with respect to the problem hoe design. Once an adequate tool was constructed, however, a single method of blade modification and hafting was widely adopted by the community and used for generations. Similarities in Lockport and Olson site hoes indicate that their design was a unique "Made in Manitoba" solution. Common use of the score and snap method of spine removal and occurrence of perforated hoe blades at the Zimmerman and Greismer sites suggests possible connections to groups in the Upper Mississippi Valley and Prairie Peninsula. Multiple formal bison scapula hoes have been recovered from the Manitoba sites, yet they are virtually absent from NEPV sites contemporaneous with Lockport.

DISCUSSION

The adoption of maize horticulture involved more than deciding to drop kernels into a hole in the ground. Maize was a cultural superfood associated with increased sedentism, preparation of fields, seeding, tending, harvesting, processing, crop storage, cuisine modification, and ritual obligations. The people who established unfortified outposts along the Upper Mississippi River valley at the Fisher Mounds and Trempealeau ca. AD 1000–1050 did so with intent. These pilgrims, missionaries, or perhaps ambassadors conveyed the package of Mississippian lifeways by demonstrating both the opportunities and the ritual responsibilities associated with maize cultivation. Perhaps they anticipated that the significance of activities, such as the construction of carefully situated platform mounds, would resonate with Late Woodland Effigy Mound builders. They may have believed that maize cultivation was more compatible with the lifeways of hunter-gatherers who constructed earthworks. The establishment of outposts in a buffer zone between different mound builder groups afforded a period of observability. Neighboring hunter-gatherers could gauge the relative advantages of food production and commensurate benefits of a reliable dietary source of cultigens, then weigh them against the complexity of the process. Strong connections with Cahokia were maintained by those who moved north and established villages in the Red Wing–Pepin locality ca. AD 1050–1100. This suggests that migrants from the American Bottom or knowledgeable converts to farming were present during the adoption process. Dozens of bison scapula hoes and numerous storage pits occur at maize farming sites. "Tail of the Thunderbird" or "Thunderer" motifs on pottery from the area may represent a blend of Algonkian and Mississippian ritual symbolism. Recoveries from the Iva site suggest the proselytization of regional Late Woodland groups continued throughout the Ramey horizon ca. AD 1100–1150. It is probable that connections were made with hunter-gatherers inhabiting the areas to the north during their 200-year residency of Red Wing–Pepin area as well.

The Lockport area was rich in wild plant and animal resources, yet the hunter-gatherers decided that the relative advantage of a reliable source of cultigens was enough to justify a major modification to their food procurement strategies and cuisine. The introduction of sophisticated horticulture into Manitoba is best explained by direct contact with villagers from the Red Wing area, or "creolized" Late Woodland people, using Boszhardt and Stoltman's (2016) term. These people may have been the descendants of hunting and gathering groups who initially converted to maize horticulture after Mississippian outposts were established in the Upper Valley. Boszhardt and Stoltman (2016) suggest that both the Red Wing and Apple River mound and village clusters, located at the north and south ends of the Driftless Area, respectively, were populated by people from multiple regions. Rodell (2003) argued that the Red Wing–Pepin locality served as a hub of Woodland social interests before the emergence of Oneota culture and outlined evidence of contact with groups to the west. It is possible that there was contact with groups to the north as well. Travel to the Red Wing area would have provided Manitoba hunter-gatherers the opportunity to observe diverse Late Woodland groups in the process of transitioning to horticulture. Travel to Manitoba would have provided the emerging horticulturalists the opportunity to assess the likelihood for successful crop production and openness of the hunter-gatherers to adopting maize cultivation. Migrants from the Red Wing area or others familiar with the practical and spiritual aspects of the production and use of this cultural superfood probably resided at the Lockport site during the introduction and initial adoption period, and possibly much longer.

In this scenario, contact would have occurred in the AD 1200s. These people were not Oneota but may have been related to, or neighbors of, the groups who later moved from the Red Wing area and established Oneota villages at La Crosse. Cultural contact before AD 1300 accounts for the differences in scapula hoe morphology observed between Manitoba and La Crosse Oneota site. The introduction of maize cultivation to Lockport predates the development of the La Crosse–style scapula hoe. Recoveries from the Lockport site include multiple bison scapula hoes, several storage pits, charred maize, and grinding stones dating from AD 1250–1450. Lockport farmers continued to take advantage of the broad spectrum of terrestrial and aquatic resources available at this aspen parkland location along the Red River. This suggests that maize cultivation was introduced by experienced horticulturalists who also had a parkland adaptation. Lockport pottery bearing chevron and punctate "tail of the raptor or Thunderbird" motifs and burials at previously constructed mounds demonstrates continuity of ritual ceremonialism from the Red Wing–Pepin area. There is evidence that the inhabitants of Lockport conveyed the spiritual aspects of maize to boreal hunter-gatherers in the region. The Rocky Cree word for maize is *manomin*, which means "god berry" (Kevin Brownlee, personal communication, 2011). Rodell (2003) suggested that ceremonies involving Ramey symbolism provided structure to the relationship between Late Woodland groups of the Red Wing–Pepin area and the American Bottom. Perhaps shared raptor/Thunderbird symbolism enabled the creation of fictive kinship relationships between groups in Manitoba and the Upper Mississippi in a similar manner.

At the time of horticultural occupation at Lockport, the northern edge of the tallgrass prairie was a short distance to the south. Horticulturalists may have followed the parkland-tallgrass prairie border northwest into Manitoba. Recent finds of elk scapula hoes with perforated blades near Bemidji, Minnesota, appear to provide support for this entry route. First Nations groups in Manitoba have an oral tradition of a "Peace Meeting" at the Forks of the Red and Assiniboine Rivers that attracted 10,000 people from as far away as Wisconsin. Estimates regarding the timing of the meeting vary from 500 to 700 years ago (Quaternary Consultants 1999; Sinclair 2019). In 2019, an exhibit opened at the Manitoba Museum identifying AD 1285 as the date of the "Peace Meeting." Fragments of bison scapula with holes in the blade have been recovered from the Forks. Participation in the "Peace Meeting" provides an explanation as to what initially drew Upper Mississippi horticulturalists to Manitoba. It is unknown how long the cessation of hostilities endured. Ebell (1988) argued that at the time of European contact, the Forks of the Red and Assiniboine Rivers represented an area of contested resources that acted as a buffer zone between competing groups. The risk of attack was high, so long-term settlements were not established; only short-term fishing, hunting, or foraging stops were possible (Ebell 1988). Bison scapula hoes from the Olson site are identical to those at Lockport, and the Olson horticultural occupation starts in the late 1400s-early 1500s, just after the Lockport site was abandoned. As with the Lockport/Fidler Mounds area, the southwest corner of Manitoba has burial mounds and other earthworks initially constructed about 2,000 years ago, then used repeatedly by later groups. Some of the Indigenous farmers of Manitoba may have returned to the Midwest, as the Zimmerman site bison scapula hoes with perforated blades postdate the Lockport occupation.

If the introduction of maize horticulture into Manitoba was due to the northward movement of NEPV complex people along the Red River; equally strong evidence of its cultivation should exist in North Dakota and predate the Lockport occupation. It does not. Cache pits were reported at only three of twelve NEPV complex sites with cultigens in North Dakota. There is no evidence of maize gardening at NEPV sites near Devils Lake, which is within the Red River drainage basin. Scapula hoes along James River sites reported by Schneider (2002) include an undated possible digging tool and hoes associated with fortified (earth lodge) villages that coincide with the latter phase of, or postdate, the Lockport occupation. Motifs identified as tail of the raptor or Thunderbird on NEPV pottery differ from those on Red Wing and Lockport vessels in that they do not include chevrons underlined by oval punctates. Toom (2004:283) called NEPV groups "villagers without villages," but before and during the occupation of the Lockport site, most NEPV people were gardeners without hoes as well.

When cast in a more prudent light, evidence shows eastern North Dakota NEPV complex groups may have been hunter-gatherers who traded bison products for maize from AD 1200 to 1400. As Michlovic (1983) indicated, Late Precontact inhabitants of the area often served as traders. Bison was the mainstay of their diet, so NEPV groups were ideally suited for procuring bison meat and scapulae, which could be exchanged for cultigens produced by horticulturalists. Trading bison products for maize was a regular feature of groups on the Northern Plains. During the late summer/early autumn, Assiniboine hunted on their way to the Mandan villages where they traded bison meat for corn. Ray (1974) considered the trip to be a usual part of their seasonal round. Alexander Henry the Younger (1988:229) noted that groups "more given to agriculture," such as the Mandan, never abandon their villages. It would have been equally advantageous for Upper Mississippi River horticultural villagers to stay close to storage pits full of the annual harvest and trade their cultigens for bison meat, scapulae, and other products. Hollinger and Falk (1996 cited in Betts 2000) previously suggested that Oneota groups in the Midwest obtained scapulae by trade. If acquired in substantial quantities, it may have been beneficial for hunter-gatherers to store their maize, beans, and squash in cache pits. The tallgrass prairie was known for supporting bison herds. It was not the best land for crop production. Hurt (1974) indicated that the Santee Dakota abandoned horticulture when they moved from the parklands and forests of Minnesota to the plains because the fertile land was occupied by the Mandan and Arikara.

Toom (2004) suggests that after AD 1400, NEPV complex groups moved to west-central North Dakota, and their sites represent the Scattered Village complex. There is general agreement between Toom (2004) and Ahler (2002) that the Scattered Village complex is associated with the Hidatsa. Ahler (2002) argues the Hidatsa resided at the Scattered Village site at the confluence of the Heart and Missouri Rivers before moving to the mouth of the Knife River.

Ahler (2002:1.17) provided an extensive review of traditional Mandan and Hidatsa information in the report on excavations at the site and remarked, "Most significant for our study of the archaeological record is the fact that all sources agree that the Hidatsa-proper arrived on the Missouri River with little knowledge or lengthy practice of corn/bean/squash horticulture." If NEPV groups were Scattered Village complex Hidatsa, they could not have introduced maize farming into Manitoba because they did not practice it.

FURTHER RESEARCH

Continued research in the Pierson WMA will provide a better understanding of the factors that lead to the voluntary adoption of maize cultivation and resulting shift in the cuisine of Manitoba hunter-gatherers, the practice and evolution of precontact Indigenous farming in Manitoba, and the relationship between the horticulturalists and earlier mound-building groups. Archaeobotanical analyses of soil cores from the Olson site mixed-grass prairie will assist with the identification of site use area and field systems. Several radiometric dates on the DgMg-40c residential debris, bison bone upright, Olson site bison, and Bemidji elk scapula hoes will better establish the Pierson WMA site chronology and the movement of Lockport farmers. No material previously recovered from burial contexts will be analyzed without permission from First Nation communities. No excavations of burial mounds will be undertaken.

While formal recognition of precontact Indigenous farming in Manitoba was delayed, its appearance at Lockport triggered reports of horticulture at several sites across the northeastern Plains. Many of these identifications appear to be the product of overexuberance rather than judicious interpretation of the archaeological record. Maize was a desirable commodity, and there are numerous accounts of hunter-gatherers arriving at horticultural villages to exchange goods, primarily bison meat, for it. Brink and Dawe (1989) even suggested intensive use of Head-Smashing-In bison jump in Alberta may be connected to the production of a surplus for trade with Middle Missouri villagers. Because the producers of maize often traded it to hunter-gatherers, its mere presence cannot be used as evidence of cultivation; it only indicates use of the cultigen. Zarillo and Kooyman (2006) used starch grain residue analysis to demonstrate the presence of maize on grinding tools from site EgPn-612, located in modern Calgary, Alberta. They (2006) argue that this was evidence of long-distance maize trading, not cultivation. The work of Zarillo and Kooyman (2006) provides an example of a measured and appropriate interpretation based on available archaeological evidence.

The occurrence of digging tools (or possible digging tools) must also be interpreted with care. In 1772, Matthew Cocking (1908) observed that tobacco was grown by hunter-gatherer groups in what is now western Saskatchewan. A modified bison scapula from the Lake Midden site (EfNg-1) could have been used for planting a patch of tobacco. The tool consists of the glenoid cavity, and the distal end of the neck is polished (Walde 1994). The blade is completely absent, and it appears to have been handheld.

Based on archaeological evidence and ethnographic accounts, it is possible to identify common traits that could serve as concrete evidence of maize cultivation. Groups who actually grew maize used formal hoes consisting of modified bison (or elk) scapula blades that were hafted onto wooden shafts and large-capacity (e.g., 1 × 1 × 1 m) crop storage pits. Previous identifications of horticulture based on the occurrence of maize or one possible digging tool need to be reconsidered. The presence of multiple, formal bison scapula hoes and crop storage pits represents additional lines of evidence that strengthen the argument. The accurate interpretations of precontact Indigenous cuisine and food patterns are predicated on the presentation of archaeological evidence in a prudent light.

Chapter 8

Nixtamalization and Cahokian Cuisine

ALLEEN BETZENHAUSER

Indigenous peoples throughout the late precontact Eastern Woodlands relied on maize to varying degrees, with corn making up significant portions of some diets (see other chapters in this volume; Ambrose et al. 2003; Cook and Price 2015; Fritz 2019; Hedman 2006; Hedman et al. 2002; Hedman et al. 2022; Lynott et al. 1986; Reber 2006; Schurr and Redmond 1991; Shuler et al. 2012). The fact that Late Woodland and Mississippian peoples, particularly those living in the American Bottom region of southwestern Illinois, generally did not suffer from severe malnutrition (Emerson et al. 2020; Hedman 2006) might indicate that they nixtamalized corn, which means that they soaked and cooked dried kernels in an alkaline solution, a process that improves the nutritional quality of the grain (Bressani et al. 1958; Bressani and Scrimshaw 1958; Briggs 2015, 2018; Katz et al. 1974; Palacios-Rojas et al. 2020).

Recent research consisting of archaeometric analyses, experimental studies, and contextual analyses of pottery and limestone from Terminal Late Woodland ([TLW] AD 900–1050) and Mississippian (AD 1050–1400) features excavated at the East St. Louis site (11S706) for an Illinois Department of Transportation project (see Schaefer, Simon, and King, chapter 9, this volume; see Emerson et al. 2018 for an overview) yielded intriguing new data that indicate that nixtamalization was practiced in the American Bottom as Cahokia grew to prominence (Betzenhauser 2018a, 2021; Betzenhauser and Evans 2022; Betzenhauser et al. 2017a, 2017b). In this chapter, I examine how processing corn in this way relates to culinary and technological choices, the development of new foodways and traditions, and efforts to create and maintain community identities.

CULINARY ALCHEMY

Nixtamalization is a culinary practice originally developed in Mesoamerica that was widely used for processing dried corn kernels throughout Central and North America for thousands of years, continuing through today (Blake 2015; Briggs 2015, 2018; Cheetham 2010; Katz et al. 1974; Myers 2006). A common method of preparation begins with shelling completely dried and fully matured corn, then boiling the kernels for a short time before soaking overnight in an alkaline solution made from hardwood ash (i.e., lye) or slaked lime made from limestone or shells (Blake 2015; Briggs 2015; Wacher 2003; Cheetham 2010; Katz et al. 1974; Khan et al. 1982; Palacios-Rojas et al. 2020; Tozzer 1910). After boiling and soaking, the kernels are rinsed to remove the caustic solution and loose hulls (Bressani and Scrimshaw 1958; Cheetham 2010; Gaviria 2021; Gomez et al. 1989; Katz et al. 1974; Myers 2006; Swanton 1946). Alternative preparations consist of grinding the dried kernels before boiling and soaking in the alkaline solution, soaking first and then boiling, or boiling for several hours without soaking (Briggs 2015; Myers 2006).

The effects of nixtamalization are magical, and some have described the process as alchemy (Andrés Garza, quoted in Ralat 2020). The kernels become enlarged and the hulls, or pericarp, are loosened, making them easier to remove and the kernels easier to grind (Cheetam 2010; Gomez et al. 1992; Katz et al. 1974; Maler 1901; Myers 2006; Tozzer 1907). If a carbonate is used to make the solution, some of it is absorbed by the kernels, providing supplemental calcium (Bressani and Scrimshaw 1958; Gaviria et al. 2017; Katz et al. 1974; Orchardson 2021). It causes partial gelatinization of starches, which allows for dough to form without gluten or the addition of binding agents (Bressani et al. 1958; Gomez et al. 1989, 1992; Khan et al. 1982; Orchardson 2021; Pflugfelder). The caustic solution also kills bacteria and mold that may have developed on the kernels during drying or storage (Katz et al. 1974; Moreno et al. 2006; Orchardson 2021). Nutrients are released or made more digestible, providing for more complete nutrition (Bressani et al. 1958; Bressani and Scrimshaw 1958; Katz et al. 1974). The color, texture, and flavor of the kernels are also altered (Briggs 2018; Cushing 1920; Gaviria 2021; Gaviria et al. 2017; Gomez et al. 1989; Khan et al. 1982; Stevenson 1909).

Nixtamalized corn can be baked, boiled, steamed, or fried and used to create a near infinite number of dishes, ranging from soups and stews to breads, beverages, and trail foods. For example, hominy is nixtamalized corn kernels left whole or cracked, while banaha is a bread the Choctaw and Chickasaw prepare by boiling ground nixtamalized corn wrapped in corn husks (see Adair

1775; Aliseda 2021; Blake 2015; Briggs 2015; Choctaw Nation Historic Preservation Department 2010; Fritz 2019; Hariot 1590; Harrington 1908; Landa 1937; Lunsford 2021; Oldmixon 1708; Parker 1910; Sahagún 1961; Spencer and Sekaquaptewa 1995; Wright 1958). Recipes may be further modified or enhanced with the addition of beans, fats, root vegetables, meats, greens, or spices. The nixtamalized kernels can be used to create a wide variety of dishes immediately or dried and stored for later use. With further processing through wet grinding, nixtamalized corn becomes a dough (i.e., masa) that can be used to make tamales and tortillas (Bressani and Scrimshaw 1958; Khan et al. 1982). Like the kernels, this dough can also be dried and stored for later use.

Nixtamalization has been, and in many cases still is, practiced by Indigenous people throughout Mesoamerica, the present-day southwestern United States, the Eastern Woodlands, Plains, and Great Lakes (Blake 2015; Briggs 2015; Myers 2006; Cheetham 2010). Archaeological and iconographic evidence suggests that the process developed in Mesoamerica more than 3,500 years ago (Blake 2015; Tate 2012). Cross-cultural studies indicate that groups who relied on corn for a significant portion of their diet nixtamalized it, but not all groups who consumed moderate amounts of corn did (Katz et al. 1974). If large amounts of nonnixtamalized corn are consumed, severe malnutrition will occur and can result in death (Katz et al. 1974; Wacher 2003). Although many different populations processed their corn in alkaline solutions, they did not all do it in the same way. In most areas documented historically, hardwood ash was used, even in areas where high calcium limestone and shell were readily available (Briggs 2015; Myers 2006).

With a few notable exceptions (see Briggs 2015, 2016, 2018; Cheetham 2010; Seligson et al. 2017a, b), discussions of nixtamalization tend to focus on how it is accomplished and the nutritional benefits rather than the production of the alkaline solutions required to complete the process. To create an alkaline solution using hardwood ash, one could simply add ashes to the water and corn kernels, or the ashes could be steeped in water first, thereby resulting in lye (Briggs 2015). Making a calcium-based alkaline solution is more complicated. First, the shell or limestone must be fired to temperatures high enough to drive off carbon dioxide (approximately 800°C), thereby converting it to quicklime (Beach et al. 2000; Oates 1998; Seligson et al. 2019). Quicklime is very caustic and volatile due its ability to absorb atmospheric water and can cause severe irritation or burning if it comes into contact with skin. If water is poured over the fired shell or limestone, it causes a chemical reaction that converts the quicklime to slaked lime and quickly releases heat resulting in temperatures exceeding 100°C (Beach et al. 2000; Oates 1998). During this process, the limestone or shell swells and disintegrates into an alkaline powder, while the water becomes a highly alkaline solution known as nejayote (Beach et al. 2000; Oates 1998; Seligson et al. 2017a). Slaked lime in liquid or powdered form is caustic but more stable than quicklime and can be stored safely. The slaked lime water can be stored as a liquid in an airtight container while the slaked lime may be dried and stored as a powder or formed into molds like historically documented salt or sugar loaves, thereby facilitating transport to more distant locales (Cheetham 2010:346). Blocks of slaked lime can also be stored underground to extend the alkaline strength (Cheetham 2010:346; Vogt 1969).

NIXTAMALIZATION IN THE AMERICAN BOTTOM

There is strong archaeological and isotopic evidence for maize agriculture and consumption during the TLW (also known as Emergent Mississippian) (AD 900–1050), and Mississippian periods (AD 1050–1400) in the American Bottom region of southwestern Illinois (Ambrose et al. 2003; Emerson et al. 2020; Hedman 2006; Hedman, Hargrave, et al. 2002; Hedman, Emerson, et al. 2022; Fritz 2019; Reber 2006; Simon et al. 2021; Witt et al. 2021), but currently the only evidence we have for nixtamalization is indirect (Benchley 2003; Betzenhauser 2021; Betzenhauser and Evans 2021). Kernel, cupule, and cob macroremains from archaeological contexts first appear in high density and ubiquity in the American Bottom during the TLW period, suggesting a widespread use of maize in addition to traditional native cultigens and other food resources (Fritz 2019; Mueller and Fritz 2016; Simon et al. 2021). Maize use continues and, in some segments of the population, becomes the primary food source during the subsequent Mississippian period; however, severe malnutrition, including among those whose diets were strongly composed of maize, was rare, suggesting that they practiced nixtamalization (Emerson et al. 2021; Fritz 2019; Hedman et al. 2022).

Innovative pottery forms also appear at the same time as maize macroremains during the TLW (Betzenhauser 2018a; Betzenhauser et al. 2018; Hedman et al. 2022; Kelly et al. 1984; Pauketat 2018). These include large pans that could have been used to bake corn bread and the enigmatic stumpware, a crudely fashioned ceramic utensil (Betzenhauser 2018a; Hedman et al. 2022; Kelly 1980; Kelly et al. 1984). Stumpware is cone-shaped, thick-walled, low-fired earthenware with projections at the base (Figure 8.1). The first published description of stumpware was provided by P. F. Titterington (1938a, b) based on examples found at Cahokia Mounds. Titterington likened their appearance

NIXTAMALIZATION AND CAHOKIAN CUISINE 183

to tree stumps, hence the name. They may be tempered with grit, grog, shell, limestone, or any combination of these various tempers, and exterior surfaces are either cordmarked or plain/smooth.

Most examples have a flat base with two projections and a continuous cone-shaped cavity extending vertically from the rim to the base, but there is considerable variation in form with some exhibiting an additional basal projection, some lacking a basal orifice, and some having a continuous cavity

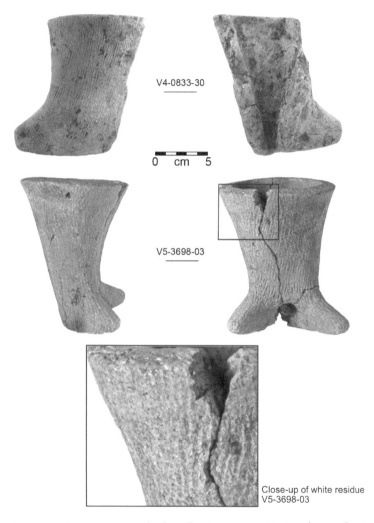

Figure 8.1. Stumpware examples from the East St. Louis Precinct (11S706) of Greater Cahokia, with close-up of white residue. (Adapted from Betzenhauser 2018a, Figure 4.56.)

extending horizontally from the front to back in addition to the vertical cavity (Betzenhauser 2018a; Titterington 1938a, b).

Stumpware has been recovered from TLW and early Mississippian contexts throughout the American Bottom region, including in high concentrations at large TLW village sites such as Cahokia, East St. Louis, and Range (Betzenhauser 2018a; Holley 1989; Kelly et al. 1990, 2007; Pauketat 1998; Pauketat 2013; Vogel 1975). They appear abruptly in ceramic assemblages during the early TLW (TLW1, AD 900–975) with no known antecedents, and increase in frequency in the late TLW (TLW2, AD 975–1050). During the early Mississippian (AD 1050–1200) period, stumpware were gradually replaced by funnels (a.k.a. Wickliffe Thick) that share some characteristics (e.g., thick walls, coarse tempers, inverted cone shape, use-wear) suggesting a similar function, but they differ in overall size and their lack of feet (Farace 2018; Holley 1989). A few stumpware have been found outside the American Bottom to the north and south along the Mississippi and Illinois River valleys in Illinois during the same time frame as the TLW (see Farnsworth et al. 1991; Hargrave 1992; Lansdell et al. 2018), but they are exceedingly rare outside the American Bottom region.

Several hypotheses concerning stumpware's functions have been posited, ranging from their use as funnels or incense burners to vessel supports in pottery firing, cooking, and/or salt production, or in the production of lime or lye (Brown 1980, 1981; Farnsworth et al. 1991; Kelly 1980; Kelly et al. 1984; Kelly et al. 1990; Eubanks and Brown 2015; O'Brien 1972). Some postulated functions may be excluded based on morphological characteristics and/ or use-wear patterns. For instance, soot is rarely observed on the exterior surfaces, indicating that they were not placed in a fire or coals, thereby excluding their use as vessel supports. Also, in nearly all cases where we have complete examples, they are more stable when placed with the feet on the ground rather than the inverse.

Stumpware frequently exhibits a white residue on the exterior surface and rim (see Figure 8.1), although this information has not been recorded systematically in most ceramic analyses. Elizabeth Benchley (2003:131) suggested that this residue, as well as similar residue observed on later Mississippian funnels, was a result of water moving through the vessel walls and leaving lime deposits on the exterior surface. She suggested that stumpware and funnels were used to process alkalis due to the presence of this residue and the thick walls that could withstand the rapid increase in temperature caused by the chemical reaction from slaking lime better than thinner-walled cooking jars (Benchley 2003:134). She indicates that stumpware could have dual purposes: (1)

to create an alkaline solution by pouring water through quicklime or wood ashes in the cavity; and (2) to contain, store, and manipulate the caustic lime (Benchley 2003:134).

NIXTAMALIZATION AT THE EAST ST. LOUIS PRECINCT

There has been much speculation over the uses of stumpware over the last century, but little systematic or quantitative research focused on determining how stumpware functioned in the past. In 2017, I initiated a multipronged pilot study with Illinois State Archaeological Survey (ISAS) colleagues (Sarah Harken, Victoria Potter, Madeleine Evans, Kjersti Emerson, and Adam Tufano) to determine whether stumpware vessels were used to process limestone for nixtamalization as Benchley (2003) suggested. The study was designed as a three-pronged approach: (1) compile contextual and ceramic data from systematic archaeological investigations; (2) perform archaeometric analysis of archaeological samples; and (3) test experimental use of stumpware. The first aspect incorporates archaeological data from recent large-scale excavations at the East St. Louis Precinct of Greater Cahokia (11S706), completed for the Illinois Department of Transportation (IDOT) and Federal Highway Administration (see Betzenhauser 2018a, b; Brennan et al. 2019; Emerson et al. 2018). The archaeometric analysis consists of elemental analysis of stumpware samples recovered from the East St. Louis Precinct. The experimental archaeology studies consist of creating and using replica stumpware to process locally available limestone. Although preliminary, the results of these three approaches presented next appear to confirm Benchley's hypothesis concerning the role of stumpware in processing limestone for use in nixtamalizing corn (Betzenhauser 2021; Betzenhauser et al. 2017a, 2017b; Betzenhauser and Evans 2021).

CONTEXTUAL AND CERAMIC ANALYSES

The extensive excavations at the East St. Louis Precinct conducted by ISAS for IDOT revealed thousands of TLW and Mississippian features (Figure 8.2) that yielded more than 1,400 stumpware examples (Betzenhauser 2018a, b; Betzenhauser et al. 2018; Brennan et al. 2018; Brennan et al. 2019). White residue was observed on the exterior surfaces of at least half of all stumpware recovered from East St. Louis. It typically appeared on the rim and exterior surfaces (Betzenhauser 2018a).

Stumpware was associated with the earliest features in this part of the site (TLW1, AD 900–975), and over 60% were from TLW2 (AD 975–1050) pits

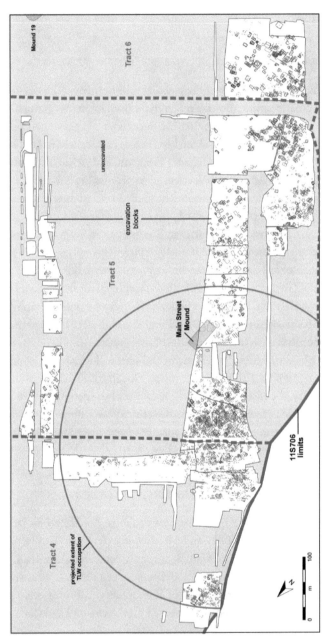

Figure 8.2. Distribution of all precontact features identified at the East St. Louis Precinct during the New Mississippi River Bridge project. TLW = Terminal Late Woodland. (Adapted from Betzenhauser 2018a, Figure 1.3.)

and structures. Another 36% were from early Mississippian (AD 1050–1200) features. When standardized by the total number of structures for each phase, this equates to roughly 1.5 and 2.5 stumpware per structure for the TLW1 and TLW2, respectively, and less than 1 per structure during the early Mississippian occupation.

Stumpware co-occurs with large concentrations of limestone at East St. Louis and at other sites in the region, with much of the limestone exhibiting evidence of burning such as having a powdery surface texture (Boles 2018; Kelly et al. 1990, 2007; Pauketat 2018). A random sample of 60 pieces of limestone from TLW contexts at East St. Louis was identified as deriving from the St. Louis Limestone formations by Zakaria Lasemi at the Illinois State Geological Survey (personal communication, 2013). According to Lasemi, St. Louis Limestone is a dense, pure, high-calcium limestone readily available at or near the surface along the bluffs and in streams in Illinois and Missouri in the American Bottom region (see also Norby and Lasemi 2000) and therefore would be conducive to making slaked lime.

ARCHAEOMETRIC ANALYSIS

A sample of 11 stumpware from features at East St. Louis with secure phase-level components (TLW2, AD 975–1050 and Lohmann, AD 1050–1100) was selected for elemental analysis based on the presence of white residue and plain surfaces, as cordmarked surfaces would likely result in lower counts due to the irregular surface. The core, exterior surface, and/or rims of seven stumpware sherds were analyzed using a Bruker portable X-ray fluorescence (pXRF) instrument with no filter and no vacuum. All samples had high iron counts, likely due to the high iron content of the locally available clays that were presumably used to create the stumpware (Table 8.1).

The elements of greatest interest for this analysis are calcium and potassium. If the stumpware were used to process limestone, there should be higher percentages of calcium, but if they were used to process hardwood ash, we would expect potassium to be more prevalent. When comparing the relative percentages of calcium obtained from the various surfaces of the same vessel, elevated calcium values were associated with the exterior and rim surfaces where white residue was observed, while the percentages for the core were lower (Figure 8.3, see Table 8.1). The vessel with the highest calcium percentages for both the core and exterior (V5-455-2) is the only one tempered solely with shell, suggesting that the shell is skewing the results. Calcium percentages of the other vessel cores are below 10% of total counts, while calcium

Table 8.1. Results of Portable X-Ray Fluorescence Analysis of Stumpware Samples from the East St. Louis Precinct (11S706)

Vessel No.	Temper	Sampled Location	Calcium (Ca) Ct./1,000	Potassium (K) Ct./1,000	Iron (Fe) Ct./1,000	Other[a] Ct./1,000	Total Ct./1,000	Percent of Total Count Ca	K	Fe
Terminal Late Woodland (900–1050 CE)										
5-3407-18	Grog-Grit	Core	198.3	218.0	2,257.0	1,952.2	4,625.4	**4.3**	4.7	48.8
5-3407-18	Grog-Grit	Exterior Base	734.7	472.6	2,339.8	2,025.5	5,572.6	**13.2**	8.5	42.0
5-3407-18	Grog-Grit	Exterior	1,928.9	387.9	2,069.7	1,902.5	6,289.0	**30.7**	6.2	32.9
5-3407-18	Grog-Grit	Rim Interior	1,019.8	471.9	2,256.1	1,973.1	5,720.9	**17.8**	8.2	39.4
4-1275-163	Grog	Core	386.4	304.1	2,133.5	1,699.1	4,523.1	**8.5**	6.7	47.2
4-1275-163	Grog	Exterior	762.0	500.2	2,637.8	2,109.8	6,009.8	**12.7**	8.3	43.9
4-1275-163	Grog	Rim	722.1	592.3	2,228.0	1,947.7	5,490.0	**13.2**	10.8	40.6
5-2975-15	Grog-Grit	Core	417.6	350.5	2,198.3	1,915.6	4,882.0	**8.6**	7.2	45.0
5-2975-15	Grog-Grit	Exterior	1,004.4	434.9	2,485.4	2,130.9	6,055.6	**16.6**	7.2	41.0
5-2975-15	Grog-Grit	Rim	1,270.4	495.4	2,338.5	2,031.0	6,135.3	**20.7**	8.1	38.1
Lohmann (1050–1100 CE)										
5-362-13	Shell/Grog	Core	186.6	194.0	1,687.7	1,483.5	3,551.8	**5.3**	5.5	47.5
5-362-13	Shell/Grog	Exterior	1,425.2	350.7	2,279.9	2,004.5	6,060.3	**23.5**	5.8	37.6
5-2641-32	Grog	Core	161.2	277.9	2,369.7	1,932.8	4,741.5	**3.4**	5.9	50.0
5-2641-32	Grog	Exterior	1,859.9	371.3	2,192.6	1,950.1	6,373.9	**29.2**	5.8	34.4
5-2641-32	Grog	Rim	1,795.2	453.8	1,932.2	1,847.1	6,028.3	**29.8**	7.5	32.1
4-217-4	Grog	Core	151.4	201.7	2,089.0	1,723.9	4,166.0	**3.6**	4.8	50.1
4-217-4	Grog	Rim	1,307.0	363.7	1,863.4	1,685.6	5,219.7	**25.0**	7.0	35.7
4-217-4	Grog	Exterior	2,347.3	407.9	1,915.1	1,778.1	6,448.4	**36.4**	6.3	29.7
5-455-2	Shell	Core	1,627.8	191.3	988.9	1,087.3	3,895.4	**41.8**	4.9	25.4
5-455-2	Shell	Exterior	3,248.0	403.3	1,517.0	1,537.6	6,705.9	**48.4**	6.0	22.6

[a]These include magnesium, aluminum, silicon, chlorine, titanium, manganese, cobalt, nickel, copper, and zinc.

percentages of the rims and exteriors consistently exceed 10% and some exceed 30%. In contrast, potassium values did not exhibit much variation within or between the specimens, with an overall range of 4.7–10.8%. These preliminary results suggest that the sampled stumpware contained carbonate-based material that was transported through the vessel wall via water, leaving lime deposits (i.e., white residue) adhering to the exterior surface as Benchley (2003:131) hypothesized.

EXPERIMENTAL ARCHAEOLOGICAL ANALYSIS

The archaeometric analysis was supplemented with experimental studies that consisted of creating replica stumpware, firing limestone to create quicklime, and pouring water over the quicklime placed in a stumpware replica (Figure 8.4). The size and morphology of the replicas were based on average

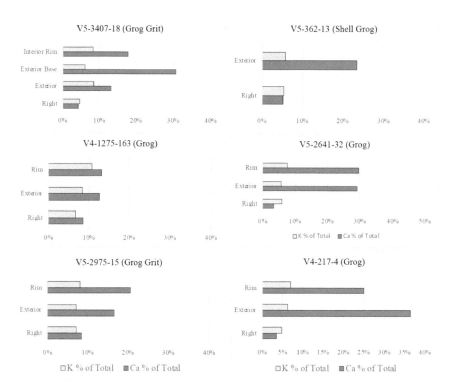

Figure 8.3. Portable X-ray fluorescence results, calcium (Ca) and potassium (K) percentages of total counts on stumpware rims, exterior surfaces, and cores. (Graphs courtesy of Alleen Betzenhauser.)

dimensions of stumpware recovered archaeologically from the East St. Louis Precinct (11S706). They were hand-built by me, Sarah Harken, and Victoria Potter using locally sourced clay (from the uplands near the Southern Illinois University campus in Edwardsville) and temper (crushed pottery made from local clays). They were fired in an open fire, reaching adequately high temperatures to convert the clay to ceramic (~700°C). High calcium limestone was collected from the bluffs near Alton, Illinois, and fired in a chiminea at a temperature high enough to convert the limestone to quicklime (~800°C). Firing temperatures were measured using a handheld infrared thermometer.

When tap water was poured over the limestone, an exothermic reaction occurred, and the limestone expanded and disintegrated, indicating that we

Figure 8.4. Experimental use of stumpware replica: (a) pouring water over burned limestone (quicklime) placed in replica, (b) slaked lime and nejayote produced, (c) litmus test of nejayote indicating it is strongly alkaline. (Photographs courtesy of Alleen Betzenhauser.)

created slaked lime. A litmus test of the solution that poured out of the basal orifice indicated that it was a strongly alkaline solution (see Figure 8.4c). The alkaline solution (i.e., nejayote) was collected and stored in a glass jar. A litmus test of this solution after storing it for over two years indicated that it was still strongly alkaline.

White deposits were observed on the stumpware after one use, but it appears to be inconsistent with the white residue observed on archaeological specimens. It is possible that the white residue observed on stumpware from archaeological contexts developed after multiple uses or while creating lime loaves. To test this, future experimental studies will include adding a small amount of water to the slaked lime powder and compressing it into the cavity in the stumpware and allowing it to dry and form a mold that can be stored for later use or be transported elsewhere.

CAHOKIAN NIXTAMALIZATION IN CONTEXT

Based on isotopic and archaeobotanical data, we can safely assume that people living in the American Bottom during the TLW and Mississippian periods nixtamalized their corn as they became more and more reliant on maize for their diets. Current research on use-wear and absorbed residues on cooking jars should aid in confirming this (Johnson et al. 2022). We can also infer that they were using locally available, high-calcium limestone to create the alkaline solution, most likely using stumpware and funnels as Benchley (2003) suggested, due to the presence of calcium-rich white residue on the exterior surfaces and thick walls that could withstand the exothermic reaction.

The stumpware count per structure ratios at East St. Louis and the small capacity of stumpware suggest that lime production for nixtamalization occurred at the household level. The wide variation in morphological characteristics and simple methods and materials that were used to create stumpware suggest that they were also produced at the household level. The variability in form also might indicate experimentation related to developing this new technology.

The available data from the research presented here and regional archaeological analyses seem to indicate that pre-Mississippian TLW people in the American Bottom adopted nixtamalization at the same time corn was becoming a staple in the diet, but they were developing new tools and methods using local resources and knowledge to accomplish this rather than importing or borrowing it from another region. Further evidence of this can be gleaned from comparisons with nixtamalization tool kits and materials in regions such as the southwestern United States and Mesoamerica (Beck 2001; Cheetham 2010; Ellwood et al. 2003; Myers 2006; Noneman et al. 2017; Spencer and Sekaquaptewa 1995). Minimally, the tools and materials required to process corn this way include dried corn kernels, a wood ash-based or carbonate-based alkaline solution, water, a container for soaking and boiling, and a colander made from ceramic, gourd, or basketry for rinsing. If the corn is to be ground, a stone or wooden mortar and pestle are required. Tortillas and other flat breads may be cooked on a griddle, or comal. Many of these items may not preserve archaeologically or might not be recognized as functioning in ways associated with preparing and cooking nixtamalized corn. However, objects similar to stumpware appear to be absent from assemblages in the southwestern United States, Mesoamerica, and other areas of the Eastern Woodlands, suggesting that they were created by and for people living in the American Bottom.

The choice to use limestone rather than ashes to create the alkaline solution is significant. Although high-calcium limestone is readily available in the American Bottom region, it takes more time and effort to create slaked lime than it does to create hardwood ash or lye. The fact that all the identified limestone from the East St. Louis Precinct was dense and pure suggests that they selected a specific type and source of limestone for nixtamalizing. This is comparable to the Maya region, where limestone sourced from Belize was considered the best for nixtamalizing corn (Thompson 1965:355, cited in Cheetham 2010).

Additionally, the alkaline material used to nixtamalize corn will affect its color and flavor. The use of limestone instead of wood ash and the selection of a particular type of limestone suggest that it was chosen for culinary and cultural reasons rather than convenience. The limestone outcrops and steep bluffs encircling the American Bottom stand out in the otherwise flat landscape of Illinois and give the region a particular character that is readily recognizable (Figure 8.5). Paired with the wide expanse of floodplain and the Mississippi River, it is rather unique. By using limestone from the bluffs flanking the American Bottom to process their corn, they were in a sense ingesting the landscape and physically becoming part of this particular place. If the slaked lime was formed into cones of dried lime, it could then be transported to other settlements and regions where others could partake in the unique flavor of the American Bottom landscape.

The adoption of a maize-based diet and the concurrent development of regionally specific tools and technology employed in nixtamalizing corn immediately before and during Cahokia's rise suggest that the hominy foodway (Myers 2006) was integral to Cahokia's urbanization (Pauketat 2018). Furthermore, cuisine is entangled with identity through the processes of procuring,

Figure 8.5. Limestone bluffs and deposits in the American Bottom region of Illinois: (a) Falling Springs near Dupo, (b) bluff face near Alton, and (c) limestone covering a creek bed near Columbia. (Photographs a and c courtesy of Madeleine G. Evans. Photograph b courtesy of Alleen Betzenhauser.)

making, sharing, and consuming foods (see Introduction; Hastorf 2016). Thus, nixtamalization and its associated tool kit were implicated in the creation of a Cahokia-specific Mississippian identity tied to the American Bottom region that was enacted and expressed through specific culinary practices.

FUTURE DIRECTIONS

The preliminary results presented here are revealing, but the project would benefit from expanding the research in several ways. Compiling data concerning intra- and intersite distributions of stumpware and funnels will aid in identifying dense concentrations of these items that might relate to differential processing of limestone or production centers (cf. Seligson et al. 2019). Fine-grained morphometric analyses of stumpware forms could reveal regional and subregional stumpware styles that could indicate minor variations in methods for processing limestone. Revisiting ceramic assemblages that did not include noting of use-wear on stumpware will likely result in the identification of more examples from sites outside the East St. Louis Precinct that could be included in additional analyses.

The archaeometric analysis could be expanded to include pXRF analysis of additional archaeological examples of stumpware from East St. Louis and other sites, and funnels. Other, more precise instruments could be used to ensure that we are analyzing only the use-wear, which would aid in alleviating the effects of carbonate tempers and uneven (i.e., cordmarked or curved) surfaces. Current research concerning analysis of absorbed residues in cooking jars could verify that the corn cooked in them was nixtamalized (Johnson and Marston 2020; Johnson et al. 2022; Santini 2021). Archaeological samples of burned limestone could also be tested to determine whether they were heated to a high enough temperature to convert it into quicklime, and then reverted back to limestone by absorbing atmospheric carbon dioxide (see Seligson et al. 2017b).

The experimental studies could be expanded by repeatedly using the replicas for both lime production and to create portable lime loaves. Additional experimentation will allow for the observation of how the residue develops and how long it takes. The replicas should also be examined archaeometrically, both before and after use, to document elemental changes resulting from use and to compare with archaeological specimens.

This research would benefit most by incorporating Indigenous sources of knowledge. These include working with descendant communities to investigate linguistic evidence for the timing of nixtamalization in the Midcontinent and working with ancestral strains of corn stewarded by seed savers (e.g., Dion-Buffalo and Mohawk 1999). Partnering with contemporary Indigenous chefs to compare flavor profiles of corn nixtamalized with limestone and corn nixtamalized with ash would aid in further investigating the consumption side of Cahokian cuisine.

CONCLUSION

Nixtamalization continues to be practiced today. In some circles, household cooks maintain long-held traditions of food processing while preparing meals for family and friends (Aliseda 2021). In others, professional Indigenous chefs are revitalizing and reconfiguring foodways using ancient techniques modified for modern palates (Brant 2020; Lunsford 2021; Ralat 2020). For many, it is a form of nostalgia and of longing for home where their mothers and grandmothers prepared the same foods when they were young. Perhaps Cahokians shared a similar sense of nostalgia and connection to place that was enacted through the production and consumption of nixtamalized corn dishes that incorporated the physical landscape of their home.

Chapter 9

The Archaeobotany of the East St. Louis Precinct of Greater Cahokia

KIMBERLY SCHAEFER, MARY SIMON, AND MARY M. KING

Plant and animal studies from Terminal Late Woodland through Mississippian Period sites in the American Bottom have noted the broad consistency in targeted resources, particularly the use of native cultivated grain crops, the addition of maize (*Zea mays*) around AD 900, and the hunting of white-tailed deer (*Odocoileus virginianus*), fish, and wildfowl by people living across the region (cf. Johannessen 1984, 1993; Kelly and Cross 1984; Kuehn 2023; Lopinot 1993; Schaefer and Simon 2023; Simon and Parker 2006). Despite the homogeneity in the types of plants and animals people consumed, the dramatic changes in social, political, and religious practices that characterized the development of the Greater Cahokian polity around AD 1050 engendered shifts in multiple aspects of cuisine. Changes occurred in the way food was procured, prepared, and shared as well as in the disposal of waste. The provisioning system was altered to accommodate a highly stratified society that included religious or political elites and specialized craftspeople not engaged in food production. This period also witnessed an influx of immigrants wanting to engage in this radical new social order. Under these conditions, cuisine was critical in establishing and maintaining social relationships.

In this chapter, we explore the interplay between changes in social organization and food procurement strategies apparent in the archaeological record from the East St. Louis (ESTL) site, one of the three major precincts making up Greater Cahokia (Figure 9.1). We first outline changes in community organization through the periods between about AD 900 and AD 1300 then summarize the plant and animal assemblages identified in specific Mississippian period neighborhoods recognized at the site. These changes would have altered the social and cultural contexts in which people were selecting ingredients for

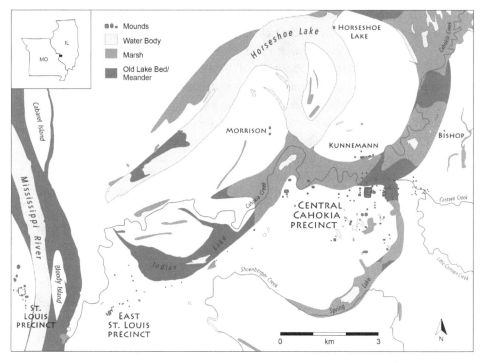

Figure 9.1. Map of the Greater Cahokia region and three major urban precincts. (Map courtesy of the Illinois Department of Transportation.)

their cuisine. We conclude with a discussion of how this work can be used as the basis for future studies of cuisine in the complex Cahokian system.

SITE BACKGROUND

The vast amount of archaeological work conducted in the American Bottom floodplain of southeastern Illinois over the past half century has revealed that human occupation of this region has been inconstant. People have been moving into and out of this landform for millennia. These movements are reflected in site distributions across the floodplain and adjacent uplands that were, in many respects, dictated by changing patterns in the fluvial regime of the Mississippi River and its many tributaries. As the main river channel slowly shifted from east to west, it left behind a ridge and swale topography that included a series of oxbow lakes and marshes as well as higher ground suitable for habitation. The Mississippi River only approached its modern channel configuration well into the Late Woodland period, about cal AD 700–900, and then extensive settlement near the modern channel was possible (Kolb 2018:100).

The earliest occupations at ESTL date to the Terminal Late Woodland I (TLWI) period, between about cal AD 900 and 975. These habitations consisted of a series of small farmsteads spread out along the western and northern edges of an island bar bordered by Cahokia Creek, the Goose Lake meander, and Indian Lake, the last two being extensions of Horseshoe Lake (see Figure 9.1). The interconnectedness of these waterways provided a direct route from the Mississippi River to ESTL and the Central Cahokia Precinct beyond.

The population of ESTL burgeoned over the Terminal Late Woodland II (TLWII) (ca. cal AD 975–1050). This period was characterized by the establishment of communities of extended kin groups, arranged in roughly circular fashions around central courtyards (Figure 9.2). In all, 38 courtyard groups have been identified (Betzenhauser 2019b; Betzenhauser et al. 2019). The dramatic population increase was fueled at least in part by an influx of immigrants from across the Midwest, drawn to the region to participate in the burgeoning social, political, and religious Cahokian phenomenon. Their presence is reflected in ceramic and lithic assemblages, which include clearly nonlocal types (Betzenhauser et al. 2018; Boles et al. 2018). It is likely that these immigrant groups would bring with them their preferred methods for selecting and preparing food.

Village life in the American Bottom underwent a dramatic change around cal AD 1050, during the Lohmann phase. This restructuring appears to have reflected a coalescence "around a political leader, religious movement, or kin-coalition that rapidly centralized the social relations and political economy of the American Bottom" (Pauketat et. al. 2002). It was characterized by massive infrastructure projects, new and specialized architectural styles, population movement into large urban centers, and an ever-increasing influx of immigrants. Change was centered at the sites of Cahokia, ESTL, and St. Louis, which together became North America's first true city, Greater Cahokia.

Greater Cahokia covered about 5.6 square miles and extended in linear fashion from the banks of Horseshoe Lake in the interior floodplain to the blufftops west of the Mississippi River (see Figure 9.1). During the Mississippian Lohmann and Stirling phases, between about cal AD 1050 and 1200, each of the precincts contained planned civic-ceremonial zones with mounds, plazas, specialized or ritual structures, and residential neighborhoods, which included garbage facilities, hearths, and domiciles for the residents. Although once thought to have been destroyed by modern development of the city of East St. Louis, excavations by the Illinois State Archaeological Survey (ISAS)

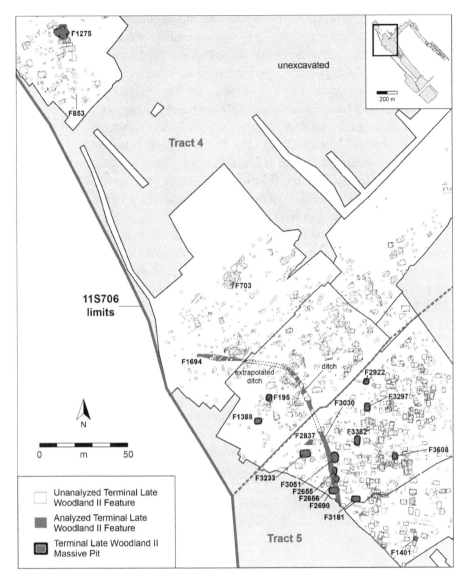

Figure 9.2. Terminal Late Woodland communities at the East Saint Louis site. (Courtesy of the Illinois Department of Transportation.)

have shown that large portions of ESTL remained intact, buried under up to 3 meters of modern fill deposit.

Outside of the urban complex, the Greater Cahokia region included outlying secondary mound centers, nodal communities, shrine complexes, and farmsteads spread across the floodplain and into the uplands. The Richland and Silver Creek uplands included farming communities that were critical in supporting urban populations (Alt 2002; Pauketat 2003). This support also facilitated the development of the massive infrastructure projects that characterized the Mississippian presence in the central Mississippi River Valley and beyond. Greater Cahokia lasted for only a few hundred years. The supporting, upland farming communities of the Silver and Richland Creek drainage areas were uninhabited by around AD 1175. At ESTL, partial abandonment took the form of intentional closure by fire, although evidence for continued use of this locale extended well into the Moorehead Phase (ca. post cal AD 1200). Regional turmoil was evidenced by the construction of a palisade around the core area at the site of Cahokia itself circa AD 1200. Along with a loss of classic iconography, shifts in mortuary practices, and other shifts in religious and social structure, the palisade may be seen to reflect an internal struggle for political and religious control or a desire to maintain some semblance of power, as well as increasing conflict. By AD 1300, Cahokia itself was virtually deserted.

MISSISSIPPIAN PERIOD SETTLEMENT ORGANIZATION AT THE ESTL SITE

The transitions in social organization during the early Mississippian period are evident in the restructuring of ESTL into neighborhoods, presumed to represent cohesive social units, with members bound by both blood ties and fictive kinship alliances (Brennan 2018c; Emerson 2018). The initial analyses in this area focused on identifying spatial patterns of plant and animal deposits by feature type within communities in an attempt to better understand community practices and organization (Kuehn 2023; Kuehn and Simon 2023; Schaefer and Simon 2023). Here we summarize those results and further explore intercommunity variances in an effort to assess variability in both cuisine and ritual resource use among these discrete social units.

Lohmann Phase

The plant and animal assemblages from Lohmann phase (ca. cal AD 1050–1100) features at the site were both extensive and diverse. Analyzed contexts included domestic and nondomestic structures, pits, hearths, and posts. Kuehn (2023:Table 4.10) identified over 22,000 skeletal fragments from 477 features. These remains included subsistence debris, especially from white-tailed deer and fish and a variety of bone tools and a large number of ritually charged fragments. Over 11,000 floral items from 93 features were also identified (Schaefer and Simon 2023:Table 3.1). As with the faunal remains, subsistence was well represented by native starchy grains—chenopod (*Chenopodium berlanderi*), erect knotweed (*Polygonum erectum*), maygrass (*Phalaris caroliniana*), and little barley (*Hordeum pusillum*)—together with maize kernels and cupule fragments, making up almost half of all botanical materials. Nutshell made up an additional 10% of all quantified materials (Schaefer and Simon 2023:Table 3.3). The assemblage was also rich in ritually charged plants, including tobacco (*Nicotiana* sp.) and morning glory (*Ipomoea* sp.) seeds. Red cedar wood (*Juniperus virginiana*) was recovered from a number of contexts, including three post pits where the remains appear to be the remains of the original post, either burned in place or redeposited after ritual extraction and combustion.

Within the greater feature assemblage, five Lohmann phase communities were identified (Figure 9.3). Feature categories follow those defined by Brennan (2018c). Public and domestic structures as well as "special purpose" structures, which may have housed nonhuman beings and/or been used for ritual or medicinal rites, were included in these communities. Internal and external pits and post pits, hearths, borrow pits, and massive pits are also represented (Table 9.1).

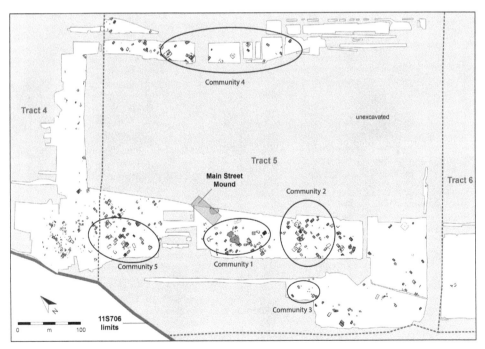

Figure 9.3. Lohman phase communities defined for this study. (Courtesy of the Illinois Department of Transportation.)

Table 9.1. Analyzed Lohmann and Stirling Phase Features by Area

Lohmann				Stirling			
Area	Tract/ Feature	Feature Type	Associated With	Area	Tract/ Feature	Feature Type	Associated With
1	F5-1801	borrow pit		1	F5-0600	circular structure	
1	F5-2133	borrow pit		1	F5-0181	domestic structure burned	
1	F5-2181	borrow pit		1	F5-0188	public structure	
1	F5-1818	circular structure		1	F5-3809	internal pit public	F5-0188
1	F5-0129	domestic structure		1	F5-3813	internal pit public	F5-0188
1	F5-1098	domestic structure		1	F5-0289	internal pit domestic	F5-0184
1	F5-1634	domestic structure		1	F5-0291	internal pit domestic	F5-0184
1	F5-1896	domestic structure		1	F5-0704	internal post pit domestic	F5-0591
1	F5-2206	domestic structure		2	F5-0327	domestic structure	
1	F5-0130	L-shaped structure		2	F5-0276	domestic structure burned	
1	F5-1099	public structure		2	F5-0324	domestic structure burned	
1	F5-0411	external pit		2	F5-0495	domestic structure burned	
1	F5-0412	external pit		2	F5-0424	internal hearth domestic	F5-0324
1	F5-1724	external pit		2	F5-0467	internal pit domestic	F5-0276
1	F5-2383	external pit		2	F5-0506	internal pit domestic	F5-0327
1	F5-0476	external post pit		2	F5-0507	internal pit domestic	F5-0327
1	F5-0501	external post pit		2	F5-1887	internal pit domestic	F5-0941
1	F5-1642	external post pit		2	F5-1888	internal pit domestic	F5-0941
1	F5-2364	external post pit		2	F5-0478	internal post pit domestic	F5-0376
1	F5-2479	internal pit domestic	F5-2206	3a	F6-0666	circular structure	
1	F5-2524	internal pit domestic	F5-1634	3a	F6-0482	domestic structure burned	
1	F5-1207	internal pit public	F5-1099	3a	F6-0717	domestic structure burned	

	Lohmann				Stirling		
Area	Tract/ Feature	Feature Type	Associated With	Area	Tract/ Feature	Feature Type	Associated With
1	F5-0418	internal pit L structure	F5-0130	3a	F6-0712	public structure	
1	F5-2077	internal post pit public	F5-2012	3a	F6-0466	storage structure	
1	F5-1897	massive pit		3a	F6-0727	internal hearth circular	F6-0666
1	F5-2000	mound		3a	F6-0816	internal hearth domestic	F6-0669
2	F5-0239	domestic structure		3a	F6-0613	internal hearth public	F6-0477
2	F5-0256	domestic structure		3a	F6-0614	internal hearth public	F6-0477
2	F5-0260	domestic structure		3a	F6-0530	internal pit public	F6-0397
2	F5-0290	external pit		3a	F6-0536	internal pit public	F6-0397
2	F5-0267	external post pit		3a	F6-0546	internal pit public	F6-0397
2	F5-1759	internal hearth public	F5-1709	3a	F6-0801	internal pit public	F6-0712
2	F5-1702	internal pit public	F5-1709	3a	F6-0533	internal pit public	F6-0397
2	F5-1704	internal pit public	F5-1709	3a	F6-0620	internal pit domestic	F6-0600
2	F5-1705	internal pit public	F5-1709	3a	F6-0640	internal pit domestic	F6-0469
2	F5-1706	internal pit public	F5-1709	3a	F6-0641	internal pit domestic	F6-0469
2	F5-1707	internal pit public	F5-1709	3a	F6-0654	internal pit domestic	F6-0469
2	F5-1708	internal pit public	F5-1709	3a	F6-0660	internal pit domestic	F6-0472
2	F5-1713	internal pit public	F5-1709	3a	F6-0673	internal pit domestic	F6-0469
2	F5-1742	internal pit public	F5-1709	3a	F6-0692	internal pit domestic	F6-0482
2	F5-1744	internal pit public	F5-1709	3a	F6-0693	internal pit domestic	F6-0482
2	F5-2388	internal pit public	F5-2371	3a	F6-0696	internal pit domestic	F6-0482
2	F5-2389	internal pit public	F5-2371	3a	F6-0808	internal pit domestic	F6-0774
2	F5-1029	internal post domestic	F5-0544	3a	F6-0815	internal pit domestic	F6-0669
3	F5-2630	domestic structure		3a	F6-0916	internal pit domestic	F6-0717
3	F5-3748	domestic structure		3a	F6-0647	internal post pit domestic	F6-0469

	Lohmann				Stirling		
Area	Tract/ Feature	Feature Type	Associated With	Area	Tract/ Feature	Feature Type	Associated With
3	F5-3782	domestic structure		3b	F6-0315	domestic structure burned	
3	F5-4117	domestic structure		3b	F6-0521	domestic structure burned	
3	F5-4137	domestic structure		3b	F6-0906	domestic structure burned	
3	F5-3880	internal pit domestic	F5-3748	3b	F6-0313	storage structure burned	
3	F5-4090	internal pit domestic	F5-3782	3b	F6-0357	internal hearth domestic	F6-0315
3	F5-4091	internal pit domestic	F5-3782	3b	F6-0362	internal pit public	F6-0336
4	F5-0001	T-shaped structure		3b	F6-0363	internal pit public	F6-0336
4	F5-0755	public structure		3b	F6-0356	internal pit domestic	F6-0315
4	F5-0656	external post pit		3b	F6-0730	internal pit domestic	F6-0521
4	F5-0634	internal pit public	F5-0569	3b	F6-0731	internal pit domestic	F6-0521
4	F5-0636	internal pit public	F5-0569	3b	F6-0906	internal pit domestic	F6-0880
4	F5-0680	internal pit public	F5-0619	3b	F6-0920	internal pit domestic	F6-0880
4	F5-0038	internal pit T-structure	F5-0001	3b	F6-0923	internal pit domestic	F6-0880
4	F 5-0039	internal pit T-structure	F5-0001	3b	F6-0927	internal pit domestic	F6-0880
4	F5-0741	internal post pit public	F5-0740	3b	F6-0928	internal pit domestic	F6-0880
5	F5-3585	burial		3b	F6-0589	internal post pit public	F6-0520
5	F5-2696	L-shaped structure		3b	F6-0652	internal post pit public	F6-0520
5	F5-3335	internal pit public	F5-2937	3c	F6-0383	T-shaped structure	
5	F5-3460	internal pit public	F5-2937	3c	F6-0386	T-shaped structure	
5	F5-2008	internal pit T-structure	F5-1410	3c	F6-0390	internal pit public	F6-0394
5	F5-2713	massive pit		3c	F6-0511	internal pit public	F6-0394
				3c	F6-0513	internal pit public	F6-0396

When taken as a whole, the floral and faunal food remains from Lohmann phase contexts at the ESTL are broadly consistent and support generalized models for the region. They show precontact groups relied on white-tailed deer, birds (particularly waterfowl), and a variety of fish from rivers and lakes. Native grains were cultivated and supplemented by sunflower (*Helianthus annuus*), squash (*Curcubita* sp.), and sumpweed (*Iva annua*). Maize was a rapid and integral addition to the agricultural system between cal AD 900 and 950, then widely used by AD 975. The assemblages also include ritually charged plant remains and the remains of unusual animals, including swan (*Cygnus* sp.), snake (Serpentes), and falcon (*Falco* sp.) (Kuehn 2023:Tables 4.1 and 4.10). Unsurprisingly, materials are inconsistently distributed across the site. While typical for archaeobotanical and faunal remains, in this case this patterning reflects the changes in social organization represented by defined neighborhoods.

Lohmann Community 1

Community 1 was located immediately south of Mound 2000 (see Figure 9.3). Analyzed features include two paired sets of one domestic and one nondomestic structure as well as associated internal and external pits, post pits, borrow areas, and one external massive pit. The external massive pit, F5-1897, measured 5.0 x 2.7 m in plan, with a volume of 17.01 m^2 and a total of 42 distinct fill zones. By comparison, typical storage and cache pits were much smaller, with an average volume of 0.572 dm^3 for external pits and 0.140 dm^3 for internal pits (Brennan et al. 2018:229–31, Tables 4.4 and 4.5). Plant and animal remains were abundant and diverse, but distributions among features by type varied considerably (Table 9.2). Subsistence items were scant or absent from domestic structures, from pits located inside structures, and, generally, from the basins of public structures. Quantities of materials from four external pits are higher, particularly for floral remains. Assuming these finds reflect the disposal of refuse from daily activities, the relative quantities and distributions of subsistence plant remains suggest they were more likely to be disposed of near food preparation areas, while noxious animal parts were discarded away from living zones in deep massive pit and reclaimed borrow pit contexts.

Two contexts, one within the massive pit F5-1897 and one in borrow feature F5-2133, are interpreted as reflecting feasting events (Kuehn 2023; Kuehn and Simon 2023). These consist of Zone K in massive pit F5-1897 and the lower zone of borrow pit F5-2133. Of the 136 faunal items distributed among 13 zones in the massive pit, almost one-half (48%) were from Zone K. The assemblage was dominated by deer and/or large-size mammals but included 24 garter snake (*Thamnophis sirtalis*) vertebrae. The borrow feature lower-level

Table 9.2. Summaries by Count of Floral and Faunal Assemblages from the Lohmann Phase Communities

	Wood	Nutshell	Maygrass	Other Starchy Grains	Maize Kernels	Maize Cupules	Deer Elements	Mammal Elements	Bird Elements	Fish Elements	Reptile/ Amphibian Elements	Mollusk Shell Fragments
Community 1												
Public Structure Group	17	—	22	7	16	23	—	11	—	—	—	7
Domestic Structure Group	1	1	6	3	5	18	—	6	—	1	—	1
L-Shaped Structure	—	—	3	—	—	1	—	—	—	—	—	—
Circular Structure	—	8	7	—	5	4	—	—	—	—	—	—
External Pits	152	370	21	7	30	32	2	13	2	1	1	30
Post Pits	11	—	7	—	13	28	2	17	1	1	—	—
Massive Pit	61	224	56	215	68	146	27	122	51	43	24	55
Borrow	17	—	26	9	3	36	34	177	7	108	10	7
Mound	1	—	—	—	—	—	—	—	—	—	—	—
Community 2												
Public Structure Group	97	6	439	80	23	21	—	5	—	—	—	—
Domestic Structure Group	192	26	367	74	99	72	9	34	17	1	—	1
Exterior Pits	13	—	13	4	18	3	—	—	—	—	—	—
Post Pit	7	—	15	1	5	6	10	11	6	88	1	—
Community 3												
Domestic Structure Group	39	—	24	5	15	22	2	21	1	5	1	8

Community 4												
T-Shaped Structure Group	1	3	6	2	1	4	—	16	—	1	—	4
Public Structure Group	60	—	460	—	10	4	—	—	—	—	—	—
External Post Pit	4	—	4	4	2	3	3	22	—	—	—	—
Community 5												
L-Shaped Structure	—	—	—	—	—	—	—	—	—	—	—	—
T-Shaped Structure	—	—	—	—	—	—	—	—	—	—	—	—
Massive Pit	290	20	406	153	56	101	6	12	31	398	4	57
Burial	230	—	760	14	46	8	2	1	4	75	—	—
External Pit	16	13	26	16	7	—	—	5	1	2	—	—

zone contained 108 faunal items, 62% of which were from white-tailed deer or unspecified large mammals (probably deer). These included three deer cranial fragments interpreted as ritual deposits. The remaining deer assemblage is largely of high-value meat portions. This not only appears to reflect selective consumption; it also suggests that butchering occurred elsewhere.

Ritually charged plant materials—red cedar and morning glory—were recovered from the massive pit and one post pit (F5–2077), while red cedar alone was present in a circular structure. F5-1818 and external pit F5-0412 (see Parker and Simon 2018 and Simon 2002 for discussions on the ritual use of cedar). Limited recovery of these two taxa from what appear to be specialized/nondomestic contexts is similar to patterns of recovery at other Mississippian sites. While Community 1 was clearly a lived-in space, the presence of nondomestic structures, ritually charged plant remains (including two possible red cedar posts), and evidence for feasting suggests that the occupants were also engaged in ritual practices. These may have included specialists who carried out the creation, maintenance, or other ritual practices associated with Mound 2000, including interment of the dead in the small, associated cemetery (Nash, Brennan, and Hedman 2016; Nash et al. 2018).

Lohmann Community 2

Community 2 included a longhouse (F5-2371) and associated plaza, post pit, and public and residential structures (see Figure 9.3). This area is notable because of the relatively high number of morning glory seeds that were recovered from two domestic structures (F5-0260 and F5-0239) and in one of the pits (F5-2388) located inside the longhouse. Based on recovery contexts and potential as an entheogen, morning glory is regarded as a ritual plant (see discussion in Parker and Simon 2018:142–45). Its presence in domestic structures suggests that use went beyond "special" structures, or these buildings may have actually housed medicinal and/or ritual practitioners.

Overall subsistence remains were well represented by feature type but of uneven distribution (see Table 9.2). The four small domestic structures yielded 34% of all fauna from the community. Taxa included the typical comestibles of white-tail deer/large-sized mammals as well as numerous small mammals, bird, and fish fragments. Plant foods were also relatively abundant in those feature fills.

In contrast, the two nondomestic structures and 11 pits inside those structures yielded only a single piece of bone, recovered from F5-1742. Plant foods were also scarce in nondomestic features, with the exception of one multizone pit, F5-2388, located within the longhouse. That assemblage was dominated by maygrass grains, and goosefoot and erect knotweed were also present as were morning glory, wild bean (*Strophostyles* sp.), and purslane (*Portulaca* sp.). The concentrated nature of that deposit suggests that it may be the remains of one or a few meals prepared in this area rather than general postoccupation refuse. Those meals incorporated the native grains, especially maygrass, and other typical plant foods. Perhaps these ingredients were prepared and served in a special manner although no evidence to that effect has been identified in this case. It may also be that these ritual meals incorporated traditional plant foods as a way to connect past and present and to assert identity with ancestors and traditions. Archaeologically, the incorporation of everyday plant foods into special meals is a well-recognized practice (Johannessen 1993; Kassabaum 2019; Pauketat et al. 2002; VanDerwarker et. al. 2007).

The nondomestic architecture also included a deep post pit (Feature 5-0267) (see Figure 9.3). Over half (65%) of the faunal assemblage was distributed among the 12 zones of this pit and reflect deposits associated with extraction of the original post. Although most were from typical subsistence taxa, a single proximal swan wing carpometacarpus was identified from an intermediate level of the post pit. As summarized by Kelly (2010:5–6), swan was highly regarded by Indigenous peoples of the Southeast, with the skin, feathers, and wings having the highest use levels for ritual or ornamental purposes. Swan bone from ESTL and other sites from the American Bottom are interpreted as reflecting ritual rather than mundane use (Kuehn 2016).

The floral assemblage from the post pit was fairly unremarkable. It included a few starchy grain seeds as well as grass seeds, nightshade seeds, and a small quantity of maize. As almost all were from the uppermost level, Zone A, it is unclear whether these remains were associated with the ritual closing of the post.

Lohmann Community 3

Community 3 consisted of five domestic houses, two internal features, and two external features that were distributed into two domestic house groups located in the northwest part of the site (see Figure 9.3). A single pit, F5-3766, located in the open area between the two domestic housing clusters, contained the only nearly complete lightning whelk (*Busycon sinistrum*) shell cup from the site (Kozuch 2023). This and other lightning whelk shell remains from the site derive from the Gulf of Mexico (Kozuch et al. 2017). It has been suggested that shell cups were used for ritual consumption of black drink (Milanich 1979), although the shell also served as raw material for bead making (Kozuch et al. 2017; Kozuch 2023).

Although interpreted as a domestic locale, food plants, including both starchy grains and maize, are poorly represented in Community 3. Approximately half (14 maize fragments and 15 starchy grain seeds) came from a structure (F5-2630) in the northern area. That structure also contained the most faunal fragments of any feature. Remains included both white-tailed deer and large mammal bone, a few fish and mollusk shell fragments, one turtle shell fragment, and one perching bird (Passeriformes) fragment. The last two taxa are rare in Lohmann phase assemblages.

The plant profile from F5-3748, a structure that was located in the southern area, is similar to the profile from F5-2630 but quantities are much lower and the only fauna recovered were five fragments of unidentifiable vertebrate. The paucity of material, especially wood, in these nine features suggests that this part of the site was not heavily occupied during the Lohmann phase. The location near the ESTL site edge, the lack of feature super positioning, and the spatial distribution of structures support this contention. It is possible that these features represent one or two small family units, perhaps even new arrivals who occupied an area on the site periphery for a short period (Betzenhauser et al. 2019; Brennan 2018a; Brennan et al. 2018).

Lohmann Community 4

Community 4 comprised a series of nondomestic structures and associated features that were distributed linearly along a rise on the northeast area of the site (see Figure 9.3) (Brennan 2018b:54, Figure 3.19). Faunal remains are scant, with a total of only 48 fragments distributed among four of the 12 features. No exotic taxa were identified. Plants are better represented but still infrequent. Maygrass is by far the most abundant plant taxa, making up almost 75% of all floral remains and nearly 99% of the starchy grain assemblage from the entire community area.

While generally considered a mundane subsistence plant, maygrass grains, along with erect knotweed and chenopod, may also have played a special role in ritual feasting in the American Bottom region, as Fritz (2014) has suggested (Fritz and Lopinot 2007; Pauketat et al. 2002). It has also been suggested that maygrass grains were used to brew a ritual beer (Schoenwetter 2001); however, to date that hypothesis is unverified (Fritz 2014; 2019).

Ritually charged plants included one morning glory seed, which was found in association with 430 maygrass seeds in a public structure (F5-0755). As mentioned, morning glory is generally viewed as having been used in ritual or medicinal activities, and its presence in a public structure is not unexpected. Red cedar is the other ritually charged plant recovered from Community 4, dominating the wood assemblage from post pit F5-0741. These remains likely represent fragments of the original post. Overall, these results support interpretation of Community 4 as a specialized ritual area.

Lohmann Community 5

Community 5 was located just north of Mound 2000 and consists of a loosely structured complex with two nondomestic structures, one domestic structure, three interior pits, one massive pit, and one deep burial pit (see Figure 9.3). The external massive pit F4-0217 was smaller than that from Community 1 but was still comparatively huge, measuring 2.5 x 1.7 m in plan and having a depth of 1.73 m with 33 distinct deposition zones (Brennan et al. 2018:229).

No plant or animal remains were identified in samples from the nondomestic structures or interior pits. The domestic structure provided a very small floral assemblage that included some starchy grains and maize but no faunal materials. In contrast, both classes of remains were abundant in both the burial feature, F5-3585, and the massive pit F4-0217. The former included a large number of starchy grains, the majority of which were maygrass, in all seven identified zones. The highest count densities were 10.5 and 10.6 seeds per liter of fill from Zone F and Zone H, respectively. These two zones also yielded almost all the faunal remains from the burial feature. The Zone H assemblage, in particular, yielded 189 fragments, almost 75% of the feature total. Most (78%) were classed as unidentifiable vertebrata. The remainder included a number of gar (*Lepisosteus* sp.) scales, as well as bullhead catfish (*Ameiurus* sp.) and bowfin (*Amia calva*) bone fragments. Only two bird bone fragments and one deer bone fragment were identified.

Fauna was even more abundant in the massive pit F4-0217, with 476 fragments distributed among 15 zones. The Zone K assemblage stands out in having 258 bone pieces, 92% of which were from seven different fish taxa. Bullhead catfish bone fragments were the most commonly identified. That assemblage also included sunfish (Centrarchidae), suckers (Catostomidae), redhorse (*Moxostoma* sp.), drum (*Aplodinotus grunniens*), and 52 unidentifiable fish cranial fragments. An additional 115 fragments (25% of the assemblage) were from Zone O. This assemblage included bullhead catfish, sunfish, redhorse, and a single northern pike (*Esox lucius*) bone fragment. Plant foods, notably maize kernel fragments and seeds of native cultivated grains, were present in both Zones K and O in numbers similar to those from the other zones overall. Both Zone H of the burial feature and Zones K and O from the massive pits may be interpreted as reflecting single or short-term episodes of

212 KIMBERLY SCHAEFER, MARY SIMON, AND MARY M. KING

deposition, resulting from large-scale feasting events, perhaps conducted as part of burial ceremonies, as the location is near a Lohmann phase cemetery.

Lohmann Phase Communities: Emerging Specialists

As summarized in Table 9.2, the plant and animal assemblages from each of the communities are variable both taxonomically and quantitatively. In Communities 1 and 3, both flora and fauna were recovered in notably low counts from domestic structure basins and from pits inside those basins. In contrast, however, the four small domestic structures in Community 2 contained more than one-third of all faunal remains from the community as well as an unusually high number of floral remains. Public and other special-use buildings tended to yield small assemblages, but again Community 2 provided an exception. Seeds, especially maygrass, were numerous in F5-2388, located inside the longhouse feature. Unsurprisingly, the greatest quantities of both plant and animal remains were from the two massive pits, one each in Communities 1 and 5. These pits included unique deposits that appear to reflect individual deposition of feasting debris. Interestingly, the Community 1 feast debris was dominated by deer bone, while that from Community 5 was dominated by fish. Feasts are special meals that have cultural meaning and value and form an important part of a group's cuisine. Assuming the differences in food choice between the communities reflect intentionality, these deposits may reflect differing identities through cuisine. They may also be the remains of feasting that took place at different times of the year or for different social purposes.

Overall, the low counts of plant and especially animal remains in most structures of any type suggest that the basin floors and even the initial soils that infilled basin depressions were kept quite clean. Garbage appears to have been disposed of away from habitation areas, even though no such dumps were identified. This concern with sanitation is understandable regarding the deposition of fetid animal parts.

As discussed, ritually charged plant and animal remains were identified in almost all communities. Of note is that ritually charged plants tend to occur in differing feature types but are notably rare from public or special function features. The recovery of morning glory seeds in Community 2 provides just one example: most seeds are from two of the small, domestic structures and only one was present in the longhouse itself. We believe that this reflects the entanglement of ritual and medicinal practices with specific practitioners rather than specific locales. The variability among communities appears to reflect a shift in social organization, which included the rise of specific elite classes and

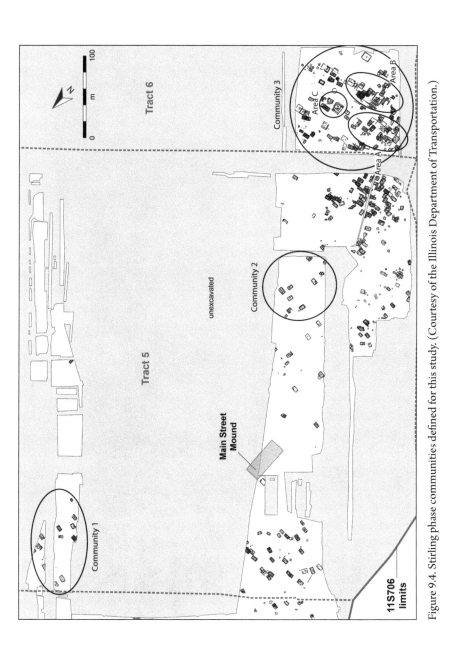

Figure 9.4. Stirling phase communities defined for this study. (Courtesy of the Illinois Department of Transportation.)

Table 9.3. Summaries by Count of Floral and Faunal Assemblages from the Stirling Phase Communities

	Nutshell	Maygrass	Other Starchy Grains	Maize Kernelsa	Maize Cupulesb	Deer Elements	Mammal Elements	Bird Elements	Fish Elements	Turtle Elements	Other Mammal-Taxon
Community 1											
Temple Structure	189	—	—	30	8	—	2	2	—	2	2
Public Structure Group	—	—	—	1	1	—	—	—	—	—	—
Domestic Structure Group	—	2	—	2	1	—	—	—	—	—	—
Circular Structure	5	17	1	—	—	1	3	2	1	—	—
Community 2											
Burned Domestic Structure Group	4	67	1	9	14	1	42	—	—	—	—
Non-Burned Domestic Structure Group	8	29	1	27	1,229	—	27	11	1	11	—
Community 3											
Area 3A											
Domestic Structure Group	1	7	3	6	3	4	11	2	1	—	—
Public Structure Group	12	3	1	4	2	1	16	1	—	6	—
Circular Structure Group	1	2	—	2	—	—	—	—	—	—	—
Storage Structure	—	—	—	—	—	—	—	—	—	—	—
Area 3B											
Domestic Structure Group	1	176	37	185	267	12	104	9	—	6	5
Public Structure Group	9	8	33	136	31	—	21	—	—	—	—
Storage Structure	1	1	—	5	1	—	—	—	—	—	—
Area 3C											
T-Shaped Structures	9	16	—	17	28	—	11	1	—	—	—
Massive Pit	8	67	9	40	68	2	30	1	—	—	—
Public Structure Group	1	1	—	4	1	—	—	3	—	—	—
Storage Structure	—	—	—	—	—	—	—	—	—	—	—

aCounts exclude mass of maize kernels from F6-0533 in Community 3.
bCounts exclude mass of cupules from F6-0533 in Community 3.

areas of specialization such as medical/ritual practitioners, craft specialists, and management of the dead.

Stirling Phase (ca. AD 1100–1200)

Five Stirling phase feature groups were identified for this study (Figure 9.4). These groups included both domestic and nondomestic structures as well as their associated features. Several burned structures are included in this phase; as a result, overall material quantities are skewed high. Table 9.1 presents a list of analyzed features in each Stirling community. Material counts by community are presented in Table 9.3, and notable aspects are summarized below.

Stirling Community 1

Community 1 was located in the far northeastern part of the site and included the area around burned temple structure F5-0181 (see Figure 9.4). The wood assemblage indicates that the temple was constructed of a variety of wood types, including oak (*Quercus* sp.), hickory (*Carya* sp.), red cedar (*Juniperus virginiana*), and cottonwood/willow (Salicaceae). An array of ritual and exotic paraphernalia was recovered from the structure, including one flint clay figurine (Brennan et al. 2018:Box 6.2). Contents also included one plaited textile fragment and masses of corn kernels and acorn nuts (Simon 2018:Figure 12.6). Structure 5-0181 also contained one left and one right polished mink (*Neogales vison*) mandible, possibly from the same animal. Context and modification suggest that these mink mandibles were ritual paraphernalia (Kuehn 2016:551). The ethnographic literature includes accounts of small carnivore cranial objects used for ritual or ornamental purposes (cf. Hudson 1976; Swanton 1946). Two turtle carapace fragments from temple structure F5-0181 do not evidence modification but nonetheless may also have been used as scoops, bowls, or even rattles. Based on size, this feature was designated as a domestic structure but one that housed important person or nonperson entities, hence its secondary designation as a "temple" (Brennan 2018b). Structure features F5-0184 and F5-0591, and F5-0188, a public structure, yielded very little in terms of plant or animal remains. In contrast, circular structure F5-0600 contained one swan wing bone fragment in addition to remains from typical comestible fauna, and almost all of the maygrass recovered from Community 1. Again, we see "mundane" foodstuffs being consumed in ritual locations, probably by religious elites.

Stirling Community 2

Community 2 consisted of a cluster of six domestic structures, interior pits, posts, and hearths (see Figure 9.4). It included three burned structures: F5-0276,

F5-0324, and F5-0495. Basin fill flotation samples from both F5-0324 and F5-0495 contained little material, suggesting that the structure was cleaned out before combustion and that burned debris was then removed. Wood was more abundant in F5-0276. Identifiable taxa primarily consist of cottonwood/willow with lesser amounts of oak and hickory. The assemblages are consistent with structural timbers from two Lohmann phase domestic structures (F5-0914 and F5-1721) at the site, which are also dominated by cottonwood/willow woods (Simon 2018). The limited assemblages contrast with the high diversity of wood types used in the construction of the burned temple, F5-0181, clearly indicating that construction material selection was a function of structure use (Simon 2018).

A mass of maize cob fragments from pit F5-1887, located inside structure F5-0091, probably reflects use of cobs for fuel. Otherwise, plant foods from basin fills and internal features across this community group were limited to low counts of maize and starchy seeds. Faunal remains were recovered in moderate quantities from basin fill in four of the six domestic structures. Those assemblages were dominated by either undifferentiated vertebrate or mammal remains. Together, the plant and animal assemblages appear quite characteristic of a Mississippian residential community.

Stirling Community 3

Community 3 comprised a ritual precinct with associated domiciles and public and/or ritual structures as well as a number of internal pits and posts (Brennan 2018a:Figure 9.4). It was divided into three spatial units for comparative purposes. Area A contained 35 features and included both domestic and special-use structures as well as associated internal pit features (see Table 9.3). Two of the domestic structures, F6-0482 and F6-0717, were burned but plant remains were scarce and no faunal remains were recovered from either structure basin or internal pit features. No flotation samples were available from five additional domestic structures, but internal pits from that group likewise contained low counts of plant food remains. White-tailed deer and/or unspecified mammal fragments were present in the basin fill of three domestic structures.

Faunal counts from public structures in Area A are comparable to those from the domestic structures. The only nonmammal taxa identified consisted of six turtle carapace fragments from F6-0533, a pit located in the basin of public structure F6-0397. This multizone pit also contained an exceptionally large quantity of floral material. Wood and seeds were distributed among the six zones, but slightly higher quantities were found in Zones D/E, F, and G. Among starchy grains, chenopods slightly outnumber maygrass, although counts are low. These three zones also yielded almost all of the maize kernels from the feature, while Zone C contained just over 1,000 cupule fragments. These materials likely represent a single episode or a series of closely spaced episodes of feasting, again incorporating mundane foods in nonmundane contexts. The circular and storage structures that were examined contained almost no floral or faunal remains.

Area B comprised 18 features that were located southeast of the screens and walls in Tract 6 (see Figure 9.4). It contained both domestic and public structures and a single storage structure. Basin fills from two burned domestic structures, F6-0315 and F6-0521, produced few subsistence plant remains. Additionally, wood was almost absent from F6-0315 basin samples. However, the lower zones of multizoned pit F6-0356, located inside F6-0315, contained almost 1,000 pieces of wood, distributed among nine zones. Red cedar was the most commonly identified, followed by hickory and oak. Identified faunal remains from structure F6-0315 were limited to two bird fragments and six turtle carapace fragments. The two complete and unmodified falcon talons recovered represent likely ritual or high-status items (Kelly 2010; Kuehn 2016). Food plants included a few maygrass and little barley seeds, but no maize was identified.

Oak wood, likely construction debris, dominated in the F6-0521 basin fill. Faunal remains, particularly white-tailed deer and large-sized mammal fragments, were also abundant. Those remains were recovered from four distinct fill zones. The largest assemblage from Zone B included 69 deer, large and indeterminate mammal bones, a few mussel shell fragments, three rodent incisors, and one bird bone. Assuming contemporary deposition, these materials may well reflect feasting associated with structure closure. The assemblage from the overlaying Zone A fill was smaller and was also almost exclusively deer.

Basin fill from the two public structures, F6-0336 and F6-0520, was not analyzed for plant remains; however, plants were identified from internal pit and post features. The assemblage from post F6-0562, located in the center of public structure F6-0520, was notable for containing over 4,000 pieces of red cedar, most likely remnants of the original post. Plant foods comprised primarily maize kernel fragments and maygrass seeds but in low counts, suggesting random garbage deposition. Faunal remains were limited to a few mussel shell fragments and pieces of mammal and indeterminate vertebrata bone.

Area C consisted of two T-shaped structures (F6-0383 and F6-0386), pits from two public structures, one storage structure, and one massive pit (see Figure 9.4). Given their shape and classification as nondomestic, ritual-use structures, it was anticipated that the T-shaped structures would contain some ritually charged floral or faunal materials, possibly discarded while the structures were in use or left behind when they were abandoned. This was not the case. Faunal remains from both F6-0383 and F6-0386 included only 11 mammal bones and one bird bone. Floral remains were typical and included a few maygrass seeds as well as maize cupules and kernels. The most unusual items were 21 persimmon (*Disopyros virginiana*) seeds from F6-0383 and cedar wood from F6-0386. In terms of floral and faunal assemblages, the presence of red cedar is the only evidence of the ritual use of this area. Likewise, the two public structures and the small storage hut yielded very few remains of any sort. There is no evidence for feasting deposits or other practices that may reflect original use or specialized closure.

A massive pit, F6-0551, was superimposed on structure F6-0383. With a measurement of 3.00 x 4.74 m and a depth of 1.55 m, this pit greatly exceeded the more common cache and storage pits of Community 3 in size (Brennan et al. 2018:241). This pit had an unusual outward flare at the top (Brennan et al. 2018:Figure 4.33), suggesting that it was partially reopened or expanded after initial filling. A total of 32 zones from this pit were analyzed for plant material, and most contained one or a few items. The faunal assemblage was dominated by mammal fragments, which were distributed among five zones. Quantitative and qualitative variability in taxa distributions among the zones of this massive pit do not approach those exhibited by other massive pits at the site; rather, the remains appear to reflect quotidian depositional episodes. This is in keeping with the interpretation that the pit was rapidly and intentionally filled in with soil from the general site area (Brennan et al. 2018:246).

Stirling Phase Communities: Urbanization

Plant and animal assemblages from Stirling phase communities vary both quantitatively and qualitatively, in keeping with the different roles inhabitants of each played within the greater system and with purported locale and feature function. The presence of elite religious, medicinal, and/or political practitioners is clearly evidenced in both Community 1 and Community 3. Temple structure F5-0181 from Community 1 was ritually closed with at least some internal furnishings in place (Brennan 2018a). Materials identified included the sacred red cedar, one figurine, and the remains of traditional foodstuffs—maize and nuts.

Public and domestic structures in Community 3 were delineated from the remainder of the site by screens, perhaps designed to both keep nonsanctioned members of the community out and to keep powerful other worldly entities in. Again, we also find ritual/sacred materials associated with F6-0315, a structure classified as domestic. These included red cedar wood and falcon talons. We also find feasting deposits of traditional foodstuffs in the form of an unusually large concentration of deer bone, identified in the basin fill of nearby domestic structure F6-0521. The inhabitants of ESTL valued deer meat and, while it was widely consumed, its value may have been both economic and symbolic. The preparation and communal consumption of large amounts of deer meat may therefore have been an important part of their cuisine.

Community 3 also included several burned structures that appear to have been wholly or partially cleared off after burning. Basins in the special purpose T-shaped buildings were also kept clean, with any ritually charged objects or material being removed before deconstruction. Based on super positioning, the single massive pit from this area postdated decommissioning of at least one of the T-shaped buildings. However, there are no deposits that clearly suggest that this was the repository of any ritual offerings or other intentional disposal practices.

Community 1 also represents at least part of a ritual area. Remains were especially abundant in the burned temple structure F5-0181. This feature was ritually closed (Brennan 2018a), but, in this case, closure was not preceded by the removal of interior furnishings. In keeping with patterns elsewhere on the site, the basins of nearby domestic structures contained very little debris.

Community 2 contrasts with Communities 1 and 3 in the near absence of ritually charged plant or animal taxa and in the recovery of modest amounts of food debris. Interestingly, the burned structures in this locale were largely constructed of cottonwood/willow with only minimal contributions of hardwoods (e.g., oak and hickory) and no red cedar. These were perhaps the domiciles of the so-called middle class kin groups, perhaps including male and female crafters and farming specialists.

FOOD PROCUREMENT STRATEGIES AND CHANGING SOCIAL ORGANIZATION

Changes in settlement organization at ESTL reflect intentional planning that culminated in the establishment of Stirling phase neighborhoods (Betzenhauser, Kitchen, and Blodgett 2018; Betzenhauser and Pauketat 2019; Betzenhauser and Potter 2019; Brennan 2018a; Brennan et al. 2018). Importantly, they reflect the desire of people to participate in a shared belief system that was the foundation of what is viewed as "Mississippian" in the Cahokian world (Alt 2018b; Emerson, Hedman, Brennan, et al. 2020). The comingling of disparate groups suggests that methods of food preparation were at least initially probably different, with people from different regions preparing food in traditional ways. With urbanization came changes in economic systems, including food procurement, distribution, and storage. As detailed, social changes also included those of land tenure or access, whether proprietary or communal, task allocations, and gender roles (Fritz 2019).

During the initial TLW I, individual family groups were presumably self-sufficient in terms of food procurement. Following the established Woodland pattern, family groups were farming nearby suitable landforms and hunting or fishing locally. During the TLW II, habitation sizes increased and there is also evidence for large-scale rebuilding of a TLW II settlement within the existing TLW I footprint at ESTL. This created a mosaic of relatively tightly spaced TLW II courtyard communities (Betzenhauser, Kitchen, and Blodgett 2018:187, 193, Figure 4.63). Field sizes required to support each community would have varied, depending on the number of individual households involved, and the increased need for cultivated plant foods would have been met by expanding the areas under cultivation farther away from the village. However, if even half of the 38 TLW II communities were occupied simultaneously, associated fields could have extended over 365,000 m^2 (approximately 90 acres) of suitable floodplain soils. These estimates provide at least some idea as to the amount of land that was required to grow agricultural crops. As a result, and with some exceptions (see Simon 2002), most remaining nearby wooded areas were probably also cleared, and it has been suggested that by the early Mississippian period, few if any forested regions remained in the northern American Bottom region (Fritz 2019). Changes in faunal availability are more difficult to determine, but it seems likely that the availability of mammals, particularly white-tailed deer, living in forested edge areas may also have declined. However, the archaeological record indicates no decrease in white-tailed deer meat consumption (Kuehn 2023 in press).

During the Lohmann phase, individual communities expanded into larger neighborhood groups (Betzenhauser and Pauketat 2019; Brennan 2018b:33). Architectural changes marking this break include the use of wall-trench construction and a dramatic increase in the number of specialized building forms (Brennan 2018b; Brennan et al. 2018). Evidence for both inter- and intra-site craft specialization also substantially increased (Pauketat 2018:470–71). Craft specialization is perhaps best represented at ESTL by the recovery of exotic marine shell and marine shell artifact-crafting workshops (see Boles et al. 2018; Kozuch 2023 in press).

It is reasonable to expect specialization also extended into existing food-production systems, in terms of floral and faunal resources. It is generally assumed that farming was the purview of women, and Fritz (2019) has argued that specialized plant cultivation among women may have resulted in the rise of female-led high-status farming societies, where they solidified critical roles in ensuring group continuity. This highlights the importance of women in the subsistence economy and the veneration of productivity, fertility, crops, women, and the earth expressed in contemporaneous Mississippian iconography.

The Lohmann phase was also characterized by an influx of farming groups into the uplands, near Richland Creek, and to the east of the American Bottom proper. Based on archaeological data, these farming groups included both migrants and relocated farming groups already living in the Greater Cahokia region. Presumably, these upland farming communities provided surplus food that was transported to Greater Cahokia to feed nonfood-producing residents (Alt 2018b; Pauketat 2003). Whether the role was undertaken willingly or under coercion is unclear (Alt 2002; Pauketat 2003:55); however, under this model, clearly there was some relationship between upland farmers and urban dwellers.

While they supplied important agricultural produce, it is unclear whether upland-dwelling family groups were also responsible for provisioning faunal resources to the residents of Greater Cahokia. Given the even distribution of high-value white-tailed deer parts found at sites located both in the floodplain and uplands, upland farmers do not seem to have been forced to give up the best cuts to an urban elite (Kuehn 2023). However, the possibility exists that white-tailed deer were so plentiful there was no need to be frugal with the best cuts.

The increased labor costs involved with provisioning one's own kin and other nonproducing persons with agricultural produce would have been considerable. The success of the system likely depended on cooperation and the exchange of valuable commodities, whether physical or spiritual, among the groups involved. For upland farmers, this may have been the opportunity to participate in the Cahokian religious system, which perhaps drew them to the area in the first place (Alt 2018b; Emerson, Hedman, Brennan, et al. 2020). In fact, the production of surplus crops, in particular, may have been viewed as participation within and crucial to the maintenance of the religious system. Successful harvests may have signified that the appropriate animate forces controlling growing conditions had been propitiated, and farmers would have been crucial in this process.

The cuisine of the Greater Cahokia area must have changed during the Lohmann phase as the result of the influx of immigrants bringing their regional cuisines and the new social context in which food was being produced and consumed. Further analysis of the individual Lohmann communities may help to distinguish differences in cuisine among them in this complicated system. However, recovered plant remains are fairly consistent between them. We can see some evidence of feasting, an important aspect of cuisine, through the presence of notable amounts of animal remains. This emphasizes the importance of looking at all available food remains to better interpret the context of their consumption. To carry on this analysis and understand cuisine more fully, we would need to incorporate other lines of evidence such as ceramics and residues for differences in the preparation, composition, and serving of dishes.

Further changes in social, and consequently spatial, organization at ESTL took place in the late Lohmann and Stirling phases. Emerson has suggested the relationships among neighborhood occupants became even more complex with the development of "house societies," defined as "corporate groups that perpetuate themselves by recruitment of outsiders using the terminology and guise of kinship" (Emerson 2018:502). Members of house societies were bound together through mutual obligations and commitment to shared values, traditions, and beliefs. Patterns of artifact recovery from across ESTL provide good evidence that some of these house societies included craft specialists, as evidenced in the identification of specific marine shell, ceramic, and lithic workshops (Boles et al. 2018). Material objects and feature footprints also indicate that house societies were ranked, with some areas clearly occupied by elites.

By the late Stirling period, the majority of the upland Richland Creek farming communities were abandoned. However, urban, nonfood-producing members of society (e.g., craftsmen, elite personages) still required provisions. Given the importance of agriculture, house societies must have included individuals or subgroups who produced crops for all members. Some house societies may have been fortunate enough to control fertile fields in the immediate bottomland, in which case farming members may have lived near or within urban centers. In other cases, farmers occupied small farmsteads scattered across the floodplain. Those groups may have been linked to their house societies through co-members living in nodal centers, who mediated productivity and exchange.

This model can be expanded to encompass faunal food procurement (Kuehn 2023). Small, floodplain farming communities may have served as bases from which fishing and hunting, particularly of waterfowl, were conducted. Upland farm sites also may have been places from which to stage hunting parties. This system would essentially ensure equal access to food, and evidence for this is present in the floral and faunal records from Mississippian sites across the region. Generally, Mississippian period archaeobotanical assemblages comprise similar complexes of crop plants and wild resources regardless of context, site type, and region. Similarly, white-tailed deer meat profiles show no evidence that people living in rural areas were relegated to consuming less optimal cuts (Kuehn 2023). In fact, we see evidence for the preferential use of high-value, meaty portions regardless of site location.

In terms of cuisine, the model presented by Emerson (2018) has several interesting implications. First, it may explain some of the patterning evident in the archaeobotanical and faunal records. Despite the homogeneity in the types of food represented in Mississippian period plant and faunal assemblages, there are also some quantitative differences in taxa representation among sites that are traditionally believed to reflect cuisine. For example, high levels of fish bones from Mississippian period floodplain farmsteads are interpreted as a group of floodplain farmers who relied more on fish protein than did contemporaneous city dwellers (Kuehn 2023). High nutshell recovery levels from upland sites, which were presumably inhabited by groups with ready access to masting trees, are in contrast to lower levels among floodplain groups (Simon and Parker 2006). For the American Bottom region, these broad interpretations based on environmental parameters are generally validated by the very large datasets analyzed. Broadly, we can assume what people ate was, to some extent, dependent on availability. However, the concept of floodplain-dwelling waterfowl eaters and upland-dwelling nut eaters is likely simplistic, particularly if these groups were engaged in food procurement for the Greater Cahokia community. If people living in nodal communities and farmsteads on the floodplain were supplying urban Cahokians with seasonal waterfowl, the abundant waterfowl remains at those sites could result in part from processing before transport. Likewise, nutshell densities could reflect processing nutmeats and nut oil for consumption elsewhere. The existence of this food procurement network also demonstrates the importance of these foods to Cahokian cuisine. People were investing time and effort into assuring access to foods that they valued and that may have had social significance to them. Perhaps they were foods that immigrants to the Greater Cahokia area had eaten before their move and wanted to continue to include in their cuisine. It is also possible that some of these foods were considered vital to specific occasions or events, like having a turkey for a modern American Thanksgiving dinner. People are often resistant to change in their cuisine and will attempt to maintain access to valued ingredients even when alternatives are available.

Also, under the house society model, female farmers may have been important and powerful members of society. From an economic standpoint, these women understood the risks of crop production and were able to ensure others within their cohort had adequate produce to meet the group's needs. Members of ranked women's agricultural societies (Fritz 2019) may have maintained strong bonds partly through the exchange of food, even if some members were dispersed across the countryside. Importantly, when those bonds broke down, a major piece of the political and economic system failed.

Specialists in any area of production or agricultural knowledge were likely interested in promoting their group and its members. The actual relationships among the individual house communities or groups are unknown, and there is plenty of evidence to support inequality and a ranked social organization at both urban centers and smaller, ceremonial nodal centers throughout the region (Betzenhauser and Pauketat 2019; Brennan et al. 2018; Emerson 2018; Pauketat 2018). Nonetheless, if food procurement was anything like the model described here, the concept of autonomous farmers being forcibly coerced to supply food to an elite, all-powerful group of leaders becomes problematic. Instead, it implies that, at the house society level, there may have been a degree of social organization and cooperation, at least for a time.

Considering cuisine from within the framework of social organization can shed light on how people work together or in opposition to sustain themselves in an urban context. This does not mean that all people had the exact same diet or that Greater Cahokia was an egalitarian community where everyone worked together to achieve a common goal or community-wide equality. Competition for status, both on the individual and group level, was undoubtedly an ongoing process.

CONCLUSION

This chapter described plant and animal remains found at the East St. Louis Precinct of Greater Cahokia and highlighted the connection between changes in social organization and food procurement strategies. The foods discussed formed the basis of the cuisine of the people of the Cahokian area. The majority of these foods were in consistent use over an extended period of time; however, there were variations in the quantities of different types of food used in different communities. Some of this variation may represent differences in cuisine between different members of the Cahokian society and reflect important aspects of identity such as regional origin or rank. We also identified a few deposits that may have been the result of feasting events, which served as an important focus of group and identity building through the use of cuisine.

The information provided in this chapter can serve as the basis for future studies of Cahokian cuisine. The social and occupational history of sites in the

Greater Cahokia area are complicated and extensive. Important distinctions in cuisine throughout the region no doubt existed, but large amounts of detailed data, like those summarized here, would be required to tease them out. It might be useful to compare the food choices made by individual communities in the Greater Cahokia precincts with those of people from sites in surrounding regions to see whether they reflect immigrants bringing their cuisine into the larger society. In addition, cuisine would be better studied through combining information about plant and animal remains with other forms of archaeological evidence such as ceramics and residue analysis. This would allow us to explore questions such as the circumstances surrounding the cooking, serving, and consumption of meals as well as their social importance and cultural context. It is likely that food preparation and consumption changed in context during the urbanization of Cahokia. Examining ceramics may help to distinguish communal from household meals. Although the information in this chapter confirms previous findings that the people of the Greater Cahokia area selected a relatively stable set of ingredients over a long period of time, we still know relatively little about how these ingredients were combined into individual dishes. Ceramic residue studies would help to identify these and explore whether recipes changed along with the social organization.

Sometime around AD 1200, ESTL was partially abandoned. Evidence for massive conflagrations a decade or two before cal AD 1200 suggests intentional, ritual closure, perhaps associated with the death or departure of prominent personages or nonhuman personages (Pauketat 2018:479). Climate change and attendant years of low crop yields may have also played a role in the dramatic collapse of Greater Cahokia (Benson et al. 2007; Benson et al. 2009). Were poor harvests seen as the failure of elites to control the weather and ensure production through intervention with powerful, other-than-human forces? On a purely economic level, crop failures meant food scarcity and the inability to maintain existing social systems, further demonstrating the importance of farming economies in maintaining a complex social system. The analysis of plant and animal remains from ESTL shows that cuisine is defined by more than food procurement, processing, and consumption; it is also an indicator of identity, power, and status.

Conclusion

Why Cuisine?

JODIE A. O'GORMAN AND SUSAN M. KOOIMAN

Nestled shoulder to shoulder around our favorite microbrewery food and spirits on a sunny pre-pandemic afternoon, our love of food abundantly apparent, our discussion revolved around the merits of cuisine as a focal point for the symposium that led to this volume. We decided to adopt an encompassing stance contrary to more exclusive definitions, such as food historian Civitello's (2011) view that cuisine developed only in "advanced civilizations" where labor specialization and food surplus allowed differentiation of cuisine from cooking for survival. In our view, cuisine conveys the cultural significance people give to food, its preparation, and its consumption. The experience of cuisine, our ideas about food, eating, cooking, sharing, and modifying to taste and circumstance, is integral to the human experience. We assume that the antiquity of the meaningfulness of cuisine and culinary practice is part of being human and is inseparable from any notion of human culture.

By focusing on cuisine we hoped to discover a more human-centered story of Native American foodways in the Midcontinent than traditional archaeological subsistence studies tend to reveal. This does not detract from the fact that subsistence studies are an integral part of how culture history, socioeconomics, and human interaction with the landscape are understood. In fact, all chapters in this volume draw on understandings based in subsistence studies in either general background or very specific ways as sources of data. Subsistence studies are foundational and have been central to Midcontinental archaeology for more than half a century; as such, their importance cannot be overemphasized.

What then, does cuisine have to offer that goes beyond subsistence studies? Perhaps a more intimate view of subsistence is one part of the answer, but foodways and its subtopic of cuisine go beyond the selection and use of foodstuffs and other resources. For example, as seen in the chapters of this volume, the focus on cuisine expands our inquiry to include such topics as explorations of the cultural embeddedness of decisions about food, how cuisine is used in signaling and negotiating identity, how people cook and choose to experiment with different practices, how and what they cook and serve for different occasions, and the relationship between everyday and special cuisines. Along the way, more unexpected (although unsurprising) themes emerge, such as women's agency around food and cooking and subregional distinctions in cuisine that are underemphasized when only foodstuffs are considered.

Before discussing the insights gained by looking through the cuisine lens, it is important to note that the chapters and our observations here are based in an anthropological archaeology perspective that lacks firsthand Indigenous knowledge. We acknowledge that our own worldview as it relates to cuisine, among other things, may be so different that key information vital to understanding Native cuisine is likely beyond our sight. An interaction with a Native student in a North American archaeology class serves as a relevant example. During a lecture about changes in subsistence strategies over time, O'Gorman was rendered speechless for a moment when a Native American student suggested that the term "exploit" (as in, "exploiting certain resources") was perhaps not the best word to use when discussing Native/environmental interactions. But was this simply a matter of semantics? After all, archaeologists probably meant *exploit* as in *use*, not as in "to benefit from unfairly." Or are the two meanings really not that different? And if so, what is a more appropriate expression that also lends some understanding to the non-Native world? We simply acknowledge this bias for the moment and reflect on its repercussions and future approaches in our final thoughts below.

CUISINE IN THE ANCIENT MIDCONTINENT

Traditional subsistence studies provide fundamental data on what plants and animals were part of foodways at any given site and their relative abundance provides data on landscape use. Often based on data gleaned from individual sites or comparative analyses through time and across space, regional subsistence patterns and their links to socioeconomic shifts are fairly well understood. When we turn our attention to cuisine, more intimate acts of food preparation, ways of cooking, and the relationships of food, land, people, and social meaning emerge.

Culinary practices within and between archaeological time periods provide new details about the social fabric of prehistory in the Midcontinent and suggest ample room for further exploration. Here, we provide a synopsis of the contributions of the volume that bring to light variations in culinary practices across the Midcontinent, between different groups of people, and across time.

Neubauer's (chapter 1) analysis of earth oven cooking in the Late Archaic on Grand Island offers an in-depth look at this poorly understood and often overlooked cooking method and its use during a time when the landscape had stabilized and become more productive. Repeated use of resource-rich areas, as documented in other parts of the Midcontinent during this time period, is linked by Neubauer to the use of earth ovens. She carefully examines the technology and provides new insights into its use, finding that the ovens were likely used to bake foods with slow and moist cooking. These ovens do not contain food remains, which is probably the result of using layers of foliage to buffer foods from the heat and provide moisture for steam. Given the evidence at contemporary sites, Neubauer suggests that nuts were baked in these ovens but acknowledges their use in other places for meat and root foods as well. Her research into the technology and discussion of variation suggest that more careful analyses to identify and understand the variation in cooking associated with earth ovens across the Midcontinent will be productive for understanding cooking before the use of pottery vessels and in later time periods when the ovens were used alongside hearth cooking.

Kooiman and Albert's (chapter 2) analysis of cuisine at the Cloudman site offers an enticing view of changing cuisine within a localized area from Middle Woodland to Late Prehistoric times. Using microbotanical identification of plant starches and phytoliths from residues on pots and cooking use-wear, they document shifts in stewing and boiling cooking modes that may be related to a shift in types of grains that were the focus over time. While both maize and *manoomin* (wild rice) were used from the Middle Woodland period onward, unlike areas of the Midcontinent farther to the south, maize is more important early on. We now know that the shift in emphasis from maize to *manoomin* is not simply a change from one grain to another but entailed linked shifts in ingredients, preparation, and cooking. Stewing of ingredients was common early on, when maize was more predominant. Boiling and then stewing became common later in time. While recognizing that many foods are unrepresented, insight into cultural sensibilities of acceptable food combinations and the growing centrality of *manoomin* emerge.

Using plant and animal macroremains along with ceramics and spatial information, Hass (chapter 3) provides another diachronic view of Middle Woodland through Late Woodland periods in a more southern location. Lake Koshkonong is roughly 450 miles from Drummond Island and less than 50 miles west of Lake Michigan. Although still considered very much a Great Lakes setting, the environment is vastly different and the local ancient cuisine provides a stark contrast to contemporary groups represented at Cloudman. Here, at the Finch site, wild rice, maize, and squash are not part of the cuisine until late in the sequence at AD 900. During the Early Woodland, cooking was done near domestic structures with some nut use. Terrestrial and aquatic animals were important for their meat and for bone grease processing. In the Middle Woodland, the addition of nut oil extraction signals culinary innovations in soups and changes in the intensity of gathering of nuts in the surrounding area. At the same time, there is more intensive processing of animal resources in the form of grease rendering in the camp farther from the house. Hass further identifies insights into preparation of dishes with nuts and fauna being processed and cooked in some pots, and only animal meat cooked in others, suggesting the possibility of specific cooking functions for some vessels within the domestic culinary sphere.

From about AD 900 onward, many groups throughout the Midcontinent incorporate more maize into their diet, and different groups of people and/or ideas appear to spread with attendant cultural interactions and shifts. Cuisine would naturally play a significant role in these developments, and the contributions in this volume focused on later time periods make clear that cuisine was an active agent of change.

In southwestern Manitoba, what appears to be an abrupt transition to maize agriculture and associated practices and symbolism illustrates the centrality of cuisine. Malainey (chapter 7) addresses a large and complex question regarding a society's decision to adopt an entirely new food production strategy and cuisine by considering both practical and spiritual aspects of that endeavor. Carefully reviewing the evidence for adoption of maize horticulture in the region, Malainey argues that hunters and gatherers in the area were introduced to maize farming and its attendant symbolic and religious practices by experienced Oneota-like horticulturalists with ties to the northern Mississippi valley around AD 1250. Use of the superfood concept highlights the multiple tendrils of cultural change and, we would note, the central role of women in these changes linked to foodways that directly impact and, at the same time, are influenced by decision-making around cuisine.

Shifts in cuisine need not be as seismic as complete replacement. From AD 1300 to 1400 Mississippian and Oneota peoples at Morton Village along the Illinois River in west-central Illinois negotiated social transformations of coalescence, and cuisine played an important role. Drawing on earlier analyses of food choice and differential cooking preferences between Oneota and Mississippian groups, Painter and O'Gorman (chapter 4) further explore serving and consumption practices via plate use at the site. This highly decorated, emblematic vessel adopted for use by Oneota potters and cooks was used throughout the site in domestic and ritual contexts. It is suggested that the plates and the foods presented on them allowed Oneota migrants to participate in cuisine-centered events that were part of the Mississippian world. While Oneota women facilitated these social negotiations as they likely made these vessels and produced the dishes presented within them, they also continued their culinary practices that were distinct from those of Mississippian women. Continuing their practice using their pottery as multipurpose implements, Oneota women used their plates significantly more than did their Mississippian neighbors for small-batch cooking of food or for warm serving.

Also at Morton Village, Nordine (chapter 6) explores the makeup of plant assemblages within refuse pits with exclusively Oneota or Mississippian pottery and those with mixed pottery. Though difficult to tease apart cuisines based largely on the same available foodstuffs, Nordine does provide evidence of the Oneota maintaining a higher diversity of kinds of plants used, which is in keeping with food choices seen elsewhere in the tradition. She also identifies what might be a preference for acorns among Mississippians. Importantly, Nordine also suggests that the observed preference for hickory versus acorns among the Oneota may reflect a divided, yet shared, responsibility for nut processing. There is also a pattern of more maize in Oneota pits, and the appearance of beans in the region corresponds with the arrival of the Oneota.

Martin (chapter 5) explores the cuisine of feasting at Morton Village through faunal remains. Based on location, structure, and contents, investigators interpreted a unique pit feature at the site, F224, as a facility related to ritual and feasting. Martin compares the large and diverse faunal assemblage to everyday food choices in the village and beyond. He finds that rather than fitting the grand, status-enhancing model of feasting seen at Cahokia and elsewhere, F224 provides evidence of more a potluck model important for fostering community relationships. The possibility that this event also includes some special animals (eagle and cormorant) and excludes others that we recognize as special (dog and bear) is also explored. Sparseness of plant foods represented in F224 is remarkable (Nordine, chapter 6), and their absence emphasizes the special activities involved in use of the pit. Likewise, nonculinary plant materials, including nightshade and tobacco, support a special use for this facility.

The emergence, apogee, and decline of the Cahokia phenomenon in the American Bottom is the most socially complex of social transformations in the

Midcontinent. Cuisine, both everyday and that associated with special events, played a major role in these transformations. With extensive archaeological investigations of the American Bottom, aided by major highway projects and a long tradition of concerted professional oversight and interpretation, a remarkable cumulative scope of subsistence studies has emerged along with copious data on ceramics and other assemblages. Building on these foundations, researchers in this volume are beginning to explore questions of cuisine and its role in social changes of the Cahokia phenomenon. This is a complex task given the scope of time, development of neighborhoods and different centers, the emergence of social hierarchy, incorporation of immigrants, and missionizing (to name some) that are associated with the phenomenon.

In our collection, Betzenhauser (chapter 8) considers the importance of the choices surrounding one cooking method in culinary practice. While the necessity of processing maize to increase its nutritional availability is critical when it is a primary food on which groups are reliant, the manner in which this chemical reaction was accomplished was variable and could be influenced by local geological factors affecting lime production. As Betzenhauser notes, this variability, along with the taste, texture, and visual changes imparted to the food, would have allowed expansion of local recipes and should be understood as part of the culinary contribution to creation and maintenance of community identity. Using contextual information, ceramic data, archaeometry, and experimental methods, Betzenhauser links this culinary practice to an innovative and heretofore curious form of pottery.

Schaefer, Simon, and King (chapter 9) take a broader approach to consider the relationship of cuisine to the context of changing social organization from before the Lohman phase (AD 1050–1150) through the Stirling phase (AD 1150–250). Detailing community-based contexts, they examine linkages between major shifts in procurement, preparation, and disposal patterns associated with the rise of urbanism and house societies. From the coming together of disparate groups with their own food traditions based in rather homogeneous resource availability, to expansion of croplands, probable specialization in production, and growing complexity of procurement patterns based in house societies, they build a framework of essential data, context, and expectations for more focused future cuisine research.

FOOD FOR THOUGHT

Several thematic areas emerge from the chapters that illustrate the importance of considering cuisine in Midcontinental archaeology: local cuisines, culinary change, social dimensions of cuisine, and women and cuisine. In *Foods of the Americas: Native Recipes and Traditions*, the Divinas write, "For American Indian people, local foods and traditional ways of preparing food have always been and remain important sources of spirituality and community. Native recipes likewise reflect the diversity and adaptability of indigenous cultures" (Divina and Divina 2004:xiii). Chapters herein suggest this is true for the ancient Midcontinent as well. Adaptability of Indigenous cultures is not a new topic in archaeology, but the study of cuisine change provides new perspectives on human agency in that adaptability vis-à-vis the role of food in economic, political, and social dynamics. Contextual data that situate culinary events, including spatial and social context, are often key. Finally, we explore how cuisine shines a light on the importance of women's work.

Local Cuisines

Although there are some important subregional variations, many plants and animals were common components of meals throughout much of prehistory across most of the Midcontinent. White-tailed deer, elk, small mammals, fish, waterfowl, and many seedy and oily plants, to name some, are common ingredients. Findings in this volume show that localized cuisines emerge, even when drawing on many of the same of ingredients, through recipes combining certain ingredients, different methods of preparation and cooking, and the state in which they are presented. In the past as in the present, local distinctions in plants and animals naturally play a role in distinctions between localized cuisines as well. For example, the whitefish and sturgeon of more northern big water areas, have taste and texture qualities quite distinct from the Mississippi valley's drum, catfish, and bowfin. Likewise, *manoomin* only grows in areas with the right water qualities and climate. Even then, local conditions can create local flavors (Vennum 1988). Focusing on cuisine rather than diet and subsistence emphasizes the nuances of local foods and the resulting differences in eating that would be experienced.

Even within a single location at one point in time Nordine (2020 and chapter 6) or across time (Schaefer, Simon, and King, chapter 9), nuanced differences in cuisine can be gleaned using traditional subsistence study identifications and careful consideration of contexts. While sampling and other issues leave some ambiguity, careful consideration of such observations can begin to build detailed comparative datasets to help identify culinary distinctions among groups. Microbotanical studies of foodstuffs (Kooiman and Albert, chapter 2) taken from cooking pots more directly inform about cuisine, although sampling issues are still relevant.

CONCLUSION

Ingredients are obviously incredibly important in cuisine, and so too are the methods of preparation. Chapters in this volume document variation in the use of common cooking methods including steaming/roasting/baking in earth ovens and stewing/boiling in ceramic vessels through time and across space (chapters 1–3). Variation between groups at a single point in the life of a village are also documented (Painter and O'Gorman, chapter 4). Cooking also includes all steps in the preparation of a dish. In our own kitchens this might include drying, chopping, tenderizing, marinating, rubbing, and so on before thermal alteration. Although it is difficult to identify different preparatory techniques of the past, Betzenhauser's (chapter 8) multipronged analysis shows that it is possible to demonstrate that certain techniques were carried out and to understand the variability in techniques.

Overall, the application of multiple datasets to questions of cuisine are necessary, as every chapter in this volume illustrates. Recognizing potential differences in cuisines via macrobotanical and other subsistence analyses, further data from microanalyses, cooking methods, presentation, and context can help identify cuisines. Experimental data can provide detailed information on the variability of cooking methods and specific chapters in this volume identify the need for further such studies to identify specific signatures (chapters 1 and 8). Although ethnohistoric literature provides clues to subregional cuisines, we wonder whether greater collaboration with traditional Native American cooks from an array of communities across the Midcontinent might provide new insights. While recognizing the profound disruptions of colonization, Indigenous histories and sharing of local practices focused on culinary traditions that may have been carefully curated over generations could illuminate deep traditions.

Culinary Change and Persistence

Perhaps because food is at once both material in nature as "a building block of the biological, ecological, and economic systems" and rich in symbolic meaning (Hastorf and Weismantel 2007:308), cuisine is at once conservative and prone to both large and small changes. The tempo and extent of culinary changes can also be quite variable. When recognizable in the archaeological record, culinary change is often closely linked to significant broader cultural shifts. Environmental changes and/or changing social situations are often linked to modifications in cuisines, and the impetuses for such shifts may also lead to or be affected by technological change. By focusing on ancient cuisine and recognizing its holistic linkages, we can better understand the role and nature of cuisine and likely gain insight into the linked contextual shifts as well.

The broadest, most revolutionary change in cuisine dealt with in this volume is the shift to maize agriculture in southern Manitoba (Malainey, chapter 7). The decision to adopt a new food—maize—and to embrace significant technological and ideological changes is one that was made by many groups across the Midcontinent. However, most shifts to maize agriculture occurred within a context of existing farming economies. The more abrupt shift in Manitoba brings into more stark contrast the attendant changes in the entire cultural package. It highlights the holistic cultural shift of marked cuisine change that goes beyond recognizing a shift in subsistence and begins to address more intimate questions of how and why. Of direct interest for our focus is that at the core of these shifts is the willingness of cooks, and those they feed, to embrace maize as a new, or more important, part of their cuisine. While further exploration is needed to detail the specifics of culinary change before, during, and after this event, we emphasize that food, and most certainly cuisine, was at the center of dynamic cultural change.

In opposition to such widespread changes, persistence of maize and its role in emerging identity can be seen in the major economic and other social shifts associated with keeping maize at the center of emerging Cahokia society (Schaefer, Simon, and King, chapter 9). There, adoption of different procurement models in the face of changing social structures enabled the persistence of maize in the culinary repertoire for most Cahokian residents.

Change and persistence are both important when migration is part of the social context. Here, cuisine of both local and migrant groups plays significant roles in inter- and intragroup dynamics. Whether the migration outcome is a brief period of coexistence or a more prolonged or even coalescent scenario, cuisine of both groups is likely to be affected if for no other reason than the food supply will have to accommodate greater numbers of people (Kowalewski 2006). Indeed, cuisine can be instrumental in bringing people together or creating and maintaining social boundaries (Graff 2018; Hastorf 2017; Twiss 2012). In the case of Cahokia, maize agriculture is an integral part of the emergence and growth of its religious phenomenon and group identity (Schaefer, Simon, and King, chapter 9). At the same time, cuisine appears to be variable among the different neighborhoods, and closer examination of cuisine within and between neighborhoods promises greater insight into diversity of traditions that were brought together and helped create the Cahokia phenomenon. Far from static, cuisine also played a vital role in the formation and support of a more hierarchical social structure, urbanization, and emergence of house societies.

In the central Illinois Valley, a smaller-scale migration event provides an opportunity to look in greater detail at the role of cuisine in social negotiations and how cuisine of a group may change. Painter and O'Gorman (chapter 4) find that local culinary traditions are incorporated into the migrant group's practices, but certain distinctive ways of cooking and eating are maintained. Food choices between the two groups appear to be similar pre- and post-migration with some nuanced distinctions (Nordine, chapter 6), but methods of preparation and serving more clearly signal differences as well as similarities.

Shared culinary practices, such as choice and combinations of foods, ways of preparing, and serving, can help build and strengthen community, differentiating one community from another (Hastorf 2017; Twiss 2007). The shift to widespread use of maize throughout the Cahokia region may have provided part of the idea that bound many migrants together. However, as in the central Illinois Valley, we might expect that different groups also used cuisine to signal a variety of distinctions. Betzenhauser (chapter 8) reminds us that cooking includes the whole of the preparation process. Practices such as different methods of corn processing create distinctive versions of cuisine; such distinctions in recipes can serve to reconnect people to shared traditions or celebrate new affiliations.

Social Dimensions of Cuisine

In addition to the intersection of cuisine and identity touched on, archaeologies of food also examine economics, status, politics, ritual, and religion (Hastorf 2017; Twiss 2019). By focusing on cuisine, lived experiences of ancient peoples in these dimensions are brought to the fore and new insights into social stability and change may emerge. Several examples illustrate how a focus on cuisine can further our understanding of the human dynamic in economies. Examining the context of storage, processing, and cooking from Early Woodland to Late Woodland, Haas (chapter 3) reveals important changes in household culinary practices and economies over time. Painter and O'Gorman (chapter 4), drawing on cooking patterns and floral and faunal studies (Nordine 2020; Painter 2022), illustrate that, without attention to culinary practices, seemingly similar subsistence economies may mask variation in household and community economics. At the same site, Nordine (chapter 6) further tentatively identifies the possibility of cooperative intergroup foci on nut procurement and processing along with nuances of intergroup economies. Schaefer, Simon, and King (chapter 9) focus on the interplay of social structure and economics with food procurement and suggest that food and cuisines played an important role in creating obligations between different segments of Mississippian society in the American Bottom.

While most chapters focus on everyday cuisine, some bring to light the importance of cuisine in ritual, religious, and other special settings. Feasting is typically attributed to these special social contexts, but identifying and understanding the variability of feasting in the archaeological record remain topics of interest (Dietler and Hayden 2001; Kassabaum 2019). Chapters in this volume illustrate a range of this culinary behavior in the Midcontinent (Martin, chapter 5; Nordine, chapter 6; Schaefer, Simon, and King, chapter 9). In the Cahokia region, status-enhancing events featuring high-value meat portions are documented along with community-based events incorporating and sometimes featuring different types of food, such as fish (Schaefer, Simon, and King, chapter 9). Further exploration of the diversity of feasting within that complex social setting could help link culinary distinctions to neighborhood identity and/or variation in ritual needs.

In a less socially complex, though multiethnic setting, Martin (chapter 5) identifies a potluck version of feasting. There, an abundance of different kinds of animals were amassed for the feast and accompanied by a few special animals, plants, and other items. Other special culinary occasions are documented at this site as well. Painter and O'Gorman's (chapter 4) work documenting the functional and contextual use of plates suggests that food and its presentation in these highly decorated dishes simultaneously allowed the immigrant group to adopt and partake in local customs involving food while signaling group identity. Together with Nordine's work (chapter 6) and Painter and O'Gorman's (chapter 4) observations on the cooking and serving vessels, Martin's research on animal involvement in the ritual associated with F224 supports the interpretation that everyday and special cuisine was used in multiple ways to negotiate community building while preserving some of the traditional culinary practices of each group.

Cuisine is and was both a tool of social integration and social distinction. Culinary traditions can be strong, yet also both subject to and an agent of political and economic change.

Women and Cuisine

Although not a focus within this volume, a common theme that independently emerged among several of the chapters is the role of women in shaping cuisine. Across the majority of the Midcontinent, women are very likely to have been the primary cooks and keepers of culinary knowledge both in everyday practice and for special events. Men have traditionally been perceived as having agency in subsistence, and they are implicitly regarded as the decision makers, but cuisine shifts our lens to the agency of women in shaping cultural practices and identity.

Women were the primary farmers, gatherers, and cooks among descendant

CONCLUSION 237

populations of Midcontinental Indigenous societies, according to the ethnographic record (Densmore 1979, 2005; Hilger 1959; Tooker 1991; Vennum 1988; Waugh 1973). In fact, they may have been the primary laborers and leaders of a great many important everyday and specialized tasks. Women were also the potters. A survey of ethnographic and ethnohistoric accounts of societies around the world found that women are generally the primary potters in communities where pottery was manufactured at the household level, which would include the majority of Indigenous societies in North America (Skibo and Schiffer 1995). Therefore, women were responsible for designing, making, and imbuing ceramic cooking, processing, and serving vessels with both symbolic and practical meaning.

Although some argue that assuming women always filled the role of cook is reductive and demeaning, this argument itself demeans and diminishes the importance of food gathering, cooking, processing, and storage, which is in many ways central to hunter-gatherer and horticultural lifeways (Brumbach and Jarvenpa 1997; Nelson 1997). Decisions regarding food selection and scheduling of food acquisition would have affected settlement patterns and ritual and social practices, providing a cultural core around which a society may have formed their identity. The manufacture of pottery would have placed women in direct control of the technology they employed for daily food-related practices and contributed an additional dimension of identity formation and communication via pottery form and style.

Our focus on cuisine in the Midcontinent during ancient times reveals the centrality of women's activities in shaping the relationships between groups and their landscapes. This is exemplified in the Woodland period Great Lakes region, where resident hunter-gatherers grappled with incorporating domesticates and low-level agricultural practices into their subsistence regimes (Kooiman and Albert, chapter 2; Haas, chapter 3); in the Central Illinois River Valley, where migrant horticultural Oneota peoples negotiated new environmental and sociopolitical landscapes (Painter and O'Gorman, chapter 4); and in the American Bottom, where Mississippian agriculturalists used food to shape their relationships to the land and to each other (Schaefer, Simon, and King, chapter 9). Women shaped cuisine, and this volume has highlighted that cuisine is connected to many other aspects of culture. Thus, those who control cuisine possess influence over society. This poses women as important decision-makers in the ancient Midcontinent. Such a revelation requires the topic of gender in relation to foodways and cuisine in the Midcontinent (in addition to considerations of more than two genders in ancient Indigenous societies) be highlighted and explored further in the future.

LOOKING FORWARD

In bringing together this collection of research focused on cuisine of the ancient Midcontinent we wanted to celebrate and share with a wider audience the insights about people of the past revealed by this perspective, and to highlight current approaches while thinking about new directions. The chapters each individually expose new information and/or ways about thinking about food in the ancient Midcontinent. Together, the chapters provide a taste of how cuisine can inform about a wide variety of social dynamics. Observations herein range from revolutionary to nuanced adjustments, but each demonstrate that what is on the plate or in the pot matters significantly. We encourage further such studies and suggest that a focus on cuisine will lead to more holistic understandings of groups within the ancient Midcontinent and the cultural shifts through time already identified by archaeology. Cuisine itself is a multifaceted endeavor, and to pursue it through archaeology requires solid traditional subsistence research, contextual data, a variety of methods to study its many different aspects, and knowledge or at least clues about its symbolic and ideological underpinnings.

Techniques used by colleagues in this volume do not exhaust all possible currently available methods for identifying foodstuffs and cooking (see Graff 2018 for a review). We encourage further use of all available techniques to address cuisine and look forward to new developments. However, works in this volume demonstrate that there are many productive ways to examine cuisine. Applying a suite of methods while examining different aspects of cuisine is a very productive approach. For example, bringing together analyses of where, what, and how by looking at spatial context along with evidence of cooking methods and botanical food remains allowed multiple insights. Use of experimental archaeology coupled with ethnography, or contextual data coupled with floral and faunal data, were effective as well.

Additional perspectives may be enlightening. Our sensory experience of food is inextricably tied to cuisine, and exploring a sensory perspective (Hamilakis 2013, 2015; Metheny 2022; Rowan 2019; Skeates and Day 2019) seems a natural next step for some of our case studies, as does pursuing Indigenous perspectives. Several of the chapters in this volume seem readily adapted to a consideration of sensorial aspects of cuisines. Malainey's research (chapter 7) on the adoption of corn agriculture in Manitoba has clear parallels to Metheny's (2022) historical case study. Through consideration of the senses involved in consumption, production, and preparation, Metheny (2022) was able to explore new understandings of identity and colonial society. Likewise, sensory aspects of feasting and serving practices at Morton Village (chapters 4, 5, 6) may provide new insights into the intercultural negotiations there. And, as Betzenhauser (chapter 8) points out, the flavor profiles of dishes where the corn is prepared with wood ash versus lime would be interesting to explore. So too might the sensory experiences of working with each of these agents during preparatory phases.

As noted at the outset of this conclusion, the incorporation of Indigenous knowledge into studies of cuisine is not represented in this volume, and this is an important avenue of future research. If we consider a Native worldview centered on interactive relationships with land, plants, and animals, it seems likely that interactions with food and cuisine in the past will have other nuanced meanings that have largely remained unexplored in archaeology of the Midcontinent. A glimpse into the rich knowledge about aspects of cuisine with which archaeologists are not engaging can be seen in the work on intersection of Native American religion and foodways (Pesantaubbee and Zogry 2021). New understandings of animism from the ontological perspective (Descola 2013; Posthumus 2017, 2018) further suggest that this different worldview of relationships with plants and animals may affect the meaning and experience of cuisine. What then are we missing when we do not understand this interactive relationship? How did these relationships affect cuisine of the past? What were the correct ways of interacting for sustenance, cooking, and serving? Exploring these meanings in the ancient past and how they reverberate in today's Indigenous cuisine will require shifts in thinking and collaborative epistemologies and methods.

We encourage future collaborative projects with Tribes across the Midcontinent so that archaeology might be brought into their service around the topic of cuisine—a topic that all around the table will find of interest though perhaps for different reasons. As archaeologists, we expect such collaboration will help us think about cuisine and Native American culture in new and more insightful ways, thereby better understanding its various connections to cultural diversity and change.

References

Adair, Mary J.

2000   Tobacco on the Plains: Historical Use, Ethnographic Accounts, and Archaeological Evidence. In *Tobacco Use by Native North Americans: Sacred Smoke and Silent Killer*, edited by Joseph C. Winter, pp. 171–85. University of Oklahoma Press, Norman.

Adams, Karen R.

2014   Little Barley Grass (*Hordeum Pusillum* Nutt.): A Prehispanic New World Domesticate Lost to History. In *New Lives for Ancient and Extinct Crops*, edited by Paul J. Minnis, pp. 139–79. University of Arizona Press, Tucson.

Ahler, Stanley A.

2002   Site Description and Previous Investigations. In *Prehistory of First Street NE: The Archaeology of Scattered Village in Mandan, North Dakota*, edited by S. A. Ahler, pp. 1.1–1.17. Research Contribution No. 40 of PaleoCultural Research Group. Submitted to the City of Mandan and the North Dakota Department of Transportation, Bismarck.

Ahler, Stanley A., and Carl R. Falk

2002   Modified Bone and Antler Remains. In *Prehistory of First Street NE: The Archaeology of Scattered Village in Mandan, North Dakota*, edited by S. A. Ahler, pp. 13.1–13.45. Research Contribution No. 40 of PaleoCultural Research Group. Submitted to the City of Mandan and the North Dakota Department of Transportation, Bismarck.

Albala, Ken

2013   *Grow Food, Cook Food, Share Food: Perspectives on Eating from the Past and a Preliminary Agenda for the Future*. Oregon State University Press, Corvallis.

Albert, Rebecca, Susan M. Kooiman, Caitlin Clark, and William A. Lovis

2018   Earliest Microbotanical Evidence for Maize in the Northern Lake Michigan Basin. *American Antiquity* 83(2):345–55.

Aliseda, Andrea

2021   Masa Today, Masa Forever: Unlocking Nixtamal. *Epicurious* (blog), June 23.

Alt, Susan M.

2002   Identities, Traditions, and Diversity in Cahokia's Uplands. *Midcontinental Journal of Archaeology* 27(2):217–35.

2006   The Power of Diversity: The Roles of Migration and Hybridity in Culture Change.

In *Leadership and Polity in Mississippian Society*, edited by Brian M. Butler and Paul D. Welch, pp. 289–308. Occasional Paper No. 33, Center for Archaeological Investigations, Southern Illinois University, Carbondale.

2018a   *Cahokia's Complexities: Ceremonies and Politics of the First Mississippian Farmers.* University of Alabama Press, Tuscaloosa.

2018b   Putting Religion Ahead of Politics. In *Archaeology and Religion in the American Midcontinent*, edited by Brad H. Koldehoff and Timothy R. Pauketat, pp. 208–33. University of Alabama Press, Tuscaloosa.

Ambrose, Stanley H., Jane Buikstra, and Harold W. Krueger

2003   Status and Gender Differences in Diet at Mound 72, Cahokia, Revealed by Isotopic Analysis of Bone. *Journal of Anthropological Archaeology* 22(3):217–26.

Anderson, E. N.

2014   *Everyone Eats: Understanding Food and Culture.* 2nd ed. New York University Press, New York.

Anderson, Jay A.

1971   Scholarship on Contemporary American Folk Foodways. *Ethnologia Europaea* 5(1):56–63.

Apfelbaum, David

2001   Jewish Cuisine. *Ethnology* 40(2):165–69.

Appadurai, Arjun

1981   Gastro-Politics in Hindu South Asia. *American Ethnologist* 8(3):494–511.

1988   How to Make a National Cuisine: Cookbooks in Contemporary India. *Comparative Studies in Society and History* 30(1):3–24.

Arranz-Otaegui, Amaia, Lara Gonzalez Carretero, Monica N. Ramsey, Dorian Q. Fuller, and Tobias Richter

2018   Archaeobotanical Evidence Reveals the Origins of Bread 14,400 Years Ago in Northeastern Jordan. *PNAS* 115(31):7925–30.

Arzigian, Constance M.

1987   The Emergence of Horticultural Economies in Southwestern Wisconsin. In *The Emergence of Horticultural Economies of the Eastern Woodlands*, edited by W. F. Keegan, pp. 217–42. Occasional Publication 7, Center for Archaeological Investigations, Carbondale.

1993   Analysis of Prehistoric Subsistence Strategies: A Case Study from Southeastern Wisconsin. Unpublished PhD dissertation, Department of Anthropology, University of Wisconsin–Madison.

Arzigian, C. M., R. F. Boszhardt, H. P. Halverson, and J. L. Theler

1994   The Gunderson Site: An Oneota Village and Cemetery in La Crosse, Wisconsin. *Journal of the Iowa Archeological Society* 41:3–75.

Asch, David L., and Nancy B. Asch

1977   Chenopod as Cultigen: A Re-evaluation of Some Prehistoric Collections from Eastern North America. *Midcontinental Journal of Archaeology* 2(1):3–45.

1978   The Economic Potential of Iva annua and Its Prehistoric Importance in the Lower Illinois Valley. In *The Nature and Status of Ethnobotany*, edited by Richard I. Ford, pp. 301–41. Anthropological Papers No. 67. Museum of Anthropology, University of Michigan, Ann Arbor.

1985   Prehistoric Plant Cultivation in West-Central Illinois. In *Prehistoric Food*

REFERENCES 243

Production in North America, edited by Richard I. Ford, pp. 149–203. Anthropological Papers No. 75. Museum of Anthropology, University of Michigan, Ann Arbor.

Atalay, Sonya, and Christine A. Hastorf

2006   Food, Meals, and Daily Activities: Food Habitus at Neolithic Catalhoyuk. *American Antiquity* 71(2):283–319.

Backhouse, Paul

2008   Campfires in Context: Hunter-Gatherer Fire Technology and the Archaeological Record of the Southern High Plains, USA. PhD dissertation, Department of Anthropology, Bournemouth University, Poole, England.

Ball, Janet

1993   Ethnobotany, Land Use Patterns, and Historic Landscape Evaluation: Grand Island, Michigan. Heritage Program Monograph No. 2. Manuscript on file, USDA Forest Service, Hiawatha National Forest, Escanaba.

Bardolph, Dana N.

2014   Evaluating Cahokian Contact and Mississippian Identity Politics in the Late Prehistoric Central Illinois River Valley. *American Antiquity* 79(1):69–89.

Bardolph, Dana N., and Amber VanDerwarker

2015   Lamb Site Archaeobotanical Remains: Reconstructing Early Mississippian Plant Collections and Cultivation in the Central Illinois River Valley. *Illinois Archaeology* 27:215–35.

Bardolph, Dana N., and Gregory D. Wilson

2015   The Lamb Site (11SC24): Evidence of Cahokian Contact and Mississippianization in the Central Illinois River Valley. *Illinois Archaeology* 27:138–49.

Barr, Kenneth

1979   An Analysis of the Faunal Assemblage from the Elam Site, an Upper Mississippian Seasonal Encampment on the Kalamazoo River in Allegan County, Michigan. Master's thesis, Department of Anthropology, Western Michigan University, Kalamazoo.

Barrett, James H., Roelf P. Beukens, and Rebecca A. Nicholson

2001   Diet and Ethnicity during the Viking Colonization of Northern Scotland: Evidence from Fish Bones and Stable Carbon Isotopes. *Antiquity* 75:145–54.

Bassie-Sweet, Karen

2008   *Maya Sacred Geography and the Creator Deities.* University of Oklahoma Press, Norman.

Beach, Robert H., A. Michelle Bullock, Katherine B. Heller, Jean L. Domanico, Mary K. Muth, Alan C. O'Connor, and Richard B. Spooner

2000   *Lime Production: Industry Profile.* Research Triangle Institute Final Report prepared for Eric L. Crump, US Environmental Protection Agency. Research Triangle Institute Center for Economics Research, Research Triangle Park, North Carolina.

Beaudry, Mary C.

2013   Feasting on Broken Glass: Making a Meal of Seeds, Bones, and Sherds. *Northeast Historical Archaeology* 42:184–200.

2017   Digging Up Dinner: Gastronomical Archaeology. Paper presented at Global Food + 2017, Boston.

Beck, Margaret E.

2001   Archaeological Signatures of Corn Preparation in the U.S. Southwest. *Kiva* 67:187–218.

2006 Midden Ceramic Assemblage Formation: A Case Study from Kalinga, Philippines. *American Antiquity* 71(1):27–51.

Becker, George C.

1983 *Fishes of Wisconsin*. University of Wisconsin Press, Madison.

Beisaw, April M.

2013 *Identifying and Interpreting Animal Bone: A Manual*. Texas A&M University Anthropology Series, College Station.

Belasco, Warren, and Philip Scranton (editors)

2002 *Food Nations: Selling Taste in Consumer Societies*. Routledge, New York.

Bell, David John

2003 Diaspora. In *Encyclopedia of Food and Culture*, Vol. 1, edited by Solomon H. Katz, pp. 513–15. Charles Scribner's Sons, New York.

Bell, David, and Gill Valentine

1997 *Consuming Geographies: We Are Where We Eat*. Routledge, New York.

Bell, R. E.

1971 Bison Scapula Skin-Dressing Tools? *Plains Anthropologist* 16(52):125–27.

1980 *Oklahoma Indian Artifacts*. Contributions from the Stovall Museum No. 4. University of Oklahoma, Norman.

Bellomo, Randy

1991 Identifying Traces of Natural and Humanly Controlled Fire in the Archaeological Record: The Role of Actualistic Studies. *Archaeology in Montana* 32(2):75–93.

Benchley, Elizabeth D.

2003 Mississippian Alkali Processing of Corn. *Wisconsin Archeologist* 84(1&2):127–37.

Benchley, Elizabeth, Derrick Marcucci, Cheong-Yip Yuen, and Kristin Griffin

1988 *Final Report of Archaeological Investigation and Data Recovery at the Trout Point 1 Site, Alger Country, Michigan*. Report of Investigations No. 89. Manuscript on file, Archaeological Research Laboratory, University of Wisconsin–Milwaukee.

Benchley, Elizabeth D., Blane Nansel, Clark A. Dobbs, Susan M. Thurston Myer, and Barbara H. O'Connell

1997 *Archeology and Bioarchaeology of the Northern Woodlands*. The Central and Northern Plains Archeological Overview. Arkansas Archaeological Survey, Fayetteville.

Bengtson, Jennifer D., and Jodie A. O'Gorman

2016 Children, Migration, and Mortuary Representation in the Late Prehistoric Central Illinois River Valley. *Childhood in the Past: An International Journal* 9(1):19–43.

2017 War at the Door: Evolutionary Considerations of Warfare and Female Fighters. In *Bioarchaeology of Women and Children in Times of War*, edited by Debra L. Martin and Caryn Tegtmeyer, pp. 27–48. Springer International Publishing, Cham, Switzerland.

Benn, David W.

1989 Hawks, Serpents, and Bird-Men: Emergence of the Oneota Mode of Production. *Plains Anthropologist* 34(125):233–60.

Benn, David W., and Joe B. Thompson

2014 What Four Late Woodland Sites Reveal about Tribal Formation Processes in Iowa. *Illinois Archaeology* 26:1–55.

Benson, Larry V., Michael S. Berry, Edward A. Jolie, Jerry D. Spangler, David W. Stahle, and Eugene M. Hattori

REFERENCES 245

2007 Possible Impacts of Early 11th, Middle 12th, and Late 13th Century Droughts on Western Native Americans and the Mississippian Cahokians. *Quaternary Science Review* 26(3–4):336–50.

Benson, Larry V., Timothy R. Pauketat, and Edward R. Cook

2009 Cahokia's Boom and Bust in the Context of Climate Change. *American Antiquity* 74(3):467–83.

Bentsen, Silje Evjenth, and Sarah Wurz

2019 Color Me Heated? A Comparison of Potential Methods to Quantify Color Change in Thermally Altered Rocks. *Journal of Field Archaeology* 44(4):215–33.

Benz, Bruce F.

1987 Seeds from the Naze Site. In *Archaeological Excavation at the Naze Site (32SN246)*, edited by Michael L. Gregg, pp. 303–28. Report prepared for the US Department of the Interior, Bureau of Reclamation by the Department of Anthropology, University of North Dakota, Grand Forks.

Beoku-Betts, Josephine

1995 We Got Our Way of Cooking Things: Women, Food, and Preservation of Cultural Identity among the Gullah. *Gender and Society* 9(5):535–55.

Betts, Colin M.

2000 Symbolic, Cognitive, and Technological Dimensions of Orr Phase Oneota Ceramics. Unpublished PhD dissertation, Department of Anthropology, University of Illinois at Urbana-Champaign.

Betzenhauser, Alleen (editor)

2018a *East St. Louis Precinct Terminal Late Woodland Ceramics*. Research Report No. 42. Illinois State Archaeological Survey, Prairie Research Institute, University of Illinois at Urbana-Champaign.

2018b *East St. Louis Precinct Terminal Late Woodland Features*. Research Report No. 46. Illinois State Archaeological Survey, Prairie Research Institute, University of Illinois at Urbana-Champaign.

2019a East St. Louis Precinct Terminal Late Woodland Features. New Mississippi River Bridge Project Technical Report No 3, Illinois State Archaeological Survey, Prairie Research Institute, University of Illinois at Urbana Champaign.

Betzenhauser, Alleen

2019b Summary and Conclusions. In *The East Saint Louis Precinct Terminal Late Woodland Ceramics*, edited by Alleen Betzenhauser, pp. 359–62. New Mississippi River Bridge Project, Technical Report No 4, Illinois State Archaeological Survey, Prairie Research Institute, University of Illinois at Urbana-Champaign.

2021 Nixtamalization and Cahokian Cuisine. Paper presented in the MAC Sponsored Symposium at the 64th Annual Meeting of the Midwest Archaeological Conference, East Lansing, Michigan.

Betzenhauser, Alleen, and Madeleine Evans

2022 Consuming the Landscape: Materials and Methods for Nixtamalization in the Cahokia Region (AD 900–1100). Manuscript on file, Illinois State Archaeological Survey, Prairie Research Institute, University of Illinois at Urbana-Champaign.

Betzenhauser, Alleen, Sarah Harken, and Victoria Potter

2017a Investigating Stumpware: Evidence for Pre-Mississippian Nixtamalization in

Illinois. Poster presented at the 74th Annual Meeting of the Southeastern Archaeological Conference, Tulsa, Oklahoma.

2017b   Investigating Stumpware: Evidence for Pre-Mississippian Nixtamalization in Illinois. Poster presented at the 61st Annual Meeting of the Midwest Archaeological
Conference, Indianapolis.

Betzenhauser, Alleen, Tamira K. Brennan, Michael Brent Lansdell, Sarah E. Harken, and
Victoria E. Potter

2018   Chronological Implications and External Connections in the East St. Louis Precinct Ceramic Assemblage. In *Revealing Greater Cahokia, North America's First
Native City: Rediscovery and Large-Scale Excavations of the East St. Louis Precinct*,
edited by Thomas E. Emerson, Brad H. Koldehoff, and Tamira K. Brennan, pp.
263–331. Studies in Archaeology No. 12. Illinois State Archaeological Survey,
Prairie Research Institute, University of Illinois at Urbana-Champaign.

Betzenhauser, Alleen, and Timothy Pauketat

2019   Elements of Cahokian Neighborhoods. *Archaeological Papers of the American Anthropological Association* 30(1):133–47.

Betzenhauser, Alleen, and Victoria E. Potter

2019   Terminal Late Woodland I Features. In *East Saint Louis Precinct Terminal Late
Woodland Features*, edited by Alleen Betzenhauser, pp. 33–68. New Mississippi
River Bridge Project Technical Report No. 3, Illinois State Archaeological Survey,
Prairie Research Institute, University of Illinois at Urbana-Champaign.

Betzenhauser, Alleen, Craig H. Kitchen, and Daniel F. Blodgett

2019   Terminal Late Woodland II Features. In *East Saint Louis Precinct Terminal Late
Woodland Features*, edited by Alleen Betzenhauser, pp. 69–288. New Mississippi
River Bridge Project Technical Report No. 3, Illinois State Archaeological Sur-
vey, Prairie Research Institute, University of Illinois at Urbana-Champaign.

Bhabha, Homi K.

1990   The Third Space. In *Identity, Community Culture, Difference*, edited by J. Rutherford, pp. 207–21. Lawrence and Wishart, London.

1994   *The Location of Culture*. Routledge, London.

Binford, Lewis, Sally Binford, Robert Whallon, and Margaret Hardin

1970   *Archaeology at Hatchery West*. Memoirs of the Society for American Archaeology
No. 24. Society for American Archaeology, Washington, DC.

Biwer, Matthew E., and Amber M. VanDerwarker

2015   Plant Subsistence at Myer-Dickson during the Woodland and Mississippian Periods.
Illinois Archaeology 27:82–117.

Black, Stephen, and Alston Thoms

2014   Hunter-Gatherer Earth Ovens in the Archaeological Record: Fundamental Concepts. *American Antiquity* 79(2):203–26.

Blake, Michael

2015   *Maize for the Gods: Unearthing the 9,000-Year History of Corn*. University of California Press, Oakland.

Blakeslee, Donald J.

1981   The Origin and Spread of the Calumet Ceremony. *American Antiquity*
46(4):759–68.

REFERENCES

Blitz, John H.
1993 Big Pots for Big Shots: Feasting and Storage in a Mississippian Community. *American Antiquity* 58(1):80–96.

Boas, Franz
1921 Ethnology of the Kwakiutl. 35th Annual Report of the Bureau of American Ethnology. Bureau of American Ethnology, Washington, DC.

Bohlen, H. David
1989 *The Birds of Illinois*. Indiana University Press, Bloomington.

Boles, Steven L. (editor)
2018 *East St. Louis Precinct Terminal Late Woodland and Mississippian Lithics*. Research Report No. 41. Illinois State Archaeological Survey, Prairie Research Institute, University of Illinois at Urbana-Champaign.

Boles, Steve, Tamira Brennan, Laura Kozuch, Steven R. Kuehn, and Mary L. Simon
2018 Crafting and Exotica at the East St. Louis Precinct. In *Revealing Greater Cahokia: North America's First Native City*, edited by Thomas E. Emerson, Brad H. Koldehoff, and Tamira K. Brennan, pp. 387–461. University of Illinois at Urbana-Champaign.

Bollwerk, Elizabeth A., and Shannon Tushingham
2016 Expanding Perspectives on the Archaeology of Pipes, Tobacco, and Other Smoke Plants in the Ancient Americas, in *Perspectives on the Archaeology of Pipes, Tobacco, and Other Smoke Plants in the Ancient Americas*, edited by Elizabeth A. Bollwerk and Shannon Tushingham, pp. 1–12. Interdisciplinary Contributions to Archaeology, Springer International Publishing, Cham, Switzerland.

Bolnick, Deborah A., and David Glenn Smith.
2007 Migration and Social Structure among the Hopewell: Evidence from Ancient DNA. *American Antiquity* 72(4):627–44.

Boszhardt, Robert F.
1994 Oneota Group Continuity at La Crosse: The Brice Prairie, Pammel Creek, and Valley View Phases. *Wisconsin Archaeologist* 75(3–4):173–237.

Boszhardt, Robert F.
1998 Additional Western Lithics for Hopewell Bifaces in the Upper Mississippi River Valley. *Plains Anthropologist* 43(165):275–86.
2002 Contracting Stemmed: What's the Point? *Midcontinental Journal of Archaeology* 27(1):35–67.
2003 *A Projectile Point Guide for the Upper Mississippi River Valley*. University of Iowa Press, Iowa City.
2004 The Late Woodland and Middle Mississippi Component at the Iva Site, La Crosse County, Wisconsin in the Driftless Area of the Upper Mississippi River Valley. *Minnesota Archaeologist* 63:60–85.

Boszhardt, Robert F., and Natalie Goetz
2000 An Apparent Late Woodland Boundary in Western Wisconsin. *Midcontinental Journal of Archaeology* 25(2):269–87.

Boszhardt, Robert F., and James B. Stoltman
2016 Petrographic Analysis of Late Woodland and Middle Mississippian Ceramics at the Iva Site (47Lc42), Onalaska, Wisconsin. *Midcontinental Journal of Archaeology* 41(2):93–126.

248 REFERENCES

Bourdieu, Pierre
1977 *Outline of a Theory of Practice*, translated by R. Nice. Cambridge University Press, Cambridge.

Boyd, Matthew J., and Clarence Surette
2010 Northernmost Precontact Maize in North America. *American Antiquity* 75(1):117–33.

Boyd, Matthew, Clarence Surette, Andrew Lints, and Scott Hamilton
2014 Wild Rice (Zizania spp.), the Three Sisters, and the Woodland Tradition in Western and Central Canada. In *Reassessing the Timing, Rate, and Adoption Trajectories of Domesticate Use in the Midwest and Great Lakes*, edited by Maria E. Raviele and William A. Lovis, pp. 7–32. Midwest Archaeological Conference Occasional Papers No. 1.

Boyd, M., C. Surette, and B. A. Nicholson
2006 Archaeobotanical Evidence of Prehistoric Corn at the Northern Edge of the Great Plains. *Journal of Archaeological Science* 33(8):1129–40.

Boyd, M., T. Varney, C. Surette, and J. Surrette
2008 Reassessing the Northern Limit of Maize Consumption at the Northern Edge of the Great Plains. *Journal of Archaeological Science* 35(9):2545–56.

Brant, Tawnya
2020 Chef Tawnya Brant: Reviving Indigenous North American and Haudenosaunee Food Culture (website), accessed October 12, 2023.

Branstner, Christine N.
1995 *Archaeological Investigations at the Cloudman Site (20CH6): A Multicomponent Native American Occupation on Drummond Island, Michigan, 1992 and 1994 Excavations*. Report on file at the Consortium for Archaeological Research, Michigan State University, East Lansing.

Brashler, Janet G., Michael J. Hambacher, Terrance J. Martin, Kathryn E. Parker, and James R. Robertson
2006 Middle Woodland Occupation in the Grand River Basin of Michigan. In *Recreating Hopewell*, edited by D. K. Charles and J. E. Buikstra, pp. 261–84. University Press of Florida, Gainesville.

Braun, David P.
1983 Pots as Tools. In *Archaeological Hammers and Theories*, edited by James A. Moore and Arthur S. Keene, pp. 107–334. Academic Press, New York.

Bray, Tamara L. (editor)
2003 *The Archaeology and Politics of Food and Feasting in Early States and Empires*. Klewer Academic/Plenum Publishers, New York.

Brennan, Tamira K.
2018a Organization of the East Saint Louis Precinct. In *East St. Louis Precinct Mississippian Features*, edited by Tamira K. Brennan, pp. 341–68. New Mississippi River Bridge Project, Technical Report No. 5, Illinois State Archaeological Survey, Prairie Research Institute University of Illinois at Urbana-Champaign.
2018b Architecture. In *East Saint Louis Precinct Mississippian Features*, edited by Tamira K. Brennan, pp. 23–190. New Mississippi River Bridge Project Technical Report No 5. Illinois State Archaeological Survey, Prairie Research Institute, University of Illinois at Urbana-Champaign.

Brennan, Tamira K. (editor)

2018c *East St. Louis Precinct Mississippian Features: New Mississippi River Bridge Project Technical Report No 5*. Illinois State Archaeological Survey, Prairie Research Institute University of Illinois at Urbana-Champaign.

Brennan, Tamira K., Alleen M. Betzenhauser, Michael Brent Lansdell, Luke A. Plocher, Victoria E. Potter, and Daniel F. Blodgett

2018 Community Organization of the East St. Louis Precinct. In *Revealing Greater Cahokia, North America's First Native City: Rediscovery and Large-Scale Excavations of the East St. Louis Precinct*, edited by Thomas E. Emerson, Brad H. Koldehoff, and Tamira K. Brennan, pp. 147–202. Studies in Archaeology No. 12. Illinois State Archaeological Survey, Prairie Research Institute, University of Illinois at Urbana-Champaign.

Brennan, Tamira K., Michael Brent Lansdell, and Alleen Betzenhauser (editors)

2019 *East St. Louis Precinct Mississippian Ceramics*. Research Report No. 45. Illinois State Archaeological Survey, Prairie Research Institute, University of Illinois at Urbana-Champaign.

Bressani, Ricardo, Ramiro Paz y Paz, and Nevin S. Scrimshaw

1958 Corn Nutrient Losses: Chemical Changes in Corn during Preparation of Tortillas. *Journal of Agricultural and Food Chemistry* 6(10):770–74.

Bressani, Ricardo, and Nevin S. Scrimshaw

1958 Lime-Heat Effects on Corn Nutrients, Effect of Lime Treatment on in Vitro Availability of Essential Amino Acids and Solubility of Protein Fractions of Corn. *Journal of Agricultural and Food Chemistry* 6(10):774–78.

Briggs, Rachel V.

2015 The Hominy Foodway of the Historic Native Eastern Woodlands. *Native South* 8(1):112–46.

2016 The Civil Cooking Pot: Hominy and the Mississippian Standard Jar in the Black Warrior Valley, Alabama. *American Antiquity* 81(2):316–32.

2018 Detangling Histories of Hominy: A Historical Anthropological Approach. In *Baking, Bourbon, and Black Drink: Foodways Archaeology in the American Southeast*, edited by Tanya M. Peres and Aaron Deter Wolf, pp. 160 73. University of Alabama Press, Tuscaloosa.

Brinkman, Adam C.

2019 Comales and Colonialism: An Analysis of Cuisine and Ceramics on a 17th-Century New Mexican *Estancia*. Master's thesis, Historical Archaeology Program, University of Massachusetts, Boston.

Brose, David S., and Michael J. Hambacher

1999 The Middle Woodland in Northern Michigan. In *Retrieving Michigan's Buried Past: The Archaeology of the Great Lakes State*, edited by John R. Halsey, pp. 173–92. Cranbrook Institute of Science, Bloomfield Hills, Michigan.

Brown, Ian W.

1980 *Salt and the Eastern North American Indian: An Archaeological Study*. Lower Mississippi Survey Bulletin No. 6. Peabody Museum, Harvard University, Boston.

1981 *The Role of Salt in Eastern North American Prehistory*. Louisiana Archaeological Survey and Antiquities Commission Anthropological Study No. 3. Louisiana Department of Culture, Recreation, and Tourism.

1989 The Calumet Ceremony in the Southeast and Its Archaeological Manifestations. *American Antiquity* 54(2):311–31.

Brown, J. A.

1961 *The Zimmerman Site: A Report on Excavations at the Grand Village of Kaskaskia, La Salle County, Illinois.* Report of Investigations No. 9, Illinois State Museum, Springfield.

Brown, James A., and Robert F. Sasso

2001 Prelude to History on the Eastern Prairies. In *Societies in Eclipse: Archaeology of the Eastern Woodlands, A.D. 1400–1700*, edited by David S. Brose, Robert C. Mainfort, and C. Wesley Cowan, pp. 205–29. University of Alabama Press, Tuscaloosa.

Brown, L. A.

1966 The Gillette Site (39ST23), Oahe Reservoir, South Dakota. *Plains Anthropologist* 11(34):239–89.

Brumbach, Hetty Jo, and Robert Jarvenpa

1997 Woman the Hunter: Ethnoarchaeological Lesson from Chipewyan Life-Cycle Dynamics. In *Women in Prehistory: North America and Mesoamerica*, edited by Cheryl Claassen and Rosemary A. Joyce, pp. 17–32. University of Pennsylvania Press, Philadelphia.

Buchanan, Meghan E.

2015 Warfare and the Materialization of Daily Life at the Mississippian Common Field Site. PhD dissertation, Department of Anthropology, Indiana University, Bloomington.

2018 Patterns of Faunal Utilization and Sociopolitical Organization at the Mississippian Period Kincaid Mounds Site. *Midcontinental Journal of Archaeology* 43(2):151–79.

2020 Diasporic Longings? Cahokia, Common Field, and Nostalgic Orientations. *Journal of Archaeological Method and Theory* 27(1):72–89.

Buchner, A. P.

1986 Archaeological Research at the Lockport Site: 1866–1985. Manuscript on file, Historic Resources Branch, Manitoba Culture, Heritage and Recreation, Winnipeg.

1988 Geochronology of the Lockport Site. *Manitoba Archaeological Quarterly* 12(2): 27–31.

Buckelew, F. M.

1911 *Buckelew, the Indian Captive; or, The life Story of F. M. Bucklew* [sic] *While a Captive among the Lipan Indians in the Western Wild of Frontier Texas, as Related by Himself* [and] *Written by S. E. Banta.* Mason Herald, Mason.

Buonasera, Tammy, Antonio V. Herrera-Herrera, and Carolina Mallo

2019 Experimentally Derived Sedimentary, Molecular, and Isotopic Characteristics of Bone Fueled Hearths. *Journal of Archaeological Method and Theory* 26(4):1327–75.

Burchill, Alexandra, and Matthew J. Boyd

2015 Analysis and Dietary Implications of Plant Microfossils on Middle Woodland Food Residues, Northern Minnesota. *Minnesota Archaeologist* 74:107–21.

Bush, Leslie L.

2019 Tobacco, Bulbs, and Other New Plant Finds from the Dixon Site (13WD8). Paper presented at the 63rd Annual Midwest Archaeological Conference, Mankato, Minnesota.

Camp, Charles
1982   Foodways in Everyday Life. *American Quarterly* 34(3):278–89.
Capes, K. H.
1963   *The W. B. Nickerson Survey and Excavations, 1912–15, of the Southern Manitoba Mounds Region.* Anthropology Papers of the National Museum of Canada 4. Ottawa.
Carney, Molly, Jade Guedes, Eric Wohlgemuth, and Shannon Tushingham
2022   Bulbs and Biographies, Pine Nuts and Palimpsests: Exploring Plant Diversity and Earth Oven Reuse at a Late Period Plateau Site. *Archaeological and Anthropological Sciences* 14(7):1–29.
Carpiaux, N.
2018   The Koshkonong Creek Village Site (47JE0379): Ceramic Production, Function, and Deposition at an Oneota Occupation in Southeastern Wisconsin. Unpublished Master's thesis, Department of Anthropology, University of Wisconsin–Milwaukee.
Carr, Christopher
2005   Rethinking Interregional Hopewellian "Interaction." In *Gathering Hopewell: Society, Ritual, and Ritual Interaction,* edited by Christopher Carr and D. Troy Case, pp. 575–623. Springer, New York.
Carr, Dillon H.
2012   Paleoindian Economic Organization in the Lower Great Lakes Region: Evaluating the Role of Caribou as a Critical Resource. PhD dissertation, Department of Anthropology, Michigan State University, East Lansing.
Charles, Douglas K., and Jane E. Buikstra
2006   *Recreating Hopewell.* University Press of Florida, Gainesville.
Cheetham, David
2010   Corn, Colanders, and Cooking: Early Maize Processing in the Maya Lowlands and Its Implications. In *Pre-Columbian Foodways: Interdisciplinary Approaches to Food, Culture, and Markets in Ancient Mesoamerica,* edited by John E. Staller and Michael Carrasco, pp. 345–68. Springer, New York.
Cheung, Sidney C. H.
2005   Consuming "Low" Cuisine after Hong Kong's Handover: Village Banquets and Private Kitchens. *Asian Studies Review* 29:259–73.
Choctaw Nation of Oklahoma Historic Preservation
2010   Choctaw Foods: History and Development. *Biskinik.*
Civitello, Linda
2011   *Cuisine and Culture: A History of Food and People.* 3rd ed. Wiley and Sons.
Clark, Jeffery J., Jennifer A. Birch, Michelle Hegmon, Barbara J. Mills, Donna M. Glowacki, Scott G. Ortman, Jeffrey S. Dean, Rory Gauthier, Patrick D. Lyons, Matthew A. Peebles, Lewis Borck, and John A. Ware
2019   Resolving the Migrant Paradox: Two Pathways to Coalescence in the Late Precontact U.S. Southwest. *Journal of Anthropological Archaeology* 53:262–87.
Clark, Jeffrey J., Deborah L. Huntley, J. Brett Hill, and Patrick D. Lyons
2013   The Kayenta Diaspora and Salado Meta-Identity in the Late Precontact U.S. Southwest. In *The Archaeology of Hybrid Material Culture,* edited by Jeb J. Card, pp. 399–424. Southern Illinois University–Carbondale, Center for Archaeological Investigations Occasional Paper No. 39. Carbondale.

REFERENCES

Cleland, Charles E.

1966　*The Prehistoric Animal Ecology and Ethnozoology of the Upper Great Lakes Region.* Anthropological Papers No. 29. Museum of Anthropology, University of Michigan, Ann Arbor.

1982　The Inland Shore Fishery of the Northern Great Lakes: Its Development and Importance in Prehistory. *American Antiquity* 47(4):761–84.

1999　Cultural Transformation: The Archaeology of Historic Indian Sites in Michigan, 1670–1940. In *Retrieving Michigan's Buried Past: The Archaeology of the Great Lakes State*, edited by John R. Halsey, pp. 279–90. Cranbrook Institute of Science, Bloomfield Hills, Michigan.

Cocking, Matthew

1908　An Adventurer from Hudson Bay: Journal of Matthew Cocking from York Factory to the Blackfoot Country, 1772–1973, edited by L. J. Burpee, pp.89–121. *Transactions of the Royal Society of Canada*, Series 3, Vol. 2, Section 2.

Conner, Michael D., and Jodie A. O'Gorman

2012　An Unusual Pit Feature at the Morton Village Site. Poster presented to the 58th Annual Midwest Archaeological Conference. East Lansing, Michigan.

Conrad, Lawrence A.

1991　The Middle Mississippian Cultures of the Central Illinois Valley. In *Cahokia and the Hinterlands: Middle Mississippian Cultures of the Midwest*, edited by Thomas E. Emerson and R. Barry Lewis, pp. 119–56. University of Illinois Press, Champaign.

Cook, Robert A., and T. Douglas Price

2015　Maize, Mounds, and the Movement of People: Isotope Analysis of a Mississippian/Fort Ancient Region. *Journal of Archaeological Science* 61:112–28.

Cook, Robert A., and Mark R. Schurr

2009　Eating between the Lines: Mississippian Migration and Stable Carbon Isotope Variation in Fort Ancient Populations. *American Anthropologist* 111(3):344–59.

Cooper, Janet

1996　*Cloudman Site (20CH6), Drummond Island, Michigan, Features 26 and 27, 1992 Excavations.* On file at the Consortium for Archaeological Research, Department of Anthropology, Michigan State University, East Lansing.

Coues, Elliot

1893　*History of the Expedition under the Command of Lewis and Clark: To the Sources of the Missouri, thence across the Rocky Mountains and down the River Columbia to the Pacific Ocean.* Francis P. Harper, New York.

Counihan, Carole M.

1999　*The Anthropology of Food and Body: Gender, Meaning, and Power.* Routledge, New York.

Counihan, Carole, and Penny Van Esterik

1997　*Food and Culture: A Reader.* Routledge, New York.

Creese, John L.

2016　Making Pipes and Social Persons at the Keffer Site: A Life History Approach. In *Perspectives on the Archaeology of Pipes, Tobacco, and Other Smoke Plants in the Ancient Americas*, edited by Elizabeth A. Bollwerk and Shannon Tushingham, pp. 27–49. Springer International Publishing, Cham, Switzerland.

Cremin, William

1980 The Schwerdt Site: A Fifteenth Century Fishing Station on the Lower Kalamazoo River, Southwest Michigan. *Wisconsin Archeologist* 61(2):280–91.

1996 The Berrien Phase of Southwest Michigan: Proto-Potawatomie? In *Investigating the Archaeological Record of the Great Lakes State: Essays in Honor of Elizabeth Baldwin Garland*, edited by Margaret Holman, Janet Brashler, and Kathryn Parker, pp. 383–413. New Issues Press, College of Arts and Sciences, Western Michigan University, Kalamazoo.

1999 Upper Mississippian Adaptation: The View from Southwestern Michigan. In *Retrieving Michigan's Buried Past: The Archaeology of the Great Lakes State*, edited by John Halsey, pp. 264–71. Bulletin 64. Cranbrook Institute of Science, Bloomfield Hills, Michigan.

Crown, P. L.

2000 Women's Role in Changing Cuisine. In *Women and Men in the Prehispanic Southwest: Labor, Power, and Prestige*, edited by P. L. Crown, pp. 226–66. School of American Research Press, Santa Fe, New Mexico.

Cutright, Robyn E.

2021 *The Story of Food in the Human Past : How What We Ate Made Us Who We Are.* University of Alabama Press, Tuscaloosa.

Dawdy, Shannon Lee

2010 A Wild Taste: Food and Colonialism in 18th Century Louisiana. *Ethnohistory* 57(3):389–414.

Davis, Simon J. M.

1987 *The Archaeology of Animals.* Routledge, Abingdon.

Deagan, Kathleen

1983 *Spanish St. Augustine: The Archaeology of a Colonial Creole Community.* Academic Press, New York.

2013 Hybridity, Identity, and Archaeological Practice. In *The Archaeology of Hybrid Material Culture*, edited by Jeb J. Card, pp. 260–78. Occasional Paper No. 39. Center for Archaeological Investigations, Southern Illinois University, Carbondale.

Deal, Michael

1985 Household Pottery Disposal in the Maya Highlands: An Ethnoarchaeological Interpretation. *Journal of Anthropological Archaeology* 4(4):243–91.

DeBoer, Warren

1988 Subterranean Storage and the Organization of Surplus: The View from Eastern North America. *Southeastern Archaeology* 7(1):1–20.

Deck, D. M., and C. T. Shay

1992 Preliminary Report on Plant Remains from the Lockport site (EaLf-1). *Manitoba Archaeological Journal* 2(2):36–49.

Defelice, Michael S.

2003 The Black Nightshades, *Solanum nigrum* L. et al.: Poison, Poultice, and Pie. *Weed Technology* 17(2):421–27.

Delacre, Marie, Daniel Lakens, and Christophe Leys

2017 Why Psychologists Should by Default Use Welch's T-Test Instead of Student's T-Test. *International Review of Social Psychology* 30(1):92–101.

Delorit, Richard J.
1970   *Illustrated Taxonomy Manual of Weed Seeds.* Agronomy Publications, River Falls, Wisconsin.

Demgenski, Philipp
2020   Culinary Tensions. *Asian Ethnology* 79(1):115–35.

Densmore, Frances
1979   *Chippewa Customs.* Minnesota Historical Society Press, St. Paul.
2005   *Strength of the Earth: The Classic Guide to Ojibwe Uses of Native Plants.* Minnesota Historical Society Press, St. Paul.

Descola, Philippe
2013   *Beyond Nature and Culture.* Translated by Janet Lloyd. University of Chicago Press, Chicago.

Dietler, Michael
2001   Theorizing the Feast: Rituals of Consumption, Commensal Politics, and Power in African Contexts. In *Feasts: Archaeological and Ethnographic Perspectives on Food, Politics, and Power,* edited by Brian Hayden and Michael Dietler, pp. 65–114. University of Alabama Press, Tuscaloosa.

Dietler, Michael, and Brian Hayden (editors)
2001   *Feasts: Archaeological and Ethnographic Perspectives on Food, Politics, and Power.* Smithsonian Institution Press, Washington, DC.

Dietler, Michael, and Brian Hayden
2001   Digesting the Feast: Good to Eat, Good to Drink, Good to Think. In *Feasts: Archaeological and Ethnographic Perspectives on Food, Politics, and Power,* edited by Brian Hayden and Michael Dietler, pp. 1–22. University of Alabama Press, Tuscaloosa.

Dion-Buffalo, Yvonne, and John Mohawk
1999   Daybreak Farm and Food Project Seeks Revitalization of White Corn Usage. In *A People's Ecology: Explorations in Sustainable Living,* edited by Gregory Cajete, pp. 175–86. Clear Light Publishers, Santa Fe.

Dirks, Robert, and Gina Hunter
2012   The Anthropology of Food. In *The Routledge International Handbook of Food Studies,* edited by Ken Albala, pp. 3–13. Taylor and Francis, New York.

Divina, Fernando, and Marlene Divina
2004   *Foods of the Americas: Native Recipes and Traditions.* Ten Speed Press, Berkeley, in Association with Smithsonian National Museum of the American Indian.

Dotzel, Krista M.
2021   Mind the Gap: Maize Phytoliths, Macroremains, and Processing Strategies in Southern New England, 2500–500 BP. *Economic Botany* 75(1):30–47.

Douglas, Mary
1966   *Purity and Danger.* Routledge, New York.
1997   Deciphering a Meal. In *Food and Culture: A Reader,* edited by Carole Counihan and Penny Van Esterik, pp. 36–54. Routledge, New York.

Driver, Harold, and W. Massey
1957   *Comparative Studies of North American Indians.* Transactions of the American Philosophical Society, New Series, Vol. 47, Part 2. American Philosophical Society, Philadelphia.

REFERENCES

Dunham, Sean B.

2014   Conclusions. In *Late Woodland Settlement and Subsistence Patterns in the Eastern Upper Peninsula of Michigan*, pp.176–208. PhD dissertation, Department of Anthropology, Michigan State University, East Lansing.

Dunham, Sean, and John Anderton

1999   Late Archaic Radiocarbon Dates from the Popper Site (FS 09-10-03-825/20AR350): A Multicomponent Site on Grand Island, Michigan. *Michigan Archaeologist* 45(1):1–22.

Dunne, Julie, Alexa Höhn, Katharina Neumann, Gabriele Franke, Peter Breunig, Louis Champion, Toby Gillard, Caitlin Walton-Doyle, and Richard P. Evershed

2022   Making the Invisible Visible: Tracing the Origins of Plants in West African Cuisine through Archaeobotanical and Organic Residue Analysis. *Archaeological and Anthropological Sciences* 14(1):1–22.

Dunsenberry, Verne

1960   The Material Culture of the Assiniboine Indian. *Ethnos* 25(1–2):44–62.

Ebell, S. B.

1988   The Red and Assiniboine Rivers in Southern Manitoba: A Late Prehistoric and Early Historic Buffer Zone? *Manitoba Archaeological Quarterly* 12(2):1–26.

Edwards, Richard W., IV

2020   *Indigenous Life around the Great Lakes: War, Climate, and Culture*. University of Notre Dame Press, Notre Dame, Indiana.

Egan-Bruhy, Kathryn C.

1988   Middle and Late Archaic Phytogeography and Floral Exploitation in the Upper Great Lakes. *Midcontinental Journal of Archaeology* 13(1):81–107.

2007   20CH6. Cloudman Site Floral Table. On file at the Consortium for Archaeological Research, Department of Anthropology, Michigan State University, East Lansing.

2014   Ethnicity as Evidence by Subsistence Patterns of Late Prehistoric Upper Great Lakes Populations. *Midcontinental Journal of Archaeology Occasional Papers 1*, edited by Maria E. Raviele and William A. Lovis, pp. 53–73. Midwest Archaeological Conference.

Ellis, Linda

1997   Hot Rock Technology. In *Hot Rock Cooking on the Greater Edwards Plateau: Four Burned Rock Midden Sites in West Central Texas*, edited by Stephen Black, Linda Ellis, Darrell Creel, and Glenn Goode, pp. 43–81. Studies in Archeology 22, Vol. 1, Archeological Studies Program, Report 2. Texas Archeological Research Laboratory and University of Texas at Austin.

Ellwood, Emily C., M. Paul Scott, William D. Lipe, R. G. Matson, and John G. Jones

2003   Stone-Boiling Maize with Limestone: Experimental Results and Implications for Nutrition among SE Utah Preceramic Groups. *Journal of Archaeological Science* 40(1):35–44.

Emerson, Thomas E.

1997a   *Cahokia and the Archaeology of Power*. University of Alabama Press, Tuscaloosa.

1997b   Reflections from the Countryside on Cahokian Hegemony. In *Cahokia: Domination and Ideology in the Mississippian World*, edited by Timothy Pauketat, pp. 167–228. E-book, University of Nebraska Press, Lincoln.

2018 Greater Cahokia—Chiefdom, State, or City? In *Revealing Greater Cahokia: North America's First Native City*, edited by Thomas E. Emerson, Brad H. Koldehoff, and Tamira K. Brennan, pp. 487–535. Illinois State Archaeological Survey, Prairie Research Institute, University of Illinois at Urbana-Champaign.

Emerson, Thomas E., Kristin M. Hedman, Tamira K. Brennan, Alleen M. Betzenhauser, Susan M. Alt, and Timothy R. Pauketat

2020 Interrogating Diaspora and Movement in the Greater Cahokian World. *Journal of Archaeological Method and Theory* 27(1):54–71.

Emerson, Thomas E., Kristin M. Hedman, Mary L. Simon, Mathew A. Fort, and Kelsey E. Witt

2020 Isotopic Confirmation of the Timing and Intensity of Maize Consumption in Greater Cahokia. *American Antiquity* 85(2):241–62.

Emerson, Thomas E., Brad H. Koldehoff, and Tamira K. Brennan (editors)

2018 *Revealing Greater Cahokia, North America's First Native City: Rediscovery and Large-Scale Excavations of the East St. Louis Precinct.* Studies in Archaeology No. 12. Illinois State Archaeological Survey, Prairie Research Institute, University of Illinois at Urbana-Champaign.

Esarey, Duane, and Lawrence A. Conrad

1998 The Bold Counselor Phase of the Central Illinois River Valley: Oneota's Middle Mississippian Margin. *Wisconsin Archeologist* 79(2):38–61.

Esarey, Duane, and Sharron Santure

1990 The Morton Site Oneota Component and the Bold Counselor Phase. In *Archaeological Investigations at the Morton Village and Norris Farms 36 Cemetery*, edited by Sharron K. Santure, Alan D. Harn, and Duane Esarey, pp. 162–66. Reports of Investigations No. 45, Illinois State Museum, Springfield.

Espenshade, C.

1999 The Trouble with Roasting Pits. *West Virginia Archeologist* 51(1–2):11–29.

Eubanks, Paul N., and Ian W. Brown

2015 Certain Trends in Eastern Woodlands Salt Production Technology. *Midcontinental Journal of Archaeology* 40(3):231–56.

Eusebio, Michelle S., Philip Piper, Fredeliza Z. Campos, T. Elliott Arnold, Andrew Zimmerman, and John Krigbaum

2022 Using Organic Compound-Specific Stable Isotope Ratios to Identify Animals in Prehistoric Foodways of Southeast Asia. In *Isotope Research in Zooarchaeology: Methods, Applications, and Advances*, edited by Ashley E. Sharpe and John Krigbaum, pp. 201–27. University Press of Florida, Gainesville.

Evans, Madeleine G., Kjersti E. Emerson, and Amanda J. Butler

2019 Burned House Floor Assemblages. In *Orendorf Settlement D: A Burned Fortified Mississippian Town in the Central Illinois River Valley*, edited by Lawrence A. Conrad, Kjersti E. Emerson, Thomas E. Emerson, and Duane E. Esarey, pp. 355–486. Illinois State Archaeological Survey Research Reports 50, University of Illinois at Urbana-Champaign.

Farace, Anthony P.

2018 A Survey and Use-Wear Analysis of Wickliffe Thick Pottery in the Southeastern United States. Master's thesis, Department of Anthropology, Southern Illinois University, Carbondale.

Farnsworth, Kenneth B., Thomas E. Emerson, and Rebecca Miller Glenn

1991 Patterns of Late Woodland/Mississippian Interaction in the Lower Illinois Valley Drainage: A View from Starr Village. In *Cahokia and the Hinterlands: Middle Mississippian Cultures of the Midwest*, edited by Thomas E. Emerson and R. Barry Lewis, pp. 83–118. University of Illinois Press, Champaign.

Faulkner, Charles H.

1970 The Late Prehistoric Occupation of Northwestern Indiana: A Study of the Upper Mississippi Culture of the Kankakee Valley. Unpublished PhD dissertation, Department of Anthropology, Indiana University, Bloomington.

1972 *The Late Prehistoric Period Occupation of Northwestern Indiana: A Study of Upper Mississippi Cultures of the Kankakee Valley*. Prehistory Research Series Vol. V, No. 1. Indiana Historical Society, Indianapolis.

Fierer, N., J. Ladau, J. C. Clemente, J. W. Leff, S. M. Owens, K. S. Pollard, R. Knight, J. A. Gilbert, and R. L. McCulley

2013 Reconstructing the Microbial Diversity and Function of Pre-Agricultural Tallgrass Prairie Soils in the United States. *Science* 342(6158):621–24.

Fishel, Richard L.

1977 Medicine Birds and Mill Creek–Middle Mississippian Interaction: The Contents of Feature 8 at the Phipps Site (13CK21). *American Antiquity* 62:538–53.

Fischler, Claude

1988 Food, Self, and Identity. *Social Science Information* 27(2):275–92.

Fishel, Richard L.

2017 Medicine Birds and Mill Creek–Middle Mississippian Interactions: The Contents of Feature 8 at the Phipps Site (13CK 21). *American Antiquity* 62:538–53.

Fitzgerald, W. R.

2001 Contact, Neutral Iroquoian Transformation, and the Little Ice Age. In *Societies in Eclipse: Archaeology of the Eastern Woodlands Indians, A.D. 1400–1700*, edited by D. Brose, C. W. Cowan, and R. Mainfort, pp. 9–18. Smithsonian Institution Press, Washington, DC.

Flynn, C.

2002 Cultural Responses to the Medieval Warm Period on the Northeastern Plains: The Example from the Lockport Site (EaLf-1). Unpublished Master's thesis, Department of Anthropology, University of Manitoba, Winnipeg.

Fortier, Andrew C.

2006 The Land between Two Traditions: Middle Woodland Societies of the American Bottom. In *Recreating Hopewell*, edited by Douglas K. Charles and Jane E. Buikstra, pp. 328–38. University Press of Florida, Gainesville.

Fortier, Jana

2001 Sharing, Hoarding, and Theft: Exchange and Resistance in Forager-Farmer Relations. *Ethnology* 40(3):193–211.

Fox, W. A.

2004 Horned Panthers and Erie Associates. In *A Passion for the Past: Papers in Honour of James F. Pendergast*, edited by J. V. Wright and J-L. Pilon, pp. 283–304. Archaeological Survey of Canada Mercury Series Archaeology Paper 164. Canadian Museum of Civilization, Gatineau, Quebec.

Frederick, Kathryn, Rebecca Albert, and William Lovis
2019   The Green Site Acorn Parching Feature: Analysis and Actualistic Replication of an Early Late Woodland Acorn Processing Pit. *Wisconsin Archeologist* 100(1–2): 48–56.

Friberg, Christina M.
2018   Cosmic Negotiations: Cahokian Religion and Ramey Incised Pottery in the Northern Hinterland. *Southeastern Archaeology* 37(1):39–57.

Fritz, Gayle J.
1990   Multiple Pathways to Farming in Precontact Eastern North America. *Journal of World Prehistory* 4(4):387–435.

2014   Maygrass (*Phalaris caroliniana* Walt.): Its Role and Significance in Native Eastern North American Agriculture. In *New Lives for Ancient and Extinct Crops*, edited by Paul J. Minnis, pp. 12–43. University of Arizona Press, Tucson.

2019   *Feeding Cahokia: Early Agriculture in the North American Heartland*. University of Alabama Press, Tuscaloosa.

Fritz, Gayle J., and Bruce D. Smith
1988a   Old Collections and New Technology: Documenting the Domestication of *Chenopodium* in Eastern North America. *Midcontinental Journal of Archaeology* 13(1):3–27.

1988b   Native Crops at Early Cahokia: Comparing Domestic and Ceremonial Contexts. In *People, Plants, and Animals: Archaeological Studies of Human-Environment Interactions in the Midcontinent, Essays In Honor of Leonard W. Blake*, edited by Robert E. Warren. *Illinois Archaeology* 15 and 16:90–111.

Fritz, Gayle J., and Neil H. Lopinot
2007   Native Crops at Early Cahokia: Comparing Domestic and Ceremonial Contexts. *Illinois Archaeology* 15 and 16:90–111.

Fritz, Gayle J., Virginia Drywater Whitekiller, and James W. McIntosh
2001   Ethnobotany of Ku-Nu-Che: Cherokee Hickory Nut Soup. *Journal of Ethnobiology* 21(2):1–27.

Fuller, Dorian Q.
2005   Ceramics, Seeds, and Culinary Change in Prehistoric India. *Antiquity* 79(306):761–77.

Gallagher, J. P., and C. M. Arzigian
1994   A New Perspective on Late Prehistoric Agricultural Intensification in the Upper Mississippi River Valley. In *Agricultural Origins and Development in the Midcontinent*, edited by William Green, pp. 171–88. Report 19, Office of the State Archaeologist. University of Iowa, Iowa City.

Gardner, Paul S.
1997   The Ecological Structure and Behavioral Implications of Mast Exploitation Strategies. In *Peoples, Plants, and Landscapes*, edited by K. J. Gremillion, pp. 161–78. University of Alabama Press, Tuscaloosa.

Garland, Elizabeth B., and Scott G. Beld
1999   The Early Woodland: Ceramics, Domesticated Plants, and Burial Mounds Foretell the Shape of the Future. In *Retrieving Michigan's Buried Past: The Archaeology of the Great Lakes State*, edited by John R. Halsey, pp. 125–46. Cranbrook Institute of Science, Bloomfield Hills, Michigan.

Gartner, William Gustav

1999   Late Woodland Landscapes of Wisconsin: Ridged Fields, Effigy Mounds, and Territoriality. *Antiquity* 73(281):671–83.

Gaviria, Jorge

2021   Making Table Tortillas from Kernel to Masa, Masienda (website), accessed October 12, 2023.

Gaviria, Jorge, Rick Bayless, Sean Brock, Amanda Gálvez, Carlos Salgado, Steve Santana, Daniela Soto-Innes, Lesley Téllez, and Blair Richardson

2017   *Nixtamal: A Guide to Masa Preparation in the United States.* Masienda and MiniSuper Studio, Mexico City.

Gibbon, Guy E.

2012   *Archaeology of Minnesota: The Prehistory of the Upper Mississippi Region.* University of Minnesota Press, Minneapolis.

Gilbert, Miles B.

1990   *Mammalian Osteology.* Missouri Archaeological Society, Columbia.

Gilbert, Miles B., Larry B. Martin, and Howard C. Savage

1996   *Avian Osteology.* Missouri Archaeological Society, Columbia.

Gingerich, Joseph A. M., and Nathaniel R. Kitchell

2014   Early Paleoindian Subsistence Strategies in Eastern North America: A Continuation of the Clovis Tradition? Or Evidence of Regional Adaptations? In *Clovis, on the Edge of a New Understanding,* edited by Thomas A. Jennings and Ashley M. Smallwood, pp. 297–318. Texas A&M University Press, College Station.

Goldstein, Lynne

1992   Middle Woodland Study Unit. In *The Southeastern Wisconsin Archaeology Program: 1991–1992.* University of Wisconsin–Milwaukee Archaeological Research Laboratory Report of Investigations No. 112. Milwaukee.

Gomez, M. H., C. M. McDonough, L. W. Rooney, and R. D. Waniska

1989   Changes in Corn and Sorghum during Nixtamalization and Tortilla Baking. *Journal of Food Science* 54(2):330–36.

Gomez, M. H., J. K. Lee, C. McDonough, R. D. Waniska, and L. W. Rooney

1992   Corn Starch Changes during Tortilla and Tortilla Chip Processing. *Cereal Chemistry* 69(3):275–79.

Goody, J.

1994   *Cooking, Cuisine, and Class: A Study in Comparative Sociology.* Cambridge University Press, Cambridge.

2006   Gordon Childe, the Urban Revolution, and the Haute Cuisine: An Anthropo-Archaeological View of Modern History. *Comparative Studies in Society and History* 48(3):503–19.

Gott, Beth, Huw Barton, Delwen Samuel, and Robin Torrance

2006   Biology of Starch. In *Ancient Starch Research,* edited by R. Torrance and H. Barton, pp. 35–44. Left Coast Press, Walnut Creek, California.

Government of Canada

2021   St. Andrews Lock and Dam—Real Property—PSPC (website).

Graff, Sarah R.

2018   Archaeological Studies of Cooking and Food Preparation. *Journal of Archaeological Research* 26(3):305–51.

2020 Archaeology of Cuisine and Cooking. *Annual Review of Anthropology* 49:337–54.

Graff, Sarah R., and Enrique Rodríguez-Alegría

2012 *The Menial Art of Cooking: Archaeological Studies of Cooking and Food Preparation.* University Press of Colorado, Boulder.

2018 Archaeological Studies of Cooking and Food Preparation. *Journal of Archaeological Research* 26(3):305–51.

Graham, R., and J. W. Ives

2019 Revisiting Besant and Sonota Era Bone Uprights in Alberta. In *Advancing Archaeology: Industry and Practice in Alberta*, pp. 1–27. Archaeological Survey of Alberta Occasional Paper No. 39, Edmonton.

Green, William, and Roland L. Rodell

1994 The Mississippian Presence and Cahokia Interaction at Trempealeau, Wisconsin. *American Antiquity* 59(2):334–59.

Gregg, M. L.

1994 Summary and Discussion. In *Horner-Kane (32RY77) Archeological Excavations, Graham Island State Park, Ramsey County, North Dakota, 1991 Field Season*, edited by M. L. Gregg, pp. 14.1–14.19. Department of Anthropology, University of North Dakota. Submitted to the US Bureau of Reclamation.

Gregg, M. L., F. E. Swenson, P. R. Picha, C. Kordecki, C. E. Haury, and C. Quinn

1987 *Test Excavations at 15 Archaeological Sites along the James River in Stutsman and LaMoure Counties, North Dakota.* Report prepared for the US Department of the Interior Bureau of Reclamation, Billings, Montana, by Department of Anthropology, University of North Dakota, Grand Forks.

Gremillion, Kristen J.

1993 Crop and Weed in Prehistoric Eastern North America: The *Chenopodium* Example. *American Antiquity* 58(3):496–509.

2004 Seed Processing and the Origins of Food Production in Eastern North America. *American Antiquity* 69(2):215–33.

Griffitts, Janet L.

2006 Bone Tools and Technology Choice: Change and Stability on the Northern Plains. Unpublished PhD dissertation, Department of Anthropology, University of Arizona, Tucson.

Gvion, Liora

2006 Cuisines of Poverty as Means of Empowerment: Arab Food in Israel. *Agriculture and Human Values* 23:299–312.

Haas, Jennifer R.

2024 Early and Middle Woodland in Southeastern Wisconsin. *Wisconsin Archeologist*, in press.

Haas, Jennifer R.

2019a Community Identity, Culinary Traditions, and Foodways in the Western Great Lakes. Unpublished PhD dissertation, Department of Anthropology, University of Wisconsin–Milwaukee.

2019b *Archaeological Data Recovery at the Finch Site (47JE0902), Jefferson County, Wisconsin.* University of Wisconsin–Milwaukee, Archaeological Research Laboratory, Report of Investigations No. 445. Milwaukee.

Haberman, Thomas W.

1984 Evidence for Aboriginal Tobaccos in Eastern North American. *American Antiquity* 49(2):269–87.

Hadden, Carla S., Gregory A. Waselkov, Elizabeth J. Reitz, and C. Fred T. Andrus

2022 Temporality of Fishery Taskscapes on the North-Central Gulf of Mexico Coast (USA) during the Middle/Late Woodland Period (AD 325–1040). *Journal of Anthropological Archaeology* 67:101436.

Hall, Robert L.

1962 *The Archaeology of Carcajou Point: With an Interpretation of the Development of Oneota Culture in Wisconsin.* Volumes 1 and 2. University of Wisconsin Press, Madison.

1991 Cahokia Identity and Interaction Models of Cahokian Mississippian. In *Cahokia and the Hinterlands: Middle Mississippian Cultures of the Midwest*, edited by Thomas E. Emerson and R. Barry Lewis, pp. 3–34. University of Illinois Press, Champaign.

1997 *An Archaeology of the Soul: North American Indian Belief and Ritual.* University of Illinois Press, Champaign.

Hally, David J.

1983 Use Alteration of Pottery Vessel Surfaces: An Important Source of Evidence for the Identification of Vessel Function. *North American Archaeologist* 4(1):3–26.

1986 The Identification of Vessel Function: A Case Study from Northwest Georgia. *American Antiquity* 51(2):267–95.

Halstead, Paul, and John C. Barrett

2004 *Food, Cuisine, and Society in Prehistoric Greece.* Oxbow Books, Oxford.

Halwas, S., E. L. Syms, and G. Monks

2019 Excavations at the Lockport Pre-European Village Site: University of Manitoba Field School May 30–June 24, 2016. *Manitoba Archaeological Journal* 29:25–44.

Hamilakis, Yannis

2013 *Archaeology and the Senses: Human Experience, Memory, and Affect.* Cambridge University Press, Cambridge.

2015 Food as Sensory Experience. In *The Archaeology of Food: An Encyclopedia*, edited by M. Beaudry and K. Metheny, pp. 205–6. Rowman and Littlefield, Lanham, Maryland.

Hamilton, S., E. L. Syms, T. Dedi, and T. Gibson

2007 *Preliminary Results of the Re-investigation of the Snyder II North and South Sites (Dg-Mg-15, 17).* Report of 2006–2007 field and lab activities prepared for Manitoba Historic Resources Branch and Manitoba Heritage Grants Program.

Hargrave, Michael L.

1992 The Ceramic Assemblage: Vessel Form, Decoration, and Regional Comparisons. In *The Petitt Site (11-Ax-253), Alexander County, Illinois*, edited by Paul A. Webb, pp. 125–82. Research Paper No. 58. Center for Archaeological Investigations, Southern Illinois University, Carbondale.

Hariot, Thomas

1590 *A Briefe and True Report of the New Found Land of Virginia.* Johann Wechel, Frankfurt. Digitized 2003, Apex Data Services, University of North Carolina, Chapel Hill.

Harrington, M. R.

1908 Some Seneca Corn-Foods and Their Preparation. *American Anthropologist* 10(4):575–90.

REFERENCES

Harris, Wendy

1996 Form and Function of Crab Orchard Tradition Pit Features in the Big Muddy River Drainage of Southern Illinois. Master's thesis, Department of Anthropology, Southern Illinois University, Carbondale.

Hart, John P., Hetty Jo Brumbach, and Robert K. Lusteck

2007 Extending the Phytolith Evidence for Early Maize (*Zea mays ssp. mays*) and Squash (*Cucurbita sp.*) in Central New York. *American Antiquity* 72(3):563–83.

Hart, John P., and C. Margaret Scarry

1999 The Age of the Common Bean (*Phaseolus vulgaris*) in the Northeastern United States. *American Antiquity* 64(4):653–58.

Hastorf, Christine A.

1988 The Use of Paleoethnobotanical Data in Prehistoric Studies of Crop Production, Processing, and Consumption. In *Current Paleoethnobotany: Analytical Methods and Cultural Interpretations of Archaeological Plant Remains*, edited by Christine Hastorf and Virginia Popper, pp. 119–44. University of Chicago Press, Chicago.

1991 Gender, Space, and Food in Prehistory. In *Engendering Archaeology: Women and Prehistory*, edited by J. M. Gero and M. Conkey, pp. 132–59. Basil Blackwell, Cambridge.

2017 *The Social Archaeology of Food: Thinking about Eating from Prehistory to the Present.* Cambridge University Press, Cambridge.

Hastorf, Christine A., and Sissel Johannessen

1994 Becoming Corn-Eaters in Prehistoric America. In *Corn and Culture in the Prehistoric New World*, edited by Sissel Johannessen and Christine A. Hastorf, pp. 427–43. University of Minnesota Publications in Anthropology No. 5. Westview Press, Boulder, Colorado.

Hastorf, Christine, and Mary Weismantel

2007 Food: Where Opposites Meet. In *The Archaeology of Food and Identity*, edited by K. C. Twiss, pp. 308–31. Center for Archaeological Investigations Occasional Paper No. 34. Southern Illinois University, Carbondale.

Hatch, Mallorie A.

2015 The Social Costs of War: Investigating the Relationship between Warfare and Intragroup Violence during the Mississippian Period of the Central Illinois Valley. PhD dissertation, Arizona State University, Tempe.

Haury, Cherie E.

1994 Vertebrate Faunal Remains. In *Horner-Kane (32RY77) Archeological Excavations, Graham Island State Park, Ramsey County, North Dakota, 1991 Field Season*, edited by M. L. Gregg, pp. 10.1–10.36. Department of Anthropology, University of North Dakota. Submitted to the US Bureau of Reclamation.

Hayden, Brian

2001 Fabulous Feasts: A Prolegomenon to the Importance of Feasting. In *Feasts: Archaeological and Ethnographic Perspectives on Food, Politics, and Power*, edited by Michael Dietler and Brian Hayden, pp. 23–64. Smithsonian Institution Press, Washington, DC.

Hayden, Brian, and Aubrey Cannon

1983 Where the Garbage Goes: Refuse Disposal in the Maya Highlands. *Journal of Anthropological Archaeology* 2(2):117–63.

REFERENCES

Hedden, John

2016   Central Plains Tradition Smoking Pipes in the Glenwood Locality of Iowa: Within a Landscape of Rising and Falling Sky. In *Perspectives on the Archaeology of Pipes, Tobacco, and Other Smoke Plants in the Ancient Americas*, edited by Elizabeth A. Bollwerk and Shannon Tushingham, pp. 135–56. Interdisciplinary Contributions to Archaeology, Springer International Publishing, Cham, Switzerland.

Hedman, Kristin M.

2006   Late Cahokian Subsistence and Health: Stable Isotope and Dental Evidence. *Southeastern Archaeology* 25:258–74.

Hedman, Kristin M., Eve A. Hargrave, and Stanley H. Ambrose

2002   Late Mississippian Diet in the American Bottom: Stable Isotope Analyses of Bone Collagen and Apatite. *Midcontinental Journal of Archaeology* 27(2):237–71.

Hedman, Kristin M., Thomas E. Emerson, Matthew A. Fort, John M. Lambert, Alleen M. Betzenhauser, and Timothy R. Pauketat

2022   Corn, Climate, and the Human Population of Greater Cahokia. In *Following the Mississippian Spread: Using Biological and Archaeological Evidence to Measure Migration and Climate Change*, edited by Robert A. Cook and Aaron R. Comstock, pp. 37–63. Springer Nature, Cham, Switzerland.

Heiser, Charles B.

1969   *Nightshades: The Paradoxical Plants*. W. H. Freeman, Kent.

Hems, David

1997   Features at the Lockport Site EaLf-1. *Manitoba Archaeological Journal* 7(2):2–7.

Hendy, Jessica, Andre C. Colonese, Ingmar Franz, Ricardo Fernandes, Roman Fischer, David Orton, Alexandre Lucquin, Luke Spindler, Jana Anvari, Elizabeth Stroud, Peter F. Biehl, Camilla Speller, Nicole Boivin, Meaghan Mackie, Rosa R. Jersie-Christensen, Jesper V. Olsen, Matthew J. Collins, Oliver E. Craig, and Eva Rosenstock

2018   Ancient Proteins from Ceramic Vessels at Çatalhöyük West Reveal the Hidden Cuisine of Early Farmers. *Nature Communications* 9(4064):1–10.

Henning, Dale R.

1970   Development and Interrelationships of Oneota Culture in the Lower Missouri River Valley. *Missouri Archaeologist* 32:1–180.

Henning, Dale R., and Dennis L. Toom

2003   Cambria and the Initial Middle Missouri Variant Revisited. *Wisconsin Archeologist* 84(1&2):197–217.

Henry the Younger, Alexander

1988   *The Journal of Alexander Henry the Younger, 1799–1814*. Vol. 1, edited by B. M. Gough, The Champlain Society, Toronto.

Henrickson, Elizabeth F., and Mary M. A. McDonald

1983   Ceramic Form and Function: An Ethnographic Search and an Archeological Application. *American Anthropologist* 85(3):630–43.

Hess, Aaron S., and John R. Hess

2017   Understanding Tests of the Association of Categorical Variables: The Pearson Chi-Square Test and Fisher's Exact Test. *Transfusion* 57(4):877–79.

Hewitt, Barbara R., E. Leigh Syms, and Robert D. Hoppa

2008   New Radiocarbon Dates for the Fidler Mounds (EaLf-3) Site, Manitoba, Canada. *Canadian Journal of Archaeology* 32:77–95.

264 REFERENCES

Hilgeman, Sherri L.
2000 *Pottery and Chronology at Angel*. University of Alabama Press, Tuscaloosa.

Hilger, Inez
1959 *Chippewa Child Life and Its Cultural Background*. Smithsonian Institution Bureau of American Ethnology Bulletin 146. Government Printing Office, Washington, DC.

Hill, Matthew
2007 Causes of Regional and Temporal Variation in Paleoindian Diet in Western North America. PhD dissertation, Department of Anthropology, University of Arizona, Tucson.

Hind, Henry Youle
1971 *Narrative of the Canadian Red River Exploring Expedition of 1857 and of the Assiniboine and Saskatchewan Exploring Expedition of 1858*. M. G. Hurtig, Edmonton.

Hofman, Jack L.
1980 Scapula Skin-Dressing and Fiber-Processing Tools. *Plains Anthropologist* 25(88):135–41.

Holland, Susan A.
1998 Evidence of the Spring Planting Ceremony to Evening Star and Her Sacred Garden. *Plains Anthropologist* 43(166):411–18.

Holley, George R.
1989 *The Archaeology of Cahokia Mounds ICT-II: Ceramics*. Illinois Cultural Resources Study No. 11. Illinois Historic Preservation Agency, Springfield.

Hollinger, R. Eric
1995 Resident Patterns and Oneota Cultural Dynamics. In *Oneota: Past, Present, and Future*, edited by William Green, pp. 141–73. Office of the State Archaeology, Iowa City, Iowa.

Holly, Donald H.
2019 Toward a Social Archaeology of Food for Hunters and Gatherers in Marginal Environments: A Case Study from the Eastern Subarctic of North America. *Journal of Archaeological Method and Theory* 26:1439–69.

Holman, Margaret B., and Kathryn C. Egan
1985 Processing Maple Sap with Prehistoric Techniques. *Journal of Ethnobiology* 5(1):61–75.

Holt, Julie
1996 AG Church Site Features and Community Organization. *Illinois Archaeology* 8:58–84.

Honigman, John J.
1961 *Foodways in a Muskeg Community: An Anthropological Report on the Attawapiskat Indians*. Northern Coordination and Research Center, Ottawa, Canada.

Hough, Walter
1926 *Fire as an Agent in Human Culture*. Smithsonian Institution, United States National Museum, Bulletin 139. US Government Printing Office, Washington, DC.

Hudson, Charles
1976 *The Southeastern Indians*. University of Tennessee Press, Knoxville.

Hunter, Andrea, and Marcel Umlauf
1989 Preliminary Analysis of Floral Remains from the OT Site (47-LC-262). In *The OT*

Site (47-LC-262) 1987 Archaeological Investigation: Preliminary Report, edited by Jodie A. O'Gorman, pp. 55–125. Wisconsin Department of Transportation, Archaeological Report No. 15. Madison.

Hurt, Wesley R.
1974   *Sioux Indians II*. Garland Publishing, New York.

Illinois Department of Natural Resources
2021   Biodiversity of Illinois (website).

Jackson, Douglas K.
1998   Settlement on the Southern Frontier: Oneota Occupations in the American Bottom. *Wisconsin Archeologist* 79(2):93–116.

Jackson, Edwin H., and Susan L. Scott
1995   The Faunal Records of the Southeastern Elite: The Implications of Economy, Social Relations, and Ideology. *Southeastern Archaeology* 14:103–19.
2003   Patterns of Elite Faunal Utilization at Moundville, Alabama. *American Antiquity* 68(3):552–72.

Jackson, Michael
1998   The Nature of Fire-Cracked Rock: New Insights from Ethnoarchaeological and Laboratory Experiments. Master's thesis, Department of Anthropology, Texas A&M University, College Station.

Jelliffe, Derrick B.
1967   Parallel Food Classifications in Developing and Industrialized Countries. *American Journal of Clinical Nutrition* 20(3):279–81.

Jeske, Robert J.
2006   Hopewell Regional Interactions in Southeastern Wisconsin and Northern Illinois. In *Recreating Hopewell*, edited by Douglas K. Charles and Jane E. Buikstra, pp. 286–309. University Press of Florida, Gainesville.
2020   The Social Landscape of Eleventh- to Fifteenth-Century Lake Koshkonong. In *Life, Death, and Landscapes at Lake Koshkonong: Oneota Archaeology in Southeastern Wisconsin*, edited by Robert J. Jeske, Richard W. Edwards IV, and Katherine Sterner, pp. 103–19. Midwest Archaeological Conference Occasional Paper No. 4. Midwest Archaeological Conference.

Jeske, Robert J., and Kira Kaufmann
2000   The Alberts Site (47Je887 & 47Je903): Excavations at a Late Archaic through Mississippian Site in Jefferson County. In *Southeastern Wisconsin Archaeology Program 1999–2000*, edited by Robert J. Jeske, pp. 79–98. University of Wisconsin–Milwaukee, Archaeological Research Laboratory, Report of Investigations No. 145. Milwaukee, Wisconsin.

Johannessen, Sissel
1984   Paleoethnobotany. In *American Bottom Archaeology: A Summary of the FAI-270 Project Contribution to the Culture History of the Mississippi River Valley*, edited by Charles J. Bareis, and James W. Porter, pp. 197–214. University of Illinois Press, Champaign.
1993   Food, Dishes, and Society in the Mississippi Valley. In *Foraging and Farming in the Eastern Woodlands*, edited by C. Margaret Scarry, pp. 182–205. University Press of Florida, Gainesville.

Johnson, Emily S., Alleen Betzenhauser, and Amber VanDerwarker
2022   *Nixtamalization and Culinary Traditions at the Ancient East St. Louis Site*. Invited

266   REFERENCES

paper presented in the symposium *Recent Advancements in Cahokia Research*, chaired by B. Jacob Skousen and Alleen Betzenhauser, at the 87th Annual Meeting of the Society for American Archaeology, Chicago.

Johnson, Emily S., and John M. Marston

2020   The Experimental Identification of Nixtamalized Maize through Starch Spherulites. *Journal of Archaeological Science* 113:105056.

Jones, Andrew M., and Colin Richards

2003   Animals into Ancestors: Domestication, Food, and Identity in Late Neolithic Orkney. In *Food, Culture, and Identity in the Neolithic and Early Bronze Age*, edited by Michael Parker Pearson, pp. 45–52. Archaeopress, Oxford.

Joyce, Rosemary A., and John S. Henderson

2007   From Feasting to Cuisine: Implications of Archaeological Research in an Early Honduran Village. *American Anthropologist*, New Series 109(4):642–53.

Kassabaum, Megan C.

2018   Social Subsistence: Integrating Analyses of Ceramic, Plant, and Animal Remains from Feltus. In *Baking, Bourbon, and Black Drink: Foodways Archaeology in the American Southeast*, edited by Tanya M. Peres and Aaron Deter-Wolf, pp. 11–29. University of Alabama Press, Tuscaloosa.

2019   A Method for Conceptualizing and Classifying Feasting: Interpreting Communal Consumption in the Archaeological Record. *American Antiquity* 84(4):610–31.

Katz, Solomon H., M. L. Hediger, and L. A. Valleroy

1974   Traditional Maize Processing Techniques in the New World. *Science* 184(4138):765–73.

Kedrowski, Brant, B. Crass, Jeffery Behm, J. Luetke, A. Nichols, A. Moreck, and C. Holmes

2009   GC/MS Analysis of Fatty Acids from Ancient Hearth Residues at the Swan Point Archaeological Site. *Archaeometry* 51(1):110–22.

Kelly, John E.

1980   Formative Developments at Cahokia and the Adjacent American Bottom: A Merrell Tract Perspective. PhD dissertation, Department of Anthropology, University of Wisconsin–Madison.

Kelly, John, Andrew Fortier, Steven Ozuk, and Joyce Williams

1987   *The Range Site: Archaic through Late Woodland Occupations. American Bottom Archaeology FAI-270 Site Reports 16.* University of Illinois Press, Champaign.

Kelly, John E., Steven J. Ozuk, Douglas K. Jackson, Dale L. McElrath, Fred A. Finney, and Duane Esarey

1984   Emergent Mississippian Period. In *American Bottom Archaeology*, edited by Charles J. Bareis and James W. Porter, pp. 128–57. University of Illinois Press, Champaign.

Kelly, John E., Steven J. Ozuk, and Joyce Williams

1990   *The Range Site 2: The Emergent Mississippian Dohack and Range Phase Occupations.* American Bottom Archaeology FAI-270 Site Reports, Vol. 20. University of Illinois Press, Champaign.

2007   *The Range Site 3: Emergent Mississippian George Reeves and Lindeman Phase Occupations.* Transportation Archaeological Research Reports, No. 18. Illinois Transportation Archaeological Research Program, University of Illinois at Urbana-Champaign.

Kelly, Lucretia S.

2001   A Case of Ritual Feasting at the Cahokia Site. In *Feasts: Archaeological and Ethnographic Perspectives on Food, Politics, and Power*, edited by Michael Dietler and Brian Hayden, pp. 334–67. Smithsonian Institution Press, Washington, DC.

2010   Zooarchaeology: A Bird's Eye View of Ritual at the Cahokia Site. In *Anthropological Approaches to Zooarchaeology: Colonialism, Complexity, and Animals*, edited by Douglas V. Campana, pp. 1–11. Oxbow Books, Oxford.

Kelly, Lucretia S., and Paula G. Cross

1984   Zooarchaeology. In *American Bottom Archaeology*, edited by Charles J. Bareis and James W. Porter, pp. 215–32. University of Illinois Press, Champaign.

Khan, M. N., M. C. DesRosiers, L. W. Rooney, R. G. Morgan, and V. E. Sweat

1982   Corn Tortillas: Corn Cooking Procedures. *Cereal Chemistry* 59(4):279–84.

King, Frances B.

1990   Geographic Setting, Past and Present Physiography, Potential Subsistence Resources. In *Archaeological Investigations at the Morton Village and Norris Farms 36 Cemetery*, edited by Sharron K. Santure, Alan D. Harn, and Duane Esarey, pp. 3–5. Reports of Investigations No. 45, Illinois State Museum, Springfield.

1999   Changing Evidence for Prehistoric Plant Use in Pennsylvania. In *Current Northeast Paleoethnobotany*, edited by J. P. Hart, pp. 11–26. State Museum Bulletin 494, University of the State of New York, Albany.

Knight, Vernon James, Jr.

2004   Characterizing Elite Midden Deposits at Moundville. *American Antiquity* 69(2):304–21.

Kobayashi, Masashi

1994   Use-Alteration Analysis of Kalinga Pottery: Interior Carbon Deposits of Cooking Pots. In *Kalinga Ethnoarchaeology: Expanding Archaeological Method and Theory*, edited by William A. Longacre and James M. Skibo, pp. 127–68. Smithsonian Institution, Washington, DC.

Koenig, Charles, and Myles Miller (editors)

2023   *Earth Ovens and Desert Lifeways: 10,000 Years of Indigenous Cooking in the Arid Landscapes of North America*. University of Utah Press, Salt Lake City.

Kolb, Michael

2018   Riverine and Anthropogenic Landscapes of the East St. Louis Area. In *Revealing Greater Cahokia: North America's First Native City*, edited by Thomas E. Emerson, Brad H. Koldehoff, and Tamira K. Brennan, pp. 95–126. Studies in Archaeology No. 12, Illinois State Archaeological Survey, Prairie Research Institute, University of Illinois at Urbana-Champaign.

Koldehoff, Brad, and Joseph Galloy

2006   Late Woodland Frontiers in the American Bottom Region. *Southeastern Archaeology* 25(2):275–300.

Koncur, Jasmine

2018   *The McClelland Site (21GD258) and the Oneota Tradition in the Red Wing Region*. Minnesota State University, Mankato.

Kooiman, Susan M.

2012   Old Pots, New Approaches: A Functional Analysis of Woodland Pottery from

Lake Superior's South Shore. Master's thesis, Department of Sociology and Anthropology, Illinois State University, Normal.

2016   Woodland Pottery Function, Cooking, and Diet in the Upper Great Lakes of North America. *Midcontinental Journal of Archaeology* 41(3):207–30.

2018   A Multiproxy Analysis of Culinary, Technological, and Environmental Interactions in the Northern Great Lakes Region. PhD dissertation, Department of Anthropology, Michigan State University.

2021   *Ancient Pottery, Cuisine, and Society at the Northern Great Lakes.* University of Notre Dame Press, South Bend, Indiana.

Kooiman, Susan M., Rebecca K. Albert, and Mary E. Malainey

2022   Multiproxy Analysis of Adhered and Absorbed Food Residues Associated with Pottery. *Journal of Archaeological Method and Theory* 29(3):795–830.

Kooiman, Susan M., Sean B. Dunham, and Christine Stephenson

2019   The Cloudman Site: A Multicomponent Woodland and Historic Period Site in the Northern Great Lakes. *Wisconsin Archeologist* 100(1–2):57–68.

Kooiman, Susan M., and Heather Walder

2019   Reconsidering the Chronology: Carbonized Food Residue AMS Dates and Compositional Analysis of a Curated Collection from the Upper Great Lakes. *American Antiquity* 84(3):495–515.

Kooyman, Brian P.

2000   *Understanding Stone Tools and Archaeological Sites.* University of Calgary Press, Calgary.

Kowalewski, Stephen A.

2006   Coalescent Societies. In *Light on the Path: The Anthropology and History of the Southeastern Indians,* edited by Thomas J. Pluckhahn and Robbie Ethridge, pp. 68–84. University of Alabama Press, Tuscaloosa.

Kozuch, Laura

2023   Exotic Marine Faunal Artifacts. In *East St. Louis Precinct Faunal and Botanical Remains,* edited by B. Jacob Skousen, pp. 265–302. Research Report No. 48, Illinois State Archaeological Survey, Prairie Research Institute, University of Illinois at Urbana-Champaign.

Kozuch, Laura, Karen J. Walker, and William H. Marquardt

2017   Lightning Whelk Natural History and a New Sourcing Method. *Southeastern Archaeology* 36(3):226–40.

Krech, Shepard, III

2009   *Spirits of the Air: Birds and American Indians in the South.* University of Georgia Press, Athens.

Kuehn, Steven R.

2016   Beyond Diet: Faunal Remains and Ritual during the Late Woodland through Mississippian Periods in the American Bottom. *Illinois Archaeology* 28:533–66.

2023   Faunal Analysis. In *East St. Louis Precinct Faunal and Botanical Remains,* edited by B. Jacob Skousen, pp. 149–264. Research Report No. 48, Illinois State Archaeological Survey, Prairie Research Institute, University of Illinois at Urbana-Champaign.

Kuehn, Steven R., and Amber M. VanDerwarker

2015   Lamb Site Zooarchaeological Analysis: Early Mississippian Faunal Exploitation in the Central Illinois River Valley. *Illinois Archaeology* 27:236–53.

REFERENCES 269

Kuehn, Steven R., and Mary L. Simon
2023 Summary and Implications. In *East St. Louis Precinct Faunal and Botanical Remains*, edited by B. Jacob Skousen, pp. 303–92. Research Report No. 48, Illinois State Archaeological Survey, Prairie Research Institute, University of Illinois at Urbana-Champaign.

LaMotta, Vincent M., and Michael B. Schiffer
1999 Formation Processes of House Floor Assemblages. In *The Archaeology of Household Activities*, edited by Penelope Allison, pp. 19–29. Routledge, London.

Landa, Diego de
1937 *Yucatan Before and After the Conquest.* Translated by William Gates. Maya Society Publication No. 20. Baltimore, Maryland.

Langlie, BrieAnna S., Natalie G. Mueller, Robert N. Spengler, and Gayle J. Fritz
2014 Agricultural Origins from the Ground Up: Archaeological Approaches to Plant Domestication. *American Journal of Botany* 101(10):1601–17.

Lansdell, Michael Brent, Sarah Harken, Mary M. King, Jolene J. Kuehn, and Victoria E. Potter
2018 *Archaeological Investigations at the Davies #1 Site (11U201) for the FAP 312/IL 3 from S. of Ware to McClure Project.* Archaeological Testing Short Report No. 499. Illinois State Archaeological Survey, Prairie Research Institute, University of Illinois at Urbana-Champaign.

Lawrence, Conrad A.
1991 The Middle Mississippian Cultures of the Central Illinois Valley. In *Cahokia and the Hinterlands: Middle Mississippian Cultures of the Midwest*, edited by Thomas E. Emerson and R. Barry Lewis, pp. 119–56. University of Illinois Press, Champaign.

Leach, Jeff, C. Britt Bousman, and David Nickels
2005 Assigning Context to Artifacts in Burned-Rock Middens. *Journal of Field Archaeology* 30(2):201–3.

Leach, Jeff, David Nickels, Bruce Moses, and Richard Jones
1998 A Brief Comment on Estimating Rates of Burned Rock Discard: Results from an Experimental Earth Oven. *La Tierra* 25(3):42–50.

Leech Lake Tribal Council Heritage Sites Program (LLHSP)
1992 *1991 Cultural Resource Survey Manistique, Munising, and Rapid River Ranger Districts Hiawatha National Forest.* Report No. 8, USDA-Forest Service, Hiawatha National Forest, Escanaba, Michigan.

Lenik, Edward J.
2010 Mythic Creatures: Serpents, Dragons, and Sea Monsters in Northeastern Rock Art. *Archaeology of Eastern North America* 38:17–37.
2012 The Thunderbird Motif in Northeastern Indian Art. *Archaeology of Eastern North America* 40:163–85.

Lepofsky, Dana, and Sandra Peacock
2004 A Question of Intensity: Exploring the Role of Plant Foods in Northern Plateau Prehistory. In *Complex Hunter-Gatherers Evolution and Organization of Prehistoric Communities on the Plateau of Northwestern North America*, edited by William Prentiss and Ian Kuijt, pp. 115–39. University of Utah Press, Salt Lake City.

Lévi-Strauss, Claude
1969 *The Raw and the Cooked.* Translated by John Weightman and Doreen Weightman. Harper & Row, New York.

1997   The Culinary Triangle. In *Food and Culture: A Reader*, edited by Carole Counihan and Penny Van Esterik, pp. 28–35. Routledge, New York.

Liebmann, Matthew

2015   The Mickey Mouse Kachina and Other "Double Objects": Hybridity in the Material Culture of Colonial Encounters. *Journal of Social Archaeology* 15(3):319–41.

Lieto, Joshua R., and Jodie A. O'Gorman

2014   A Preliminary Analysis of Oneota and Mississippian Serving Vessels at the Morton Village Site, West-Central Illinois. *North American Archaeologist* 35(3):243–55.

Lints, Andrew

2012   Early Evidence of Maize (*Zea mays* ssp. *mays*) and Beans (*Phaseolus vulgaris*) on the Northern Plains: An Examination of Avonlea Cultural Materials (AD 300–1100). Unpublished Master's thesis, Environmental Studies, Department of Northern Environments and Cultures, Lakehead University, Thunder Bay, Ontario.

Liu, Kinyi, and Rachel E. B. Reid

2020   The Prehistoric Roots of Chinese Cuisines: Mapping Staple Food Systems of China, 6000 BC–220 AD. *PLoS ONE* 15(11):e0240930.

Logan, Brad

2022   Late Woodland Feasting and Social Networks in the Lower Missouri River Region. *North American Archaeologist* 1–46.

Long, Lucy M.

2004   Culinary Tourism: A Folkloristic Perspective on Eating and Otherness. In *Culinary Tourism*, edited by Lucy M. Long, pp. 20–50. University of Kentucky Press, Lexington.

2009   Introduction. *Journal of American Folklore* 122(483):3–10.

Lopinot, Neal H.

1992   Spatial and Temporal Variability in Mississippian Subsistence: The Archaeobotanical Record. In *Late Prehistoric Agriculture*, edited by William I. Woods, pp. 44–94. Studies in Illinois Archaeology No. 8, Thomas E. Emerson, general editor. Illinois Historic Preservation Agency, Springfield.

Lopinot, Neal H., Timothy Schilling, Gayle J. Fritz, and John E. Kelly

2015   Implications of Plant Remains from the East Face of Monks Mound. *Midcontinental Journal of Archaeology* 40(3):209–30.

Lovis, William A., Kathryn C. Egan-Bruhy, Beverly A. Smith, and G. William Monaghan

2001   Wetlands and Emergent Horticultural Economies in the Upper Great Lakes: A New Perspective from the Schultz Site. *American Antiquity* 66(4):615–32.

Lovis, William A., Gary R. Urquhart, Maria E. Raviele, and John P. Hart

2011   Hardwood Ash Nixtamalization May Lead to False Negatives for the Presence of Maize by Depleting Bulk $\delta13C$ in Carbonized Residues. *Journal of Archaeological Science* 38(10):2726–30.

Lundy, Jasmine, Lea Drieu, Antonio Meo, Viva Sacco, Lucia Arcifa, Elena Pezzini, Veronica Aniceti, Girolamo Fiorentino, Michelle Alexander, Paola Orecchioni, Alessandra Mollinari, Martin O. H. Carver, and Oliver E. Craig

2021   New Insights into Early Medieval Islamic Cuisine: Organic Residue Analysis of Pottery from Rural and Urban Sicily. *PLoS ONE* 16(6):e0252225.

Lunsford, Mackensy

2021 Handmade Tortillas and Hominy Grits: Meet 3 Georgia Chefs Rethinking Corn. Southern Kitchen (website), accessed October 15, 2023.

Lyman, R. Lee

1994 *Vertebrate Taphonomy*. Cambridge Manuals in Archaeology. Cambridge University Press, Cambridge.

Lynott, Mark, Thomas W. Boutton, James E. Price, and Dwight E. Nelson

1986 Stable Carbon Isotope Evidence for Maize Agriculture in Southeast Missouri and Northeast Arkansas. *American Antiquity* 51(1):51–65.

Mackenzie, Alexander

1927 *MacKenzie's Voyages from Montreal through the Continent of North America to the Frozen and Pacific Oceans, 1789 and 1793*, edited by J. W. Garvin. Master-works of Canadian Authors Volume 3. The Radisson Society of Canada, Toronto.

MacNeish, Richard S.

1958 *An Introduction to the Archaeology of Southeastern Manitoba*. National Museum of Canada, Bulletin 157. Ottawa.

Malainey, M. E., R. Przybylski, and B. L. Sherriff

2001 One Person's Food: How and Why Fish Avoidance May Affect the Settlement and Subsistence Patterns of Hunter-Gatherers. *American Antiquity* 66(1):141–61.

Malainey, Mary E.

2011 Lipid Residue Analysis. In *A Consumer's Guide to Archaeological Science,* edited by Mary E. Malainey, pp. 201–18. Springer, New York.

2019 The Olson Site (DgMg-167): Investigating Precontact Indigenous Cultivation in the Melita Area. Paper presented at the Interprovincial Archaeology Conference, Flin Flon, Manitoba.

2020a *Report on the Testing and Assessment of the Olson site (DgMg-167) Pierson Wildlife Management Area, SE 29-2-27WPM in the Rural Municipality of Two Borders. Heritage Permit No. A06–19, Wildlife Management Area Use Permit WB22754, Work Permit 2019-03-42-001*. Report submitted to Manitoba Historic Resources Branch and Manitoba Sustainable Development and Manitoba Agriculture and Resource Development.

2020b 2019 and 2020 Investigations of the Olson Site (DgMg-167): A Joint Project of Brandon University and the Manitoba Archaeological Society. Paper presented at the Manitoba Archaeological Society Conference.

2021a The Olson Site (DgMg-167): Initial Investigations of a Pre-contact Indigenous Farming Site near Melita, Manitoba by M. E. Malainey. Paper presented at the Canadian Archaeological Association Annual Meeting.

2021b *Report on 2020 Archaeological Research at the Olson site (DgMg-167) Pierson Wildlife Management Area, SE 29-2-27WPM in the Rural Municipality of Two Borders. Heritage Permit No. A42-20, Wildlife Management Area Use Permit WB24583, Work Permit 2020-03-42-002*. Report submitted to Manitoba Historic Resources Branch and Manitoba Sustainable Development and Manitoba Agriculture and Resource Development.

2021c Introducing the Olson site (DgMg-167): Initial Investigations of a Late Pre-European Contact Indigenous Agriculture Site in Southwest Manitoba. *Manitoba Archaeological Journal* 31(1&2):91–116.

2021d   Bison Hoes and Bird Tails: Reconsidering the Introduction of Maize Farming into Manitoba. Paper presented at the Midwest Archaeological Conference, East Lansing, Michigan.

2021e   We've Only Just Begun: 2021 Archaeological Investigations in the Pierson Wildlife Management Area. Paper presented at the Manitoba Archaeological Society Conference.

Malainey, Mary, and Timothy Figol

2014   *Analysis of Lipid Residues Extracted from Archaeological Sediment.* Report on file, Anthropology Program, Illinois State University, Normal.

2017   *Analysis of Lipid Residues Extracted from Early and Middle Woodland Pottery from Southeast Wisconsin.* Report on file, Department of Anthropology, University of Wisconsin–Milwaukee.

2019   *Analysis of Lipid Residues Extracted from Pottery from 47JE00902 (Finch), Jefferson County, Wisconsin.* Report on file, Department of Anthropology, University of Wisconsin–Milwaukee.

Malainey, Mary E., and Eric Olson

2018   Looking Back and Looking Forward: Evidence of Precontact Cultivation near Melita, Manitoba. Paper presented at the Manitoba Archaeological Society Conference, Winnipeg.

Malainey, Mary E., Roman Przybylski, and Barbara L. Sherriff

1999   Identifying the Former Contents of Late Precontact Period Pottery Vessels from Western Canada Using Gas Chromatography. *Journal of Archaeological Science* 26(4):425–38.

Malainey, Mary E., and Barbara L. Sherriff

1996   Adjusting Our Perceptions: Historical and Archaeological Evidence of Winter on the Plains of Western Canada. *Plains Anthropologist* 41(158):333–57.

Malinowski, Bronislaw

1950   *Argonauts of the Western Pacific.* E. P. Dutton, New York.

Manne, Tiina

2012   Vale Boi 10,000 Year of Upper Paleolithic Bone Boiling. In *The Menial Art of Cooking: Archaeological Studies of Cooking and Food Preparation*, edited by Sarah R. Graff and Enrique Rodríguez-Alegría, pp. 173–99. University of Colorado Press, Boulder.

Marshall, Fiona

2001   Agriculture and Use of Wild and Weedy Greens by the Piik op Oom Okiek of Kenya. *Economic Botany* 55(1):32–46.

Martin, A. C., and W. D. Barkley

1961   *Seed Identification Manual.* University of California Press, Berkeley.

Martin, Terrance J., and Mary Carol Masulis

1993   Faunal Remains from the Weaver Component. In *Rench: A Stratified Site in the Central Illinois River Valley*, edited by Mark A. McConaughy, pp. 274–307. Reports of Investigations No. 49, Illinois State Museum, Springfield.

Martin, Terrance J., and Kathryn E. Parker

2017   Ritual Feasting at Cahokia?: Animal and Plant Remains from an Early Eighteenth-Century Illinois Occupation on the First Terrace of Monks Mound. In *Cahokia and Beyond: Essays in Honor of Thomas E. Emerson*, edited by John A. Walthall and David J. Nolan, pp. 301–54. Illinois Archaeology 29.

REFERENCES

McConaughy, Mark A.

1993   Excavation and Analytical Methods. In *Rench: A Stratified Site in the Central Illinois River Valley*, edited by Mark A. McConaughy, pp. 274–307. Reports of Investigations No. 49, Illinois State Museum, Springfield.

McDowell-Loudan, Ellis

1983   Fire-Cracked Rocks: Preliminary Experiments to Determine Its Nature and Significance in Archaeological Contexts. *Chesopeian* 21(1):20–29.

McElrath, Dale L., with Thomas E. Emerson, and Andrew C. Fortier

2000   Social Evolution or Social Response? A Fresh Look at the "Good Gray Cultures" after Four Decades. In *Late Woodland Societies: Tradition and Transformation across the Midcontinent*, edited by Thomas E. Emerson, Dale L. McElrath, and Andrew C. Fortier, pp. 3–36. University of Nebraska Press, Lincoln.

McHale Milner, Claire

1998   Ceramic Style, Social Differentiation, and Resource Uncertainty in the Late Precontact Upper Great Lakes. Unpublished PhD dissertation, Department of Anthropology, University of Michigan, Ann Arbor.

McKern, William C.

1942   The First Settlers of Wisconsin. *Wisconsin Magazine of History* 25:153–69.

McLeester, Madeleine, and Mark R. Schurr

2020   Uncovering Huber Lifeways: An Overview of Findings from Four Years of Excavations at the Huber Phase Middle Grant Creek Site (11WI2739) in Northern Illinois. *Midcontinental Journal of Archaeology* 45(2):102–29.

McParland, Pat

1977   Experiments in the Firing and Breaking of Rocks. *Calgary Archaeologist* 5(3):31–33.

Mead, Margaret

1964   Food Habits Research: Problems of the 1960s. *National Academy of Sciences Vol. 1225*. National Research Council, Washington, DC.

1997   The Changing Significance of Food. In *Food and Culture: A Reader*, edited by Carole Counihan and Penny Van Esterik, pp. 11–19. Routledge, New York.

Meinholz, Norman M., and Jennifer Kolb

1997   *The Statz Site: A Late Woodland and Archaic Workshop in Dane County, Wisconsin*. Archaeology Research Series No. 5. Museum Archaeology Program, Madison, Wisconsin.

Messner, Timothy

2011   *Acorns and Bitter Roots: Starch Grain Research in the Prehistoric Eastern Woodlands*. University of Alabama Press, Tuscaloosa.

Metheny, Karen Bescherer

2022   Sensory Perspectives on Maize and Identity Formation in Colonial New England. *Historical Archaeology* 56:227–43.

Metzke, Brain A., Brooks M. Burr, Leon C. Hinz Jr., Lawrence M. Page, and Christopher A. Tayler

2022   *An Atlas of Illinois Fishes: 150 Years of Change*. University of Illinois Press, Champaign.

Michlovic, Michael G.

1983   The Red River Valley in the Prehistory of the Northern Plains. *Plains Anthropologist* 28(99):23–31.

1988   The Archaeology of the Red River Valley. *Minnesota History* 5(2):55–62.

Michlovic, Michael G., and Fred E. Schneider

1993   The Shea Site: A Prehistoric Fortified Village on the Northeastern Plains. *Plains Anthropologist* 38(143):117–37.

Milanich, Jerald T.

1979   Origins and Prehistoric Distributions of Black Drink and the Ceremonial Drinking Cup. In *Black Drink: A Native American Tea*, edited by C. M. Hudson, pp. 83–119. University of Georgia Press, Athens.

Milburn, Douglas, Uyen Doan, and Joanna Huckabee

2009   Spatial and Temporal Distributions of Archaeological Heated-Rock Cooking Structures in the Transverse Mountain Ranges: Proposed Markers of Land-Use Shifts since the Early Holocene. *Society for California Archaeology Proceedings* 22:1–21.

Miller, Jessica R.

2015   Interior Carbonization Patterns as Evidence of Ritual Drink Preparation in Powell Plain and Ramey Incised Vessels. *American Antiquity* 80(1):170–83.

Miller, Melanie J., Helen L. Whelton, Jillian A. Swift, Sophia Maline, Simon Hammann, Lucy J. E. Cramp, Alexandra McCleary, Geoffrey Tayler, Kirsten Vacca, Fanya Becks, Richard P. Evershed, and Christine A. Hastorf

2020   Interpreting Ancient Food Practices: Stable Isotope and Molecular Analyses of Visible and Absorbed Residues from a Year-Long Cooking Experiment. *Nature: Scientific Reports* 10(1):1–16.

Milner, George R.

1999   Warfare in Prehistoric and Early Historic Eastern North America. *Journal of Archaeological Research* 7(2):105–51.

Milner, George R., Eve Anderson, and Virginia G. Smith

1991   Warfare in Late Prehistoric West-Central Illinois. *American Antiquity* 56(4):581–603.

Minnis, Paul E.

2003   *People and Plants in Ancient Eastern North America.* Smithsonian Institution, Washington, DC.

Mintz, Sidney

1985   *Sweetness and Power: The Place of Sugar in Modern History.* Viking, New York.

1996   *Tasting Food, Tasting Freedom: Excursions into Eating, Culture, and the Past.* Beacon Press, Boston.

Mintz, Sidney, and Christine M. Du Bois

2002   The Anthropology of Food and Eating. *Annual Review of Anthropology* 31:99–119.

Moerman, Daniel E.

1998   *Native American Ethnobotany.* Timber Press, Oregon.

Monaghan, G. William, Timothy M. Schilling, and Kathryn E. Parker

2014   The Age and Distribution of Domesticated Beans (*Phaseolus vulgaris*) in Eastern North America: Implications for Agricultural Practices and Group Interactions. *Midwest Archaeological Conference Occasional Papers* No. 1:33–52.

Montanari, Massimo

2006   Identity, Exchange, Traditions, and "Origins." In *Food Is Culture*, pp. 133–37. Columbia University Press, New York.

Montgomery, Frederick H.
1977   *Seeds and Fruits of Eastern Canada and Northeastern United States*. University of Toronto Press, Toronto.

Montgomery, Henry
1908   Prehistoric Man in Manitoba and Saskatchewan. *American Anthropologist* 10(1):33–40.

Montón Subías, S.
2002   Cooking in Zooarchaeology: Is This Issue Still Raw? In *Consuming Passions and Patterns of Consumption*, edited by P. Miracle and N. Milner, pp. 7–16. McDonald Institute for Archaeological Research, Cambridge.

Moore, Katherine M.
2012   The Archaeology of Food. In *The Routledge International Handbook of Food Studies*, edited by Ken Albala, pp. 3–13. Taylor and Francis, New York.

Moreno, Luis Latournerie, John Tuxill, Elaine Yupit Moo, Luis Arias Reyes, Jairo Cristobal Alejo, and Devra I. Jarvis
2006   Traditional Maize Storage Methods of Mayan Farmers in Yucatan Mexico: Implications for Seed Selection and Crop Diversity. *Biodiversity and Conservation* 15(5):1771–95.

Morin, Eugène, and Marie-Cécile Soulier
2017   New Criteria for the Archaeological Identification of Bone Grease Processing. *American Antiquity* 82(1):96–122.

Morrow, Juliet E.
2014   Early Paleoindian Mobility and Watercraft: An Assessment from the Mississippi River Valley. *Midcontinental Journal of Archaeology* 39(2):103–29.

Mueller, Natalie G.
2013   *Mound Centers and Seed Security: A Comparative Analysis of Botanical Assemblages from Middle Woodland Sites in the Lower Illinois Valley*. Springer Briefs in Plant Science, New York.
2017   Seeds as Artifacts of Communities of Practice: The Domestication of Erect Knotweed in Eastern North America. PhD dissertation, Department of Anthropology, Washington University in St. Louis.

Mueller, Natalie G., and Gayle J. Fritz
2016   Women as Symbols and Actors in the Mississippi Valley: Evidence from Female Flint-Clay Statues and Effigy Vessels. In *Native American Landscapes: An Engendered Perspective*, edited by Cheryl Claassen, pp. 109–48. University of Tennessee Press, Knoxville.

Mueller, Natalie G., Gayle J. Fritz, Paul Patton, Stephen Carmody, and Elizabeth T. Horton
2017   Growing the Lost Crops of Eastern North America's Original Agricultural System. *Nature Plants* 3(7):1–5.

Myers, Thomas P.
2006   Hominy Technology and the Emergence of Mississippian Societies. In *Histories of Maize: Multidisciplinary Approaches to the Prehistory, Linguistics, Biogeography, Domestication, and Evolution of Maize*, edited by John E. Staller, Robert H. Tykot, and Bruce F. Benz, pp. 511–20. Academic Press, Boston.

Nash, Lenna M., Tamira K. Brennan, and Kristin M. Hedman
2016   Burials and Human Remains. In *Main Street Mound: A Ridgetop Monument at the*

East St. Louis Mound Complex, edited by Tamira K. Brennan, pp. 57–88. Research Report No. 36, Illinois State Archaeological Survey, Prairie Research Institute, University of Illinois at Urbana-Champaign.

Nash, Lenna M., Kristin M. Hedman, and Mathew A. Fort

2018 The People of East Saint Louis. In *Revealing Greater Cahokia: North America's First Native City*, edited by Thomas E. Emerson, Brad H. Koldehoff, and Mathew A. Fort, pp. 219–62. Illinois State Archaeological Survey, Prairie Research Institute, University of Illinois at Urbana-Champaign.

Nelson, Erin Stevens, Ashley Peles, and Mallory A. Melton

2023 A Mississippian Example of Harvest Renewal Ceremonialism. In *Ancient Foodways: Integrative Approaches to Understanding Subsistence and Society*, edited by C. Margaret Scarry, Dale L. Hutchinson, and Benjamin S. Arbuckle, pp. 152–82. University Press of Florida, Gainesville.

Nelson, Michael

2020 *Statistics in Nutrition and Dietetics*. John Wiley and Sons, Hoboken, New Jersey.

Nelson, Sarah Milledge

1997 Gender and the Division of Labor. In *Gender in Archaeology: Analyzing Power and Prestige*, edited by Sarah Milledge Nelson, pp. 85–112. AltaMira Press, Walnut Creek, California.

Neubauer, Fernanda

2013 Field Journal of the 2012–2013 Excavations on Grand Island, MI. Manuscript on file, USDA-Forest Service, Hiawatha National Forest, Gladstone, Michigan.

2016 Late Archaic Hunter-Gatherer Lithic Technology and Function (Chipped Stone, Ground Stone, and Fire-Cracked Rock): A Study of Domestic Life, Foodways, and Seasonal Mobility on Grand Island in Michigan's Upper Peninsula. PhD dissertation, Department of Anthropology, University of Wisconsin–Madison.

2017 Late Archaic Hunter-Gatherer Lithic Technology and Function (Chipped Stone, Ground Stone, and Fire-Cracked Rock): A Study of Domestic Life, Foodways, and Seasonal Mobility on Grand Island in Michigan's Upper Peninsula. *Revista de Arqueología* 30(1):260–62.

2018a Use-Alteration Analysis of Fire-Cracked Rocks. *American Antiquity* 83(4):681–700.

2018b Hunter-Gatherer Fall Social Aggregation: A Late Archaic Seasonal Mobility Model for Grand Island and Michigan's Upper Peninsula in the Great Lakes Region. *Wisconsin Archeologist* 99(1):41–53.

2019 Fire-Cracked Rock Experiments: A Comparison of Use-Alteration and Fracture Patterns between Stone Boiling/Wet Cooling and Hearth/Dry Cooling. *Wisconsin Archeologist* 100(1–2):35–47.

Neubauer, Fernanda, James Skibo, and Eric Drake

2010 Sítio Arqueológico Popper: Um Estudo da Tecnologia Lítica do Período Arcaico Tardio em Grand Island, Michigan, E.U.A. In *Proceedings of the 15th National Congress of the Society for Brazilian Archaeology (SAB)*, 2009 Sept. 20–23, Belém, PA, Brazil, Trabalhos Completos: Comunicações, vol. 1, pp. 44–62.

Neuman, Robert W.

1975 *The Sonota Complex and Associated Sites on the Northern Great Plains*. Nebraska

State Historical Society Publications in Anthropology No. 6. Nebraska State Historical Society, Lincoln.

Nicholson, Bev A.

1990 Ceramic Affiliations and the Case for Incipient Horticulture in Southwestern Manitoba. *Canadian Journal of Archaeology* 14:33–60.

1991 Modelling a Horticultural Complex in South-Central Manitoba during the Late Prehistoric Period: The Vickers Focus. *Midcontinental Journal of Archaeology* 16(2):163–88.

1994 Interactive Dynamics of Intrusive Horticultural Groups Coalescing in South-Central Manitoba during the Late Prehistoric Period—The Vickers Focus. *North American Archaeologist* 15(2):103–27.

Nicholson, Bev A., Scott Hamilton, Matt Boyd, and Sylvia Nicholson

2008 A Late Plains Woodland Adaptive Strategy in the Northern Parklands: The Vickers Focus Forager-Horticulturists. Invited Paper for Papers in Northeastern Plains Prehistory, edited by Michael G. Michlovic and Dennis L. Toom. *North Dakota Journal of Archaeology* 8:19–34.

Nicholson, Bev A., Scott Hamilton, Garry Running IV, and Sylvia Nicholson

2006 Two Cultures—One Environment: Vickers Focus Adaptations Contrasted with Blackduck Adaptations in the Tiger Hills. *Plains Anthropologist* 51(199):335–53.

Nicholson, Bev A., and Mary E. Malainey

1994 Pits, Pots, and Pieces of China: Results of the Archaeological Testing of Two Shallow Depressions near Melita, Manitoba. *Manitoba Archaeological Journal* 4(1&2):128–67.

Nicholson, Bev A., David Meyer, Gerry Oetelaar, and Scott Hamilton

2011 Human Ecology of the Canadian Prairie Ecozone circa 500 BP: Plains Woodland Influences and Horticultural Practice. In *Human Ecology of the Canadian Prairie Ecozone 11,000 to 300 BP*, edited by B. A. Nicholson, pp. 153–80. Canadian Plains Research Center, Regina, Saskatchewan.

Noneman, Heidi, Christine VanPool, and Andrew Fernandez

2017 Examination of Organic Residues and Tribochemical Wear in Low Fired Casas Grandes Pottery Vessels. Poster presented at the 81st Annual Meeting of the Society for American Archaeology, Vancouver, British Columbia.

Norby, Rodney D., and Zakaria Lasemi (editors)

2000 *Paleozoic and Quaternary Geology of the St. Louis Metro East Area of Western Illinois.* ISGS Guidebook 32, Illinois State Geological Survey, Urbana-Champaign.

Nordine, Kelsey

2020 Building Communities: Interpreting Oneota and Mississippian Interaction through Paleoethnobotanical Analysis at the Morton Village Site (11F2), West-Central Illinois. PhD dissertation, Department of Anthropology, Washington University in St. Louis.

Oates, Joseph A. H.

1998 *Lime and Limestone: Chemistry and Technology, Production and Uses.* Wiley-VCH, New York.

O'Brien, Patricia J.

1972 *A Formal Analysis of Cahokia Ceramics from the Powell Tract.* Monograph 1. Illinois Archaeological Survey. Springfield.

O'Gorman, Jodie A.

2016 A Pilot Study to Examine Mississippian and Oneota Foodways at the Morton Village Site. *Illinois Antiquity* 51(4):1–5.

O'Gorman, Jodie A., Jennifer D. Bengtson, and Amy R. Michael

2020 Ancient History and New Beginnings: Necrogeography and Migration in the North American Midcontinent. *World Archaeology* 52(1):16–34.

O'Gorman, Jodie A., and Michael D. Conner

2023 Making Community: Implications of Hybridity and Coalescence at Morton Village. *American Antiquity* 88(1):79–98.

O'Gorman, Jodie A., and W. A. Lovis

2006 Before Removal: An Archaeological Perspective on the Southern Lake Michigan Basin. In *The Potawatomi Removal*, Special Issue Guest Edited by Mark Schurr. *Midcontinental Journal of Archaeology* 31(1):21–56.

Ohnuki-Tierney, Emiko

1993 *Rice as Self: Japanese Identities through Time.* Princeton University Press, Princeton, New Jersey.

Oldmixon, John

1708 *The British Empire in America: Containing the History of the Discovery, Settlement, Progress and Present State of All the British Colonies on the Continent and Islands of America. Volume 1.* John Nicholson and Benjamin Tooke, London. Digitized 2014, National Library of the Netherlands.

Orchardson, Emma

2021 What Is Nixtamalization? Water, Heat, and Lime Transform Grain in a Traditional Central American Maize Processing Method. CIMMYT (website), accessed October 12, 2023.

Oras, Ester, Mari Tõrv, Tõnno Jonuks, Martin Malve, Anita Radini, Sven Isaksson, Andy Gledhill, Ott Kekisev, Signe Vahur, and Ivo Leito

2018 Social Food Here and Hereafter: Multiproxy Analysis of Gender-Specific Food Consumption in Conversion Period Inhumation Cemetery at Kukruse, NE-Estonia. *Journal of Archaeological Science* 97:90–101.

O'Shea, John M., and Clare McHale Milner

2002 Material Indicators of Territory, Identity, and Interaction in a Prehistoric Tribal System. In *The Archaeology of Tribal Societies*, edited by W. A. Parkinson, pp. 200–226. International Monographs in Prehistory, Ann Arbor, Michigan.

O'Sullivan, Aidan

2003 Place, Memory, and Identity among Estuarine Fishing Communities: Interpreting the Archaeology of Early Medieval Fish Weirs. *World Archaeology* 35:449–68.

Ozker, Doreen B.

1982 *An Early Woodland Community at the Schultz Site 20SA2 in the Saginaw Valley and the Nature of the Early Woodland Adaptation in the Great Lakes Region.* Anthropological Papers No. 70. Museum of Anthropology, University of Michigan, Ann Arbor.

Painter, Autumn M.

2022 Coalescence and Animal Use: Examining Community Building at the Multi-Ethnic Morton Village Site. PhD dissertation, Department of Anthropology, Michigan State University, East Lansing.

Painter, Jeffrey M.

2021 Cooking and Coalescence: Exploring the Construction of Community and Cuisine at Morton Village. PhD dissertation, Department of Anthropology, Michigan State University, East Lansing.

Painter, Jeffrey M., and Jodie A. O'Gorman

2019 Cooking and Community: An Exploration of Oneota Group Variability through Foodways. *Midcontinental Journal of Archaeology* 44(3):231–58.

Palacios-Rojas, Natalia, Laura McCulley, Mikayla Kaeppler, Tyler J. Titcomb, Nilupa S. Gunaratna, Santiago Lopez-Ridaura, and Sherry A. Tanumihardjo

2020 Mining Maize Diversity and Improving Its Nutritional Aspects with Agro-Food Systems. *Comprehensive Reviews in Food Science and Food Safety* 19(4):1809–934.

Palliser, John

1968 *The Papers of the Palliser Expedition: 1857–1860*, edited by I. M. Spry, Champlain Society, Toronto.

Papakosta, Vasiliki, Ester Oras, and Sven Isaksson

2019 Early Pottery Use across the Baltic—A Comparative Lipid Residue Study on Ertebølle and Narva Ceramics from Coastal Hunter-Gatherer Sites in Southern Scandinavia, Northern Germany, and Estonia. *Journal of Archaeological Science: Reports* 24:142–51.

Parachini, Kathryn

1981 The Paleoethnobotany of the Upper Mississippian Component at the Elam Site, a Seasonal Encampment on the Lower Kalamazoo River. Master's thesis, Department of Anthropology, Western Michigan University, Kalamazoo.

Parker, Arthur C.

1910 *Iroquois Uses of Maize and Other Food Plants*. Education Department Bulletin No. 482. University of the State of New York, Albany.

Parker, Kathryn E.

1992 The Oneota, Bold Counselor Complex Component: Archaeobotany. In *The Sponemann Site 2: The Mississippian and Oneota Occupations*, edited by Douglas K. Jackson, Andrew C. Fortier, and Joyce A. Williams, pp. 485–96. American Bottom Archaeology FAI-270 Site Reports, Vol. 24. Illinois Department of Transportation by the University of Chicago Press, Chicago.

1996 Three Corn Kernels and a Hill of Beans: The Evidence for Prehistoric Horticulture in Michigan. In *Investigating the Archaeological Record of the Great Lakes State*, edited by Margaret B. Holman, Janet G. Brashler, and Kathryn E. Parker, pp. 307–40. Western Michigan University Press, Kalamazoo.

Parker, Kathryn E., and Mary L. Simon

2018 Magic Plants and Mississippian Ritual. In *Archaeology and Ancient Religion in the Midcontinent*, edited by Brad H. Koldehoff and Timothy R. Pauketat, pp. 117–66. University of Alabama Press, Tuscaloosa.

Parmalee, Paul W.

1957 Vertebrate Remains from the Cahokia Site, Illinois. *Transactions of the Illinois Academy of Science* 50:235–42.

1975 A General Summary of the Vertebrate Fauna from Cahokia. In *Perspectives in Cahokia Archaeology*, pp. 137–55. Bulletin No. 10. Illinois Archaeological Survey, University of Illinois at Urbana-Champaign.

1977 The Avifauna from Prehistoric Arikara Sites in South Dakota. *Plains Anthropologist* 22:189–222.

Pauketat, Timothy R.

1998 *The Archaeology of Downtown Cahokia: The Tract 15a and Dunham Tract Excavations.* Illinois Transportation Archaeological Research Program, Studies in Archaeology, No. 1. University of Illinois at Urbana-Champaign.

2004 *Ancient Cahokia and the Mississippians.* Cambridge University Press, New York.

2003 Resettled Farmers and the Making of a Mississippian Polity. *American Antiquity* 68(1):39–66.

2013 *The Archaeology of Downtown Cahokia II: The 1960 Excavation of Tract 15B.* Illinois State Archaeological Survey, Studies in Archaeology, No. 8. Prairie Research Institute, University of Illinois at Urbana-Champaign.

2018 Thinking through the Ashes, Architecture, and Artifacts of Ancient East St. Louis. In *Revealing Greater Cahokia, North America's First Native City: Rediscovery and Large-Scale Excavations of the East St. Louis Precinct,* edited by Thomas E. Emerson, Brad H. Koldehoff, and Tamira K. Brennan, pp. 463–86. Studies in Archaeology No. 12. Illinois State Archaeological Survey, Prairie Research Institute, University of Illinois at Urbana-Champaign.

Pauketat, Timothy R., and Thomas E. Emerson

1991 The Ideology of Authority and the Power of the Pot. *American Anthropologist* 93(4):919–41.

Pauketat, Timothy R., Robert F. Boszhardt, and Danielle M. Benden

2015 Trempealeau Entanglements: An Ancient Colony's Causes and Effects. *American Antiquity* 80(2):260–89.

Pauketat, Timothy R., Robert F. Boszhardt, and Michael Kolb

2017 Trempealeau's Little Bluff: An Early Cahokian Terraformed Landmark in the Upper Mississippi Valley. *Midcontinental Journal of Archaeology* 42(2):168–99.

Pauketat, Timothy R., Lucretia S. Kelly, Gayle J. Fritz, Neal H. Lopinot, Scott Elias, and Eve Hargrave

2002 The Residues of Feasting and Public Ritual at Early Cahokia. *American Antiquity* 67(2):257–79.

Peace, Adrian

2011 Barossa Dreaming: Imagining Place and Constituting Cuisine in Contemporary Australia. *Anthropological Forum* 21(1):23–42.

Peacock, Sandra

2002 Perusing the Pits: The Evidence for Prehistoric Root Resource Processing on the Canadian Plateau. In *Hunter-Gatherer Archaeobotany: Perspectives from the Northern Temperate Zone,* edited by Sarah Mason and Jon Hather, pp. 45–63. Institute of Archaeology Occasional Publications. Archetype Publications, London.

Pearsall, Deborah M.

2015 *Paleoethnobotany: A Handbook of Procedures,* 3rd ed. Left Coast Press, Walnut Creek, California.

Peck, Trevor R.

2011 *Light from Ancient Campfires: Archaeological Evidence for Native Lifeways on the Northern Plains.* Athabasca University Press, Edmonton.

REFERENCES

Peles, Ashley, and Megan C. Kassabaum
2020 Reexamining the Evidence for Bear Ceremonialism in the Lower Mississippi Valley. In *Bears: Archaeological and Ethnohistorical Perspectives in Native Eastern North America*, edited by Heather A. Lapham and Gregory A. Waselkov, pp. 235–55. University Press of Florida, Gainesville.

Peres, Tanya M.
2017 Foodways Archaeology: A Decade of Research from the Southeastern United States. *Journal of Archaeological Research* 25(4):421–60.

Peres, Tanya M., and Aaron Deter-Wolf (editors)
2018 *Baking, Bourbon, and Black Drink: Foodways Archaeology in the American Southeast.* University of Alabama Press, Tuscaloosa.

Pesantubbee, Michelene E., and Michael J. Zogry
2021 *Native Foodways: Indigenous North American Religious Traditions and Foods.* State University of New York Press, Albany.

Petraglia, Michael, Susan Bupp, Sean Fitzell, and Kevin Cunningham (compilers)
2002 *Hickory Bluff: Changing Perceptions of Delmarva Archaeology.* DelDOT Archaeology Series No. 175. Report on file, Delaware Department of Transportation, Dover.

Pflieger, William L.
1975 *The Fishes of Missouri.* Missouri Department of Conservation, Jefferson City.

Picard, Jennifer
2013 Northern Flint, Southern Roots: A Diachronic Analysis of Paleoethnobotanical Remains and Maize Race at the Aztalan Site. Unpublished Master's thesis, Department of Anthropology, University of Wisconsin–Milwaukee.

Picard, Jennifer, and Jennifer R. Haas
2019 Ceramic Analysis. In *Archaeological Data Recovery at the Finch Site (47JE0902), Jefferson County, Wisconsin*, edited by Jennifer R. Haas, pp. 241–310. University of Wisconsin Archaeological Research Laboratory, Report of Investigations No. 445. Milwaukee.

Piperno, Dolores R.
2006 *Phytoliths: A Comprehensive Guide for Archaeologists and Paleoecologists.* AltaMira Press, Lanham, Maryland.
2009 Identifying Crop Plants with Phytoliths (and Starch Grains) in Central and South America: A Review and an Update of the Evidence. *Quaternary International* 193(1–2):146–59.

Pitts, Martin
2015 The Archaeology of Food Consumption. In *A Companion to Food in the Ancient World*, edited by John Wilkins and Robin Nadeau, pp. 95–104. Wiley Blackwell, Malden, Massachusetts.

Popper, Virginia S.
1988 Selecting Quantitative Measures in Paleoethnobotany. In *Prehistoric Archeology and Ecology Current Paleoethnobotany: Analytical Methods and Cultural Interpretations of Archaeological Plant Remains*, edited by Christine A. Hastorf and Virginia S. Popper, pp. 53–71. Prehistoric Archeology and Ecology. University of Chicago Press, Chicago.
2019 Cuisine of the Chinese at Market Street Chinatown (San Jose, California): Using

Cookbooks to Interpret Archaeological Plant and Animal Remains. *Vegetation History and Archaeobotany* 28:347–55.

Posthumus, David C.

2017 All My Relatives: Exploring Nineteenth-Century Lakota Ontology and Belief. *Ethnohistory* 64(3):379–400.

2018 *All My Relatives: Exploring Lakota Ontology, Belief, and Ritual.* University of Nebraska Press, Lincoln.

Province of Manitoba

1963 Archaeological Salvage Set for Lockport Site, Department of Industry and Commerce, April 11 (website), accessed October 12, 2023.

n.d. History of Flooding in Manitoba (website), accessed October 12, 2023.

Quaternary Consultants

1999 *Impact Assessment and Archaeological Monitoring of the Forks Access Project: South of Water Avenue (DILg-33:97A).* Report submitted to Reid Crowther and Partners, Winnipeg.

Quigg, Michael

2003 New Analytical Approaches to South Texas Cultural Assemblages. *La Tierra* 30(3–4):15–23.

Quigg, Michael, Mary Malainey, Roman Przybylski, and Gregory Monks

2001 No Bones about It: Using Lipid Analysis of Burned Rock Groundstone Residues to Examine Late Archaic Subsistence Practices in South Texas. *Plains Anthropologist* 46(177):283–303.

Ralat, José R.

2020 The Tex-Mexplainer: Nixtamalization Is the 3,500-Year-Old Secret to Great Tortillas. *Texas Monthly.*

Raviele, Maria E.

2010 Assessing Carbonized Archaeological Cooking Residues: Evaluation of Maize Phytolith Taphonomy and Density through Experimental Residue Analysis. PhD dissertation, Department of Anthropology, Michigan State University, East Lansing.

2011 Experimental Assessment of Maize Phytolith and Starch Taphonomy in Carbonized Cooking Residues. *Journal of Archaeological Science* 38(10):2708–13.

Ray, Arthur J.

1974 *Indians of the Fur Trade.* University of Toronto Press, Toronto.

Reber, Eleanora A.

2006 A Hard Row to Hoe: Changing Maize Use in the American Bottom and Surrounding Areas. In *Histories of Maize: Multidisciplinary Approaches to the Prehistory, Linguistics, Biogeography, Domestication, and Evolution of Maize,* edited by John E. Staller, Robert H. Tykot, and Bruce F. Benz, pp. 235–48. Academic Press, Boston.

Reber, Eleonora A., and Richard P. Evershed

2004 How Did Mississippians Prepare Maize? The Application of Compound-Specific Carbon Isotope Analysis to Absorbed Pottery Residues from Several Mississippi Valley Sites. *Archaeometry* 46(1):19–33.

Redmond, Brian G., Bret J. Ruby, and Jarrod Burks (editors)

2020 *Encountering Hopewell in the Twenty-First Century, Ohio and Beyond: 2. Settlements, Foodways, and Interaction.* University of Akron Press, Ohio.

Reilly, F. Kent, III

2004   People of Earth, People of Sky: Visualizing the Sacred in Native American Art of the Mississippian Period. In *Hero, Hawk, and Open Hand: American Indian Art of the Ancient Midwest and South*, edited by Richard F. Townsend and Robert V. Sharp, pp. 125–38. Art Institute of Chicago, Chicago.

Reitz, Elizabeth J., Lee A. Newsom, and Sylvia J. Scudder

1996a   Issues in Environmental Archaeology. In *Case Studies in Environmental Archaeology*, edited by Elizabeth J. Reitz, Lee A. Newsom, and Sylvia J. Scudder, pp. 3–16. Plenum Press, New York.

Reitz, Elizabeth J., Lee A. Newsom, and Sylvia J. Scudder (editors)

1996b   *Case Studies in Environmental Archaeology*. Plenum Press, New York.

Reitz, Elizabeth, Irvy R. Quitmyer, H. Stephen Hale, Sylvia J. Scudder, and Elizabeth S. Wing

1987   Application of Allometry to Zooarchaeology. *American Antiquity* 52(2):304–17.

Reitz, Elizabeth, and Elizabeth S. Wing

2008   *Zooarchaeology: Second Edition*. Cambridge Manuals in Archaeology. Cambridge University Press, Cambridge.

Rice, Prudence M.

1987   *Pottery Analysis: A Sourcebook*. University of Chicago Press, Chicago.

Richards, Audrey I.

1939   *Land, Labour, and Diet in Northern Rhodesia, an Economic Study of the Bemba Tribe*. Oxford University Press, London.

Richards, John D.

1992   Ceramics and Culture at Aztalan: A Late Prehistoric Village in Southeast Wisconsin. Unpublished PhD dissertation, Department of Anthropology, University of Wisconsin–Milwaukee.

Roberts, Linda J.

1991   Bison Scapula from the Lockport Site, EaLf-1. *Manitoba Archaeological Journal* 1(2):1–21.

Robson, Harry K., Raminta Skipityté, Giedré Piličiauskiené, Alexandre Lucquin, Carl Heron, Oliver E. Craig, and Gytis Piličiauskas

2019   Diet, Cuisine, and Consumption Practices of the First Farmers in the Southeastern Baltic. *Archaeological and Anthropological Sciences* 11(8):4011–24.

Rodell, Roland

1997   The Diamond Bluff Complex: Time and Tradition in the Northern Mississippi Valley. Unpublished PhD dissertation, Department of Anthropology, University of Wisconsin–Milwaukee.

Rodríguez-Alegría, Enrique, and Sarah R. Graff

2012   Introduction: The Menial Art of Cooking. In *The Menial Art of Cooking: Archaeological Studies of Cooking and Food Preparation*, edited by Sarah R. Graff and Enrique Rodríguez-Alegría, pp. 1–19. University Press of Colorado, Boulder.

Rogers, Edward S.

1962   *The Round Lake Ojibwa*. Occasional Paper 5, Art and Archaeology Division, Ontario Department of Lands and Forests for the Royal Ontario Museum, Toronto.

Rusch, Lynn A.

1988   *The Early and Late Woodland Occupations at the Bachmann Site (47 Sb-202) in*

284   REFERENCES

East-central Wisconsin. Museum Archaeology Program, Research Report in Archaeology. Madison, Wisconsin.

Rogers, Everett M.

1995   *Diffusion of Innovations.* 4th ed. Free Press, New York.

Rowan, Erica

2019   The Sensory Experiences of Food Consumption. In *The Routledge Handbook of Sensory Archaeology,* edited by Robin Skeates and Jo Day, pp. 293–314. Taylor and Francis Group, New York.

Rutherford, A. A., J. Wittenberg, and B. C. Gordon

1984   University of Saskatchewan Radiocarbon Dates X. *Radiocarbon* 26(2):241–92.

Ruxton, Graeme

2006   The Unequal Variance T-Test Is an Underused Alternative to Student's T-Test and the Mann-Whitney U Test. *Behavioral Ecology* 17(4):688–90.

Sahagún, Bernardino de

1961   Book 10: The People, No. 14, Part 11. In *Florentine Codex: General History of the Things of New Spain,* translated by Arthur J. O. Anderson and Charles E. Dibble. School of American Research and the University of Utah, Santa Fe and Salt Lake City.

Salkin, Philip H.

1986   Lake Farms Phase: The Early Woodland Stage in South-Central Wisconsin as Seen from the Lake Farms Archaeological District. In *Early Woodland Archeology,* edited by Kenneth B. Farnsworth and Thomas Emerson, pp. 92–120. Center for American Archeology, Kampsville, Illinois.

1987   A Reevaluation of the Late Woodland Stage in Southeastern Wisconsin. *Wisconsin Academy Review* 33(2):75–79.

2000   The Horicon and Kekoskee Phases: Cultural Complexity in the Late Woodland Stage of Southeastern Wisconsin. In *Late Woodland Societies,* edited by Thomas E. Emerson, Dale L. McElrath, and Andrew C. Fortier, pp. 525–42. University of Nebraska Press, Lincoln.

Salzer, Robert J.

N.d.   The Waukesha Focus: Hopewell in Southeastern Wisconsin. Manuscript on file, Department of Anthropology, University of Wisconsin–Milwaukee.

1965   The Highsmith Site (Je4): An Early, Middle, and Late Woodland Site in the Upper Rock River Drainage. Master's thesis, Department of Anthropology, University of Wisconsin–Madison.

Santini, Lauren M., Sadie L. Weber, John M. Marston, and Astrid Runggaldier

2021   First Archaeological Identification of Nixtamalized Maize, from Two Pit Latrines at the Ancient Maya Site of San Bartolo, Guatemala. *Journal of Archaeological Science* 143:105581.

Santure, Sharron K., and Duane Esarey

1990   Analysis of Artifacts from the Oneota Mortuary Component. In *Archaeological Investigations at the Morton Village and Norris Farms 36 Cemetery,* edited by Sharron K. Santure, Alan D. Harn, and Duane Esarey, pp. 75–110. Reports of Investigations No. 45, Illinois State Museum, Springfield.

Santure, Sharron K., Alan D. Harn, and Duane Esarey

1990   *Archaeological Investigations at the Morton Village and Norris Farms 36 Cemetery.* Reports of Investigations No. 45, Illinois State Museum, Springfield.

Sassaman, Kenneth E.

1993   *Early Pottery in the Southeast: Tradition and Innovation in Cooking Technology*. University of Alabama Press, Tuscaloosa.

Saul, Hayley, Marco Madella, Anders Fischer, Aikaterini Glykou, Sönke Hartz, and Oliver E. Craig

2013   Phytoliths in Pottery Reveal the Use of Spice in European Prehistoric Cuisine. *PLoS ONE* 8(8):e70583.

Saylor, B. J.

1976   Fidler Mounds (EaLf-3): Analysis of a Mound Population and Its Associations. Unpublished Master's thesis, Department of Anthropology, University of Manitoba, Winnipeg.

Scarry, C. Margaret

2003   Patterns of Wild Plant Utilization in the Prehistoric Eastern Woodlands. In *People and Plants in Ancient Eastern North America*, edited by Paul E. Minnis, pp. 50–104. Smithsonian Books, Washington, DC.

Scarry, C. Margaret, and Elizabeth J. Reitz

2005   Changes in Foodways at the Parkin Site, Arkansas. *Southeastern Archaeology* 24(2):107–20.

Schaefer, Kimberly, and Mary L. Simon

2023   Floral Analysis. In *East St. Louis Precinct Faunal and Botanical Remains*, edited by B. Jacob Skousen, pp. 41–148. Research Report No. 48, Illinois State Archaeological Survey, Prairie Research Institute, University of Illinois at Urbana-Champaign.

Schneider, Fred

1982   A Model of Prehistoric Cultural Development in the James River Valley of North Dakota. *Journal of the North Dakota Archaeological Association* 1:113–34.

2002   Prehistoric Horticulture in the Northeastern Plains. *Plains Anthropologist* 47(180):33–50.

Schoenwetter, James

1998   Rethinking the Paleoethnobotany of Early Woodland Caving. *Midcontinental Journal of Archaeology* 23(1).23–44.

Schroeder, Sissel

2004   Current Research on Late Precontact Societies of the Midcontinental United States. *Journal of Archaeological Research* 12(4):311–72.

Schurr, Mark R., and Brian G. Redmond

1991   A Stable Isotope Analysis of Incipient Maize Horticulturalists from the Grand Island 2 Site. *Midcontinental Journal of Archaeology* 16(1):69–84.

Scott, Elizabeth M.

1996   Who Ate What? Archaeological Food Remains and Cultural Diversity. In *Case Studies in Environmental Archaeology*, edited by Elizabeth J. Reitz, Lee A. Newsom, and Sylvia J. Scudder, pp. 357–74. Plenum Press, New York.

Seeman, Mark F., Nils E. Nilsson, Garry L. Summers, Larry L. Morris, Paul J. Barens, Elaine Dowd, and Margaret E. Newman

2008   Evaluating Protein Residues on Gainey Phase Paleoindian Stone Tools. *Journal of Archaeological Science* 35(10):2742–50.

Seligson, Kenneth, Tomás Gallareta Negrón, Rossana May Ciau, and George J. Bey III

2017a   Lime Powder Production in the Maya Puuc Region (A.D. 600–900): An Experimental Pit-Kiln. *Journal of Field Archaeology* 42(2):129–41.

2017b   Using Multiple Lines of Evidence to Identify Prehispanic Maya Burnt-Lime Kilns in the Northern Yucatán Peninsula. *Latin American Antiquity* 28(4):558–76.

Seligson, Kenneth E., Soledad Ortiz Ruiz, and Luis Barba Pingarrón

2019   Prehispanic Maya Burnt Lime Industries: Previous Studies and Future Directions. *Ancient Mesoamerica* 30(2):199–219.

Sengupta, Jayanta

2010   Nation on a Platter: The Culture and Politics of Food and Cuisine in Colonial Bengal. *Modern Asian Studies* 44(1):81–98.

Shay, C. Thomas

1980   Food Plants of Manitoba. In *Directions in Manitoba Prehistory: Papers in Honour of Chris Vickers*, edited by L. Pettipas, pp. 233–90. Association of Manitoba Archaeologists and Manitoba Archaeological Society, Winnipeg.

Shoda, Shinya, Alexandre Lucquin, Chi Ian Sou, Yastami Nishida, Guoping Sun, Hiroshi Kitano, Joon-ho Son, Shinichi Nakamura, and Oliver E. Craig

2018   Molecular and Isotopic Evidence for the Processing of Starchy Plants in Early Neolithic Pottery from China. *Nature: Scientific Reports* 8(1):1–9.

Shuler, Kristina A., Shannon C. Hodge, Marie E. Danforth, and Danielle N. Cook

2012   In the Shadow of Moundville: A Bioarchaeological View of the Transition to Agriculture in the Central Tombigbee Valley of Alabama and Mississippi. *Journal of Anthropological Archaeology* 31(4):586–603.

Silliman, Stephen W.

2013   What, Where, and When Is Hybridity? In *The Archaeology of Hybrid Material Culture*, edited by Jeb J. Card, pp. 486–500. Occasional Paper No. 39. Center for Archaeological Investigations, Southern Illinois University, Carbondale.

Simon, Mary L.

1998   Archaeobotanical Assemblage. In *The Rock River Sites: Late Woodland Occupation along the Middle Rock River in Northern Illinois*, edited by A. R. Titelbaum, pp. 223–29. Transportation Archaeological Research Reports No. 57. Illinois Transportation Archaeological Research Program, University of Illinois at Urbana-Champaign.

2000   Regional Variations in Plant Use Strategies in the Midwest during the Late Woodland. In *Late Woodland Societies*, edited by Thomas E. Emerson, Dale L. McElrath, and Andrew C. Fortier, pp. 37–75. University of Nebraska Press, Lincoln.

2002   Red Cedar, White Oak, and Bluestem Grass: The Colors of Mississippian Construction. *Midcontinental Journal of Archaeology* 27(2):273–308.

2009   A Regional and Chronological Synthesis of Archaic Period Plant Use in the Midcontinent. In *Archaic Societies: Diversity and Complexity across the Midcontinent*, edited by Thomas E. Emerson, Dale L. McElrath, and Andrew C. Fortier, Pp. 81–114. State University of New York Press, Albany.

2018   Plants and Burned Structures at the East St. Louis Precinct. In *Revealing Greater Cahokia: North America's First Native City*, edited by Thomas E. Emerson, Brad H. Koldehoff, and Tamira K. Brennan, pp. 445–61. University of Illinois at Urbana-Champaign.

REFERENCES

Simon, Mary L., Kandace D. Hollenbach, and Brian G. Redmond
2021   New Dates and Carbon Isotope Assays of Purported Middle Woodland Maize from the Icehouse Bottom and Edwin Harness Sites. *American Antiquity* 86(3):613–24.

Simon, Mary, and Kathryn Parker
2006   Prehistoric Plant Use in the American Bottom: New Thoughts and Interpretations. *Southeastern Archaeology* 25(2):170–211.

Sinclair, Niigaan
2019   Archaeology Unearths Proof of Huge 1285 Meeting. *Winnipeg Free Press* (website), November 25.

Skeates, Robin, and Jo Day
2019   *The Routledge Handbook of Sensory Archaeology*, edited by Robin Skeates and Jo Day. Taylor & Francis Group, New York.

Skibo, James
1992   *Pottery Function: A Use-Alteration Perspective*. Plenum, New York.
1994   The Kalinga Cooking Pot: An Ethnoarchaeological and Experimental Study of Technological Change. In *Kalinga Ethnoarchaeology: Expanding Archaeological Method and Theory*, edited by William A. Longacre and James M. Skibo, pp. 113–26. Smithsonian Institution, Washington, DC.
2013   *Understanding Pottery Function*. Manuals in Archaeological Methods, Theory, and Technique. Springer, New York.
2015   Pottery Use-Alteration Analysis. In *Use-Wear and Residue Analysis in Archaeology*, edited by J. M. Marreiros, J. F. Gibaja Bao, and N. F. Bicho, pp. 189–98. Springer, New York.

Skibo, James M, T. C. Butts, and Michael B. Schiffer
1997   Ceramic Surface Treatment and Abrasion Resistance: An Experimental Study. *Journal of Archaeological Science* 24(4):311.

Skibo, James M., and Mary Malainey
2013   Residue. In *Understanding Pottery Function*, by James M. Skibo, pp. 161–89. Springer, New York.

Skibo, James, Mary Malainey, and Eric Drake
2009   Stone Boiling, Fire-Cracked Rock, and Nut Oil: Exploring the Origins of Pottery Making on Grand Island. *Wisconsin Archeologist* 90(1–2):47–64.

Skibo, James M, Mary E. Malainey, and Susan M. Kooiman
2016   Early Pottery in the North American Upper Great Lakes: Exploring Traces of Use. *Antiquity* 90(353):1226–37.

Skibo, James M., and Michael B. Schiffer
1995   The Clay Cooking Pot: An Exploration of Women's Technology. In *Expanding Archaeology*, edited by James M. Skibo, William H. Walker, and Axel E. Nielsen, pp. 80–91. University of Utah Press, Salt Lake City.

Smith, Beverly A.
2004   The Gill Net's "Native Country": The Inland Shore Fishery in the Northern Lake Michigan Basin. In *An Upper Great Lakes Archaeological Odyssey: Essays in Honor of Charles E. Cleland*, edited by William A. Lovis, pp. 64–84. Wayne State University Press, Detroit.

Smith, Bruce D.

2006 Eastern North America as an Independent Center of Plant Domestication. *Proceedings of the National Academy of Sciences* 103(33):12223–28

2011 The Cultural Context of Plant Domestication in Eastern North America. *Current Anthropology* 52(S2):S471–S484.

Smith, Bruce D., C. Wesley Cowan, and Michael P. Hoffman

2007 *Rivers of Change: Essays on Early Agriculture in Eastern North America.* University of Alabama Press, Tuscaloosa.

Smith, Bruce D., and Richard A. Yarnell

2009 Initial Formation of an Indigenous Crop Complex in Eastern North America at 3800 B.P. *Proceedings of the National Academy of Sciences* 106(16):6561–66.

Smith, G. H.

1972 *Like-a-Fishhook Village and Fort Berthold, Garrison Reservoir, North Dakota.* Anthropological Papers 2. National Park Service, US Department of the Interior, Washington, DC.

Smith, Kevin, Sebastian Wärmläander, René Vellanoweth, Chelsea Smith, and William Kendig

2015 Residue Analysis Links Sandstone Abraders to Shell Fishhook Production on San Nicolas Island, California. *Journal of Archaeological Science* 54:287–93.

Smith, Marion F.

1988 Function from Whole Vessel Shape: A Method and Application to Anasazi Black Mesa, Arizona. *American Anthropologist* 90(4):912–23.

Smith, Monica L.

2006 The Archaeology of Food Preference. *American Anthropologist* 108(3):480–93.

Sohodoleanu, Adriana

2020 The Production of the "New Romanian Cuisine": Elite Local Taste and Globalisation. *Journal of Comparative Research in Anthropology and Sociology* 11(2):49–64.

Speck, Frank G.

1909 *Ethnology of the Yuchi Indians.* University of Pennsylvania University Museum Anthropological Publications No. 1. University of Pennsylvania, Philadelphia.

Spencer, Victoria, and Marlene Sekaquaptewa

1995 Piki of the Hopi Indians. *Expedition* 37(1):19–24.

Spero, George

1979 The Allegan Dam Site: An Upper Mississippian Occupation in the Lower Kalamazoo River Basin. Master's thesis, Department of Anthropology, Western Michigan University, Kalamazoo.

Speth, John

2015 When Did Humans Learn to Boil? *PaleoAnthropology* 2015:54–67.

Staeck, John P.

1995 Oneota Archaeology Past, Present, and Future: In the Beginning, Again. In *Oneota Archaeology: Past, Present, and Future,* edited by William Green, pp. 3–9. Office of the State Archaeologist, University of Iowa, Iowa City.

Stahl, Ann

1985 *The Dohack Site (11-S-642). American Bottom Archaeology FAI-270 Site Reports 12.* University of Illinois Press, Champaign.

Stark, Richard

2002a   Comidas de la Tierra: An Ethnoarchaeology of Earth Ovens. PhD dissertation, Department of Anthropology, University of Texas at Austin.

2002b   Fire-Cracked Rock Experiments: The Potential of Three Analytical Techniques. *La Tierra* 29(4):12–28.

Steadman, Dawnie Wolfe

2008   Warfare Related Trauma at Orendorf, A Middle Mississippian Site in West-Central Illinois. *American Journal of Physical Anthropology* 136(1):51–64.

Steinbring, Jack

1998   Aboriginal Rock Painting Sites in Manitoba. *Manitoba Archaeological Journal* 8(1&2):i–viii; 1–156.

Stencil, Zachary R.

2015   Vertebrate Evidence for Diet and Food-Processing at the Multicomponent Finch Site (47 JE-0902) in Jefferson County, Southeastern Wisconsin. Master's thesis, Department of Anthropology, University of Wisconsin–Milwaukee.

Steuber, Karin I.

2018   Geochemical Characterization of Brown Chalcedony during the Besant/Sonota Period. Unpublished PhD dissertation, Department of Anthropology, University of Saskatchewan. Saskatoon.

Stevenson, Katherine P., Robert F. Boszhardt, Charles R. Moffat, Philip H. Salkin, Thomas C. Pleger, James L. Theler, and Constance M. Arzigian

1997   The Woodland Tradition. *Wisconsin Archeologist* 78:140–201.

Stiner, Mary C., Steven L. Kuhn, Stephen Weiner, and Bar Bar-Yosef

1995   Differential Burning, Recrystallization, and Fragmentation of Archaeological Bone. *Journal of Archaeological Science* 22(2):223–37.

Stockhammer, Philipp W.

2012   Conceptualizing Cultural Hybridization in Archaeology. In *Conceptualizing Cultural Hybridization: A Transdisciplinary Approach*, edited by Philipp W. Stockhammer, pp. 43–58. Springer, New York.

Stoltman, James B.

1990   The Woodland Tradition in the Prairie du Chien Locality. In *The Woodland Tradition in the Western Great Lakes: Papers Presented to Elden Johnson*, edited by Guy G. Gibbon, pp. 239–59. Publications in Anthropology No. 4. University of Minnesota, Minneapolis.

2005   Tillmont (47CR460): A Stratified Prehistoric Site in the Upper Mississippi River Valley. *Wisconsin Archeologist* 86(2):1–113.

2006   Reconsidering the Context of Hopewell Interaction in Southwestern Wisconsin. In *Recreating Hopewell*, edited by Douglas K. Charles and Jane E. Buikstra, pp. 310–27. University Press of Florida, Gainesville.

St-Pierre, Christian G., and Robert G. Thompson

2015   Phytolith Evidence for the Early Presence of Maize in Southern Quebec. *American Antiquity* 80(2):408–15.

Struever, Stuart

1962   Implications of Vegetal Remains from an Illinois Hopewell Site. *American Antiquity* 27(4):584–87.

1964   The Hopewell Interaction Sphere in Riverine–Western Great Lakes Culture

History. In *Hopewellian Studies*, edited by J. R. Caldwell and R. Hall, pp. 86–106. Scientific Papers 12. Illinois State Museum, Springfield.

Styles, Bonnie W.

1981   *Faunal Exploitation and Resource Selection: Early Late Woodland Subsistence in the Lower Illinois Valley*. Scientific Papers No. 3, Northwestern University Archeology Program, Evanston, Illinois.

Styles, Bonnie W., and Frances B. King

1990   Faunal and Floral Remains from the Bold Counselor Phase Village. In *Archaeological Investigations at the Morton Village and Norris Farms 36 Cemetery*, edited by Sharron K. Santure, Alan D. Harn, and Duane Esarey, pp. 56–65. Reports of Investigations No. 45, Illinois State Museum, Springfield.

Styles, Bonnie W., and R. Bruce McMillan

2009   Archaic Faunal Exploitation in the Prairie Peninsula and Surroundings Regions of the Midcontinent. In *Archaic Societies: Diversity and Complexity across the Midcontinent*, edited by Thomas E. Emerson, Dale L. McElrath, and Andrew C. Fortier, pp. 39–80. State University of New York Press, Albany.

Sutton, Keith

2000   *Fishing Arkansas: A Year-Round Guide to Angling Adventures in the Natural State*. University of Arkansas Press, Fayetteville.

Swanton, John R.

1946   *The Indians of the Southeastern United States*. Smithsonian Institution Bureau of American Ethnology Bulletin 137. United States Government Printing Office, Washington, DC.

Swenson, Fern E., and Michael L. Gregg

1988   A Devils Lake–Sourisford Mortuary Vessel from Southeastern North Dakota. *Journal of the North Dakota Archaeological Association* 3:1–15.

Syms, E. Leigh

1974   History of a Refuse Pit: Interpreting Plains Camp Activity at a Microcosmic Level. *Plains Anthropologist* 19(66):306–15.

1977   Cultural Ecology and Ecological Dynamics of the Ceramic Period in Southwestern Manitoba. Memoir 12. *Plains Anthropologist* 22(76, pt. 2):1–160.

1978   *Aboriginal Mounds of Southern Manitoba: An Evaluative Overview*. Manuscript Report 323. Canadian Parks Service. Ottawa.

1979   The Devils Lake–Sourisford Burial Complex on the Northern Plains. *Plains Anthropologist* 24(86):283–308.

Syms, E. Leigh, and Sara Halwas

2019   The Lockport Site, a History of Recovery: Past, Present, and Future. *Manitoba Archaeological Journal* 29:1–23.

Taché, Karine, and Oliver E. Craig

2015   Cooperative Harvesting of Aquatic Resources and the Beginning of Pottery Production in North-Eastern North America. *Antiquity* 89(343):177–90.

Taggart, David

1981   Notes on the Comparative Study of Fire-Cracked Rock. In *Report of Phase I and II Archaeological Survey of Proposed M-275 Right-of Way through Western Oakland County*, edited by Doreen Ozker and David Taggart, pp. 142–52. Museum of Anthropology, University of Michigan, Ann Arbor.

REFERENCES

Talalay, Laurie, Donald R. Keller, and Patrick J. Munson
1984   Hickory Nuts, Walnuts, Butternuts, and Hazelnuts: Observations and Experiments Relevant to Their Aboriginal Exploitation in Eastern North America. In *Experiments and Observations on Aboriginal Wild Plant Food Utilization in Eastern North America*, edited by P. J. Munson, pp. 338–59. Indiana Historical Society, Indianapolis.

Tate, Carolyn E.
2012   *Reconsidering Olmec Visual Culture: The Unborn, Women, and Creation*. University of Texas Press, Austin.

Tekiela, Stan
1999   *Birds of Illinois Field Guide*. Adventure Publications, Cambridge, Minnesota.

Teller, James T., and Lee Clayton (editors)
2003   *Glacial Lake Agassiz*. Geological Society of Canada, St. John's, Newfoundland.

Theler, James
2021   Bison Scapula Hoes by Dr. James Theler—MVAC Lab. Video Mississippi Valley Archaeology Center at University of Wisconsin–La Crosse, YouTube video.

Theler, James L., and Robert F. Boszhardt
2000   The End of the Effigy Mound Culture: The Late Woodland to Oneota Transition in Southwestern Wisconsin. *Midcontinental Journal of Archaeology* 25(2):289–312.

Thompson, John Eric Sidney
1965   Archaeological Synthesis of the Southern Maya Lowlands. In *Handbook of Middle American Indians, Volume 2. Archaeology of Southern Mesoamerica, Part 1*, edited by Gordon R. Willey, pp. 331–59. University of Texas Press, Austin.

Thoms, Alston
1989   The Northern Roots of Hunter-Gatherer Intensification: Camas and the Pacific Northwest. PhD dissertation, Department of Anthropology, Washington State University, Pullman.

2003   Cook-Stone Technology in North America: Evolutionary Changes in Domestic Fire Structures during the Holocene. In *Le feu Domestique et ses Structures au Néolithique et aux Âges des Métaux: Actes du Colloque de Bourg-en-Bresse et Beaune, 7 et 8 octobre 2000*, edited by M. Frère Sautot et al., pp. 87–96. Monique Mergoil, Montagnac.

2008a   Ancient Savannah Roots of the Carbohydrate Revolution in South-Central North America. *Plains Anthropologist* 53(205):121–36.

2008b   The Fire Stones Carry: Ethnographic Records and Archaeological Expectations for Hot-Rock Cookery in Western North America. *Journal of Anthropological Archaeology* 27(4):443–60.

2009   Rocks of Ages: Propagation of Hot-Rock Cookery in Western North America. *Journal of Archaeological Science* 36(3):573–91.

2015   Earth-Oven Cookery: Historical Background and Introduction to the Fort Hood Microfossil Study. In *Earth Ovens, Geophytes, and Microfossils: Investigating Burned Rock Features and Archeobotanical Remains on Fort Hood, Central Texas*, edited by Alston Thoms, Douglas Boyd, and Karl Kibler, pp. 1–11. Research Report 65, Archeological Resource Management Series. US Army, Fort Hood.

Thoms, Alston, Laura Short, Masahiro Kamiya, and Andrew Laurence
2018   Ethnographies and Actualistic Cooking Experiments: Ethnoarchaeological

Pathways toward Understanding Earth-Oven Variability in Archaeological Records. *Ethnoarchaeology* 10(2):76–98.

Thrush, Coll

2011 Vancouver the Cannibal: Cuisine, Encounter, and the Dilemma of Difference on the Northwest Coast, 1774–1808. *Ethnohistory* 58:1–35.

Titterington, Paul F.

1938a *The Cahokia Mound Group and Its Village Site Materials.* Privately published, St. Louis, Missouri.

1938b For Identification. *American Antiquity* 3(4):354–55.

Tooker, Elisabeth

1991 *An Ethnography of the Huron Indians, 1615–1649.* Syracuse University Press, Syracuse, New York.

Toom, Dennis L.

2004 Northeastern Plains Village Complex Timelines and Relations. *Plains Anthropologist* 49(191):281–97.

Torrance, Robin

2006 Description, Classification, and Identification. In *Ancient Starch Research*, edited by R. Torrance and H. Barton, pp. 115–44. Left Coast Press, Walnut Creek, California.

Tozzer, Alfred M.

1910 *A Comparative Study of the Maya and the Lacandones.* Archaeological Institute of America. Macmillan, London.

Trigger, Bruce G.

1996 *A History of Archaeological Thought.* Cambridge University Press, New York.

Tsafou, Evgenia, and Juan José García-Granero

2021 Beyond Staple Crops: Exploring the Use of "Invisible" Plant Ingredients in Minoan Cuisine through Starch Grain Analysis on Ceramic Vessels. *Archaeological and Anthropological Sciences* 13(8):1–16.

Tubbs, Ryan M.

2013 Ethnic Identity and Diet in the Central Illinois River Valley. PhD dissertation, Department of Anthropology, Michigan State University, East Lansing.

Twiss, Katheryn

2007a *The Archaeology of Food and Identity.* Center for Archaeological Investigations, Southern Illinois University Carbondale Occasional Paper No. 34. Southern Illinois University, Carbondale.

2007b We Are What We Eat. In *Archaeology of Food and Identity*, edited by Katheryn C. Twiss, pp. 1–16. Center for Archaeological Investigations Occasional Paper No. 34. Southern Illinois University, Carbondale.

2008 Transformations in an Early Agricultural Society: Feasting in the Southern Levantine Pre-Pottery Neolithic. *Journal of Anthropological Archaeology* 27(4):418–42.

2012 The Archaeology of Food and Social Diversity. *Journal of Archaeological Research* 20(4):357–95.

2019 *The Archaeology of Food: Identity, Politics, and Ideology in the Prehistoric and Historic Past.* Cambridge University Press, Cambridge.

United States Department of Agriculture

2017 Plants Database (website).

VanDerwarker, Amber M.

1999 Feasting and Status at the Toqua Site. *Southeastern Archaeology* 18:24–34.

VanDerwarker, Amber, Dana Bardolph, Kristin Hoppa, Heather Thakar, Lana Martin, Allison Jaqua, Matthew Biwer, and Kristina Gill

2016 New World Paleoethnobotany in the New Millennium (2000–2013). *Journal of Archaeological Research* 24(2):125–77.

VanDerwarker, Amber M., and Tanya M. Peres

2010 *Integrating Zooarchaeology and Paleoethnobotany*. Springer, New York.

VanDerwarker, Amber, C. Margaret Scarry, and Jane M. Eastman

2007 Menus for Families and Feasts: Household and Community Consumption of Plants at Upper Saratown, North Carolina. In *The Archaeology of Food and Identity*, edited by Katheryn Twiss, pp. 16–49. Occasional Paper No. 34, Southern Illinois University, Carbondale.

VanDerwarker, Amber M., and Gregory D. Wilson

2016 War, Food, and Structural Violence in the Mississippian Central Illinois Valley. In *The Archaeology of Food and Warfare*, edited by A. M. VanDerwarker and G. D. Wilson, pp. 75–105. Springer International Publishing, Cham, Switzerland.

VanDerwarker, Amber M., Gregory D. Wilson, and Dana N. Bardolph

2013 Maize Adoption and the Intensification in the Central Illinois River Valley: An Analysis of Archaeobotanical Data from the Late Woodland to Early Mississippian Periods (A.D. 600–1200). *Southeastern Archaeology* 32(2):147–68.

Vennum, Thomas

1988 *Wild Rice and Ojibway People*. Minnesota Historical Society Press, St. Paul.

Vogel, Joseph O.

1975 *Trends in Cahokia Ceramics: Preliminary Study of the Collections from Tract 15A and 15B*. Bulletin No. 10. Illinois Archaeological Survey, University of Illinois at Urbana-Champaign.

Vogt, Evon Z.

1969 *Zinacantán: A Maya Community in the Highlands of Chiapas*. Belknap Press of Harvard University Press, Cambridge.

Wacher, Carmen

2003 Nixtamalization, a Mesoamerican Technology to Process Maize at Small-Scale with Great Potential for Improving the Nutritional Quality of Maize Based Foods, pp. 735–44. 2nd International Workshop Food-Based Approaches for Healthy Nutrition, Ouagadougou, Burkina Faso.

Wagner, Gail E.

2000 Tobacco in Prehistoric Eastern North America, in *Tobacco Use by Native North Americans: Sacred Smoke and Silent Killer*, edited by Joseph C. Winter, pp.185–204. University of Oklahoma Press, Norman.

Wagner, Gale E., and Peter H. Carrington

2014 Sumpweed or Marsheld (*Iva annua*). In *New Lives for Ancient and Extinct Crops*, edited by Paul E. Minnis, pp. 65–101. University of Arizona Press, Tucson.

Walde, Dale A.

1994 The Mortlach Phase. Unpublished PhD dissertation. University of Calgary.

Walde, Dale, David Meyer, and Wendy Unfreed

1995 The Late Period on the Canadian and Adjacent Plains. *Revista de Arqueología Americana* 9:7–9, 11–66.

Wallis, Neill J., and Meggan E. Blessing

2015 Big Feasts and Small Scale Foragers: Pit Features as Feast Events in the American Southeast. *Journal of Anthropological Archaeology* 39:1–18.

Wallis, Wilson D., and Ruth Sawtell Wallis

1955 *The Micmac Indians of Eastern Canada.* University of Minnesota Press, Minneapolis.

Walter, Richard, and Bryon Schroeder

2023 Late Paleoindian Earth Ovens in the Texas Big Bend. In *Earth Ovens and Desert Lifeways: 10,000 Years of Indigenous Cooking in the Arid Landscapes of North America,* edited by Charles Koenig and Myles Miller, pp. 9–23. University of Utah Press, Salt Lake City.

Walz, Gregory

1991 The Paleoethnobotany of Schwerdt (20AE127): An Early Fifteenth Century Encampment in the Lower Kalamazoo River Valley. Master's thesis, Department of Anthropology, Western Michigan University, Kalamazoo.

Wandsnider, LuAnn

1997 The Roasted and the Boiled: Food Composition and Heat Treatment with Special Emphasis on Pit-Hearth Cooking. *Journal of Anthropological Archaeology* 16(1):1–48.

Warwick, Matthew C.

2002 A Diachronic Study of Animal Exploitation at Aztalan, A Late Prehistoric Village in Southeastern Wisconsin. Unpublished Master's thesis, Department of Anthropology, University of Wisconsin–Milwaukee.

Watson, Patty Jo

1969 *The Prehistory of Salts Cave, Kentucky.* Illinois State Museum Reports of Investigation 16, Springfield.

1974 *Archaeology of the Mammoth Cave Area.* Academic Press, New York.

Watson, Patty Jo, and Mary C. Kennedy

1991 The Development of Horticulture in the Eastern Woodlands of North America: Women's Role. In *Engendering Archaeology: Women and Pre-history,* edited by Joan M. Gero and Margaret W. Conkey, pp. 255–75. Blackwell, Oxford.

Watts, Christopher M., Christine D. White, and Fred J. Longstaffe

2011 Childhood Diet and Western Basin Tradition Foodways at the Krieger Site, Southwestern Ontario, Canada. *American Antiquity* 76(3):446–72.

Waugh, F. W.

1973 *Iroquois Foods and Food Preparation. Anthropological Series No. 12,* Memoir 86, Canada Department of Mines, Geological Survey, Ottawa.

Wedel, Mildred Mott

1963 Notes on Oneota Classification. *Wisconsin Archeologist* 44:118–22.

Welch, Paul D., and C. Margaret Scarry

1995 Status-Related Variation in Foodways in the Moundville Chiefdom. *American Antiquity* 60(3):397–419.

Weller, Daniel L., and David Turkon

2015 Contextualizing the Immigrant Experience: The Role of Food and Foodways in

Identity Maintenance and Formation for First- and Second-Generation Latinos in Ithaca, New York. *Ecology of Food and Nutrition* 54:57–73.

Weltfish, G.

1965 *The Lost Universe: Pawnee Life and Culture.* University of Nebraska Press, Lincoln.

Wheeler, Alwyne, and Andrew K. G. Jones

1989 *Fishes.* Cambridge Manuals in Archaeology. Cambridge University Press, Cambridge.

Whelan, C. S., A. R. Whitaker, J. S. Rosenthal, and E. Wohlgemuth

2013 Hunter-Gatherer Storage, Settlement, and the Opportunity Costs of Women's Foraging. *American Antiquity* 78(4):662–78.

Wiersum, Wayne Edward

1968 The Cooper's Shore Site (R02): A Late Havana-Hopewell Village Site in South-central Wisconsin. Master's thesis, Department of Anthropology, University of Wisconsin, Madison.

Wiessner, Polly

1983 Style and Social Information in Kalahari San Projectile Points. *American Antiquity* 48(2):253–76.

Wilk, Richard

1999 "Real Belizean Food": Building Local Identity in the Transnational Caribbean. *American Anthropologist* 101(2):244–55.

2012 The Limits of Discipline: Towards Interdisciplinary Food Studies. *Physiology and Behavior* 107:471–75.

2016 The Ambiguous (but Important) Materiality of Food. In *Exploring the Materiality of Food "Stuffs": Transformations, Symbolic Consumption, and Embodiments,* edited by Louise Steel and Katharina Zinn, pp. 287–98. Routledge, New York.

Wilkins, John, and Robin Nadeau

2015 Introduction. In *A Companion to Food in the Ancient World,* edited by John Wilkins and Robin Nadeau, pp. 1–16. John Wiley and Sons, West Sussex, UK.

Wilson, Douglas, and David DeLyria

1999 The Experimental Reduction of Rock in a Camas Oven: Towards an Understanding of the Behavioral Significance of Fire-Cracked Rock. *Archaeology in Washington* 7:81–89.

Wilson, Douglas, and Amber VanDerwarker

2015 The Functional Dimensions of Earth Oven Cooking: An Analysis of an Accidently Burned Maize Roast at the C. W. Cooper Site in West-Central Illinois. *Journal of Field Archaeology* 40(2):166–75.

Wilson, Gilbert L.

1924 The Horse and the Dog in Hidatsa Culture. *Anthropological Papers of the American Museum of Natural History* 15:125–311. American Museum of Natural History, New York.

1987 *Buffalo Bird Woman's Garden: Agriculture of the Hidatsa Indians.* Minnesota Historical Society Press, St. Paul.

Wilson, Gregory D., and Mallory A. Melton

2019 Features. In *Orendorf Settlement D: A Burned Fortified Mississippian Town in the Central Illinois River Valley,* edited by Lawrence A. Conrad, Kjersti E. Emerson, Thomas E. Emerson and Duane E. Esarey, pp. 63–89. Illinois

REFERENCES

State Archaeological Survey Research Reports 50, University of Illinois at Urbana-Champaign.

Winter, Joseph C.

2000 Traditional Uses of Tobacco by Native Americans. In *Tobacco Use by Native North Americans: Sacred Smoke and Silent Killer*, edited by Joseph C. Winter, pp. 9–58. University of Oklahoma Press, Norman.

Witt, Kelsey E., Karthik Yarlagadda, Julie M. Allen, Alyssa C. Bader, Mary L. Simon, Steven R. Kuehn, Kelly S. Swanson, Tzu-Wen L. Cross, Kristin M. Hedman, Stanley H. Ambrose, and Ripan S. Malhi

2021 Integrative Analysis of DNA, Macroscopic Remains, and Stable Isotopes of Dog Coprolites to Reconstruct Community Diet. *Scientific Reports* 11(1):1–16.

Wobst, H. M.

1977 Stylistic Behavior and Information Exchange. In *Papers for the Director: Research Essays in Honor of James B. Griffin*, edited by C. E. Cleland, pp. 317–42. Anthropological Paper 61. University of Michigan, Museum of Anthropology, Ann Arbor.

Wood, W. Raymond

1971 *Biesterfeldt: A Post-Contact Coalescent Site on the Northeastern Plains*. Smithsonian Institution Press, Washington, DC.

Wrangham, Richard W., N. James, Holland Jones, Gregory Laden, David Pilbeam, and Nancy Lou Conklin-Brittain

1999 The Raw and the Stolen: Cooking and the Ecology of Human Origins. *Current Anthropology* 40(5):567–94.

Wright, Muriel H.

1958 American Indian Corn Dishes. *Chronicles of Oklahoma* 36(2):155–66.

Wright, Patti J.

2008 Understanding the Carbonization and Preservation of Sunflower and Sumpweed Remains. *Midcontinental Journal of Archaeology* 33(2):139–53.

Wymer, Dee Anne, and Elliot Abrams

2003 Early Woodland Plant Use and Gardening: Evidence from an Adena Hamlet in Southeastern Ohio. *Southeastern Archaeology* 28(2):175–94.

Yarnell, Richard A.

1972 *Iva annua* var. *macrocarpa*: Extinct American Cultigen. *American Anthropologist* 74(3):335–41.

Yerkes, Richard

2005 Bone Chemistry, Body Parts, and Growth Marks: Evaluating Ohio Hopewell and Cahokia Mississippian Seasonality, Subsistence, Ritual, and Feasting. *American Antiquity* 70(2):241–65.

Yoder, Don

1972 Folk Cookery. In *Folklore and Folklife: An Introduction*, edited by Richard M. Dorson, pp. 325–50. University of Chicago Press, Chicago.

Yoshida, Kunio, Dai Kunikita, Yumiko Miyazaki, Yasutami Nishida, Toru Miyao, and Hiroyuki Matsuzaki

2013 Dating the Stable Isotope Analysis of Charred Residues on the Incipient Jomon Pottery (Japan). *Radiocarbon* 55(2–3):1322–33.

Yost, Chad L., and Mikhail S. Blinnikov

2011 Locally Diagnostic Phytoliths of Wild Rice (*Zizania palustris* L.) from Minnesota,

REFERENCES

USA: Comparison to Other Wetland Grasses and Usefulness for Archaeo-botany and Paleoecological Reconstructions. *Journal of Archaeological Science* 38(8):1977–91.

Zalucha, L. Anthony

1988   Paleoethnobotanical Analysis of the Bachmann Site (47SB202), Sheboygan County, Wisconsin. In *The Early and Late Woodland Occupations at the Bach-mann Site (47 Sb-202) in East-Central Wisconsin*, edited by L. A. Rusch, Appendix. Museum Archaeology Program, Research Report in Archaeology, Madison, Wisconsin.

Zarillo, Sonia, and Brian Kooyman

2006   Evidence for Berry and Maize Processing on the Canadian Plains from Starch Grain Analysis. *American Antiquity* 71(3):473–99.

Zurel, Richard

1979   *Brief Comments Regarding the Nature of Fire Cracked Rock on Aboriginal Sites in the Great Lakes Area.* Working Papers in Archaeology No. 3. Laboratory of Archaeology, Oakland University, Rochester, Michigan.

Contributors

Rebecca K. Albert is a paleoethnobotanist specializing in microbotanical analysis. Her work has focused mostly on subsistence practices, foodways, and identity in the Great Lakes region of North America.

Alleen Betzenhauser is coordinator of the Illinois State Archaeological Survey's American Bottom Field Station within the University of Illinois Prairie Research Institute. Her research interests include the Terminal Late Woodland–Mississippian transition in the American Bottom, ceramic analysis, experimental archaeology, and engagement with local communities. She is coeditor of *Reconsidering Mississippian Communities and Households*.

Jennifer R. Haas is the director of the Archaeological Laboratory Research Center and NAGPRA Coordinator at the University of Wisconsin–Milwaukee. Haas manages the cultural resource management program, serves as curator of the archaeological repository, and is graduate faculty in the Department of Anthropology.

Mary M. King is a senior scientific specialist, archaeobotany, for the Illinois State Archaeological Survey.

Susan M. Kooiman is an assistant professor of anthropology at Southern Illinois University, Edwardsville. Her research is focused on pottery, food, cooking, and human-environmental interactions in the ancient Indigenous Midwest.

Mary E. Malainey is an archaeology professor at Brandon University and lipid residue analyst. For the past several years, her research has focused on precontact Indigenous farming in Manitoba. She is the author of *A Consumer's Guide to Archaeological Science: Analytical Techniques*.

Terrance J. Martin is a curator emeritus of anthropology at the Illinois State Museum in Springfield and an adjunct faculty member in the Department of

Anthropology at Michigan State University. He is author or coauthor of numerous articles and book chapters on zooarchaeology in the Midwest and Upper Great Lakes region.

Fernanda Neubauer is a lecturer in anthropology at the University of California, Los Angeles. Her research includes lithic analysis, hot-rock cooking, foodways, gender, and decolonizing methods as well as long-term projects carried out in collaboration with Indigenous communities in North and South America.

Kelsey Nordine is a paleoethnobotanist broadly interested in the intersections of social identity, cuisine, and subsistence. Her work has focused on Historic and Precontact sites in the Midwest.

Jodie A. O'Gorman is an associate professor of anthropology at Michigan State University. She specializes in archaeology of the Midwest and has long been interested in the intersection of food, gender, and community.

Autumn M. Painter is an archaeologist with a regional focus of the Eastern Woodlands of North America and broad interests in zooarchaeology, foodways, social interaction, and coalescent communities.

Jeffrey M. Painter is an archaeologist for the Natural Resources Conservation Service in New Hampshire. His research broadly focuses on foodways, social interaction, community development and integration, and ceramic analysis.

Kimberly Schaefer is an assistant research scientist in archaeobotany for the Illinois State Archaeological Survey.

Mary Simon served as chief archaeobotanist for the Illinois State Archaeological Survey at the University of Illinois, Urbana-Champaign, from 1998 through 2021. She is the author or coauthor of numerous technical reports, articles, and book chapters focusing on plant use practices by Native peoples living in the Eastern Woodlands of North America.

Index

abundance metrics, 72

acorn (*Quercus* sp.), 34–35, 66, 68, 70, 72–73, 84, 139–40, 144, 149–50, 230

agriculture, 9, 16–17, 64, 142. *See also* gardening; maize cultivation

Ahler, Stanley A., 172, 176–77

Algonquin peoples, 163, 173

Alt, Susan M., 91

American Bottom, 16–17, 96, 98, 106, 152, 173, 175, 179–95, 197–200, 221, 230–31, 237; nixtamalization in, 182–85

American coot, 114

American lotus (*Nelumbo lutea*), 143

AMS (accelerator mass spectrometry), 61, 64–65, 111, 159–60

Anderson, Jay, 3

animal components of cuisine, in CIRV, 119–26

animism, 239

Anishinaabe people, 22, 59

anthropological archaeology, 227

anthropology, 1–2

Antler River, 160

Apple River, 174

archaeobotanical analysis of soil cores, 177

archaeobotanical assemblages, 32, 222–23. *See also* plant remains assemblages

archaeobotany, 131

archaeological assemblage, at Site 914 (Grand Island, MI), 22–24

archaeological signatures of earth ovens with FCR, 37

archaeometric analysis, 179, 185, 187–89, 194

archaeozoological analysis, 92. *See also* faunal assemblages

Arikara people, 169, 176

Arikara sites (South Dakota), 128

artifact scatter, at Finch site, 66

artifact studies, 130

Arzigian, C. M., 171

Assiniboine people, 176

Assiniboine River, 156

Atalay, Sonya, 7

Aztalan (SE Wisconsin), 168

baking, 36–37. *See also* earth oven

bald eagle, 114, 121, 127–28

banaha, 180–81

Barrett, John C., 7

bead making, 209

beans, 16, 41. *See also* common bean; wild bean

Beaudry, Mary C., 6–7

beaver, 114, 124

Becker, George C., 67

beechnut, 34–35

beer, 210

Belize, 192

Bellomo, Randy, 24

Bemidji, Minnesota, 170, 175

Benchley, Elizabeth, 184–85, 189, 191

Benz, Bruce F., 166
Besant/Sonota occupation, at DgMg-40c, 160–62
Besant/Sonota people, 160, 166
Binford, Lewis, 26
biomass, 111
birds, 16, 114, 127–28, 205, 210, 217. *See also common names of species*
bird symbolism, 96, 98, 127
bison, 13, 16, 166, 176
bison scapula hoes, 156, 158–59, 168, 173, 175; morphology, 169–74
bitternut hickory (*Carya cordiformis*), 70
black bass, 118
black bear, 127
black drink, 209
Blackduck occupation, at Lockport site, 158
black walnut (*Juglans nigra*), 68, 70, 72–73, 84–85, 140
Blessing, Meggan E., 126
bobcat, 124
boiling, 44, 48, 57, 59–60, 79, 94, 228; plus stewing, 44, 49, 52, 56. *See also* nixtamalization
Bold Counselor phase, 98, 110–54. *See also* Morton Village site (WC Illinois)
bone grease rendering, 65–66, 84, 86–87, 124, 172, 229
bone tools, 200
Boszhardt, Robert F., 165–69, 174
bottle gourd (*Lagenaria siceraria*), 141, 148–49
bow and arrow, 15
bowfin (*Amia calva*), 118, 122–24, 128–29, 211
Branstner, Christine N., 43
Brennan, Tamira K., 201
brewing, 210
Buchanan, Meghan E., 96
Buchner, A. P., 158–59, 163
Buckelew, F. M., 25
buffer zones, 173, 175
bullhead catfish (*Ameiurus* sp.), 118, 122, 211
burial ceremonies, 212
burning, 149–50, 200, 225

butternut (*Juglans cinerea*), 140

caching/cache pits, 35, 66, 85, 87, 167, 175–76
Cahokia Creek, 198
Cahokia culture, 15–17, 96, 168, 173, 184; and nixtamalization, 179–95. *See also* Greater Cahokia complex
Cahokia Mounds, 128, 182
Calgary, Alberta, Canada, 177
Calumet ceremonialism, 144
Cambria sites (SW Minnesota), 167
Canada goose, 114
carbonization, 44–45, 47–50, 52, 54–56, 79–82, 99–100, 103–4
Carpiaux, N., 165
catfish (Ictaluridae), 118, 122
cemeteries, 92–93, 127
Central Cahokia Precinct, 198
ceramic assemblages, 15–16, 48, 198; at Cloudman site, 44, 48–49, 61; at Finch site, 65–68, 78–82, 88; at Morton Village site, 110–11, 146, 148–50
ceramic decoration: Mississippian *vs.* Oneota, 100–101; "tail of the raptor"/ Thunderbird motifs, 163–65, 173–76
ceramic distribution, at Morton Village site, 92, 105–7
ceramic manufacture, in Northern Great Lakes, 59–60
ceramic morphological analysis, 63
ceramic use-wear analysis, 10, 63, 85–86, 88, 94, 106, 184, 191, 194
ceramic vessel forms, 13–14, 79, 87, 101, 104–5, 107; bowls, 107, 109; broad-rimmed plates, 90–109, 230, 236; cooking vessels, 101; funnels, 184, 191, 194; jars, 15, 78–79, 94, 96–97; mortuary vessels, 164; pans, 182; serving vessels, 94–95, 100–101, 105, 107; storage vessels, 100; stumpware, 182–92, 194
ceramic wares: collared wares, 66; Diamond Bluff Complex, 165; Havana wares, 65; Honey Creek Corner notched, 66; Initial Variant Middle Missouri Tradition, 163; Madison

INDEX 303

Triangular, 66; Madison ware, 64, 66; Perrot Punctate, 165; Ramey Incised, 96, 168; Rock ware, 65; Shorewood Cord Roughened, 66; Traverse Ware, 61; Wells Incised, 96
ceremonial centers, 14
ceremonialism, 156
channel catfish *(Ictalurus punctatus),* 76, 118
charcoal, 30–31
chemical residue analysis, 63, 79, 81–82, 130–31, 153, 191, 194, 225. *See also* lipid residue analysis
chenopod *(Chenopodium berlanderi),* 201, 210, 216
cherry *(Prunus serotina),* 143
Cheyenne people, 166
Chippewa people, 166
Chopunnish (Nez Perce) people, 25
CIRV (Central Illinois River Valley), 90–154, 234–35, 237
Civitello, Linda, 226
Clark, Jeffrey J., 91
clay figurines, 215, 218
climate change, 13, 225
coalescence, 90–109, 133–34, 198, 229–30, 234
Cocking, Matthew, 178
collaboration, with Indigenous experts, 194–95, 233
common bean *(Phaseolus vulgaris),* 140, 145, 149, 230
Conner, Michael D., 148
contextual analysis, 179, 238
cooking, 4–5, 11–17, 24; at Cloudman site, 56–57; dry/wet mode, 81–83, 100; in earth oven, 19–38; at Finch site, 66; and ingredients, 40. *See also* cuisine
cooking facilities, 10. *See also* earth oven
cooking methods, 42, 44, 47–49, 55–56. *See also* baking; boiling; roasting; simmering; steaming; stewing
cooking pits, at Finch site, 65–66, 84–85. *See also* pit features
cooking pots, 36, 41–42. *See also* food residues, associated with ceramic cooking pots

cooking style, diachronic change in, 57–59
corn. *See* maize *(Zea mays)*
cosmology, 96
cottontails, 124
cottonwood/willow (Salicaceae), 215–16, 219
Coues, Elliot, 25
Counihan, Carol, 3, 5
courtyard groups, 198, 220
craft specialization, 220, 223
creolization, 133–34, 151, 169, 174
crop failures, 225
crop/weed relationship, 142
cross-cultural studies, 181
cuisine, 3–6, 8, 10–11, 17, 39–40, 110, 154, 226; Cahokian, 179–95, 224–25; and coalescence, 90–109; earth oven, 19–38, 228; everyday *vs.* special, 126–30; high and low, 4; and hybridity, 90–109; and lipid residue analysis, 34–36; local, 232–33; Northern Great Lakes, 39–62; and social interaction/identity, 60–61, 132–54, 235–36; Southeastern Wisconsin, 63–89; Woodland tradition, 63–89
culinary archaeology, 7
culinary change: diachronic, 57–60; and persistence, 233–35
culinary practice, 4–5, 10–11; in CIRV, 110–31. *See also* nixtamalization
culinary studies, in archaeology, 7–8
cultural anthropology, 3–4
cultural connections, 169; and ceramic decoration motifs, 163–65
cultural superfoods, 155, 229
Cutright, Robyn E., 5

Dakota Sioux people, 166
Deagan, Kathleen, 133
deer/deer meat, 13, 16, 219–21, 223. *See also* white-tailed deer *(Odocoileus virginianus)*
DeLyria, Davie, 32
Densmore, Frances, 54
Devils Lake, 166, 176
Devils Lake–Sourisford Burial Complex, 160, 164

Diamond Bluff site complex, 168
diet, 2, 42; at Cloudman site, 43–44
diet reconstruction, 10
dish, and recipe, 40, 44
dishes, at Cloudman site, 56–57
diversity, 17, 72, 150–51
Divina, Fernando and Marlene, 232
domestication, of plant species, 142. *See also* maize *(Zea mays)*; maize cultivation
Dotzel, Krista M., 58
double-crested cormorant, 114, 121, 127–28
Drake, Eric C., 22
Driftless Area, 174
Driver, Harold, 29
drum *(Aplodinotus grunniens)*, 211
dry/wet mode cooking, 81–83, 100
duck, 114, 121
Dunham, Sean B., 47, 58

EAC (Eastern Agricultural Complex), 9, 13, 15–17, 60, 88, 136, 141–43, 149, 151, 158
eagle feathers, 127. *See also* bald eagle
Early Archaic period, 13
Early Woodland period, 13–14, 64
earthen cap, for earth oven, 30
earth oven, 13, 19–38, 228
eastern black nightshade *(Solanum ptychanthum)*, 144, 146, 149–53
East St. Louis Precinct, 127–28, 184–91, 196–225; Lohmann Community 1, 205–8; Lohmann Community 2, 208–9; Lohmann Community 3, 209–10; Lohmann Community 4, 210–11; Lohmann Community 5, 211–12; Stirling Community 1, 215; Stirling Community 2, 215–16; Stirling Community 3, 216–18
eating events, 129
Ebell, S. B., 175
economy of effort, 102
elk *(Cervus canadensis)*, 16, 73, 83, 175
elk scapula hoes, 170, 175
"emerging specialists," Lohmann

phase communities as, 212–15
Emerson, Thomas E., 169, 222–23
environmental archaeology, 130
erosion, 158
Espenshade, C., 27
ethnicity, 8, 40
ethnoarchaeological data, 102, 139
ethnobotanical literature, 152–53
ethnographic data, 25–26, 32, 39, 47, 52–56, 59, 62–63, 86–89, 102, 215, 237
ethnography, 2, 238
ethnohistoric accounts, 25–26, 39, 52–56, 59, 144, 233
even-toed ungulate (Artiodactyl), 73–76
excavations, 160; at East St. Louis Precinct, 185; at Finch site, 64; at Lockport site, 158; at Morton Village site, 92, 101–3, 107
exchange networks, 14, 166, 169, 176–77
experimental studies, 179, 185, 189–91, 194, 238; cooking in ceramic pots, 47; earth ovens, 32–34
exploit/exploitation, use of term, 2, 227
exterior carbonization, of ceramic vessels, 79–80
exterior sooting, of ceramic vessels, 79–80

falcon *(Falco* sp.*)*, 205
falcon talons, as ritual/high-status items, 217, 219
Falk, Carl. R., 172
farming. *See* agriculture; maize cultivation
Faulkner, Charles H., 170
faunal analysis, 63
faunal assemblages, 9, 44, 222–23, 230; at Finch site, 66–67, 73–78; at Lamb site, 120–26; at Lohmann phase East St. Louis Precinct, 200–212; at Morton Village site, 110–31
faunal availability, changes in, 220
faunal food procurement, 222–23
FCR (fire-cracked rock), 19–38
feasting, 7, 106, 129, 145–50, 168, 205, 208, 210, 212, 217, 219, 222, 224, 230, 235–36; in CIRV, 110–31

Federal Highway Administration, 185
fictive kinship relations, 175
field sizes, 220
fire-renewal ceremony, 130
Fischler, Claude, 5
fish, 76, 78, 83–84, 88, 118–19, 121–22, 200, 205, 210–12, 223. *See also common names of species*
Fisher Mounds Site Complex, 168, 173
fishing, 9, 13–14, 16, 24, 66
fishing camp, 158
flathead catfish, 118
flooding, 158–59
floodplain resources, 17
Flynn, C., 158–59, 163
folklore studies, 3
food, archaeology of, in Midcontinent, 8–17
food choice, 2, 4–5, 10, 86–87, 92, 130, 139
food combinations, 49–52, 61
food culture, 39–40
food/foodways studies, 3–4, 9, 17–18
food procurement models, 234
food procurement strategies, 196, 219–24
food residues, associated with ceramic cooking pots, 8, 41–42; absorbed residues, 41–42, 61; adhered residues, 39–62; carbonized, 42, 47–48; and pottery typologies, 61. *See also* chemical residue analysis; lipid residue analysis
food residue studies, 34–36
food scarcity, 225
foodways, 3–4, 9
foodways, changing, at Finch site, 84–89
foraging, 14
fracture patterns, of FCR, 29–30
Frederick, Kathryn, 35
freshwater mussels, 120–21, 129
Fritz, Gayle J., 11, 17, 221
fruits, 43, 66, 143
Fuller, Dorian Q., 4, 7
functional analysis, 98–101, 107

Gainsborough Creek, 159–60
gar (*Lepisosteus* sp.), 118, 211
garden hunting, 14, 126

gardening, 85, 87–88, 166
garter snake (*Thamnophis sirtalis*), 205
gastronomic archaeology, 7
gathering, 14, 24. *See also* hunter-gatherers
gendered patterns, in cuisine, 93. *See also* women, roles of
Gilbert, Miles B., 67
Glacial Lake Agassiz, 166
Goltz, Grant, 170
Goody, Jack, 4
goosefoot/lamb's quarters (*Chenopodium berlandieri* ssp. *jonesianum*), 141, 144, 148–51, 209
Goose Lake, 198
Graff, Sarah R., 132
Graham, R., 162
Grand Island, Michigan, 19–38, 228
Grand Island Archaeological Program, 22
grape (*Vitis* sp.), 143
grasses, 149
great blue heron, 114
Greater Cahokia complex, 184, 196–225, 230–31, 234. *See also* Cahokia culture; East St. Louis Precinct
Great Horned Serpent, 164
Great Lakes, 12–13; Northern, 39–62
Gregg, M. L., 166–67, 170–71
Gremillion, Kristen J., 142
Griffitts, Janet L., 172
ground-breaking ceremonies, 169
ground-penetrating radar, 160
gruel, 54
Gulf of Mexico, 209

Halstead, Paul, 7
Halwas, S., 159
Hamilton, S., 159
hardwood ash, used in nixtamalization, 180–81, 187, 192
Harken, Sarah, 190
harvest ceremonies, 130
Hastorf, Christine A., 4–7, 129
Haudenasaunee (Iroquois) peoples, 163
Haury, Cherie E., 171
hawk-falcon-Thunderer symbolism, 98
hawk-men symbolism, 98

306 INDEX

hazelnut (*Corylus* sp.), 34–35, 66, 70, 72–73, 139–40
Head-Smashing-In bison jump, 177
hearth: at Finch site, 85; at Lockport site, 158. *See also* earth oven
Heart River, 172, 176
heat: direct/indirect, 26; in earth ovens, 27
Hems, David, 158–59
Henning, Dale, 166–67
Henry, Alexander, the Younger, 176
hickory (*Carya* sp.): nut, 66, 70, 72–73, 83–88, 139, 150, 230; wood, 215–17
Hidatsa people, 166–67, 169, 172, 176–77
hides, animal, 124
Hilger, Inez, 54
Ho-Chunk (Winnebago) people, 26
holistic approaches, 10
hominy, 54–55, 57, 180
hominy foodway, Cahokia and, 192
Honigman, John, 3
Hopewell culture, 14, 60, 166
Horseshoe Lake, 198
"horticultural interlude," at Lockport site, 158–59
horticultural occupation, at Pierson WMA, 159–60
Hough, Walter, 26, 35
houses, at Finch site, 84–85
house size, in Oneota tradition, 134
house societies model, 222–24
hunter-gatherers, 237; and introduction of maize cultivation, 155–78, 229
hunting, 9, 12–16, 24; garden hunting, 14, 126
hunting parties, 222
hunting practices, 14
Hurt, Wesley R., 176
hybridity, 91, 98, 133–34
hybridization processes, 142
hydrolysis, 59

identification, of foodstuffs, 9
identity, and cuisine, 5–6, 8, 10, 60–61, 192–93. *See also* social identity
Illinois, 15, 26; northwestern, 168; southwestern, 179–95; west-central, 90–109, 132–54, 229. *See also* CIRV (Central Illinois River Valley)
Illinois Department of Transportation, 179, 185
Illinois River, 119–26, 229
Illinois State Archaeological Survey, 185, 198
Illinois State Geological Survey, 187
Illinois State Museum, Research and Collections Center, 111
Indiana, 26–27
Indian Lake, 198
Indigenous knowledge and perspectives, 194–95, 233, 238–39
ingredients, 40, 42, 44, 46–47. *See also* chemical residue analysis; lipid residue analysis; nixtamalization
integrated analyses (ceramic, faunal, botanical), 153–54
"intensification through diversification" model, 16
interior carbonization, of ceramic vessels, 79–81
Iowa, 15, 26, 153
Iroquoian groups, 53–57, 59, 61
Ives, J. W., 162

Jackson, Douglas K., 31
James River, 166–67, 171, 176
Jelliffe, Derrick B., 155

Kalispel people, 25
Kansas, 172; northeastern, 129
Kassabaum, Megan, 129
Kelly, Lucretia S., 128, 209
Kenya, 152
King, Frances B., 120
King, Francis, 140
knapping station, 160
Knife River, 176
Knife River flint/obsidian, 160, 166–67, 172
knotweed (*Polygonum erectum* ssp. *watsoniae*), 141, 201, 209–10
Kooyman, Brian, 177
Koshkonong Locality, 152

INDEX

Kuehn, Steven R., 124, 127, 200

La Crosse, Wisconsin, 165, 169, 174
Lake Koshkonong (Rock River), Wisconsin, 64, 229
land-use intensification, and earth oven cooking, 25
La Salle, Robert Cavelier de, 25
Lasemi, Zakaria, 187
Late Archaic period, 19–38
Late Precontact period, 15
Late Woodland period, 14–15, 64
Leach, Jeff, 30
Leech Lake Tribal Council, Heritage Sites Program, 22
Lepofsky, Dana, 25
Lewis phase, 168
lifeways, changing, 84–89
lightning whelk (*Busycon sinistrum*), 209
limestone, 187, 190–92
Lipan Apache people, 25
lipid hydrolysis, 59
lipid residue analysis, 34–36, 61–62, 82–84, 109, 130–31, 153
lithic analysis, and earth oven technology, 27–32
lithic assemblages, 198
little barley (*Hordeum pusillum*), 141, 143–44, 201, 217
local cuisines, 232–33
Logan, Brad, 129
Lohmann phase, 168, 198; at East St. Louis Precinct, 200–215, 221
Lovis, William, 162

Mackenzie, Alexander, 157
MacNeish, Richard S., 158, 163
macrobotanical analysis, 63
macrobotanical remains, 9; at Finch site, 66–67. *See also* plant remains assemblages
"magic plants," 143, 152–53. *See also* ritually charged plants
maize (*Zea mays*), 14–17, 41, 56–57, 66, 70–73, 83–84, 87–89, 92, 120, 130, 136, 140, 144–45, 148–49, 151, 196,

205, 218, 228–30; as cultural superfood, 155, 173; and diachronic culinary change, 57–59; eight-row variety (Maize de Ocho, Northern Flint corn), 72, 158; ethnographic accounts, 54–55; in food combinations, 49–52; as food residue, 46–47
maize cobs, 216
maize culinary package, 60
maize cultivation, 155–78, 229, 234
maize phytoliths, 46–47
maize-planting ceremonies, 169
maize processing, 58. *See also* nixtamalization
maize trading, 177
malnutrition, 179–95
mammal procurement, 64
mammals, unidentified, 84
Mandan people, 176–77
Manitoba, Canada, introduction of maize cultivation to, 155–78, 229, 234
Manitoba Historic Resources Branch (HRB), 158
Manitoba Museum, 175
manoomin, 175. *See also* wild rice
Maple River, 171
marrow extraction, 84, 86–87, 124
Martin, Terrance J., 111
Massey, W., 29
material culture, 65–66, 68–82; at Morton Vilage site, 134–35
Maya region, 192
maygrass (*Phalaris caroliniana*), 141, 143, 149, 151, 201, 209–12, 215–17
meal, 6–7
medicinal practices, 212
Metheny, Karen Bescherer, 238
Michigan, 15, 26–27
Michigan State University, 43
Michlovic, Michael G., 166, 171, 176
microbotanical analysis, 41–42, 45, 62, 109, 232
microbotanical remains, 41, 61. *See also* plant remains assemblages
microfaunal remains, 126. *See also* faunal assemblages

Midcontinental, use of term, 8–10
Middle Archaic period, 13
Middle Woodland period, 13–14, 64
Middle World, 128
Midwest Archaeological Conference, 8
migration, 141, 146, 198, 221–22, 234–35. *See also* coalescence
Miller, Melanie J., 42
mink *(Neogales vison)*, 215
mink mandibles, as ritual paraphernalia, 215
Minnesota, 15, 26, 53, 156, 166
Minnesota River, 167
Mintz, Sidney, 4
missionaries/pilgrims/ambassadors, 168–69, 173
Mississippian period/culture, 15–16, 90–154, 173, 219, 230
Mississippian Southeastern Ceremonial Complex, 160
Mississippi River, 197–98
Missouri River, 167, 172, 176
mixed economy, at Finch site, 88
MNI (minimum number of individuals), 111
mobility, 14–15; decreasing, 87–88
moisture content, for earth ovens, 29–30
mollusk shell, 210
Monaghan, G. William, 141
Moore, Katherine M., 6
Moorehead phase, 200
morning glory *(Ipomoea* sp.), 143, 201, 208–10, 212
Morton Village site, 90–154, 229–30; Feature 152, 136; Feature 174, 136; Feature 175, 106; Feature 209, 136; Feature 213, 136, 144; Feature 214, 136, 144; Feature 224, 106, 110–31, 145–50; Structure 20, 106; Structure 25, 120; Structure 34, 106
mortuary goods, 159
mounds and mound building, 16, 160–62, 168, 173; burial mounds, 160, 166, 175, 177; effigy mounds, 64, 168, 173
multicultural community, Morton Village as, 139

muskrat *(Ondatra zibethicus)*, 76
musk turtle (stinkpot; *Sternotherus odoratus*), 118
mustelids, 124

Nebraska, 172
neighborhood groups, 220
nejayote, 182, 191
Nelumbo lutea (American lotus), 35
NEPV (Northeastern Plains Village) complex, 163, 165–67, 171–73, 175–77
New York, 53
Nicholson, Bev A., 170
nightshade family (Solanaceae), 68. *See also* eastern black nightshade *(Solanum ptychanthum)*
NISP (number of identified specimens), 67
nixtamalization, 10, 54–55, 59–60, 179–95, 231
nonuse alteration of FCR, 27
Nordine, Kelsey, 92, 119
North American plum *(Prunus americana)*, 143
North Dakota, 156, 166–67, 172, 175–76
Northern Great Lakes, 39–62
Northern Late Woodland people, 141
northern pike *(Esox lucius)*, 122, 211
nostalgia, 195
NSP (number of specimens), 113
nut assemblages, at Finch site, 72–73
nut harvesting, 85–86
nut oil, 82, 86–87, 229
nut processing, 66, 84, 86–88, 139–40, 150
nuts/nutshells, 13, 34–36, 43, 68–73, 83, 85, 136, 139–41, 148–49, 201, 218, 223, 228. *See also common names of species*

oak *(Quercus* sp.), 215–17. *See also* acorn *(Quercus* sp.)
O'Gorman, Jodie A., 104, 111, 134, 148, 150
Ohio Valley, 27
Ojibwe people, 53–57, 60
Okiek people, 152
Oklahoma, 172
Olson, Eric, 159

Oneota tradition, 15–16, 90–154, 163, 169–71, 174, 176, 229–30, 237
Ontario, Canada, 53
oral tradition, of "Peace Meeting" at Forks of Red and Assiniboine Rivers, 175
organic residue analysis, 62
other, the, 6

packing material, for earth ovens, 29–30
Painter, Autumn M., 92, 94, 104, 119–20, 124, 134
paleoethnobotanical analysis, 92, 132–54
paleoethnobotany, 2
Paleoindian period, 12
palisade construction, 200
parching, 47–48
Parker, Kathryn E., 31, 111, 143, 152
parkland-tallgrass prairie border, 156, 175
Parmalee, Paul, 127–28
patterning, in archaeobotanical and faunal records, 223
Pauketat, Timothy R., 168–69
"Peace Meeting" at Forks of Red and Assiniboine Rivers, 175
Peacock, Sandra, 25
persimmon (Diospyros virginiana), 143, 218
phytoliths, 41, 45
Pierson Wildlife Management Area (WMA), 156–63, 177
pit features, 26, 230; at 47PI2 site, 168; at East St. Louis, 201, 205; at Morton Village site, 92, 106, 110, 132–54. See also caching/cache pits; earth oven; storage pits
pitting, 100
Pitts, Martin, 7
Plains societies, 15, 141
Plains Village tradition, 171
plant food ratio, as abundance metric, 72, 85
plant remains assemblages, 85, 222–23, 230; at Finch site, 68–73; at Lohmann phase East St. Louis, 200–212; at Morton Village site, 113
plant resources, increasing commitment to, 87–88

plant use patterns, at Morton Village site, 150
pond turtle family (Emydidae), 118
positionality, 5–6
postmigration interactions, 90–109
Potagannissing River, 42
potluck model, 129, 230, 236
Potter, Victoria, 190
potters, women as, 237
pottery. See under ceramic
Prairie Peninsula, 134, 173
projectile points, 66
proto-Odawa people, 61
purslane (Portulaca sp.; Portulaca oleracea), 144, 148, 209

quartzite, 27
quicklime, 181, 189, 194

rabbit, 13, 124
raccoon (Procyon lotor), 76
radiocarbon dating, 43, 92, 111, 158–60
Ray, Arthur J., 176
recipes, 40, 44, 49–52; at Cloudman site, 56–57
red cedar (Juniperus virginiana), 201, 208, 210, 215, 217–19
redhorse (Moxostoma sp.), 211
Red River, 156–57, 163, 166–67, 174–75
Red Wing occupation, 168, 174
Red Wing–Pepin area (Minnesota/Wisconsin), 156, 165, 173–75
refuse deposits, 230; at Morton Village site, 110–31
refuse disposal, 205, 212
regional perspective, on Woodland tradition foodways, 84–89
Reitz, Elizabeth J., 130
religious system, Cahokian, 221
reptile (Testudines), 84
residue patterns, associated with cooking methods, 42, 45
resource exploitation, 2
rice. See wild rice
Richland Creek, 200, 221, 223
ritual ceremonies, 169

310 INDEX

ritual closure, 209, 225
ritual deposits, 208
ritually charged plants/plant materials, 201, 205, 208, 210, 212
ritual meals, 209
ritual practices, 208, 212
ritual space, 106; at Morton Village site, 92
roasting, 47
roasting pits, 26–27, 129
Roberts, Linda J., 169
Rodell, Roland, 165, 168, 174–75
Rogers, Edward S., 55

sagamité, 56–57
salvage excavations, 160
sampling issues, 232
Santee Dakota, 176
scapula hoes: bison, 156, 158–59, 168–73; elk, 170
Scattered Village complex, 172, 176–77
Schneider, Fred E., 166–67, 171–72, 176
Schroeder, Sissel, 134
scratches, 100
seasonal activities, 37–38; at Grand Island (Michigan) sites, 24
seasonal habitation, 13, 84–85, 87; at Finch site, 64–66
seasonality indicators, 130
seasonally mobile foragers, 64
seasonal resettlement, 134
seasonal resources, 15
sedentism, 159
seeds, 43
seed savers, 194
selective pressures, 142
sensory perspective, 238–39
serving practices, 94
settlement patterns, Mississippian, 16–17
settlements, Oneota, 134
shagbark hickory (*Carya ovata* sp.), 72
shared culinary practices, 235
shell cups, 209
shell-tempered pottery, 15
Sheyenne River, 171
Silver Creek, 200
simmering, 48, 59, 85, 94

Simon, Mary L., 143, 152
site abandonment, 200, 223
site formation processes, 30
site function, interpreting, 36
sites: 32LM104 (SE North Dakota), 164; 754 (Grand Island, MI), 34–36; 914 (Grand Island, MI), 19–38; 929 (Grand Island, MI), 34–36; Adams (47PI12), 165, 168; Aztalan (47JE0001), 88; Bartron (21GD02), 165, 168; Bendish (32M02), 172; Biesterfeldt, 166; Bryan, 168; Burnside School (21GD159), 165; Cloudman (Drummond Island, Lake Huron, Michigan), 39–62, 228; Common Field (EC Missouri), 96; Cross Ranch (320L14), 172; C. W. Cooper (WC Illinois), 35; Deapolis (32ME5), 172; DgMg-15, 159; DgMg-17, 159; DgMg-40a, 160; DgMg-40c, 160; DgMg-162, 159; DgMg-168, 159–60; Dixon (Iowa), 152; East St. Louis, 127–28, 179–225 (*See also separate entry*); EgPn-612, 177; Fidler Mounds (EaLf-3), 160; Finch (47JE0902; SE Wisconsin), 35, 63–89, 229; Green (S Lower Michigan), 35; Greismer site (Indiana), 169–70, 173; Gundersen site, 171; Hatchery West (Illinois), 26; Hendrickson III (32SN403), 164, 167, 171; Horizon (S Saskatchewan), 164; Horner-Kane (32RY77), 171–72; Ituhu (32SN110), 165; Iva, 168, 173; Jonas, 170; Koshkonong Creek Village (47JE0379; Wisconsin), 165; Lake Midden (EfNg-1), 178; Lamb (Schuyler County, IL), 119–27, 139; Larson, 94, 104; Larson (32BL9), 172; Larson (32SN106), 167, 170–71; Little Bluff Platform Mound Complex (47TR32), 168; Lockport (EaLf-1), 155–63, 165, 169–70, 172–75, 177; Lovstrom (DjLx-1), 170; Lowton, 170; McClelland (21GD258), 165; Mero (21PI02), 165; Moose Creek (Central Alaska), 24; Morton Village (11F2; WC Illinois), 90–154, 229–30 (*See also separate entry*);

Naze (32SN246), 165–67; Norris Farms 36, 92–93, 127; Olson (DgMg-167), 155, 159, 169–70, 172–73, 175, 177; Orendorf, 103; OT (SW Wisconsin), 152; Parchman Place (22C0511; Yazoo Basin, NW Mississippi), 129–30; Phipps (NW Iowa), 127; Pierson Wildlife Management Area (WMA), 156–63, 177; Range, 184; Rench (11P4), 128; Reston (SW Manitoba), 164; Scattered Village (32MO31), 172; Schwerdt (SW Lower Michigan), 35; Shea (32CS101), 167, 171; Silvernale (21GD03), 168; Tony Glas (32EM3), 172; Tremaine Complex, 94; Zimmerman (Illinois), 169–70, 173, 175

Skibo, James M., 22, 34
slaked lime, 181–82, 187, 191–92
small mammals, 16
smoldering, 146, 149, 153
smudging, 105
snake (Serpentes), 205
SNE (seed number estimates), 135–36
soaking. *See* nixtamalization
social contexts of cuisine, 10
social identity, 108–9, 132–54
social interaction, 60–61
social organization, and food procurement strategies, 196, 219–24
solanine, 151–52
Sonota people, 160
sooting, 100, 184
soups, 55
Souris River, 159–60
spatial analysis of ceramic vessels, 101–3, 105
specialization, in food production systems, 220–21
species composition, in faunal assemblage, 120
Spoon River, 168
squash (*Cucurbita* sp.), 16, 41, 56–57, 66, 68, 70, 73, 84, 141, 148–49, 205; ethnographic accounts, 54–55; in food combinations, 49–52; as food residue, 46–47
squirrel, 13, 124

stable isotope analysis, 61
starches, 41, 45
starch grain residue analysis, 177
steaming, 25–26
Stencil, Zachary R., 67
stewing, 44, 47–48, 55–57, 59, 124, 228. *See also* boiling
Stirling phase, 198, 215–19
Stoltman, James B., 174
storage pits, 173, 176, 178; bell-shaped, 158
striped skunk (*Mephitis mephitis*), 76
structures: single-post, 92, 106; "special purpose," 201; wall trench, 92
stumpware, 182–92, 194
Styles, Bonnie W., 120, 122
stylistic pottery analysis, 43, 104
subsistence, archaeology of, in Midcontinent, 11–17
subsistence, use of term, 2
subsistence patterns, 10; Oneota tradition, 16
subsistence regimes, 64
subsistence studies, 1–2, 8–9, 226–27, 231–32
succotash, 55–56
sucker (Catostomidae), 118, 122, 211
sumac (*Rhus* sp.), 143
sumpweed/marshelder (*Iva annua* var. *macrocarpa*), 141–43, 205
sunfish (Centrarchidae), 211
sunflower (*Helianthus annuus*), 141–42, 144, 150, 205
sun symbolism, 96–97
surface treatment analysis, 101, 105, 107
surplus crops, production of, 221
swan (*Cygnus* sp.), 205, 209
sweat lodge, at Morton Village site, 106
Syms, E. Leigh, 159–60

"tail of the raptor"/Thunderbird motifs, 163–65, 173–76
taphonomy, 58
tassimanonny, 56–57
taxa representation, quantitative differences in, 223
textile, plaited, 215

312   INDEX

Theler, James, 167, 171
"third space," 91
Thoms, Alston, 25, 36–37
"Three Sisters" agricultural systems, 141
Thunderbird, 163–65, 173–76
timescales, for food preparation and cooking time, 31
Titterington, P. F., 182–83
tobacco (*Nicotiana* sp.), 70, 144, 178, 201
Toom, Dennis L., 165–67, 171–72, 176
trade networks, 14, 166, 176–77
trade relations, 14, 58, 61
trees. *See common names of species*
tree squirrel, 124
Trempealeau, 168, 173
tropical cultigens, 136, 140–41. *See also* maize *(Zea mays)*
Tubbs, Ryan M., 92–93
tubers/bulbs, cooked in earth ovens, 25
turtle (Testudines), 76, 84, 114
turtle shell, 210, 215–17
Twiss, Katheryn, 7, 146

ubiquity, as abundance metric, 72, 85
Under World, 96, 128
University of Wisconsin–Madison, Zoology Museum, 67
University of Wisconsin–Milwaukee, Department of Anthropology, 67
upland farming communities, Cahokian, 221
Upper Mississippian society, 15
Upper Mississippi Valley, 156, 173; evidence of horticulture, 167–73
Upper World, 96–98, 128
urbanization, Cahokian, 218, 225
use-alteration analysis, 19, 42, 44, 62, 79, 83, 98–101, 103–4
use-alteration traces, 41–42
use lateration, of FCR, 27–29
use-wear analysis, 10, 63, 85–86, 88, 94, 106, 184, 191, 194
US Forest Service, 22

VanDerwarker, Amber M., 124, 126
Vennum, Thomas, 54–55

verbena, 148
villages, 15
village sites, in Oneota tradition, 16
violence, periodic short-term, 126

Wallis, Neil J., 126
wall-trench construction, 220
walnut (Juglandaceae), 70, 72–73, 84–86, 139–40
Wandsnider, LuAnn, 26
wapiti, 114, 124, 126
Washington University, 136; Paleoethnobotany Laboratory, 135
waterfowl, 13, 114, 121, 205, 209
Wendat people, 53–56
wetland resources, 13
white-tailed deer (*Odocoileus virginianusi*), 73–76, 83–84, 114, 120, 124, 126, 196, 200, 205, 208, 210, 212, 216–17, 220–21, 223
wild bean (*Strophostyles* sp.), 209
wild plants, 13. *See also* foraging
wild rice (*Zizania aquatica*), 56–57, 60–61, 66, 70, 73, 87, 155, 228; ethnographic accounts, 54–55; in food combinations, 49–52; as food residue, 46–47
wild seeds, 70, 72, 143
wild turkey, 114, 121
Wilk, Richard, 2
Wilson, Douglas, 32–33
Wilson, Gregory D., 126
Wisconsin, 15, 26, 53, 63–89, 153, 156
wolf/coyote/dog (*Canis* sp.), 73, 124, 127
women, roles of, 60, 87, 108–9, 221, 223, 227, 236–38
wood charcoal, 136, 149
wood fuel, for earth ovens, 30–32

year-round habitation, 64, 119–20
Yoder, Don, 3

Zarillo, Sonia, 177
zooarchaeological analysis, 110–31
zooarchaeological assemblages, at Finch site, 67, 73–78
zooarchaeology, 2, 131